UNION SISTERS

Women in the Labour Movement

EDITED BY
Linda Briskin
&
Lynda Yanz

The
Women's
·Press·

CANADIAN CATALOGUING IN PUBLICATION DATA

Main entry under title:
Union sisters

Bibliography: p.
ISBN 0-88961-079-7

1. Women in trade-unions – Canada. 2. Trade-unions – Canada.
I. Briskin, Linda, 1949- II. Yanz, Lynda, 1951-

HD6079.2.C3U54   331.88'0971   C83-098577-8

Edited by Jane Springer
Cover and book design by Liz Martin
Assembly by Sharon Nelson
Lithographed by union labour at
Charters Publishing Co. Ltd.
Brampton, Ontario
Printed and bound in Canada
Published by the Women's Educational Press
16 Baldwin Street
Toronto, Ontario, Canada

Second edition 1985

CONTENTS

ACKNOWLEDGMENTS

Our first opportunity to bring together the experiences of union women was provided by *Resources for Feminist Research* (July 1981), when we edited a special issue of *RFR* on women and unions. We would like to thank the Editorial Board for their encouragement.

Many people contributed to *Union Sisters*. We would like to thank Leslie Cotter and Liza McCoy for spending long hours typing difficult manuscript copy; John Ford from the Ontario Ministry of Labour History and Ann Wardrop from the Industrial Relations Information Service for providing recent statistical information; Josée Lamoureaux for making contacts with Quebec authors; Deirdre Gallagher from United Steelworkers, Art Heathcote from the Ontario Public Service Employees Union, Alan Pryde from the Ontario Federation of Labour, Michael Lyons from the Metro Labour Council and David Kidd for their help in finding suitable photographs. We would especially like to thank Judy McClard and the reading group at the Women's Press, who patiently read and gave us important feedback on the first draft of articles and Jane Springer, whose involvement and commitment to the book went far beyond her responsibilities as copyeditor.

Union Sisters is a first attempt to record and analyze the experiences of women in unions in Canada. We hope it will contribute to an ongoing discussion of strategy amongst all those committed to women's liberation.

Linda Briskin & Lynda Yanz

INTRODUCTION

Linda Briskin & Lynda Yanz

Women's activism in unions has increased dramatically in the last decade, creating a sense of renewed vitality and excitement in the trade union movement. *Union Sisters* is an attempt to document the struggles and victories of the movement of union women as well as to provide some direction to women and unions as they fight to defend the interests of working people.

More than 900,000 women in Canada belong to unions and in the last ten years our numbers in the union movement have almost doubled. In 1972 we represented 24.2 percent of trade unionists while today more than 30 percent of union members are women. As our numbers have grown so has our strength and organization. Women unionists have been at the forefront of struggles for the right to unionize and the right to strike, for equal pay and equal job access, for maternity and parental leave and around issues relating to technological change. We have pushed unions to be more responsive to the needs and concerns of women; to fight on issues they have traditionally shied away from — issues like sexual harassment, support of lesbian and gay rights and abortion — and to make alliances with and learn from the women's movement and other community movements.

This changed relation of women to unions has made this book possible. We have only just begun to record and, more importantly, to analyze the daily struggles to organize women inside unions and in the workplace. For such an analysis to lay the basis for future political directions, it must be firmly rooted in the actual experience of organizing. It is therefore significant that the majority of this collection of articles is written by activists who have directly participated in these struggles.

The book is divided into six sections: Background, Union Issues, The Challenge of the Unorganized, Inside Unions, The Power of Alliances and Resources.

The first section presents an overview of the contemporary situation of women at work and in unions and of the historical struggle of women for union rights. These articles dispel any notion that the situation for women in the workplace is improving. Women have made almost no gains in equalizing their wages with men, are still limited to a narrow range of jobs, and with the combined impact of the general economic crisis and the new technology, are likely to be squeezed further. Although women have made tremendous progress in unionizing, less than a third of women workers are unionized.

Many of the traditionally accepted union issues, such as the right to strike and first contract legislation, have different implications for women because of their specific location in the work force, in the family and in a society dominated by patriarchal ideology. This means that women have a unique perspective on these issues. Furthermore, the discrimination women face in the work force creates a set of particular concerns, such as sexual harassment and affirmative action, that the trade union movement has long ignored.

In the second section, *Union Issues,* union activists look at the union movement's treatment of affirmative action, microtechnology, part-time work, sexual harassment, sexual orientation, the right to strike and contract negotiations. These articles describe current controversies and outline strategies to enable union women to make gains in these areas.

The third section, *Challenge of the Unorganized,* deals with the obstacles to organizing women, and in particular, the special problems facing immigrant women and domestic workers. In the last quarter century the union movement has not taken the task of organizing the unorganized seriously. Rather than seeing itself as the leadership and defender of all workers, organized or not, the union movement has defended the rights and interests of its membership, often to the detriment of the unorganized.

The militancy of the public sector workers – of the Public Service Alliance of Canada clerks, Canadian Union of Public Employee hospital workers and most recently of Quebec teachers – has forced us to reexamine the common assumption that the basis of union strength and militancy is in the industrial sectors. Clerical and service workers will be subjected to extensive layoffs and job redefinition over the next ten years as a result of technological change, making them a number one organizing priority.

Given this situation, the economic crisis and the attacks by government and employers, the union movement must aggressively try to organize all workers as well as represent the interests of the unemployed. This is a tall order, and it is unclear whether or not the union movement is ready to take up this challenge.

Inside Unions, the fourth section, considers the experience of women unionists. One of the most significant changes in the last decade has been the development of women's committees, which openly address the problems women face in becoming active in unions. They have helped to bring women into union structures but in the process women have often confronted the structural and political limitations of unions as a vehicle for social change.

The fifth section, *The Power of Alliances,* examines the relationship between the trade union movement and the day care movement, the women's movement, the NDP and wives' committees. The union movement has historically been isolationist. But in recent years, as a result of the crisis of the labour movement and the growing perception by other groups of the potential of uniting with the labour movement, both unions and community organizations have tried to develop coalition politics. The experience of the women's movement in building large and effective coalitions and in mobilizing thousands of women without the aid of a large institutional structure recognized by the state will be crucial to the success to these alliances.

The last section, *Resources,* provides three bibliographies: an annotated cineography of films and videos on women, work and unions; a list of materials on women, including documents, research reports and briefs available from Canadian unions; and finally, a selected bibliography on women and unions.

This is a difficult period to be demanding more of the union movement, which is itself under serious attack. The economic crisis has meant widespread layoffs and reduction in union membership. At the same time the government is imposing limitations on collective bargaining and the right to strike, which make it all the harder for unions to defend their members. When unions do try to go on the offensive they are met with ever more sophisticated forms of union and strike busting.

Nevertheless we are demanding more. We are fighting harder than ever before as unionists – and in the process we are challenging the unions to better defend our interests in both the immediate and the long term. We don't have easy answers of how this should be done, nor do we always agree. However, there is no doubt that the experiences, analysis and politics of women activists is having a dramatic influence on the direction of the union movement.

I BACKGROUND

WOMEN AT WORK IN CANADA

Lynda Yanz and David Smith

We are in the middle of a prolonged economic and social crisis qualitatively more severe than any since the Second World War. Living in a capitalist society we are used to the cyclical, or boom and bust, nature of the economy. However, this crisis is not simply a short-term recession with hope for recovery around the corner. Unemployment rates are the highest since the Great Depression and are not expected to fall below ten percent until at least the end of 1985. In fact, each time the economy is at a peak point in its periodic upswing the unemployment rate is higher than at the previous peak in the cycle. This has been the case over the last fifteen years as we've had to accept higher and higher "normal" unemployment rates. There is little reason to expect this to change soon.

In addition to chronically high unemployment, inflation means that the wages of those who do have jobs buy less. Yet there is mounting pressure from the state and employers to make our wage packages stretch even further. In recent months both provincial and federal governments have brought in programs of wage controls for government workers and, at the same time, private sector employers are demanding wage concessions — from even the most organized sections of the working class. The effects of the crisis are being complicated by the rapid introduction of microtechnology, which threatens to eliminate between one and two million Canadian jobs by 1990.[1]

Given this rather grim scenario, what are the prospects for women? How do present developments affect women's situation in the paid work force? What implications do they have for the struggles women are waging? Just as no one really knows how the economic crisis is going to work itself out, there are no easy answers about the consequences for women. The outcome in part lies outside the realm of economics and inside the political battles now being waged by the union and women's movements around a whole range of issues aimed at securing women's economic independence and equality. This article is a first step in tackling some of these questions: it sets the stage for the articles that follow by highlighting some of the most significant economic pressures that determine women's situation in the labour force.

When we look at women's position in the labour force in the Eighties it is important to keep two things in mind: first, women are integrated into the waged work force to an extent that was inconceivable thirty years ago. Today women represent over forty percent of the labour force and that percentage is still climbing. Secondly — and this is no surprise — <u>women continue to be severely disadvantaged at work.</u> Neither women's rapid integration into paid work nor their political struggles of the last fifteen years have been able to substantially alter their inequality in the labour force. The range of jobs in which women can work is severely limited: women tend to be segregated into clerical, personal service or jobs in the "caring" professions, and into a relatively small number of industries — the "service" as opposed to goods producing sectors. Furthermore, work in these "job ghettos" is consistently the lowest paid. Despite our efforts to win equal pay with men we still earn roughly sixty percent of what men earn for full-time work. In fact, based on a recent assessment, men receive higher average incomes "for every occupational group, for every age group, for part- and full-time workers, for every educational level and in every region in Canada."[2]

Women's high participation rate in the labour market in combination with their weak wage position creates contradictory economic and political pressures, especially in this time of crisis. Women's numbers in paid work have continued to increase dramatically despite the discouragement of increasing unemployment and continuing recession. This contradiction is mirrored in the political realm, where the state limits our economic options by making it harder, for example, to collect UIC, get day care subsidies or take manpower training courses. At the same time the state is forced to concede unprecedented gains — such as around the issue of maternity leave. Women's position in the labour force is a product of these contradictory pressures.

If we are going to mobilize effectively to counteract these pressures aimed at locking us more tightly into dead-end and disadvantaged positions in the work force it is important that we understand the dynamics giving shape to our work lives. We are in a period of transition and unless we understand the peculiar difficulties it creates we shall be unable to bring about the changes needed to give women a full place in society.

Traditionally analyses have focused on women's weak attachment to wage work. These have, for example, stressed women's role as a reserve labour force, pulled into the work force when there is a shortage of men and pushed back into the home when the shortage ends. The most graphic example of this was women's experience in both wars, when as soon as the men came home, women were abruptly dismissed from "men's jobs" with, at best, a "thank you ladies you've done enough." This analysis identifies women in a simple way as being "last hired first fired" or as "bearing the brunt of the economic crisis." These assessments are true in certain contexts, but the reality is much more complex and becoming increasingly so as the crisis deepens.

*   *   *   *   *

Women's current situation in the work force is qualitatively different from their position in any earlier economic crisis. <u>Women now have a permanent (if unequal) attachment to the labour force</u>. In the past women had a more transitory relation to wage work; they earned wages, but often only until they got married. Women could expect to work for only a short period of their lives and the married woman who continued in the labour force was a rarity. This has changed dramatically. <u>Since the Second World War there has been a consistent and accelerating increase in the percentage of Canadian women in the labour force</u>. In 1966 35.4 percent of Canadian women were in the work force; by 1980 the figure was 50.3 percent. Or if we step back even further: the number of working women has more than doubled since 1950 and has nearly tripled since 1940. At present six out of ten of the "new entrants" to the labour market are women and this is expected to increase to eight out of ten in the next ten years. If participation trends continue, women will be in the labour force at the same rate as men by 2000.[3]

It is significant that the participation rates of married women are rising faster than any other single group. This is an about-turn from the earlier part of the century, when the majority of women workers were young and single. Today married women represent sixty percent of female income earners. Obviously far fewer women are dropping out of the labour force when they marry and if they do drop out their absence is shorter. Today a woman can expect to spend nearly five times as many years outside the home as she does full-time in the home. In short, whether we like it or not, the days when women's place was in the home are gone. We have gradually but very definitely undermined the possibility of defining women solely in domestic terms.

The dramatic expansion of women's labour force participation took place relatively smoothly due to the growth of the service sector that coincided with it. The service producing industries grew rapidly after the Second World War and women filled most of the jobs in them. During the 1970s alone 83 percent of labour force growth was in this sector. In 1941, 40 percent of the labour force was in the service sector; by 1981 it was 65 percent. In 1982 women filled 49 percent of these jobs as compared with 23 percent of jobs in the goods producing sector.[4] In 1980, the service sector accounted for 81 percent of all women in the labour force. Most significant perhaps is the fact that the growth of the service sector allowed women to enter wage work without competing directly with men for jobs, something that sparked considerable controversy in the past.

Women's integration into the labour force through the creation of a women's ghetto, in part provides the basis for their permanence. In spite of the fact that we are in the midst of a serious economic crisis and the expansion of the traditional service sector appears to be coming to an end, women are not facing a serious threat of being excluded from paid work. We are unlikely to witness the conscious and successful alliance of government, state institutions and employers to oppose women's right to work that we did in the Thirties and after 1945. In fact, some of the characteristics of women's vulnerability – the segregation of the labour force into men's and women's jobs, women's characteristic low and unequal pay vis à vis men, and general lack of unionization – can work to make women preferred as workers by employers.

Women are now in a very different situation in the trade union movement. Whereas in the late Forties unions sometimes collaborated (but more often were complicit) with attempts to push women out of the labour force and into the home, it would be impossible for unions to take up a position so blatantly opposed to women's interests. Quite the contrary; with women representing 30 percent of union members, unions are being pushed to make women's issues a priority – quite an accomplishment in a period of recession.

In addition, women's own life possibilities have altered significantly since the early Fifties. Women's entry into wage work was not just a response to an increase in demand for our labour power. For one thing, it has become more difficult for the family to survive on the male wage. And just as importantly, the family as an institution is much less stable than it was. The traditional family with a husband supporting his wife and children has changed and continues to change. Divorce rates are high and marriage is less socially compulsory. Many women are forced or are choosing to have and support their children alone or with other women. Alternative families are becoming common rather than the exception in our society. The women's movement has changed the way women see themselves, and the fact that women are not under as much financial and social pressure to live with a man as in the past is a victory. These developments reinforce the absolute necessity of paid work; if women can't get jobs they are more likely to see themselves as unemployed than to become housewives, an option less of us have or would choose.

Unemployment is of course a major concern for both men and women workers. Between 1967 and 1981 women's unemployment rates were higher than men's in all but two years. Many feminist analyses have assumed this pattern will continue and get worse as the recession intensifies. This does not seem to be the case. In 1982, when the economy almost collapsed, women's unemployment rate was marginally lower than the male unemployment rate (10.8 percent as compared to 11.1 percent). The significance of what may seem a miniscule difference is that women's unemployment rates have not risen disproportionately and thus it is difficult to make a convincing argument that the unemployment of women is specifically women's unemployment. Different male and female unemployment rates are rather a result of unemployment, which varies by industry and occupation.

It is ironic but women's segregation into a narrow range of industries and occupations has given them some protection from the effects of the crisis. The service sectors are traditionally less subject to unemployment than the goods producing sectors, where women have been concentrated in the past. This is because the service sectors are less sensitive to declines in the level of demand. Banks don't lose as much business in recessions as do mining or steel companies. The contradictory nature of women's employment possibilities come out to some extent if we disaggregate the unemployment rates by sector. In doing this we find the peculiar situation in which the overall female unemployment rate is lower *despite* the fact that in almost every sector of the economy the female rate is higher.

Women's unemployment rate is lower across the board because women are segregated into the low employment (also low wage) service sector. For example, in 1982 the unemployment rates in the predominantly male goods producing sectors was 14.9 percent, while the unemployment rate in the service sector, where most women work, was a relatively low 8.5 percent. The female rates were marginally higher in both sectors. Thus if we look at each sector individually women are discriminated against in unemployment but in terms of the economy as a whole women's chances of being unemployed are slightly lower than men's. The only sectors where women's unemployment rates are lower are the sectors where male and female jobs are clearly differentiated into male jobs in production and female jobs in clerical work. While a company can shut down production it cannot shut down its administrative operations unless it goes out of business completely. A forestry firm may lay off the workers in its pulp mill but it won't lay off the clerical and administrative staff in its head office to the same degree. In general the work of women is more concerned with keeping the company going than with keeping production going. Thus in the primary goods sector (not including agriculture) and the construction industry where, in 1980, 60 percent and 72 percent respectively of women's jobs were clerical, women had lower rates of unemployment than men.[5]

Of course the economic crisis also creates pressures that heighten women's vulnerability. At the same time as women's segregation into a narrow range of industries and occupations ensures they will not be pushed out of the work force, it also underlines the precariousness of their position by determining the jobs they have access to and the wages they receive. Opportunities for getting out of the job ghettos are decreasing. Cutbacks in social services are limiting the professional opportunities we've had as nurses or teachers, as well as the better-paid unionized positions in the public sector. These setbacks are likely to be very consequential for women since these are precisely the jobs where women have been able to earn the best wages. The possibilities of access to better rates of pay through non-traditional jobs are becoming more remote as massive layoffs and unemployment hit the "male" jobs in the trades and heavy industry. The seniority principle of "last hired, first fired" works to exclude women, wiping out even the small gains made over the past few years. The result is increased competition among women for clerical and service jobs at a time when women are still entering the labour force and the growth in the service sector is leveling off sharply. More women competing for fewer jobs makes it easier for employers to keep wages low and even decrease them.

There are other aspects of our work lives that protect us from absolute unemployment but as a result increase our insecurity in terms of wages and working conditions. One of the most serious is that women are still substantially underrepresented in unions, whether it be in small light manufacturing or electronic shops or in huge offices, restaurants or department stores. Our wages suffer almost automatically as a result of not being unionized. For example, on average the wage differential between women and men in unionized jobs is only 20 percent as compared with 40 percent in non-unionized jobs. And it is women, especially immigrant women, who predominate in occupations — like domestic and farm work — which do not have even the basic rights provided by provincial and federal labour legislation, let alone strong unions backing them. As well, women who are wives and mothers are less mobile, less likely to move to follow jobs or to find other work and more inclined to accept part-time work without the benefits or rights that go with full-time jobs.

*   *   *   *   *

The attempts of government and business to find solutions to the problems of the economy are proceeding along a number of lines, none of them particularly beneficial to women. First, employers are engaged in an offensive against workers' wages and at the same time attempting to make production more efficient, particularly by the introduction of microtechnology. In both areas governments are providing legislative support. All across the country and without regard to political affiliation, governments have introduced wage controls for public sector workers. In addition, governments are trying to "rationalize" their own operations through cutbacks in the public service, by giving support to the microtechnology industry and by subsidizing firms that introduce microtechnology into the workplace. How are these "solutions" affecting women?

To begin with it is clear that the government measures are having a severe effect on women's jobs in the public sector. On the one hand, the cutbacks in jobs severely affect women's professional opportunities. On the other hand, wage controls keep women from improving their wages in the only sector where they are widely enough unionized to fight for better pay. Furthermore, unlike the wage controls imposed in 1976-78 these controls have no provision for exceptions to allow women to catch up with men.

Despite the seriousness of these problems in the short run, it is the introduction of microtechnology that may pose the most serious threat. The postwar expansion of jobs has stopped and no sectors have opened up to replace the service sector as a source of new jobs. Unemployment is soaring and the new technology is eliminating or changing many of the jobs that remain. While microelectronics will affect sectors like manufacturing and thus "male" jobs, its potential uses are much greater in the service sectors and particularly in women's occupations, which involve much more of the "information processing" that microtech is designed to perform.

The introduction of mini-computers, word processors and other types of new equipment will eliminate many of the jobs women have been able to depend on. The present higher male unemployment rate suggests that the effects of the introduction of microtech have not yet had as severe an effect on jobs as the overall economic slowdown, but we cannot expect this to continue. Some studies indicate that the microtechnological revolution could eliminate as many as 80 percent of office jobs.[6] Government and business usually argue that these will be replaced by new jobs on a large scale, but it seems unlikely that the economy is going to produce the jobs that women need at least until the economy makes a real recovery.

In the sectors where microtech is being introduced the segregation of men's and women's jobs is reproduced in classic form. The jobs in data entry, and sometimes in computer programming, are going to women, while the more technical, highly-paid software jobs are still primarily men's. What we may see then, is new openings for men (albeit not in large numbers) in the service sectors, in very specialized information processing occupations, while the numbers employed in clerical work (mostly women) decrease. Women, on the other hand, can be expected to end up working in new, probably less skilled and certainly lower-paid clerical occupations and in production in high technology industry itself.

Unless the economies of the advanced countries regain the relative vigour that characterized them in the post World War II period, the jobs lost to microtech are unlikely to be replaced. Women are locked into a narrow range of occupations that they could depend on in the past. Now these sectors are being transformed, with the probability of widespread job loss. Because of women's segregation and the stagnation of the goods producing sectors, they have nowhere to move. Retraining that would enable women to fill some of the new and better-paid jobs in the high tech industry is a possibility, but prospects are not encouraging.

This is particularly true in light of government policies on training. The old federal government Training Act placed a major emphasis on considerations of "equity." That is, disadvantaged groups such as women were considered to be prime candidates for training for skilled jobs, to which their access had been limited historically. The effects of this Act were minimal, but under a new Training Act, introduced in 1981, the situation is worse. Its emphasis is on the efficiency with which people can be trained for new skill areas. This means focusing on the people who are already most qualified for the jobs, who, in general, are not women. Training in basic skills such as mathematics and sciences, which are critical to women if they are to enter the new computer-oriented fields, has been downplayed. This Act reduces the already slim possibilities for women to make significant advances in the microtech field.

Another problem women can expect to face is that the changes in the skills involved in jobs that will accompany the introduction of microtech are likely to hinder their fight for equal pay. It has been difficult to make gains in terms of equal pay in part because the skills women had were not recognized. In clerical work, for example, women typically had well-developed skills in writing, reading, use of numbers, recording in an accurate and methodical fashion, organization and social skills. These skills were often hidden by the fact that the job requirements stressed "typing" as the only acknowledged and thus marketable skill. To counter this women began to fight for "equal pay for work of equal value," the recognition in wages of our skill, education, experience and responsibility.

This struggle was successful in a few cases, but in general, employers resisted demands for job evaluations because they knew it would result in a higher wage bill. With the introduction of microtech whole classifications are being wiped out, and the jobs that are left are being reorganized to force workers to do more work. In many instances the level of skill is being reduced, with the result that employers are downgrading classification levels and attempting to lower wages. Employers now think job evaluations might not be such a bad idea. After all, if job evaluation will allow them to pay women less, why object?

Women's place in society has been fundamentally altered in the last seventy years. The resulting changes in women's lives reflect the wider changes in capitalism itself. Where women were once confined to being housewives, with only short periods of paid work, most of them are now wage workers. Whatever the level of unemployment women's return to the home will not deal with it. The economy will continue to need women, although the form that will take may alter.

Yet despite women's increasing labour force participation, their chances of getting decent and decently paid jobs is limited by unemployment and is becoming more so. If anything, women's segregation into low-paid sectors seems likely to increase with the introduction of microtechnology. And it can also be expected to eliminate the "protection" from unemployment that the segregated labour market has offered women up until now.

The economic squeeze is exacerbated by the cutbacks and political pressures that are blind to the realities of women's lives. Social services that make it possible, or more accurately bearable, for women to work are being unremittingly cut back. Cuts in UIC, job training allowances and family benefits all limit women's possibilities for economic independence. They make women more dependent on nuclear families. Restrictions on abortion and day care also make us less available for work and limit our work options.

These money-saving cutbacks, by making women less available for work, both hide unpopularly high levels of unemployment in the family and save the state money by having women take on the extra work that state services used to provide. The state has been unable to impose a wholesale campaign of cutbacks aimed at "bolstering" the traditional family. Not only have women and unions successfully opposed the most extreme attempts, but as we've seen, women play too central a role in the work force for this to be a real option. But these cutbacks and the corresponding glorification of family ideology ensure that women have fewer and fewer alternatives either at work or in the family. At the same time as they are pressured to rely on families and particularly on men for support, these kinds of relations are more and more unstable. Families today need two wages to survive; many family arrangements do not hold up over the long term and women, especially, end up supporting their children alone. Thus women make "choices" under conditions that often impoverish their own and their children's lives, increasing the stress on households.

These contradictory political and economic developments are the backdrop for women's increasingly militant role in the women's and labour movements. Women workers have pushed both movements to recognize that each has a stake in the political struggles of the other, and that women cannot separate their interests as workers from their interests as women. These contradictory pressures and women themselves are challenging both movements to find new strategies as the economy and state policies shift the grounds of struggle beneath our feet.

With the introduction of microtechnology we can expect the fight for jobs to increasingly be a fight for women's jobs and against forced part-time jobs with little or no benefits. The jobs that are at most risk are predominantly not unionized. How can women push the union and women's movements to cooperate on what is a central issue for women? Microtechnology threatens to make organizing more difficult, but it also presents us with new possibilities. While beginning organizing drives in times of high unemployment is not a popular idea we should remember that the industrial unions in the automobile industry originated during the Depression and that they too were in part a response to the introduction of a new technology – assembly line production.

Equal pay and desegregation of the labour force are essential if women are going to make qualitative gains over the next years. Yet it is clear that our old strategies for equal pay and affirmative action haven't worked and may be obsolete as wage controls, cutbacks and rising unemployment radically change the context in which we are mounting these battles. What can we learn from our failures in the past ten years? How can the union and women's movements work together on the issues that both have identified as priorities?

More important than any single issue is recognizing that the issues are interconnected. Our job is not only to link equal pay and affirmative action but to bring them together with the fight against wage controls, for full union rights, the organizing of the unemployed and with the issues like abortion and day care so many want to treat as secondary. And we need to recognize the importance of building broad-based campaigns – involving both women and men and the combined might of the union, women's and unemployed movements in this country – to fight for these issues.

A crisis is a time of decision, a turning point. The kind of society we shall have and women's place in it are uncertain. There is no doubt that women will continue to be wage workers. What is not clear is whether in the years to come women will make progress towards equality with men or whether they will be forced into new job ghettos, with equality remaining only a dream. The outcome for women in this crisis is not decided; it will be the struggles over the next few years, how we wage them and with whom, that will determine our status in the labour force in the years to come.

NOTES

We would like to thank Linda Briskin, Marcie Cohen, Leslie Cotter, David Kidd, Liza McCoy and Jane Springer for critical comment and helpful suggestions.

1 *Globe and Mail,* May 4, 1983, p. 1.

2 Paul Phillips and Erin Phillips, *Women and Work, Inequality in the Labour Market* (Toronto: James Lorimer, 1983), p. 52.

3 For more detailed statistical information on trends for women at work, see *A Working Majority, What Women Must Do for Pay* by Pat Armstrong and Hugh Armstrong (Ottawa: Canadian Advisory Council on the Status of Women, 1983); *Women and Work, Inequality in the Labour Market* by Paul Phillips and Erin Phillips (Toronto: James Lorimer, 1983)

and *Women and Part-Time Work* by Julie White (Ottawa: Canadian Advisory Council on the Status of Women, 1983).

4 See Pat Connelly, *Last Hired, First Fired* (Toronto: Women's Press, 1978) p. 95; Statistics Canada, *Update* from 1981 Census (March 1983); and Statistics Canada, *The Labour Force* (Dec. 1982).

5 Statistics Canada, *The Labour Force*.

6 See *Your Job in the Eighties, A Woman's Guide to the New Technology* by Ursula Huws (London: Pluto Press, 1982) and *Women and the Chip, Case Studies of the Effects of Informatics on Employment in Canada* by Heather Menzies (Montreal: The Institute for Research on Public Policy, 1982).

WOMEN AND UNIONS IN CANADA:
A STATISTICAL OVERVIEW

Linda Briskin

This article examines the statistics on women's participation in unions in Canada. The statistical information is divided into sections: union organization and union membership.[1] Although the statistics provide a useful context from which to examine the changing character of union activity by women, the numbers themselves indicate very little about the actual experience of women in unions. And the statistics are no substitute for an analysis of the social and political forces confronting union women. The daily struggles of women, recounted in this book, bring the statistics to life and establish a more viable basis for understanding the political contradictions.

UNION ORGANIZATION

The percentage of the paid female work force[2] that is unionized increased marginally between 1974 and 1979, from 22.7% to 23.7%.[3] However, for male workers it declined, from 40.4% in 1974 to 38.5% in 1979 (see Table 1). Between 1974 and 1979, the number of paid female workers increased by 25%; in the same period the number of women unionized increased by 31%.

For men, there has been a 12% increase in the number of paid workers but only a 7% increase in the number unionized. During this period the unionization of the male workers did not keep up with the numbers entering the work force. More women than men are entering the work force and women are unionizing at a faster rate than they are entering the work force. Thus the increased number of unionized women is not simply a result of more women entering the work force. This pattern is borne out if we look at the figures for the years between 1970 and 1980. During this ten-year period, there was an 81.7% increase in the number of women unionized, but the number of employed women increased by only 58.8%. For men, there was 23% increase in union members, just slightly higher than the increase in the numbers of employed men (22.2%).

Table 1
Union Members as a Percentage of Paid Workers, by Sex,
1974 and 1979

	Paid Workers	Union Members	Union Members as % of paid workers
TOTAL			
1974	7,946,000	2,682,939	33.8
1979	9,318,000	3,035,752	32.6
		+192,326*	
		3,228,078	34.6
FEMALE			
1974	2,980,000	676,939	22.7
1979	3,749,000	890,365	23.7
		+102,457*	
		992,822	26.5
MALE			
1974	4,965,000	2,006,000	40.4
1979	5,569,000	2,145,387	38.5
		+89,869*	
		2,235,256	40.1

* (teachers)

* The Corporation and Labour Unions Returns Act (CALURA), up until 1983 when the legislation was changed, required only those organizations whose original function was as a trade union to report on their membership. Since many teachers' unions began as professional associations, most teachers are not included in the report. This should be remedied in the next CALURA Report.

I have shown the impact of including teachers on the percentage of the paid work force that is unionized. Figures are from *Key Characteristics of Teachers in Public Elementary and Secondary Schools, 1972-73 to 1980-81*, Canadian Teachers' Federation, 1981, pg. 33.

Table 2 looks at union members as a percentage of paid workers broken down by province. Although in a given province a high percentage of paid female workers may be unionized, this may represent only a small number of women. For example, in Saskatchewan in 1979, 26.6% of paid female workers were unionized but this accounted for only 34,000 women. In Ontario, although the percentage of unionized female workers was considerably smaller — only 20.3% — it represented 307,000 union members.[4]

Table 2
Union Members as a Percentage of Paid Workers, by Sex and Province, 1979

	% Women	% Men	% Total
Quebec	30.8	38.8	35.7
Newfoundland	28.9	61.5	49.3
British Columbia	27.4	48.2	40.1
Saskatchewan	26.6	32.4	29.6
Manitoba	24.5	35.6	30.7
Ontario	20.3	38.1	30.7
Prince Edward Island	20.0	23.8	21.6
Yukon and Northwest Territories	20.0	27.8	25.0
New Brunswick	18.8	40.3	32.1
Nova Scotia	17.0	37.4	29.5
Alberta	16.9	26.4	22.5
Canada	23.7	38.5	32.6

The percentage of unionized women and men workers differs quite dramatically in some provinces. For example, in Newfoundland, only 28.9% of women workers are unionized, compared to 61.5% of male workers; in British Columbia, only 27.4% of women workers are unionized, compared to 48.2% men. Three factors — available work, sex-differentiated patterns of employment and the degree of unionization in a particular industrial sector — explain these differences. For example, in British Columbia, the wood industry, which is unionized, is not only the major industry in the province but an area that employs very few women. This explains the 20.8% difference in unionization between women and men. This pattern is also evident in the unionization rates by industrial sector.

Before we turn to the unionization rates by industrial sector, it is important to explain that Statistics Canada in the *Standard Industrial Classification* has broken down the economy into the eight sectors referred to in Table 3. Some of these are quite straightforward, such as "manufacturing;" "construction," which includes the skilled trades; and "mining." The titles of the rest are not self-explanatory, however.

Table 3

Union Organization by Sector and by Sex, 1980

Sectors	% of all Workers Unionized	Women as a % of all Workers	Women as % of Union Membership	Unionized Women as % of Women Workers	Unionized Women as % of all Women Unionists
Community, Business and Personal Service	24.2	60.8	63.6	25.3	46.9
Trade	8.9	44.3	35.6	7.2	5.8
Manufacturing	43.2	26.0	19.0	31.6	18.0
Finance, Insurance and Real Estate	2.5	61.6	63.8	2.6	1.0
Public Administration	67.8	34.0	33.8	67.2	18.2
Transportation, Communication and other Utilities	53.2	22.0	20.0	48.3	9.4
Construction	57.6	9.6	0.6	3.8	0.2
Mining	32.5	13.0	2.8	7.0	0.2

"Transportation, communication and other utilities" includes air, rail, water transport and buses, taxis and trucking. It also includes radio, TV, telephone and post office operations as well as electric, gas and water utilities. "Trade" refers not to skilled trades but to wholesale trade, such as the distribution of food, farm products, dry goods and coal and to the entire range of retail stores: shoes, clothing, food, hardware, books, cars, etc. "Finance, insurance and real estate" comprises the banks, trust, insurance and real estate companies and the Bank of Canada.

The "community, business and personal service" sector is extensive and includes education, health and welfare agencies, religious organizations, amusement and recreation, business management services, accommodation and food services, labour organizations and a range of personal services such as laundries, barber shops and funeral services. Finally, "public administration" includes all areas of federal, provincial and local government administration such as defence, labour, employment and immigration, the legal system and the police.

Two points emerge from this overview of the sectors of the economy. First, they cannot be neatly divided into public and private sectors. For example, transportation includes a whole range of services in the public sector such as city buses and the CN Railway, as well as the private trucking industry. Second, each of these sectors contains a variety of job classifications. For example, a secretary could be working in the public administration sector, in the finance sector or in the transportation sector.

With the exception of construction and mining[5] and perhaps transportation, most sectors of the economy contain areas of work that are both traditional and non-traditional for women. The figures in Table 3 indicate the percentage of the work force in each sector of the economy who are women. In looking at these figures, keep in mind that each sector is not made up of homogeneous occupational groups; however, we still see that women workers dominate in certain sectors: service, finance, trade and manufacturing.

In fact, in 1980, three sectors of the economy — service, manufacturing and trade — employed 68.5% of all workers and 76.9% of women workers. However these are not the sectors with the highest degree of unionization; in 1980, only 24.2% of service workers, 43.2% of manufacturing workers and 8.9% of trade workers were unionized. The highest degree of unionization is in the area of public administration, where 67.8% of workers were unionized, followed by 57.6% of construction workers and 53.2% of transportation and communication workers.

Is the degree of unionization in each sector attributable to the sex of the work force? If sex were a critical factor, we would expect for example, that the higher the proportion of women workers in a particular sector, the lower the degree of unionization. However this is not the case. Table 3 shows that service and finance both have an approximately 60% female work force. However, 24.2% of all service workers and only 2.5% of finance workers are unionized. In public administration, where 34% of the work force are women, 67.8% of the workers are unionized. Thus no general pattern emerges on the basis of sex.[6]

This is reinforced by the fact that the percentage of the union membership that is women is in most cases almost equal to the percentage of women workers in that sector. Table 3 shows that 63.6% of the union membership in the service areas are women, slightly higher than the 60.8% of the female work force in that sector; similarly, women make up 20% of the union membership in the transportation sector and 22% of the workers. We can conclude that the sector of the economy has more impact on unionization rates than the sex of the worker. To increase the numbers of unionized women, we must look to those sectors with low rates of unionization.

A sectoral analysis shows that two sectors that have a very low degree of unionization employ large numbers of women workers. In finance, 358,00 women are employed, mostly by the banks. However, only 9,412 women — 2.6% — are unionized. In trade, there are 746,000 women employed but only 7.2% — 53,411 — are in unions. There is no doubt that unionizing drives in these areas are desperately needed. Even in the service sector, where 25.3% of women workers are unionized, women workers not in unions total 1,289,478.

We know that some unionizing is occurring and for women workers at a rate faster than they are entering the work force. If we look back to Table 1 we can see that between 1974 and 1979, 213,426 joined unions. The majority of these — 120,000 — were in the service sector; 54,000 in public administration; 16,000 in transportation and 11,000 each in trade and manufacturing. Noticeably absent was any successful organizing in the finance sector.

Finally, Table 3 shows that 46.9% of all women unionists are in the service sector. In fact, 83% of all women unionists are in manufacturing, service and public administration. It is therefore no surprise that unions in these sectors are taking the lead in addressing the concerns of women workers.

Table 4
Rate of Unionization of Women 1965-80

	Number of Women Members	Percentage of all Members
1965	292,056	16.6
1970	513,203	22.6
1975	711,102	26.0
1979	890,365	29.3
1980	932,883	30.2

UNION MEMBERSHIP

Let us turn from the contrast between unionized and non-unionized workers to the make-up of the union membership. By 1979 women made up 40.2% of the work force but Table 4 shows that only 29.3% of union membership were women. On the positive side, in the 15 years between 1965 and 1980, the number of women unionists increased by 219%.

Table 5 looks at the distribution of union membership in three types of unions: international, national and government employees' organizations.

Table 5
Union Membership in International, National and Government Employees' Organizations, by Sex 1970, 1980

Women as a Percentage of the Membership

	1970	1980
International	14.3	18.5
National	39.0	42.7
Government	27.5	40.3

Distribution of Union Membership, by Sex and Type of Union

1970	Women	Men	Total
International	38.6	67.6	61.0
National	47.4	21.6	27.5
Government	14.0	10.8	11.5
	100.0	100.0	100.0

1980	Women	Men	Total
International	30.8	58.6	50.2
National	47.8	27.7	33.8
Government	21.4	13.7	16.0
	100.0	100.0	100.0

International unions are based in the United States with offices in Canada. Most are affiliated to the American Federation of Labour and

Congress of Industrial Organizations (AFL-CIO) as well as to the Canadian Labour Congress (CLC). Although an international union may have many members in Canada, the Canadian component of the entire union is small. For example, in 1979 only 8.2% of the membership of the United Auto Workers (UAW) were Canadian yet the UAW was one of the largest unions in Canada, with 131,163 members. Similarly, the United Food and Commercial Workers has 145,177 members in Canada but this represents only 11.7% of its total membership. In 1979, 1,573,807 Canadian workers were in international unions.

International unions tend to dominate in the major industrial areas. In 1980, 50.2% of total union membership in the industrial sector belonged to international unions. In fact, 43% of all unionists in international unions were in the manufacturing sector, 16.1% were in construction and 13.5% were in transportation.

In contrast, national unions tend to organize public sector workers such as hospital workers, teachers and communication workers. In 1979, 966,777 unionists were in national unions, the largest of which was the Canadian Union of Public Employees (CUPE), with 252,040 members.

Government employees' organizations represent 495,168 people who work directly for the federal or provincial governments. In 1979, the largest government workers' union was the Public Service Alliance of Canada (PSAC) with 152,725 members.

The percentage of women's membership in the three types of unions reflects different patterns of male-female employment — women primarily in the public sector and service areas and men in the industrial areas. It is therefore not surprising that in 1980 women made up only 18.5% of the membership of the international unions, only a 4% increase since 1970 (see Table 5). In contrast, women constituted 42.7% of national unions and 40.3% of government unions. And while 30.8% of women unionists were in international unions, almost double — 58.6% of male unionists — were in international unions.

Since the late Sixties there has been an upsurge of unionization among government workers, teachers and hospital workers, many of whom are women. This has meant a shift in the balance of power from the international unions, which predominate in the industrial sectors, to the national unions, which are organizing these groups of workers. In 1970 the international unions represented 61% of all unionists but by 1980 this figure had dropped to 50.2%.

Since a large number of those unionizing were women, the distribution of female membership in the three groups of unions has also shifted. There has been a decline in the percentage of women unionists belonging to international unions, from 38.6% in 1970 to 30.8% in 1980. At the same time the percentage of women unionists in government employees' unions has risen from 14% in 1970 to 21.4% in 1980.

Table 6
Provincial Distribution of Women Union Members, 1980

	Women members	% Women members of regional union membership	% of all Women members
Ontario	314,117	28.3	33.7
Quebec	294,264	33.9	31.5
British Columbia	121,107	27.2	13.0
Alberta	65,011	30.7	7.0
Manitoba	42,883	35.0	4.6
Saskatchewan	36,310	38.1	3.9
Nova Scotia	21,888	25.9	2.3
New Brunswick	16,795	23.3	1.8
Newfoundland	14,971	22.1	1.6
Prince Edward Island	3,320	37.9	0.3
Yukon and Northwest Territories	2,217	30.6	0.3
Canada	932,883	30.2	100.0

The provincial breakdown of women unionists (see Table 6) shows that 78.2% of all women unionists are in Ontario, Quebec and British Columbia; however, 78% of *all* unionists are in these three provinces. It is here that we find the most powerful union movements and also the strongest movements of union women.

Table 6 also shows that the union movements in Saskatchewan and Prince Edward Island have the highest percentage of women members in their ranks. About 38% of unionists in these provinces are women, in comparison to a national average of 30.2%. Newfoundland and New Brunswick have the smallest percentage of women members, 22% and 23% respectively, significantly less than the average.

One of the ways of assessing the success of women unionists in penetrating the traditionally male-dominated unions is to look at their election to union positions. However, the figures in Table 7 include only those members of central leadership bodies. All other elected officials of unions – at local and regional levels – are not included. For example, in the Ontario Public Service Employees Union (OPSEU), each of the 410 locals will have 5 to 8 executive members. None of these are included in the figures in Table 7. This explains why, in total, there were only 944 Canadian executive board members in 1980.

In both the national and government workers' unions there is approximately one board member for every 1850 members; in the international unions there was one board member for 14,661 members. (Not only are women underrepresented on the boards of international unions, all Canadian members are underrepresented.)

Table 7
Executive Board Members by Type of Union and Sex,
1972-80

	1980	1979	1978	1977	1976	1975	1972
International							
EBM	106.0	108.0	120.0	112.0	158.0	142.0	132.0
Women EBM	4.0	2.0	4.0	5.0	8.0	6.0	5.0
% of Total EBM	3.8	1.9	3.3	4.5	5.1	4.2	3.8
National							
EBM	578.0	552.0	619.0	636.0	589.0	541.0	460.0
Women EBM	126.0	168.0	145.0	155.0	99.0	74.0	65.0
% of Total EBM	21.8	30.4	23.4	24.4	16.8	13.7	14.1
Government							
EBM	260.0	255.0	238.0	443.0	402.0	483.0	413.0
Women EBM	30.0	23.0	22.0	39.0	29.0	36.0	24.0
% of Total EBM	11.5	9.0	9.2	8.8	7.2	7.5	5.8
Total							
EBM	944.0	915.0	977.0	1191.0	1149.0	1166.0	1005.0
Women EBM	160.0	193.0	171.0	199.0	136.0	116.0	94.0
% of Total EBM	17.0	21.1	17.5	16.7	11.8	9.9	9.4

In 1980, although women were approximately 30% of unionists, they made up only 17% of executive board members (EBM) (see Table 7). In government employees' unions, women made up 40.3% of members but only 11.5% of EBM. In national unions women made up 42.7% of the membership and only 21.8% of EBM; in international unions women made up 18.5% of membership and 3.8% of EBM. The actual numbers reinforce the degree of underrepresentation. Of the 944 executive board members of all these unions, 160 were women.

Representation has improved only slightly in the last decade. In 1972, 3.8% of EBM in international unions were women. In 1980 the figure is exactly the same. However, given the actual number of board members, this represented a decline of one! In the government unions there was a decline in board members between 1977 and 1978, due to a change in government reporting guidelines. However, in 1977 there were 39 women EBM, which was 8.8% of the total; in 1980 there were 30 women EBM, which was 11.5% of the total. It is difficult to assess whether or not the percentage increase is a victory!

Although an increase in women's representation on central leadership bodies is necessary, the low representation is not indicative of the activity and success of women in unions. In government politics, women are always better represented at the municipal than at the federal level. This is also true in unions. OPSEU conducted a study that showed that in 1981 36.5% of all local executive committee members were women – up from 30.7% in 1976.

> Women are assuming more key positions. In 1976 only 75 women were local presidents; by 1981 this number had increased to 96. Of the 31 additional presidents in 1981 fully two thirds (21) were women. This again points to increased participation by women as a source of new strength.[7]

And although there has been a sharp decline in the membership of the United Steelworkers due to the recession (from 203,000 in 1980 to 183,000 in 1983),[8] the percentage of women in local executive positions has increased dramatically in the same period. For example, there has been a 44.7% increase in the number of female presidents of locals between 1979 and 1982 (from 38 to 55), and in just a three-year period, the percentage of women local executive members rose from 8.9% to 11.6%.[9]

We often picture a union meeting as a room full of men with a few women. However, the limited participation of women is not necessarily a result of women being numerically disadvantaged in the union. Table 8 shows that although 47.8% of labour organizations had less than 30% women members, only 14.2% of all women unionists were in these unions (which probably represented workers in sectors with many job areas non-traditional for women, such as construction and mining). It is true that women activists in these unions would certainly be isolated.

Table 8
Unions by Proportion of Women Members, 1980

Percentage of women members	Labour organizations		Women members	
	No.	%	No.	%
No women members	14	7.7	–	–
Under 10%	47	25.8	42,421	4.5
10%–19.9%	27	14.9 } 47.8	72,055	7.7 } 14.2
20%–29.9%	13	7.1	18,933	2.0
30%–39.9%	18	9.9	126,951	13.6
40%–49.9%	18	9.9	204,502	21.9 } 68.5
50%–59.9%	12	6.6 } 33.5	121,840	13.1
60%–69.9%	13	7.1	185,643	19.9
70%–79.9%	4	2.2	16,611	1.8
80%–89.9%	8	4.4 } 11.0	56,419	6.1 } 17.3
90%–99.9%	8	4.4	87,508	9.4
All women members	–	–	–	–
Total	182	100.0	932,883	100.0

However, 68.5% of all women unionists were in unions where they made up between 30% and 70% of the membership; and 17.3% of women unionists were in unions consisting almost exclusively of women. The latter unions represented female job ghettos like nursing. This means that 85.8% of women unionists were in unions with at least 30% female membership.

Women workers are ghettoized in certain occupational classifications such as clerical and sales jobs. However because unions usually organize by sector and industry rather than by job, members of unions, especially national and government employees' organizations, do a wide variety of jobs. This means that the ghettoization of female occupations is not totally reproduced inside the union movement.

The picture of the union meeting as a room full of men and a few women may be accurate but the underrepresentation of women in union activity is by and large not a result of numerical isolation. Traditionally women have not chosen, have not been able to, or have not been encouraged to get involved in union activity; however, this book documents that a dramatic change is taking place. The fact that the majority of women unionists are in unions with a sizable female membership means that there is enormous potential for them to have an impact on the policies and practice of their unions.

Table 9
Unions with 25,000 or more Members or with 10,000 or more Women Members, 1979

	Number of members	Number of women members	Women as % of total membership
OVER 25,000 MEMBERS			
International Unions:			
Steelworkers	187,089	13,264	7.0
Food and Commercial Workers	145,177	55,578	38.3
United Auto workers	131,163	16,522	12.5
Teamsters	87,740	6,796	7.7
Carpenters	81,452	2,213	2.7
Electrical Workers	71,442	8,887	12.4
Machinists	61,876	5,928	9.5
Woodworkers	62,845	4,279	6.8
Service Employees	61,010	41,222	67.5
Labourers	52,980	329	0.6
Plumbers	41,136	16	—
Operating Engineers	34,586	1,549	4.5
Musicians	34,716	4,477	12.8
Hotel and Restaurant Employees and Bartenders	31,897	16,230	50.8
Clothing and Textile Workers	31,935	20,925	65.5
Retail Wholesale Union	27,770	9,921	35.7
Subtotal	1,144,814	208,136	18.2
National Unions:			
Public Employees (CUPE)	252,040	109,847	43.5
Public Service Alliance	152,725	58,763	38.5
Quebec Teaching Congress	84,301	52,575	62.4
Ontario Public Service Employees Union	67,290	33,719	50.0
Social Affairs Federation	67,983	47,197	69.4
Paperworkers Union	63,675	3,488	5.5
British Columbia Government Employees Union	42,678	17,404	40.8
Alberta Union of Provincial Employees	38,939	20,988	53.9
Railway, Transport and General Workers	38,821	5,261	13.5
Quebec Government Employees	48,949	19,489	39.8
Nurses Association of Ontario	27,640	27,459	99.3
Public Service Employees	27,233	10,374	38.0
Communication Workers of Canada	26,570	8,869	33.4
Congress of Democratic Trade Unions	18,343	2,910	15.9
Subtotal	957,187	418,343	43.7

Table 9 (cont.)	Number of members	Number of women members	Women as % of total membership
10,000 OR MORE WOMEN MEMBERS			
International Ladies Garment Workers	22,522	18,887	83.8
Hospital Employees Union	21,444	17,154	80.0
Canadian Telephone Employees Association	17,097	16,561	96.8
Registered Nurses Association of British Columbia	14,491	14,248	98.3
Federation of Quebec Professional Union of Nurses	13,585	12,938	95.2
Office and Professional Employees International	22,798	12,715	55.8
Subtotal	111,937	92,503	82.6
Total of 3	2,213,938	718,982	32.5
All other unions	821,814	171,383	20.9
Total	3,035,752	890,365	29.3

Table 9 reinforces this point. It identifies the 30 largest unions in Canada — 16 international and 14 national or government employees' unions. Although women make up 30% or more of the membership in only 5 of the 16 international unions, in 11 of the largest national unions the percentage of women members ranges from 33% to 99%. If we also include the six additional unions (listed at the bottom of the table), which have large numbers of women members, we find that 80.8% of all women unionists are in these 36 unions.

In conclusion, the number of women in unions is increasing — faster than the numbers of men and faster than women are entering the work force. At the grass roots level inside the labour movement women are playing more of a leadership role. It is clear from these figures that women's presence in unions and their potential impact on them is growing. Nonetheless it is important to end on a sombre note. Only 23.7% of paid women workers are in unions. This means that 76% of women workers are not unionized. The strength, and perhaps the survival of the labour movement — and surely the success of women's struggles for equal rights in the workplace — will depend on unionizing those 3 million women workers.

NOTES

1 The sources for statistical material are:
  Statistics Canada, *Corporations and Labour Unions Returns Act, Part II, Labour Unions*, Cat. No. 71-202 (CALURA); Statistics Canada, *Corporations and Labour Unions Returns Act, Part II, Labour Unions, Supplement*, Cat. No. 71-202S; Women's Bureau, Labour Canada, *Women in the Labour Force*, Cat. No. L38-30; Statistics Canada, *Historical Labour Force Statistics – actual data, seasonal factors, seasonally adjusted data*, Cat. No. 71-201; Statistics Canada, *Standard Industrial Classification*, Cat. No. 12-501E.

  Some of the charts use 1979 figures and some use 1980 figures. The 1983 edition of *Women in the Labour Force*, which includes figures on the percentage of the work force that is unionized, uses 1979 data. The 1982 CALURA Report, the latest available, uses 1980 figures. This accounts for the slight discrepancy in some of the figures.

2 Labour Canada's definition of paid workers is "persons entitled to or receiving remuneration from employers for labour or services performed (does not include the self-employed)." Another classification called "employed workers," refers to "any work for pay or profit that is paid work in the context of an employer-employee relationship or self-employment. It also includes unpaid family work." See *Women in the Work Force*.

  If the figures for employed workers are used to calculate the unionized percentage of the work force, the percentage declines dramatically. Compare these figures for 1979 to those in Table 1: total employed female workers unionized, 29.3%; employed female workers unionized, 22%; employed male workers unionized, 33.8%.

3 Figures taken from Women's Bureau, Labour Canada publications have previously shown a higher percentage of female paid workers who were unionized (see 1976 and 1977). Until 1978 they were using unpublished data from Labour Canada to calculate these figures; since then they have been using figures from the CALURA reports. Earlier books on women and unions, such as Julie White, *Women and Unions* (Ottawa: Advisory Council on the Status of Women, 1980) used the earlier Labour Canada figures and show a higher percentage of unionized women.

4 The numbers of the unionized women in each province shown in Table 6 are slightly higher because they are 1980 figures. See note one for further explanation.

5 In 1975, Labour Canada reported no paid women workers in mining; by 1980, 25,000 women were working in this sector.

6 Julie White makes this point in *Women in Unions*.

7 "Women in OPSEU – A Statistical Analysis of Participation in Union Affairs by Women," President's Report, OPSEU, Feb. 1982.

8 Labour Canada, *Directory of Labour Organizations in Canada* (Ottawa: Minister of Supply and Services, 1980 and 1983 [unpublished data].

9 "Women of Steel – Equality in the Economy, on the Job and in the Union," Research Report, United Steelworkers, 1983, p.21.

NO PROPER DEAL: WOMEN WORKERS AND THE CANADIAN LABOUR MOVEMENT, 1870-1940

Ruth Frager

In the past, Canadian women workers faced enormous barriers that hindered their participation in union and strike activities. Labour spokespeople often blamed women's relatively low level of participation on the allegedly inherent traits of womankind. For example, an 1897 Ontario labour journalist stressed "the *natural* timidity among women to enter into [unions]."[1] Such sexist explanations ignored the realities of the situation which women workers faced, realities which significantly limited the possibilities of protest. Some of these limitations applied to unskilled male workers as well, but women workers were under special constraints. Nevertheless, there were important cases where women workers were able to protest militantly against their exploitation and domination.

The following analysis of the period from the late 19th century to World War II focuses on both the difficulties faced by women workers and on some of the situations in which they engaged in tenacious strikes. Because the manufacturing sector was of central importance to the labour movement in this period, this article deals chiefly with women in that sector. This anaylsis is necessarily a tentative one, however, for the available evidence is still fragmentary.[2]

During this period, Canada's women workers, like many male workers, endured long hours of monotonous, often hazardous labour. Workers in the textile industry, for example, worked long hours for low pay, and were plagued by inadequate ventilation, high humidity, considerable noise, and poor sanitary facilities as well as the employers' incessant pressure to speed up the work. Turn-of-the-century women laundry workers did heavy work, on their feet for hours on end. The noxious fumes, which they breathed, produced headaches and sore eyes. Workers in the fur industry toiled in foul-smelling, dimly lit shops where clouds of hair from the fur floated around their heads. Tuberculosis was not uncommon, and harsh chemicals produced skin rashes.[3]

Female workers were characteristically underpaid throughout this period. As today, they received a fraction of what males earned, even when doing the same jobs as men. In 1921, Canadian women who engaged in paid employment earned, on average, 54% of men's wages, and in 1931, they earned 60%. In the manufacturing sector, this proportion was as low as 44%.[4] It was rare for a woman worker to make enough money to be economically self-sufficient. Thus in 1913, a commentator noted that the average female factory worker in Montreal earned $4.50 to $5.50 per week, at a time when the lowest estimate of the minimum living wage was $7.00 per week.[5]

Women, like unskilled male workers, frequently "voted with their feet" to protest their harsh working conditions and low pay. Women moved from one type of factory work to another and from factory work to jobs such as waitressing and fruit-picking, and perhaps back to the factories again.[6] In many cases, such individual means of expressing discontent may have been the only available recourse, but transiency made it difficult for women to organize themselves collectively into unions. Another significant factor undercutting the possibilities of organization was the large number of unskilled women competing for jobs. Where women did begin to organize, employers often broke their unions by firing and replacing the militants. In numerous cases, employers defeated strikes of the unskilled by replacing the strikers en masse with scab labour.

These weaknesses plagued unskilled male workers as well. With heroic exceptions, such as the transitory Industrial Workers of the World and the One Big Union, it was not until the rise of the Congress of Industrial Organizations (CIO) in the late 1930s that unskilled workers were able to organize in substantial numbers. Prior to this, the strongest unions were generally those of the craft workers, whose solidarity and militancy stemmed from craft pride and a relatively high demand for their skills. Thus it was the unskilled — both female and male — who faced the gravest difficulties in organizing during most of the period under consideration.[7]

Yet women workers have almost always borne additional burdens and had to deal with greater barriers than male workers. The problems women confronted in organizing were compounded by the demands of childrearing and housekeeping. Thus it was that women workers in this period were generally young and single. For most, marriage marked their exit from the world of paid labour. The fact that most women workers had relatively little workplace experience may well have made it harder for them to engage in collective protests. It is not surprising that few seasoned female union leaders emerged under these circumstances. [8]

As today, married women who did do work for wages were burdened with additional household responsibilities. They normally had little time or energy for active participation in union or strike activities. Seeking out jobs that were as compatible as possible with their household labour, they tended to take in laundry, accept boarders, or do home sewing for clothing contractors. In such cases, the woman's isolation in the home meant that it was very difficult for her to participate in collective forms of protest. Those few married women who did work outside their homes frequently moved in and out of the paid labour force. These shifts back and forth were often regulated by pregnancies. After a baby was weaned, a woman might return to her paid job, only to leave it when the next child was born. As the children grew older and were able to contribute to the family income, a woman might concentrate on her domestic responsibilities, perhaps only to return to paid labour when her children had left home. [9] Thus these married women workers, like many single workers, tended not to build up continuous workplace experience.

In order to understand why women workers faced special difficulties in organizing, it is also important to realize that many women were working as domestic servants. This was particularly true at the turn of the century, when over a third of Canadian women workers were in domestic service. [10] This is a sector that was difficult to organize because women who served in private homes were extremely isolated. The hours of work were unusually long and often irregular, thereby making it difficult for these workers to attend organizing meetings. In addition, the servant's relation to her employer was often fairly personal, and she was under close supervision. Those who boarded in their employers' homes were in a vulnerable position if their employers sought retaliation for organizing activities or slow-downs. [11]

In general, women workers were more vulnerable than male workers to intimidation by their employers. Employers were probably particularly intransigent with their female employees because often the very reason they had hired women in the first place was because they could pay them lower wages. Employers in highly competitive areas such as the garment industry were dependent on low-wage female labour and therefore likely to be especially opposed to organizing activities on the part of their female employees. Moreover, employers were frequently able to pursue a "divide and conquer" strategy by buying off male workers at the expense of the women.

In 1897, according to William Lyon Mackenzie King's newspaper report, when a manufacturer of ready-made clothing was asked what he paid his help, he replied:

I don't treat the men bad, but I even up by taking advantage of the women. I have a girl who can do as much work, and as good work as a man; she gets $5 a week. The man who is standing next to her gets $11. The girls, however, average $3.50 a week, and some are as low as two dollars. [12]

Earlier, around 1870, male shoeworkers in Toronto found that management's opposition to their union dramatically increased when the union began to organize the women shoeworkers as well. Solidarity between female and male workers represented a threat that was potentially very costly to the owners. [13]

Successful unionization and demands for higher pay presented their own dangers to women. They provided an incentive for employers to switch to all-male work forces. In a significant number of cases where unions did succeed in obtaining better pay and better working conditions for both women and men, the employers simply fired the women. [14]

For all these reasons – transiency, lack of skill, lack of experience in the workplace, the extra demands of household responsibilities, isolation on the job, and the particular intransigency and "divide and conquer" tactics of the employers – women commonly faced extraordinary barriers to their participation in unions and strikes. For male workers, active participation in the labour movement required time, energy, and dedication that was often extraordinary. For female workers, it was often impossible.

* * * * *

"Woman's work, outside of her home, is one of the sad novelties of the modern world; it is a true social heresy," the Chief Factory Inspector for Quebec pontificated in 1922. "Woman, outside of her home, appears to us as a being out of place, a woman without a country," he huffed.[15] He was not alone in these views, of course, not then or now. Part of this prejudice reflected a fear among male workers that the employment of women would worsen job competition, thereby allowing employers to undercut wages. But there were other social roots to this prejudice; at the heart of male supremacist ideology lies the notion that a woman's "proper place" is in the home ("a man's castle").

Historically, this ideology of female domesticity held sway across Canada but was especially prominent in Quebec, where the traditional family was usually seen as crucial to the survival of the French-Canadian way of life. The Quebec clergy played a prominent role in opposing the entry of women into the paid labour force, fearing that such changes would undermine masculine authority and wreak havoc on the traditional family. The fears associated with women entering the paid labour force became sharper as unemployment (a worse threat to the maintenance of family life) tore apart the social fabric. The MP for Hull expressed this deepening anxiety in the midst of the depression of the 1930s:

> We must correct a completely abnormal situation: one sees girls and even their mothers leaving the house to work, while the husbands and the male youths stay at home, looking after the children, and even doing the cooking.[16]

In both English and French Canada, it was less socially unacceptable for single women to engage in paid labour than for married women. In fact, in the 1920s, there was a growing expectation that single women would enter the paid labour force for a few years until they got married.[17] Once she married, however, the domestic ideology continued to prevail. Those who violated these norms were commonly thought to do so for "pin money," and this made it more difficult for women workers to gain sympathy in their struggles for better pay.

For women workers, the prevalence of the domestic ideology in society at large meshed with the realities of the world of paid labour. Since women were usually unable to earn enough to live on, it made sense for them to hope that their stint in the paid labour force would only be temporary, a hope that was reinforced by the harsh working conditions. Thus the young woman worker, expecting soon to become a full-time housewife, might well have hesitated to invest time and energy in the labour movement. As a male labour spokesperson explained in 1895, bemoaning women's reluctance to agitate for higher pay:

> in too many cases [women workers] look to marriage as the door through which they will escape from toil, and not expecting to be permanently in the labour market, they do not insist on keeping it up to a high standard.[18]

This argument was also made by female commentators. In 1913, the *Labour Gazette*'s female correspondent from Toronto, agreeing with remarks made earlier by the Vancouver correspondent, wrote that the rarity of labour organization on the part of women must be seen, in part, as "an absence in general on the part of women workers of looking to their occupation as a life work."[19] In 1929, a Communist Party organizer, Florence Custance, argued in a similar vein that one of the major problems in organizing women was that "women do not take wage earning seriously. To them it is only a temporary necessity ..."[20]

Under widespread social pressure to be relatively passive and to obey men, women workers had more social inhibitions to overcome in their struggles against male employers. Nor were unions generally considered respectable, especially for proper young ladies. Thus Leonora Barry, General Investigator of Women's Work for the Knights of Labour and organizer of women workers in both Canada and the United States, reported in the late 1880s that her attempts to organize women floundered on:

> *the habit of submission* and acceptance without question of any terms offered them, with the pessimistic view of life in which they see no ray of hope .... *Many women are deterred from joining labor organizations by foolish pride,* prudish modesty and religious scruples; and a prevailing cause, which applies to all who are in the flush of womanhood, is the *hope and expectancy that in the near future marriage will lift them out of the industrial life* to the quiet and comfort of a home, foolishly imagining that with marriage their connection with and interest in labor matters end ...[21]

Similar themes on women's social conditioning are apparent in a poem written in 1886 by a female unionist from Belleville, Ontario. It urged women to join the Knights of Labour, proclaiming:

> It is not any women's part (sic)
> We often hear folks say
> And it will mar our womanhood
> To mingle in the fray.

> I fear I will never understand
>   Or realize it quite
> How a woman's frame can suffer
>   In struggling for the right.[22]

This poem indicates that there was, in fact, concern that a "true woman" should not "mingle in the fray," and it is unlikely that all women workers agreed with the poet in dismissing this concern.

*   *   *   *   *

For those women who were able to overcome these barriers of prejudice and circumstance, there were still further hurdles. In their struggles against employers, many female workers were faced with much less than total solidarity from their "fellow" workers and "brother" unionists.

As firms grew in size and financial clout, employer aggression kept male unionists on the defensive. In many cases, unions were unable to hold their own, and, in fact, unionized men constituted a small proportion of all male workers. Inadequate wages and the threat of unemployment were very real concerns. Employers used their power to chip away at the much-prized skills of craft workers through the introduction of new machinery. Old skills were carved up and the pieces handed out to less skilled — and cheaper — workers. Although many women workers were confined to traditional female job ghettos (i.e., jobs that were done exclusively by women), women were sometimes brought into traditionally male workplaces in order to work at some of the newly simplified tasks.

This "divide and conquer" strategy used women, as it also used unskilled male immigrants, to keep workers in a competitive scramble for scarce jobs. Women were sometimes hired as scabs during male workers' strikes as, for example, during the employer assault on the printing trade in turn-of-the-century Toronto.[23] Yet we still do not know how extensively women were used as strike-breakers. In these cases, it is unlikely that male craft unionists were able to appeal sincerely and effectively to women's sentiments of working-class solidarity because the men themselves were frequently pursuing exclusionary policies.

Male craft unionists in the late 19th and early 20th centuries frequently sought to exclude women from the paid labour force in general and from their own trades in particular. These craftsmen were usually affiliated with the American Federation of Labour (AFL), which had a strong influence on the Trades and Labour Congress (TLC), the most important central labour body in Canada at the time. As the international treasurer of the AFL explained in 1905, "the great principle for which we fight is opposed to taking ... the women from their homes to put them in the factory and the sweatshop."[24] Although there was a humanitarian side to this, it was distinctly paternalistic. Morever, the main issue was probably not the humanitarian dimension but rather the fears that competition from women would undermine the men's positions. Thus a labour organization in Ontario explained in 1910 that "we think that women should not be allowed to work in the foundries, as it has a tendency to degrade them, to lower the wages of the men and to keep a number of young men out of work."[25] In some cases, as in the Montreal bookbinders' strike in 1904, male unionists led strikes to force employers to fire the women.[26]

In the late 19th century, such exclusionary policies had been elevated to a formal principle of the Trades and Labour Congress. The TLC's platform of principles called for the "abolition of ... female labour in all branches of industrial life, such as mines, workshops, factories, etc." This "principle" was not changed until 1914 when it seemed that many women were needed to fill the places of male workers who went off to war. The new TLC plank called for "equal pay for equal work for men and women."[27]

Yet the TLC's antipathy to the use of women in "men's jobs" continued to be apparent during the First World War, for male unionists insisted that women should only be used as a last resort. As male workers of different nationalities were sent to battle each other in the trenches, employers in war-related industries amassed super-profits. In the name of patriotism, Canadian workers were called upon to make greater and greater sacrifices, both at home and at the front, while employers continued to play off male workers against female workers. As more women were drawn into the work force, employers continued their attacks on the craft workers' skills, wages, and working conditions. Male craft unionists reacted by trying to restrict the use of female labour. Thus, in June 1917, the TLC's "Pronouncement of Organized Labour in Canada on War Problems" condemned "the unnecessary dilution of labour by the introduction of female labour before proper steps had been taken to utilize available skilled mechanics." From their point of view, the situation was particularly deplorable in munitions plants, where there was "indiscriminate use of female labour."[28]

The same theme was taken up again at the 1918 Annual Convention of the TLC when a report was delivered on the "Conference on War Problems" between government and labour representatives. The report proclaimed:

> We called upon the Government for the protection of women who enter industries to replace men, and suggested that *they should only be placed there after full investigation had proven that all available man power had been absorbed* .... Reports by women inspectors, in conjunction with representatives of men's organizations, as to the advisability of women undertaking any class of work (with the view of their responsibility towards the nation, as the mothers of our future citizens), should be a contingent condition of their employment in any industry.[29]

Such careful protection of women was, no doubt, a way of keeping women out of jobs that males saw as rightfully belonging to themselves. The labour representatives at the conference also called upon the government to support equal pay for equal work, and this, too, may have been a way of keeping women out of "men's jobs."

The issue of equal pay for equal work was a particularly slippery one. On the one hand, many unions did nothing to promote equal pay, thereby failing to help women who earned one-third to one-half less money for doing the same work as their male counterparts. On the other hand, some unions may have adopted the strategy of calling for equal pay as a way of actually trying to keep women out of particular workplaces. Although it is difficult to document deliberate motivation in such cases, we do know of a number of cases where a union's insistence on equal pay meant that women were no longer hired. For example, one late 19th-century commentator stated:

> In Toronto there are very few women employed in cigar-making. The reason being that all the employés (sic) belong to a union which insists on all workers being paid alike, and the employers prefer to employ men, because they are likely to remain longer in the business.[30]

One cannot help but suspect that the men in this union had anticipated this result. After all, given the way employers tended to use women as low-wage labour, it was probably evident to the male workers that this would be the outcome of pursuing an equal pay strategy. Thus, supporting a union could, in such cases, actually work to the immediate disadvantage of women. Women workers were, therefore, hurt both in situations where they received significantly lower pay than men performing similar work and in situations where unions' insistence on equal pay, without programs like affirmative action, served to drive women out of the workplace.

During World War I, support for equal pay, by helping to remove the low-wage incentive for hiring women, may have been an attempt to ensure that all available men would be hired before employers would resort to using women. Support for equal pay may also have been a way of helping to make sure that, when the war ended, women workers would be replaced by returning men. Indeed, during the war male unionists often insisted that, in cases where women had taken over "men's jobs," these jobs must revert to men once the war was over. Women, they argued, should then be returned to the home.[31]

Craft unionists sometimes opposed the organization of women in a variety of ways. Recent scholarship has revealed that in the turn-of-the-century United States, women workers who organized and applied for a charter from the international union in their trade, were sometimes rejected or ignored. If they then appealed to the top leadership of the AFL, these leaders did nothing to rectify the situation. High initiation fees were also used in the United States to keep women out of particular unions, since women generally earned so much less than men.[32] Although we do not yet know how common these practices were in Canada, it is likely that the international unions pursued similar policies with respect to women on both sides of the border. After all, these unions tended to be quite centralized.

Although the story of male unionists' relationship with women workers is a far cry from class solidarity, it was not wholly a battle between the sexes. There were recognizable, common class interests, which produced a certain ambivalence in the relationship. Some men, who felt that women should not engage in paid labour, began to acknowledge that the women who were in the labour force needed union support. The Ontario labour press in the early 20th century, for example, did show concern for women workers, noting the need to improve the women's working conditions. Yet at the same time, this press stressed women's role in the home, and there was considerable apprehension that women's wage labour would ruin the family.[33]

At the turn of the century, male craft unionists who shared this fundamental ambivalance often gave only half-hearted support to women workers' struggles. The International Brotherhood of Electrical Workers (IBEW), for example, had asserted its jurisdiction over women telephone operators but appears to have been relatively uninterested in organizing them. The executive board of the union often refused requests to help organize the operators. Although, in the pre-World War I period, there were a few IBEW locals of women telephone operators in the U.S., they were not given the autonomy and the voting rights normally afforded to the male locals. Skilled men in this union probably were afraid that if many operators were organized, the women would eventually outnumber the men and would therefore take control of the organization. The men seemed particularly to fear that unskilled operators might make poor decisions with regard to craft issues.[34]

Another international union that gave only limited support to women in its jurisdiction was the United Garment Workers (UGW). Female members seem to have had little influence on UGW policies, which were at times actually detrimental to them. The union's main approach to organizing was to convince employers to use the union label, on the grounds that more workers would then buy those employers' goods. The union label was to be used as leverage to get particular employers to make their shops conform to union standards, and the label was thus, of course, supposed to be issued only to those employers who conformed. Sometimes, however, as in Chicago in 1907, the UGW issued labels to shops in which women worked under extremely poor working conditions.[35] It is likely that examples of this practice could be uncovered in Canada as well.

The general ambivalence toward women workers was also reflected in male unionists' reluctance to permit women to become involved in decision-making and leadership roles within the labour movement. Consider this account of a 1915 meeting between the officers of the National Women's Trade Union League, an American organization, and the Executive Council of the AFL. The point of view of Samuel Gompers, international president of the AFL, is related by the female president of the League:

> The Executive Council of the AFL recognized the need of organizing women, but they did not think women were qualified to organize women, that, in the first place, women were very difficult to organize,

even if they could be organized at all; that, secondly, women organizers were rarely worth anything, that they had a way of making serious mistakes — and [he] used some other language which, frankly, I don't want to repeat.[36]

Similarly, male union leaders in early 20th-century Vancouver hesitated to include women workers in their policy deliberations. When the Vancouver Trades and Labour Council, at the request of the Royal Commission on Labour Conditions in B.C., formed a committee to submit suggestions regarding legislation for working women, the male unionists turned to middle-class women's organizations such as the Local Council of Women. Helena Gutteridge, one of the few women union leaders in British Columbia, was not invited to join the committee. Moreover, when the male union leader of the committee did his own investigation on this subject, he apparently relied on evidence from the women's employers, totally neglecting to ask the women workers themselves.

Several years later, Gutteridge met with disapproval when she proposed to the Vancouver Trades and Labour Council that women from various unions be brought together to discuss the eight-hour day, a minimum wage for women, and mothers' pensions. The male members of the Council objected to such an irregular arrangement, arguing that the elected delegates were the only ones who could legitimately represent their unions, even when it was just a matter of discussion. It was therefore decided that an existing committee of men would deal with these issues in accordance with the established procedures.[37]

Pearl Wedro, a Jewish immigrant who was active in the International Fur Workers' Union in Winnipeg and Toronto in the 1920s through the 1940s, probably expressed the disappointment of a number of women activists when, looking back over her life in the labour movement, she stated:

I always felt, it's left with me now that even [in] progressive-led unions, a woman's chances are less than a man's. There's always somehow resentment to let to the very top a woman. And although our International was led by progressives and our own union, but I don't think, due to my ability and contribution, that I got a proper deal. If I was a man I think I would have been placed with the highest responsibility and having a chance not to sit in the shop but really make the *full* contribution. But that was not the case.[38]

Wedro explained that she never married because she was always so involved in the labour movement, and she described how her aunt used to tell her that she was destroying her own life by remaining unmarried. Women labour organizers, as in so many other careers, often had to choose, then as now, between a family and a career. (Needless to say, most men did not have to make such a choice.) And when some women did make the sacrifice to work as committed union activists, they faced discriminatory attitudes on the part of male unionists. That women such as Wedro were able to carry on under such conditions is eloquent testimony to their dedication and strength of will.

In general, the male culture of the labour movement probably served as a significant impediment to women's full participation in unions. At the turn of the century in particular, if the "real woman" belonged at home, it was the "real man" who belonged in the union. Skilled workers in particular tended to view manliness and notions of the inherent dignity of manhood as fundamental ideological elements in their struggle. Thus in 1909, skilled male workers denounced strike-breakers as those who "were prevailed upon to betray their manhood."[39] For a significant number of male trade unionists, their sense of dignity – and indeed their conception of unionism – was bound up with their gender identity. The notion of the manly union member, indeed the very notions of "fraternity" and "brotherhood," defined women as outsiders.

The atmosphere of union meetings and the patterns of union socializing could only have been deterrents to women's participation. At the turn of the century, for example, the members of a Toronto labour council committee felt that women members of the council did not come to the meetings because the atmosphere of the meetings was "repellent."[40] Unions commonly met in smoke-filled bar-rooms, normally a masculine preserve of boozy camaraderie and sexist jokes. It is hardly mysterious that women's participation in such union meetings was so infrequent.

There were, however, some exceptional occasions where male unionists proved to be particularly supportive of women workers. When women shoe workers struck five major factories in Toronto in 1882, demanding union recognition and better wages, the city's labour movement, including the various craft unionists, provided considerable support. Male shoemakers went out in sympathy and provided the women strikers with advice and money. However, despite the men's support, the settlement was disappointing.[41]

The Knights of Labour, a late 19th-century labour organization that sought to organize both skilled and unskilled, was more progressive than the craft unions in its attempts to organize women workers. There is evidence, however, that the male Knights were not as progressive as their rhetoric suggests. Thus Leonora Barry, the previously mentioned head of the Knights' women's department, maintained that the "selfishness" of the male Knights was partly to blame for the problems in organizing women.[42]

Generally, the support women received from male-dominated unions was half-hearted and sporadic. Women workers faced the same disparaging sexism from their fellow male unionists that permeated Canadian society as a whole.

*   *   *   *   *

Despite all of this — the barriers that faced them as workers and the disheartening sexism of both employers and many trade unionists — women were sometimes able to battle for union rights and better working conditions, not only for themselves but for men as well. They set up soup kitchens and, at times, barricades, sometimes actively fighting scabs and police. Thus, when the United Mine Workers led a strike for union recognition in Cardiff, Alberta in 1922, women backed their husbands, brothers, and fathers. While the men guarded the entrance to the mine, the women marched ahead. Armed with sticks, they attacked the scabs head on. Although the strike was lost, the militancy and solidarity of these women was remarkable.[43]

Women also fought for union rights on their own behalf. At the turn of the century, in cities such as Toronto and Vancouver, they struggled to organize themselves in a vast array of jobs. Efforts were made to organize female telephone operators, retail clerks, bookbinders, laundry workers, candy factory hands, hotel and restaurant employees, stenographers, garment workers, and even domestic servants. That most of these attempts collapsed, in the face of all the obstacles that women confronted, does not detract from their efforts.[44] That women were willing to take on such odds in the first place is an indication of the quality and strength of their spirit.

Too few of the fights that women waged in this period are adequately documented. One that does emerge from the buried past of women's struggles is the 1907 Bell Telephone strike in Toronto. For female telephone operators, the pace of work was gruelling, and there were serious health hazards such as electrical shocks. The pay was low. On top of all this, management was conducting an efficiency drive and demanding a reduction in hourly pay. Without union affiliation and with little chance to plan, four hundred women operators struck. Bell brought scabs in from its branches in other cities and stone-walled, refusing to negotiate or to be bound by a Royal Commission established to investigate the dispute. Although Bell's powerful resources prevailed in the end, these young women maintained an impressive solidarity throughout the strike. Strikers who lived in families with other breadwinners, for example, gave money to those who lived alone. The militancy of the strikers was created and maintained without the benefit of strong allies or years of experience in union organizing.[45]

Another dramatic example of women's militancy is the 1929 textile strike at the Canadian Cottons Mill in Hamilton, Ontario. This five-week strike began, apparently spontaneously, among the women workers. It started when the company tried to force each female spinner to tend more machines. They refused to accept this increased workload, and the strike spread to other workers. The strike committee consisted of three women and three men, and women apparently played an important role in sustaining the strike. The 600 strikers engaged in mass picketing, demanding the abolition of the increased workload, the re-hiring of all the workers who had lost their jobs because of the new efficiency measures, and an across-the-board 25% wage increase. Although, confronted by a powerful employer, the workers ultimately lost the strike, their militancy and solidarity in the face of such power was impressive.[46]

Another important battle was the three-week strike of several thousand female dressmakers in Montreal in 1937. When the International Ladies' Garment Workers' Union (ILGWU) began its organizing drive in Montreal in this year, one of the international's female organizers, Rose Pesotta, came to Montreal to help with the drive because, as she explained, "the dressmakers needed a woman's approach."[47] Although the vast majority of dressmakers were women, the official leadership of the strike was mostly male. Pesotta reported that, as the organizing drive progressed, the "pent-up resentment [of the female dressmakers] against existing conditions flared forth, and they trooped into the union office, pressing us to call strikes in their shops."[48] The union responded by calling a general strike in the trade.

The ILGWU faced enormous opposition. In addition to the resistance of the dress manufacturers, the strike also faced opposition from the provincial government and the Catholic union in Quebec's clothing trades. The Catholic unionists denounced the ILGWU "foreigners" and urged the women workers, who were mostly French Canadian, to return to work. Priests apparently joined in the denouncing of the ILGWU during their Sunday sermons, and the provincial government threatened to arrest the strike leaders. Nevertheless, it seems that most of the dressmakers joined the ILGWU's strike. In an unusual display of solidarity, the male dress cutters, skilled members of the ILGWU who had a separate collective aggreement with the manufacturers, joined the women. Dress production ground to a complete halt. The employers, anxious to be able to market the new summer dresses, finally settled. For once, women's solidarity and militancy had won out, this time with genuine support from male fellow workers and a male-dominated union leadership.[49]

* * * * *

For the most part, women workers faced serious constraints that significantly limited the possibilities of organization and protest during the period from the late 19th century to World War II. They were held down, and indeed often overpowered, both as workers and as women. As unskilled workers, women were in a particularly vulnerable position. Their employers were often uncompromising because these men depended on the cheapness of female labour, especially in labour-intensive industries. Because the women tended to be young and inexperienced, they were less prepared to deal with this heightened intransigence. In addition, many women workers were in the domestic service sector, a sector which has been especially difficult to organize because of the very nature of the work. Furthermore, given the hardships of the women's work situations, it is no wonder that women workers tended to internalize the domestic ideology. They often hoped to marry and leave paid employment, and this meant that they underemphasized efforts to improve their lot as workers.

Women workers could not normally count on the strong support of male unionists. At times, male unionists were openly hostile to them. Turn-of-the-century male craft unionists, who themselves faced serious management assaults, tended to regard women as unwanted intruders; they sought to exclude the women from "men's jobs" and from the union "brotherhoods," drawing on the notions of woman's "proper place" to buttress their arguments. Although other male unionists were less hostile toward women workers, their general ambivalence meant they seldom supported women's struggles wholeheartedly. Furthermore, there were cases where joining and supporting a male-dominated union would, in fact, have been detrimental to the immediate interests of the women involved. Women workers, in a history that is only beginning to be uncovered, confronted enormous obstacles — it is remarkable that they were sometimes able to fight back.

NOTES

Special thanks to the friends who have helped me clarify my thinking on these issues.

1 *Industrial Banner,* July 1897, cited in Craig Heron, "Working-Class Hamilton, 1895-1930," Ph.D.Thesis, Dalhousie University, 1981, p. 432 (emphasis added).

2 Not only have women workers been frequently ignored by historians, but they were also frequently ignored by their contemporaries. Male labour journalists and male union leaders seldom referred to them, even when these men were writing or speaking about industries in which a significant proportion of the workers were women. And the women themselves seldom recorded their own experiences. A significant number of strikes were never recorded, and existing strike records are often very sketchy, particularly with regard to the role of women. In addition, there is often little available information on other types of resistance. Sabotage, because of its covert nature, is, of course, difficult to examine, and it is particularly difficult to find out about practices of informal workplace solidarity. Informal methods of resistance may have been relatively more

important to women workers, yet evidence concerning these methods is particularly difficult to find. The search, however, has only just begun in earnest.

3   See, for example, Marie Lavigne and Jennifer Stoddart, "Women's Work in Montreal at the Beginning of the Century," in Marylee Stephenson, ed. *Women in Canada* (Don Mills, Ont.,1977), p. 133; Heron, pp. 403-424; Wayne Roberts, *Honest Womanhood: Feminism, Femininity and Class Consciousness Among Toronto Working Women, 1893-1914* (Toronto, 1976), pp.17-18; and the *Masses* (Toronto), Sept. 1933, p. 5.

4   Veronica Strong-Boag, "The Girl of the New Day: Canadian Working Women in the 1920's," *Labour / Le Travailleur,* (1979), p.147.

5   Lavigne and Stoddart, p. 134. See also Heron, p.392. For additional wage information, see Terry Copp, *The Anatomy of Poverty: The Condition of the Working Class in Montreal, 1897-1929* (Toronto, 1974), p. 32.

6   See *Labour Gazette,* May 1913, p.1209; *Toronto Star,* June 4, 1912, cited in Irving Abella and David Millar, eds., *The Canadian Worker in the 20th Century* (Toronto, 1978), p. 169; Strong-Boag, p . 137; Heron, p. 430.

7   The relatively more powerful position of skilled workers is revealed, for example, by Terry Copp's analysis of strike patterns of early 20th-century Montreal. Copp found that most of the few strikes that were successful involved highly skilled craft unions (Copp, p. 129).

8   In 1911, for example, over half of Canada's female workers were under 25. See Star Rosenthal, "Union Maids: Organized Women Workers in Vancouver, 1900-1915," B.C. *Studies,* 41 (Spring 1979), p. 40. See also Copp, p. 45. In 1931 and 1941, roughly 80% of Canada's women workers were single. (Canada, Department of Labour, *Women at Work in Canada* (Ottawa, 1965), p.21.)

9   This pattern predominated, for example, among female, French-Canadian textile workers in early 20th-century Manchester, New Hampshire. See Tamara K. Hareven, "Family Time and Industrial Time: Family and Work in a Planned Corporation Town, 1900-1924," in Tamara K. Hareven, ed., *Family and Kin in Urban Communities, 1700-1930* (New York, 1977) pp. 192, 198-99.

10 Patricia Connelly, *Last Hired, First Fired: Women and the Canadian Work Force* (Toronto, 1978), p. 92.

11 See Genevieve Leslie, "Domestic Service in Canada, 1880-1920," in Janice Acton *et al.,* eds., *Women at Work: Ontario, 1850-1930* (Toronto, 1974), pp. 110-11.
    As the 20th century progressed, a significant number of women turned to clerical work. Historically, this sector, like domestic service, has been difficult to organize, but more research is neccessary in order to ascertain

why clerical workers have only recently begun to organize in large numbers.

12 *The Daily Mail and Empire* (Toronto),Oct. 9, 1897, p. 10, cited in Michael Cross, ed., *The Workingman in the 19th Century* (Toronto, 1974), pp. 132-33 (emphasis added).

13 See Gregory S. Kealey, *Toronto Workers Respond to Industrial Capitalism*, 1867-1892, (Toronto, 1980), pp. xvi, 43-44.

14 See, for example, Roberts, pp. 1-2.

15 *Annual Report of the Quebec Department of Labour,* 1922, pp.87-88, cited in Copp, p. 49.

16 *La Presse,* 23 janvier 1935, cited in Marie Lavigne and Jennifer Stoddart, "Ouvrières et Travailleuses Montréalaises, 1900-1940," in Marie Lavigne and Yolande Pinard, eds., *Les Femmes dans la Société Québécoise* (Montréal,1977), p. 141. (The quotation has been translated from the French.)

17 Mary Vipond, "The Image of Women in Mass Circulation Magazines in the 1920's," in Susan Mann Trofimenkoff and Alison Prentice, eds., *The Neglected Majority: Essays in Canadian Women's History* (Toronto, 1977), p. 117 and Strong-Boag, p. 163.

18 *Canada Farmers Sun,* Nov. 13, 1895, cited in Roberts, p. 2.

19 *Labour Gazette,* May 1913, p. 1209 and April 1913, p. 1079.

20 F. Custance, "Our Tasks Among Women," Kenney Papers, Box 2, cited in Heron, p. 430.

21 Report of General Instructor and Director of Woman's Work, *Proceedings of the Knights of Labour,* 1889, p. 2, cited in Eleanor Flexner, *Century of Struggle* (New York, 1974), p. 200. On Barry's activities in Toronto, see Kealey, pp. 187-88.

22 *Journal of United Labour,* April 25, 1886, cited in Kealey, p. 189.

23 See Roberts, p.23.

24 "Talks on Labor," *American Federationist,* 12 (Nov. 1905), p. 846, cited in Alice Kessler-Harris, "'Where are the Organized Women Workers?'", *Feminist Studies,* Vol. 3, No. 1/2 (Fall 1975), p. 97.

25 Bureau of Labour Report, Ontario, 1910, p. 152, cited in Alice Klein and Wayne Roberts, "Besieged Innocence: The 'Problem' and Problems of Working Women — Toronto, 1896-1914," in Acton *et al.,* p. 220.

26 Lavigne and Stoddart, "Ouvrières et Travailleuses...," p. 140.

27 Cited in H.A. Logan, *Trade Unions in Canada* (Toronto, 1948), p. 399.

28 The text of this pronouncement appeared in the *Industrial Banner,* June 22, 1917, p. 6. The pronouncement also expressed concern that the women were getting lower wages for performing "men's work."

29 *Labour Gazette,* Oct. 1918, p. 833.

30 Jean Scott Thomas, "The Conditions of Female Labour in Ontario," *University of Toronto Studies in Political Science,* ed. W.J. Ashley, 1889, Series III, cited in Ramsay Cook and Wendy Mitchinson, eds., *The Proper Sphere: Woman's Place in Canadian Society* (Toronto, 1976), p. 178.

31 See, for example, the excerpt from the 1916 *B.C. Federationist* in Marie Campbell, "Sexism in B.C. Trade Unions, 1900-1920," in Barbara Latham and Cathy Kess, eds., *In Her Own Right: Selected Essays on Women's History in B.C. (Victoria,* B.C., 1980), p. 182.

Despite all the war-time concern expressed over women in "men's jobs," it appears that, during this war, women did not replace male workers to the extent which has been commonly assumed. On this issue, and on other aspects of the position of women workers during this war, see Ruth Frager, "Deluded Assumptions about Diluted Labour" (unpublished paper).

32 Alice Kessler-Harris, *Out to Work: A History of Wage-Earning Women in the United States* (New York, 1982), pp. 157-58.

33 Joan Sangster, "The 1907 Bell Telephone Strike: Organizing Women Workers," *Labour / Le Travailleur,* Vol. 3 (1978), p. 127.

34 *Ibid.,* p. 126. On the generally limited support given to women workers' struggles in Hamilton, Ontario, see Heron, pp. 455, 458.

35 On the UGW in Hamilton, see Heron, pp. 431-36. For a discussion of the shortcomings of the UGW in the American context, see Philip S. Foner, *Women and the American Labor Movement: From Colonial Times to the Eve of World War I* (New York, 1979), pp. 321-22, 350-54, 376.

36 National Women's Trade Union League, "Proceedings: N.Y. Convention, 1915," p. 100 (NWTUL Papers, Schlesinger Library). The NWTUL came into considerable conflict with the AFL as it pressured AFL leaders to appoint more women organizers.

37 Campbell, pp. 172-74.

38 Interview with Pearl Wedro by E. Mitchell on Sept. 14, 16, 17, 1971 (I. Abella Tape Collection).

39 *Industrial Banner,* April 1909, p. 4, cited in Craig Heron and Bryan Palmer, "Through the Prism of the Strike: Industrial Conflict in Southern Ontario, 1901-1914," *Canadian Historical Review,* Vol. 58, No. 4 (Dec. 1977), p. 450. On the general importance of manliness to male unionists, see Kealey, pp. 57-58, 78.

40 Roberts, p. 44.

41 See Kealey, pp. 50, 179.

42 For Barry's remarks, see Alice Henry, *The Trade Union Woman* (New York, 1915), p. 29. We do not yet know very much about the Knights' activities in Canada. (One hopes that the forthcoming book by Gregory S. Kealey and Bryan D. Palmer on the Knights will prove useful in clarifying the position of women in this organization in Ontario.)

There are other important gaps in our knowledge of Canadian male unionists' attitudes towards women workers. This issue has not yet been explored with regard to the Workers' Unity League, the Communist trade union centre during the late 1920s and early 1930s. Nor have we yet begun to explore the position of women with regard to the rise of the CIO in Canada in the late 1930s.

The radical unions of the early 20th century, the Industrial Workers of the World and the One Big Union, seem to have been largely confined to sectors such as logging and railroad construction, which involved mostly single men.

43 Anne B. Woywitka, "A Pioneer Woman in the Labour Movement," *Alberta History*, Vol. 26, No. 1 (Winter 1978), pp. 12-16.

44 For the details of these organizing drives, see Rosenthal, pp. 41-53 and Roberts, pp. 15, 18, 21-22, 26-28, 41.

45 Sangster, pp. 109-116, 118, 120-21, 123, 125-29.

46 Heron, pp. 442, 446-50.

47 Rose Pesotta, *Bread Upon the Waters* (New York, 1944), p. 253.

48 *Ibid.*, p. 260.

49 The settlement provided for an across-the-board wage increase of 10%, the 44-hour week, time and a half for overtime, union recognition, and a grievance procedure. See Pesotta, pp. 253-76 and Evelyn Dumas, *The Bitter Thirties in Québec* (Montreal, 1975), pp. 56-69.

II UNION ISSUES

OUT OF THE GHETTOS: AFFIRMATIVE ACTION AND UNIONS

Jackie Larkin

A woman worker who took a training course and got a job in a non-traditional area as a mine inspector was soon afterwards divorced. Down in the mine one day she heard men whispering, "Giving women these jobs causes divorces." She responded, "Having this job didn't cause my divorce. It just made it possible."

At my first International Woodworkers of America union meeting, I walked into a room of approximately seventy men and two other women. Intimidating enough. I sat down. A brother walked up to me and asked, "Can I sit here?" Thinking he meant the empty seat beside me, I said "yes." He then sat on my lap. When I pushed him off, angry and humiliated, but not wanting to make a "scene," he turned to his buddies and delivered his line, "Well, after all, it's the best seat in the house."

Affirmative action is what feminists and supporters of women's rights in North America describe as the special measures taken to encourage female entry into jobs that are traditionally male-dominated.[1] For decades, indeed centuries, the vast majority of women have been systematically denied entry into a considerable number of occupations where the pay rates are high. In order to reverse this "systemic" discrimination, proponents of affirmative action have supported a variety of different programs, including priority in hiring (preferential hiring), special training and education to challenge the prevailing myths about women's ability to perform such jobs.

Winning equal job access, especially through affirmative action, is slowly gaining popular acceptance. This is not solely a product of a growing feminist consciousness that rejects traditional roles. Women *need* higher-paying jobs in order to survive economically. Today, most couples find it difficult to manage on the one-and-a-half family wage brought in when both are working (the male often paid twice as much as the female). The growing number of female single parents can barely manage, if at all. The urgency to gain access to new fields will increase under the impact of microchip technology as more and more women lose jobs in the traditional areas of female employment.

In addition to these major economic pressures, there is another impetus for change. Unionized women workers have been undergoing an important radicalization in recent years. Feminism has spread beyond its student and professional origins and is being embraced and redefined by working women. And small but growing numbers of male unionists are also beginning to fight actively for women's rights. It has taken some time for this radicalization to be reflected in a demand for the labour movement to actively support affirmative action, but the situation is changing and a few successful struggles have won broad attention and support.

However, this support remains small compared to the breadth of support for other women's demands. Feminists and unionists must undertake a serious discussion of the merits of affirmative action and the best strategies for winning gains in this area. This article focuses on unions as the main vehicle to fight existing job segregation and addresses some of the central issues concerning affirmative action that have been raised in the labour movement. It does not discuss affirmative action programs designed to help women break into top management and executive positions. It is concerned with the possibility of changes for the majority of women, not for the few who would make their way to the top to join with men in perpetuating the existing power relationships. Too often, employers have coopted affirmative action and turned it into a showpiece program to demonstrate that women can be bosses too. While this article is concerned with affirmative action for women, many of the same barriers exist for racial and ethnic minorities and much of what is said here is relevant to the struggle against racial job ghettos. For women in racial minorities it is doubly applicable.

THE CASE FOR AFFIRMATIVE ACTION

Women should have the right to work at any job. Without it, we accept the intent behind job segregation: low wage ghettos, which maintain our economic dependence on male wages. Without it, we perpetuate deeply-held attitudes that women are incapable of many types of work. Without it, we are denied access to sectors of industry where profits (and therefore often wages) have traditionally been high and where union organization has been extensive and powerful. The gender division of the labour force also weakens the ability of all workers to fight for improvements in wages and working conditions. It divides women and men, who defend their petty "privileges" and see the work that women do as less important, less deserving of a decent wage. Because the occupational segregation by sex is often so extreme, neither understands the real problems faced by workers of the other sex.

Gaining access to the male-dominated sectors will not be easy. An intimidating line-up of opposition faces us. Employers and governments resist any serious efforts to eliminate the job ghettos, which are so profitable to those who want cheap labour. Systemic discrimination in both hiring and training policies is widespread and so deeply ingrained that it is seldom conscious. Women themselves often lack confidence in their ability to perform certain jobs; they know they risk male disapproval if they apply for "men's" jobs, if they do dirty work, if they develop muscles. Women often find the effort of surviving in dominantly male environments too great: coping with the macho style, sexual harassment, physically difficult working conditions (which take a different form than in traditional female sectors). Especially in industrial jobs, the high incidence of shift work makes it difficult to organize domestic labour and child care. (This is also a problem in some female sectors.)

Although male workers' attitudes are changing, men seldom lead a fight for female job access without being pushed hard by the women who want the jobs. Since women are not working in these sectors (or their numbers are few) they are in a weak position to do the pushing. In hard economic times when male workers feel their own jobs are threatened, it is especially difficult to convince men to fight for programs such as affirmative action.

Finally, the scope of the job segregation problem is enormous. Obviously, any perspective to effect a major breakthrough must be a long-term one. This only underlines the necessity of a general strategy and clear specific proposals for how to fight most effectively. There are three general ways in which affirmative action programs can be implemented: a) voluntary employer affirmative action, b) government-enforced affirmative action and c) union-won affirmative action.

VOLUNTARY EMPLOYER AFFIRMATIVE ACTION

This type of program deserves the briefest comment. Several years of government encouragement of voluntary affirmative action programs by employers has produced only token results. This is not surprising — why would employers voluntarily provide the effort, training, reeducation of staff and funds necessary for a program designed to undermine the low-wage ghettos that benefit them? The futility of this route is obvious when we note that the voluntary affirmative action program initiated by the Ontario government in 1975 has resulted in only .05 percent of companies introducing such plans![2]

GOVERNMENT-ENFORCED AFFIRMATIVE ACTION

Governments have introduced programs of affirmative action through human rights legislation, through apprenticeship and training programs, and through requirements built into contracts negotiated between the government and companies receiving contracts or funding from the government.

Human rights legislation is extremely limited. Only in Saskatchewan does it allow for enforced affirmative action to overcome past discrimination. Generally, individuals can file complaints under human rights legislation and if they win, be given the job, but companies cannot be forced to put full-scale programs into place. Unlike the u.s. 1964 Civil Rights legislation, Canadian legislation does not allow for suits that would permit whole groups of women or racial minorities to challenge past discrimination and receive compensation. In 1973, for example, the u.s. legislation allowed the successful pursuit of a suit that forced AT&T and its subsidiaries to reimburse arrears of $53 million to their employees in discriminated categories.

Most Canadian human rights branches do not actively seek out cases. Instead, they wait until approached by individuals. Discrimination against that particular individual must then be proved. As an Ontario Federation of Labour (OFL) document on affirmative action notes: "The one by one complaint system presently used places undue hardship on the complainant, and is ineffective in uncovering systemic discrimination."[3]

Provincial and federal governments have also introduced small-scale affirmative action training programs for women seeking non-traditional skilled jobs. Although the programs are token (e.g., allocating two seats for women in vocational pre-apprenticeship programs) they are a step in the right direction. *Ontario Labour* points out that: "Only 174 Ontario women were enrolled in non-service sector apprenticeship programs in 1981, compared to 36,000 men."[4] Pre-apprenticeship training is essential for giving women confidence in their ability to do the work. Clearly, these programs should be introduced on a much broader scale, and yet the present programs are being cut or threatened.

The final method of mandatory affirmative action has seen its only serious implementation in the U.S.: enforced programs for companies with federal contracts that require them to hire a certain percentage of women or blacks or other victims of group discrimination. While the impact of such programs is limited to certain corporations, they serve nevertheless to legitimize women's right to non-traditional jobs and in some cases actually win access to jobs for a substantial number of women. In the U.S., the combination of civil rights legislation and federal government mandatory programs had, for some time, a considerable effect. In order to avoid imposed programs and costly suits, a number of companies negotiated voluntary programs with unions. For example, in the American steel industry in 1974-75, nine major companies and the United Steelworkers of America (USWA) signed a voluntary program in order to remedy the near total absence of women and minorities from better-paid positions.

Even if limited, such programs should receive support from the unions. It is seldom that governments in this country, or the U.S., act to defend the interests of the most exploited workers against the hiring policies of large corporations. However, mandatory affirmative action of the American variety has not been introduced in Canada and unless a broad campaign to win it is waged by the unions and the women's movement it is not likely to be. In this regard the American experience is instructive. The major impetus for affirmative action in the U.S. resulted from the 1964 civil rights legislation, which itself was generated by the impact of the growing civil rights movement. Especially during the 1970s, blacks and women benefited from the programs introduced under that legislation, and a number of unions actively supported its principles. Like any other legislation, however, it can be reinterpreted, even withdrawn. Thus, if the unions and the women's movement do mount a successful campaign for mandatory affirmative action legislation in Canada, its implementation will be dependent on constant pressure.[5] Without legislation of this sort, there are no avenues for women seeking access to non-traditional jobs in non-unionized sectors, in newly opened industries or in situations where the union is unwilling to fight for real job access for women.

There is increasing acceptance within the labour movement for legislated action. The main objection to government programs stems from a concern that the government will be interfering with union rights. In most instances, this is simply not a problem, since few unions have encroached on management rights in the hiring field. It *can* become an issue in the skilled trades, where the unions retain some control over who is admitted to apprenticeship programs. Obviously, in this case, the best solution is for the unions to adopt the non-sexist policies that would give women access to these highly paid jobs. If, however, unions are not prepared to adopt programs to overcome past discrimination, then women or members of racial minorities should have the right to use legal means to correct the situation. Surely, if a union continues to accept unequal pay rates for men and women doing the same job and refuses to change its stance, few would oppose the right of the women involved to use equal pay legislation to force the employer to accept the principle of equal pay.

UNIONS AND AFFIRMATIVE ACTION

A few unions have fought for women's right to jobs from which they have been historically excluded. The Women Back Into Stelco Campaign, which was supported by Local 1005 of the Steelworkers in Hamilton, effectively publicized the fact that women had worked at Stelco during the war, but had not been hired since. In the ten years prior to 1980, 10,000 women had applied to Stelco. None had been hired. As a result of the campaign, a ten percent hiring quota was established and 130 women were hired. Unions and groups of women have also initiated affirmative action programs in plants in Hamilton, Sudbury, Fort Erie, in relation to CN in Toronto and Montreal, and in the open pit mines in Elkford in northern B.C.

These campaigns represent only small beginnings, and in many cases the gains made have already been wiped out by layoffs. They are nevertheless important victories. They demonstrate that large corporations can be forced to reverse discriminatory practices, especially when groups of determined women, with the active support of the union, are prepared to make the fight. They are also testimony to the way in which the attitudes of male unionists have begun to change.

At the policy level, many unions have begun to discuss affirmative action in a serious way. Most provincial and national federations have adopted policy statements in support of equal opportunity, including support for affirmative action. As early as 1977, the Canadian Union of Public Employees (CUPE) published a manual as a guide for union members, and in the years since, many other unions have produced documents dealing with the issue.

Some union organizations define affirmative action to include "any action designed to overcome and compensate for past and present discrimination."[6] Such definitions cover hiring and promotion policies and practices, equal pay for work of equal value, training and education, and terms and conditions of employment. Some unions come out strongly in favour of effective government legislation to enforce affirmative action. Most talk about negotiating programs through collective bargaining by establishing some sort of joint union-employer committee. A few unions have also begun to look at affirmative action from the point of view of racial minorities and handicapped persons.

Under the impact of the successful fights to get women into non-traditional jobs in Ontario and the growing strength of feminist consciousness among union women, in 1982 the Ontario Federation of Labour held a conference on affirmative action attended by 200 participants. The conference discussion paper, "Our Fair Share: Affirmative Action and Women" is perhaps the most comprehensive treatment of affirmative action to have received wide circulation among union women.[7] Without detracting from the few fights, which stand as an example to the rest of the labour movement, it has to be acknowledged that few unions have undertaken campaigns for affirmative action or made it a bargaining priority. Why is there such reluctance? Most union leaderships are slow to take initiatives unless they are under pressure from their membership to do so. Trade union bureaucracies tend to be conservative, especially when it comes to issues that are a radical challenge to the status quo. Thus in the largely male unions the leadership sees little reason to rock the boat. Such a stance does not necessarily rule out a rhetorical commitment to affirmative action. For example, in the bargaining conference that prepared for the 1981 contract negotiations between the International Woodworkers of America (IWA) and forest companies in B.C., the union for the first time adopted a proposal to establish joint union-management affirmative action committees. However, the discussion on the resolution was extremely brief, there was no education of the membership, and the demand quickly disappeared when the talks got down to business. Women are of course on the outside of these unions or constitute a small percentage of their membership and are therefore in a weak position to apply pressure to get them to take the issue seriously.

Yet as the Stelco experience has demonstrated, victories can be won — provided the union is willing to ally itself with women prepared to wage a campaign for jobs. Big gains can also be made in those job situations where unions organize both male and female workers, but where the work is segregated on the basis of sex. Such unions have the greatest potential leverage for winning affirmative action, because of the weight of the female membership. Yet in these unions, equal pay for work of equal value, not affirmative action, has been the major demand raised by women. (I will return to this point later in the article.)

The next section outlines a strategy for labour movement action towards breaking down job segregation. It takes up five major points: membership education, collective bargaining, quotas, seniority, and the relationship between equal pay and affirmative action.

MEMBERSHIP EDUCATION

Without education that takes up the fundamental questions involved in winning real equality for women in the labour force, unions will not be able to fight consistently for affirmative action. A conscious and committed membership is always the most important element in winning a fight and ensuring that it stays won.

A clear example of what can happen in the absence of good internal education and policies committed to equal rights for women workers was the post World War II collaboration of male unionists and employers to push women out of industrial jobs they had performed during the war. In this regard, the record of the American United Auto Workers (UAW) has been well documented: women were denied seniority rights with the tacit consent of local unions, were fired when they married, and had grievances discouraged or rejected by the union.[8]

Especially in the male-dominated unions where affirmative action is most needed, education would involve questions such as: why are women workers ghettoized? What would real economic equality for women imply? What role have unions played in maintaining job segregation? What should unions do to make women feel welcome as members? A discussion of these questions would inevitably stimulate far-reaching debate, and might very well upset the base of support that the union leaderships enjoys among male workers in these job areas.

The education process is not just a question of explaining why women need affirmative action; it must explore the best ways for winning the demand and for integrating women into the union once it is won. It means looking to labour federation women's committees and similar committees in local unions for assistance in the educational process. It could mean inviting local women's groups to participate in the process. The union itself should be prepared to establish a women's committee if affirmative action is won and women start joining the union. This would enable women to support one another, to express their particular needs as they begin working in the new jobs and to continue the process of membership education.

COLLECTIVE BARGAINING

If both public and private sector unions make affirmative action a priority in the collective bargaining process, this route can have a broader impact than all other methods. First, it is where workers can most effectively bring to bear their organized strength, where they can force management to change hiring practices without having to resort to lengthy and costly legal procedures that utilize limited and cautious legislation. Secondly, if they choose to make affirmative action a clear priority, instead of a few women gaining access to a plant (as is often the case with limited mandatory government programs), hundreds of women could gain jobs. Instead of a few small gains, private and public sector unions could win widespread programs in a broad variety of workplaces. Thirdly, if the unions undertake a serious fight for female access to non-traditional jobs, it will indicate to hundreds of thousands of unorganized workers how unions can improve their situation.

Finally, by fighting for affirmative action in a given plant or industry, the union can make real links with the surrounding community, demonstrating that unions can be concerned with the needs of all workers. The possibility of winning is much greater when *both* the union and groups of women (wanting jobs and willing to organize to get them) confront the company openly. The Stelco campaign was effective precisely for this reason: it captured the interest of the city and provided a focus for women who wanted jobs in the steel mill.

Union position papers often promote the establishment of joint management-union committees as the major mechanism for getting programs established. This route has all the pitfalls that such committees have exhibited when applied to equal pay for work of equal value. It ties up the union in lengthy discussions with management over criteria, methods of evaluation and implementation procedures. Often, the result is merely bureaucratic tangles and delays. The real decisions are taken out of the hands of the membership of the union. The most effective route to winning affirmative action is for the union to determine what kind of program it wants and to make that a demand in the collective bargaining process – just as it does for wages and benefits.

SETTING QUOTAS

Union leaders have often opposed the introduction of specific quotas for affirmative action plans. One of their favourite arguments is to propose vaguely defined "goals" rather than quotas, on the grounds that the latter would be a form of "reverse discrimination." Yet the whole idea of affirmative action involves "discriminating" in favour of a group that has been the victim of many years of negative discrimination. The OFL discussion paper puts it well: "We must remember that our present system is based on the fact that men have had affirmative action for 2000 years. Are we going to begrudge it to women for a few decades?"[9] *Of course* affirmative action means that if women are hired where they were not hired previously, men will not get those jobs. That's the way it will have to be if there is to be any change at all. The failure to define numbers or percentages of women to be hired, timetables for the realization of such quotas, and concrete support measures such as training programs and necessary facilities makes it impossible to hold management accountable.

Quotas have also been rejected on the grounds that there are no universal criteria for establishing them, that quotas may not reflect the realities of available skilled labour, that they can be used as ceilings, and that it will be difficult to get management to agree to any quotas proposed by the union. The criteria to be applied for establishing quotas should not be plucked from the sky; they should be based on concrete consideration of the pattern of discrimination of a given company and the available labour force. For example, the Stelco quota was based on the percentage of women who had applied in preceding years. Through a process of debate and discussion within the union, criteria for quotas can be developed and used to motivate the bargaining demand.

Naturally, it will be very difficult to gain management acceptance of any action that involves hiring policies. Management will actively resist any infringement of what they consider to be their sole prerogative — to determine who is hired. They will resist quotas precisely because quotas make them accountable.

SENIORITY

The question of seniority is probably the most contentious one raised in connection with affirmative action. Many partisans of affirmative action argue that it is possible to support affirmative action programs without altering existing seniority rights. They contend that special training programs and hiring quotas are essential but that seniority should not be tampered with. Under seniority systems, layoffs must occur according to last hired, first laid off; access to more skilled jobs within a plant must be on the basis of bidding determined by seniority.

This position is probably the majority view among affirmative action supporters within the labour movement. Yet even this modest view encounters strong resistance. The opponents of affirmative action have too often reasoned that anyone supporting hiring policies that act in women's favour is automatically in support of violating seniority rights. Yet this argument becomes a smokescreen to avoid doing anything to break down exisitng barriers. It deliberately plays on men's fears that their jobs will be threatened and avoids the prior question — how to get women the jobs in the first place.

However, there are those, myself included, who argue that effective affirmative action *does* require modification of seniority rights in order to defend the gains that have been won. Evaluating the merits of such a position requires a closer look at what seniority means for workers. Seniority represents a very important gain for the working class. It protects workers from arbitrary firing by employers on the basis of a worker's political views or refusal to tolerate unfair treatment. It ensures that older workers who would have difficulty finding jobs elsewhere because of their age have the greatest job protection and also that they will be less and less required to do the heavier jobs. It stops workers from competing with one another within a plant or office for higher-paying jobs. Under a seniority system, employer favouritism or assessment of merit plays little or no role. The employer is required to train the worker for the job to which she or he is entitled on the basis of seniority. Seniority rights thus help prevent conflicts between workers – which can only work to the benefit of the employer. However, like many gains of the working class, the impact is contradictory. Seniority discriminates against younger, newly hired workers. It perpetuates the existing stratification in many job situations, protecting the white, male workers who originally formed many unions. Thus seniority systems make it extremely difficult to overcome past discrimination. This is compounded by the failure of unions to take action to reverse systemic discrimination. There are few historical examples of unions in traditional male occupations campaigning actively for affirmative action during good economic times. In those boom periods substantial hiring of women would have given them a more secure foothold. Instead, as layoffs occur women have lost the few gains recently made because of their low place on the seniority list.

Let's look at the least disputed proposals for remedying the situation. Most important is winning plant or company-wide seniority (rather than departmental seniority) as a means of improving women's ability to move into traditionally male-dominated areas. Departmental seniority tends to keep women segregated and confined to lower-paid jobs.

The document prepared for the OFL conference on affirmative action makes a number of other proposals to improve women's seniority status. They include the accumulation of seniority during parental leave and the bridging of service clauses, which would allow a parent to leave the work force for an extended period of time to care for a child, and when reemployed to be credited with the length of seniority that had been accrued prior to termination. In fact, this latter proposal would be a first step in recognition of the socially necessary role women play in reproducing the future labour force – a role for which they are presently penalized in relation to job security. The OFL discussion paper also proposes encouraging unions to bargain "thirty and out" (retirement and full pension after thirty years) to encourage a faster turnover and the opening up of jobs for younger workers and new entrants to the work force.

The same document also endorses legal provisions under human rights codes that would give back-dated seniority to women who are proven to be victims of sex discrimination in hiring. This proposal, while supportable, would do little for the vast majority of women, since discrimination is difficult to prove some time after the fact.

The foregoing proposals are all necessary, but they do not address the central problem: how to protect gains made through affirmative action programs when layoffs occur. Virtually all the victories of recent years have been wiped out by layoffs.

Women have argued that the few gains they have made should be protected by the introduction of dual or parallel seniority lists that would maintain the *percentage* of women who have won access to non-traditional jobs. There are two kinds of responses to this. The first is that seniority is inviolable, a principle that should not be tampered with and that attempts to do so will produce resentment and anger on the part of male workers. There is an important truth contained in this argument and it is the following: workers fought long and hard for the seniority system that they now have and no institution – the government or any other agency – should have the right to change that system. But the workers themselves can change it. If, in their democratic majority they decide that a modified seniority system that strengthens the position of women and minorities who have recently been hired is desirable, then that is their decision to make. Of course it should not be imposed, and it cannot occur without the kind of serious political education that was outlined earlier. A politically conscious membership committed to overcoming past discrimination against sectors of workers will be able to evaluate the degree to which the seniority system is in contradiction with other important goals and act to change it if necessary. This is exactly what happened between USWA and Kaiser Corporation in the u.s., although it affected seniority in relation to training for skilled jobs rather than layoffs. The negotiated program established an integrated seniority list by factory *and* ordered access to training positions in the course of employment according to a quota policy. This latter provision violated strict seniority in relation to access to higher-paid positions.

The second argument made against modifying seniority through dual seniority lists takes the following approach: workers should fight all layoffs, but if they occur, it is not up to the union to determine who will and will not get laid off. The first part of the argument is correct — the union should actively fight all layoffs. Today, there are many possible programs for fighting layoffs and unemployment, which unions have not introduced. Indeed the fightback against massive increases in unemployment has been virtually non-existent. As capitalism's economic difficulties place a growing burden on workers' backs, this failure means that *all* workers, not just recently hired women and younger workers, are under the threat of layoffs. On the second part of the argument: unions do not really administer layoffs under any circumstances, but they have fought for a seniority system that determines how layoffs will be administered by management. In that sense, unions have determined that in general, younger workers will be laid off before older ones. Seniority systems represent a bottom-line union policy on layoffs. If the workers themselves decide upon it, that policy can be changed and additional criteria included.

The issues we have looked at up to this point — joint committees, quotas, seniority — cannot be dealt with in an abstract way. What can be won in any workplace depends on many factors — the level of union consciousness, the history of the union's activity in favour of affirmative action, the degree of management resistance and the nature of the surrounding community. Tactics must be designed to take these factors into account. For example, insisting on quotas in the first stages of a union debate might result in a detrimental early polarization. Similarly, demanding that dual seniority lists be established right away, before the union has begun to wage a fight for affirmative action, may lose more support than could be gained through an insistence on principle. It's not a question of abandoning general principles, but rather of recognizing that union members will be won to the ideas through a process of debate and concrete experience.

THE LINK WITH EQUAL PAY FOR WORK OF EQUAL VALUE

In strategy debates, there is often a polarization between those who argue that the central task is to raise the existing wages of female workers, primarily through winning equal pay, and those who argue that the key is getting women into the non-traditional areas – especially those sectors of high profitability and a strong union tradition. Indeed, the two fights have to be seen as two prongs of an overall strategy for winning equal rights for women workers. In recognition of this, the OFL Affirmative Action Conference included both equal pay and affirmative action under the general rubric of affirmative action.

The role of the equal pay fights, especially in the public sector, cannot be underestimated. It is where women workers are most concentrated that they must fight for monetary recognition of the importance of the work they do. Women need decent wages, wherever they work. But it is not only in the interests of women to win the fight for equal pay. As long as there are low-paid sectors, they act to depress the wages in the higher-paid jobs. As the economy goes into crisis this becomes more obvious. Lower-paid workers are made to bear the heaviest burden, and the low wages are used to justify lower settlements in the more profitable sectors of private industry.

The demand for equal pay has already had a huge impact within and without the labour movement. This is especially true in mixed occupational groups where women workers are confined to certain jobs. For example, women work in clerical jobs, men work as maintenance and outside workers in municipalities; women work as clericals and operators, men work in plant and installation in the telephone companies. Women's right to equal pay can be made forcefully and effectively in these situations because there is enough knowledge of the type of work done by male and female members of the union to make it difficult to sustain arguments that a male worker who digs flower beds should receive higher wages than a woman who works at a video display terminal. When the Telecommunications Workers Union in Vancouver occupied the B.C. Telephone Co. offices during their 1981 strike and continued to maintain telephone service, some of the male workers saw the pressure involved in the work of the operators, and began to question whether male workers "deserve" more wages than women.

The right to equal pay can also be presented forcefully in mixed job situations because of the considerable concentration of women workers. When it comes to winning support for demands, numbers count, both with the union and with the boss. Where women are in the majority they have the greatest power to fight for their demands and to ensure that the union doesn't subordinate their interests.

In British Columbia, during 1980-82, the fight for equal pay focused on the demand for equal base rates (i.e., equal starting salaries), and struck a responsive chord. The equal base rates demand avoids complex negotiations over the definition of equal value and at the same time is easily comprehensible to the union membership and to the public. The point was brought home rather forcefully in the 1981 Vancouver municipal strike of the CUPE and Vancouver Municipal and Regional Employees Union (VMREU) when it was revealed that women clericals required more education to get a job, yet received considerably lower starting salaries than male "outside" workers. During these strikes there was broad public support for the demands of women, even though there was inadequate organized support for the unions.[10]

A few examples illustrate how equal pay fights can be linked successfully to the struggle for affirmative action. Consider again the mixed occupational situation where unions straddle traditional male and female job areas. There are many examples of this: communications, public sector unions that organize inside and outside workers, industrial locations where plants and offices are in the same union, factories where men have the more skilled jobs. It is in these workplaces that lateral movement under plant or company-wide seniority systems can be used to break into the male-dominated areas. At present, many job situations have departmental seniority arrangements that correspond to job ghettos. Breaking down these seniority barriers is an important means of winning job access for women, especially in situations where the company is doing little hiring. The union can also insist that any new jobs opened up in the nontraditional areas be open first to women who have been working in traditional female jobs in the plant. Combined with equal pay victories that would then make some of the traditional female jobs more attractive to men, such arrangements combat job segregation.

Unfortunately, unions have not linked equal pay and affirmative action in such contexts, and employers are then able to counterpose the two demands. Recently the Employers Council of B.C. advanced the position that getting women into non-traditional jobs is the correct and only feasible alternative to equal pay:

> The Employers Council of British Columbia is not opposed to the concept of "equal pay for work of equal value." However, the practical implementation of such a process on even a limited scale presents substantial and perhaps insurmountable difficulties. There are serious questions as to whether or not equal pay for work of equal value can be implemented without causing a massive disruption in the existing labour market and in historical collective bargaining relationships. We believe that the desired goal of equitable treatment can be achieved more expeditiously by ensuring equality of opportunity. The positive steps that employers should institute are discussed later in this paper and in another council document entitled Affirmative Action ....
>
> Whether we like it or not, or whether we agree with it or not, the labour market produces a hierarchy, a continuum of wage rates. By definition, there will always be positions at the bottom of the scale.[11]

This kind of employer ideological offensive (which remains in the realm of ideology because few firms are interested in *real* affirmative action) underlines the importance of unions fighting on both fronts. Rather than denying the affirmative action fight just because the employers are making token arguments in that direction, unions should be pressing joint affirmative action and equal pay demands.

A second example demonstrates situations where winning equal pay can work against women workers it if is not combined with affirmative action. This is most likely to occur in sectors where women are a small minority. Historically, there are a number of instances of equal pay victories resulting in employers refusing to hire women. There are cases of male unionists supporting equal pay as a means of preventing women workers from being used as cheap labour competition, but with the expectation that this would result in women being excluded from jobs once equal pay was won.

In more recent years, the IWA in B.C. fought for equal pay but did not combine it with affirmative action. In 1966, the union finally succeeded in wiping out discriminatory pay categories for women workers. This was an important victory, but the union did not wage a

simultaneous battle to get women hired. The result was predictable –
some employers simply stopped hiring women and their numbers
declined in those mills.

PROSPECTS FOR THE FUTURE

This article's approach to affirmative action may seem utopian, especially in the present economic context. It is true that the resistance of
employers to both affirmative action and equal pay is greater than it has
ever been. Employers and governments are using a gamut of measures
such as wage controls, cutbacks and layoffs to drive down the real
wages of all workers and to force higher productivity. In such a context, demands that seek to qualitatively improve women's situation are
difficult to win. We've already seen a retreat from equal pay demands in
the past year in B.C. For example, in early 1982, the Hospital Employees Union launched an effective public education program to explain
why it was making equal pay a major bargaining demand. Soon afterwards the Social Credit government introduced wage controls. The
union, faced with fighting a difficult battle, opted for binding arbitration. Equal pay lost its high profile.

It *is* difficult to make gains when workers are faced with defending
what they have already won, but the only way out of the present crisis
is for the union movement to develop an effective fighting program
that represents all workers' interests and is an overall solution to the
economic crisis. To defend ourselves against widespread unemployment we have no other option than to fight for job creation programs
and social services that involve a fundamental reorganization of the
economy. While it is not within the scope of this article to outline such
a program, it should be increasingly evident that a real defence requires
policies that prefigure a society organized to meet human needs, not
those of profit-hungry banks and corporations. Demanding the
nationalization of corporations that threaten to shut down because
their profit margin is too narrow, fighting for major job creation projects (including affirmative action programs) and for a shorter work
week without loss in pay to redistribute the amount of work – these are
only a few examples of what we must begin to put forward as alternatives to the present attack on our living standards.

An essential part of the way forward involves uniting workers. It
means recognizing that unity can only be built through an active com-

mitment to fight for equality for women and minority groups. A false unity, built on subordination of the needs of women workers, will not stand the test of coming years. This is not a time to be saying to women: "Your needs will have to wait." The opposite is demanded. And women will stand for no less. By fighting for equal pay, for affirmative action, by organizing the unorganized, the unions will be in a stronger position to defend themselves.

Building this unity also requires a recognition that unions can no longer go it alone, that they need the organizing solidarity of other unions and of social movements – such as the women's movement – in order to win. The labour movement must reach out to the millions of unorganized workers who have no unions to defend them and who may adopt anti-union stances in the absence of policies that address their interests. It must join hands with feminists who are committed to fighting for women's rights but who are not union members, helping to build a women's movement that embraces the majority of working-class women, whatever their job or union situation. In the same way, feminists must recognize that they will not win equality without the mobilized support of the labour movement as a whole. The forces in opposition are tremendous: they command almost unlimited financial and legal resources (quite aside from their ultimate willingness to use force). Our greatest strength will be realized through the building of a unity that is based on a fight for equality.

NOTES

1 In Britain the term for affirmative action is "positive action."

2 "Affirmative Action Conference Breaks Ground," *Ontario Labour*, July-August 1982, p. 1.

3 "Our Fair Share: Affirmative Action and Women," Discussion Paper prepared for the OFL Conference on Affirmative Action, 1982, p. 18.

4 "Affirmative Action Conference," p. 1.

5 Instructive on this point was the announcement by the Reagan administration in 1981 that it would no longer require companies doing business with the government to draw up detailed plans for hiring and

promoting women and blacks. "Government officials privately describe the new rules as an attempt to test how far it is politically safe ... to abandon the current concept of affirmative action." "Every Man for Himself," *Time*, Sept.7, 1981, p. 14.

6 Research Report on Affirmative Action, National Union of Provincial and Government Employees, p. 1.

7 "Our Fair Share."

8 Nancy Gabin, "Women Workers and the UAW in the Post World War II Period, 1945-54," *Labour History*, Vol. 21 (Winter 1979-80), pp. 5-30.

9 "Our Fair Share," p. 11.

10 See Patricia J. Davitt, "When All the Secretaries Demand What They Are Worth," in *Still Ain't Satisfied*, eds. M. FitzGerald, M. Wolfe and C. Guberman (Toronto: Women's Press, 1982), pp. 195-209, for a detailed description of this strike.

11 Employers Council of British Columbia, "A Review of Equal Pay for Work of Equal Value," 1981, pp. 1, 7.

"ACTION POSITIVE" IN THE QUEBEC TRADE UNION MOVEMENT

Hélène David

The last days of 1982 will remain in Quebec memories as a graphic indication of the about-turn of the Parti Québécois government against the labour movement. The government unilaterally ended the bargaining process with the common front of public sector employees (public service, health and education workers — two-thirds of whom are women) through an exceptional piece of legislation. Bill 105 imposed cutbacks as well as lowering of wages and a worsening of many other working conditions; it also did away with the right to bargain and to strike for unionized public sector employees. Yet during this same time period the PQ government passed amendments to the Charter of Human Rights and Freedoms, making it possible for the Quebec Human Rights Commission to impose affirmative action programs on employers.

This article examines how the Quebec government came to adopt such a policy around affirmative action, as yet unique in Canada; and also why a major part of the labour movement has supported the Quebec Human Rights Commission's demands for legislation imposing affirmative action under certain conditions. It also looks at the potential impact of affirmative action programs in the light of the deteriorating conditions facing working women in Quebec.

A UNIQUE SITUATION WITHIN CANADA

The amendments to the Charter of Human Rights and Freedoms by Quebec's National Assembly, along with the regulations currently in preparation will make Quebec the only Canadian province in which affirmative action programs may be imposed on employers proven guilty of discrimination by the Human Rights Commission.[1] Before it was amended, Quebec's Charter of Rights and Freedoms was more restrictive than that of any other province or the Canadian Human Rights Act. All other charters (except that of Newfoundland) specify that affirmative action programs must not contravene the law. The absence of any such formulation in the Quebec Charter made any affirmative action attempt, even those undertaken on a voluntary basis, liable to be contested in court.

The Quebec government, after lagging considerably behind the rest of Canada or other advanced capitalist countries, has enacted path-breaking legislation or initiated social programs in other cases as well. This is true of issues such as maternity leave, child care, equal pay for work of equal value and the right to strike for public employees, as well as equalization of salaries across Quebec in the construction industry. While it is beyond the scope of this article to explain this phenomenon, we might note that it is in part linked to class relationships in Quebec, and to the fact that the question of nationalism, which gives the Quebec state a primary role not common to other provinces, cuts across all social movements. Wide popular support is necessary in order to make governments yield to demands, and the process of broadening the struggles has been easier in Quebec, due to the already broadly based nationalist consciousness.

When the Quebec government proclaimed the Charter of Human Rights and Freedoms in 1976, Quebec was the only province without legislation against salary discrimination. Early versions of the bill contained the "classic" provision found in all provinces, the United States and other nations, which prohibits unequal pay for men and women for *equal* or same work. This formulation makes a mockery of International Agreement No.100 adopted by the International Labour Organization (ILO) in 1953 and ratified by Canada in 1972, which recognizes the right to equal pay for work of equal *value*. The trade union movement and several women's groups protested the equal work provision and it was subsequently modified by the government. (Several years later, the same scenario was repeated at the federal level when the Canadian Human Rights Act was under consideration.[2]) In order to give the Quebec Charter's provision the scope of the ILO's agreement, the notion of *equivalent work* was retained in the final version of the bill that became law in June 1976.

The Charter had barely been adopted and the first rulings handed down in cases of discriminatory salaries for women when the Human Rights Commission, along with the trade union movement and various women's rights groups, began to point out the limits the Charter imposed on the Commission's work. In a brief published in December 1980, the Commission demanded an amendment that would enable it to recommend the establishment of affirmative action programs designed to prevent, eliminate or reduce any form of discrimination against any group following either a complaint or an investigation carried out by the Commission on its own initiative, and the right to impose such a program on a recalcitrant party through court action. The Commission also demanded the right to develop regulations to determine the scope and content of such programs and to supervise their implementation. Compliance with these regulations would be required by the various agencies or organizations requesting contracts, permits, licences and government grants as a necessary condition. Failure to comply with the Commission's regulations would be considered a violation of the Charter and, as such, liable to prosecution. Finally, the Commission also recommended that the Quebec Public Service set up an affirmative action program.[3]

Due to the dissatisfaction expressed by the Human Rights Commission and the pressure from numerous groups, a first, inadequate bill to the Charter of Human Rights and Freedoms gave rise to a parliamentary committee in the fall of 1981 and was replaced by a second bill in June 1982. In September 1981, the Quebec Employers' Council appeared before the parliamentary committee opposing the recommendations of the Human Rights Commission on the grounds that it would constitute an "unacceptable intrusion into the internal management of business."[4] However, the majority of trade union and women's groups upheld the Commission's demands, and would have endorsed more forceful measures.

TRADE UNION DEMANDS

Union support for the Commission's positions on affirmative action programs was not unconditional. They wanted to have input into the content of the programs and to ensure that affirmative action did not become a cover-up for political inaction on crucial policy issues concerning women. The union fully recognized the limitations of this form of struggle against institutional discrimination and emphasized the need to accompany affirmative action programs with systematic policies towards equality. For example, the Quebec Teachers' Federation stated that affirmative action programs were

> one of several tools of justice and equality, limited but useful [since] it is not through magic quotas and deadlines that the situation will be set right; at the same time, new policies must be established in areas such as the organization of work, the "desexing" of the structure and content of

training, family services and collective facilities [such as child care centres], the redefinition of relations between men and women, and many others. [5]

The Quebec Council of the Canadian Union of Public Employees (CUPE) saw affirmative action programs as "an element of the solution to the problems of discrimination which victimize women in the workforce." CUPE called for full employment and declared that the nonsexist, egalitarian society the amendments to the Charter should be working towards "cannot be conceived until we begin to understand the waste of resources that the unemployed represent." [6]

In its brief, the Confederation of National Unions (CSN) outlined the union's role in the implementation of affirmative action programs. While allowing that the Commission should order employers to implement a corrective program, specify the program's goals, determine the criteria for hiring, approve programs and supervise their implementation, it asserted that the *union* must be involved in negotiating the terms of the program with the employer, retaining the right to veto it in case of dispute with the employer. [7]

Rank and File, a group that defends the rights of non-unionized workers, recommended more far-reaching regulations. This group considered corrective affirmative action programs to be "one of the least ineffective forms of struggle against systemic discrimination," and proposed the imposition of affirmative action programs not just at the level of individual businesses but throughout the labour force of a given region, in particular economic sectors and in particular job categories. This represented quite a different perspective, one which attempted to deal with the situation of non-unionized working women, who do not benefit from the rights normally assured by a collective agreement. [8]

Most trade union groups agreed that the Commission should be able to recommend affirmative action programs directly or enforce their implementation through court action in the case of both private business and the public service. However, the Quebec Federation of Labour was opposed to this. According to the FTQ/QFL, to place faith in the Commission was "to admit the utter failure of trade unionism and the collective bargaining process as tools in the defence and promotion of workers." The QFL preferred the perspective of the initial bill, which permitted the establishment of voluntary affirmative action, although it wished to see that provision coupled with the recognition of "the essential role of the union in all matters concerning working conditions." [9]

The newly amended Charter gives the Human Rights Commission the power to recommend affirmative action programs or impose them through the courts. The Commission also has the power to investigate and approve programs, to supervise their implementation and to request ongoing reports. The task of developing regulations falls to the government, although it must consult with the Commission. The government has removed the public service from the jurisdiction of the Commission, stating that it is bound to establish affirmative action programs within its ministries, but in its own time, and there is no provision concerning contract compliance.

The amendment partly accommodated the recommendations of the Human Rights Commission and the demands of the groups that supported it. But until the regulations are formally adopted it is unclear whether or not the government has given the Commission an efficient instrument to correct the wrongs done to members of oppressed groups such as women, or whether this is just a high-class burial of the affirmative action issue. An equally important factor will be the strength of the human and financial resources furnished to the Commission to carry out its new responsibilities.

WHY DEMAND AFFIRMATIVE ACTION PROGRAMS?

Since about 1975, committees on the status of women have played a very important role in the trade union movement in Quebec. Since 1976, trade union women's committees, and other groups outside the union movement committed to defending the rights of women, have been working together. Joint action was at its peak in 1979, when two Etats généraux — two-day conferences that brought together unionized and non-unionized women and feminist groups — were held. These women adopted a platform that brought forward demands for the real recognition of the right of women to paid work. The second Etats généraux created action committees, most of which brought forward working papers that defined shared perspectives. This joint undertaking formed the basis for demand-setting, around which ad hoc common fronts grouped themselves on women's issues like child care, as well as on the issue of unionization.[10]

The demands and gains of unionized men and women workers in the public sector continued to lead the way for the private sector. Examples of this are the twenty-week paid maternity leave, the gains (however minimal) in the area of child care in the workplace, and the elimination of some of the more blatant forms of discrimination against women in the workplace (such as sex-identified job titles or classifications). However, while awareness of the various mechanisms that keep women in a state of super-exploitation on the job has been steadily growing, the actual situation of women has been deteriorating. On the basis of this fact, Quebec women's committees came to agree that in spite of their limitations, affirmative action programs can be of some value.

In their briefs on affirmative action, one by one, the various trade union organizations stated that 1) although the most obvious forms of discrimination – such as separate seniority lists for men and women – are on the wane, the most systematic mechanisms of discrimination remain untouched; 2) the means available to the trade union movement in its fight against discrimination are ineffective, often due to legal constraints; and 3) the battles around women's rights in recent years have resulted in many employers hiring fewer women, because there are fewer advantages and because of fears that hiring women will be a source of new union demands and conflicts.[11]

In the public sector, the government of Quebec's professional staff union (Syndicat des professionnels du gouvernment du Québec – SPGQ) attempted in vain to negotiate, over a period of several years, for an end to the inequities of the salary scales in a number of professions that were women's ghettos, such as librarians, dieticians, translators, cultural agents, information officers and social workers. These workers earn less than their colleagues with equivalent educational experience working in more "male" professions. The union submitted a grievance to the Commission of Human Rights on this issue, citing article 19 of the Quebec Charter, which charges every employer with the obligation to pay equal salaries for equivalent work. SPGQ points out that there are twice as many women as there should be in the lowest salary categories and this situation has remained unchanged despite the government's establishment of a policy of equal opportunity employment for women in the public sector.[12]

In the manufacturing sector, the question has been posed in a different way. In factories that become automated or close a department, women are often the first to be fired, in spite of relatively high seniority. This is because in order to displace someone with lower seniority in another department, they must apply for the job at the bottom of the scale, which is often that of labourer. They may also join the "reserve," alternating work with unemployment at the will of the employer. Many employees work on call, not knowing from week to week or even from one day to the next how many hours of work they will get.

Two recent cases of women deciding to take the necessary measures to guarantee a permanent full-time job illustrate the problems women and their unions face when they turn to action to end a discriminatory condition. At Kruger, a plant of 250 employees, all the women who produced products finished in cardboard worked on call. According to their collective agreement, the fourteen women's seniority gave them neither the right to displace less senior employees nor to apply for vacant positions. Furthermore, there were roughly equal job categories with a difference of twenty-five cents per hour between men and women.

In 1979, one of the women lodged a complaint with the Human Rights Commission. Her grievance was based solely on the restrictions on seniority rights for reserve employees that prevented them from obtaining regular positions. However, the Commission found, during its investigation, that there were sex-classified jobs in the workplace and discriminatory salary differences; and ruled that the corresponding clause in the contract was illegal. Although the union – affiliated to the CNTU/CSN – had supported the grievors and had requested the Commission's investigation in order to bring the collective agreement into conformity with the Charter, it was the Commission's decision that the signatory parties to the agreement should share equal responsibility and asked the court to divide the costs incurred by lost salary between them. Since the contract had been signed for the union by the local union *and* the professional federation to which the local was affiliated, the sharing of expenses meant that the union had to assume two-thirds of the costs!

This decision involved a number of disastrous consequences for the women as well as for the local union, not to mention the loss of confidence in the Charter and in the Commission. First of all, the Commission had at no time considered the possible consequences of its decision to eliminate sex-determined job classifications and salaries. In effect, the imposition of salary parity destroyed the implicit understanding that the employer would not ask women to take on certain of the more physically demanding jobs.[13] Secondly, the fact that the

Commission placed the greater part of the responsibility on the union was a source of conflict inside the union as well as between the women who had lodged the complaint and the other female employees. Ultimately the trade union movement concluded that it would have been better trusting its own means than appealing to an external authority.

This is what happened in the second case, at the Perkins paper products factory in 1981. There also, the rules governing the actions of the staff and the actual content of certain tasks had a discriminatory effect against women. The women, who made up about a third of the 150 employees, had regular positions but were concentrated in three job categories within a single department. These were the lowest-paid positions in the whole factory. The women wanted to get out of them not only to get better salaries and to ensure they would not be laid off but to gain access to other jobs that they found more interesting. Because access to positions was governed by departmental seniority and lines of progression, if they changed departments, they would have to start at the bottom of the list in the new department. The jobs at the bottom required physical effort that was often excessive even for the men, who had to be fairly young and in top physical condition to be able to handle them.

The women who had brought up the issue with the help of the women's committee of the CNTU/SCN to which they are affiliated, analyzed the requirements of every job in the factory. They then divided up the jobs according to their accessibility to women and the type of modifications that would have to be made (degree of technical difficulty of the modifications, costs, etc.). They concluded that a considerable number of jobs presented no particular impediment, several would require only minor external modifications to the mechanical process, and a minority of others would require more costly modifications involving changing pieces of certain machines. And finally, some remaining jobs, such as labourer's jobs, did not appear to be accessible in the short run.

The women then formulated a set of demands that were presented at the membership meeting with the support of the union executive. The main points were: 1) demands for certain technical changes; 2) a proposal that the progression line be eliminated to allow a person to change departments without having to start over at the lowest position on the scale, normally a labourer's position; and 3) demands to bring up the salary level of the jobs where the women are concentrated to at least the starting level for the jobs in production departments, which are nearly all held by men. Although the discussion was contentious, several men recognized that the proposed changes would improve their own working conditions, which were so demanding that they became worn out very young or developed chronic health problems.

Because of the economic crisis and the rising rate of unemployment, the union had no success in the area of technical changes. However, the employer accepted the elimination of the departmental progression line through the ranks, allowing women with high seniority to get jobs as operator-aides and operators as soon as there are openings. However, because of the enormous amount of energy expended in this process and the limits imposed by management "right," which the union came up hard against in negotiations, it seems impossible to imagine this approach carrying over to the rest of the trade union movement without some legislation to impose affirmative action programs on employers. Supporting measures are also necessary, since unions do not have the resources to carry out the wide-scale investigations and analysis needed to identify discriminatory practices at their root and propose egalitarian measures to replace them.

Furthermore, the issue of hiring women has become crucial as women now face deliberate decisions on the part of employers not to hire them, decisions that are becoming more firm as women have become more vocal in demanding improved working conditions.[14] In the two cases mentioned above, for instance, no women have been hired for several years. This is true in many other workplaces as well. In hospitals, for example, the reaction of administrators to blending hospital aide categories, previously sex-determined, has been to hire only men, claiming that men were needed to lift the patients.

Automation has accelerated this process in factories, because women are often concentrated in the finishing departments, or as inspectors or wrappers in departments where the work is still done by hand or mechanically. Automation will now be replacing them in traditional jobs while, despite their high seniority, many will likely face layoffs as a result of the seniority regulations described above.

For these reasons, most of the trade union movement in Quebec has offered conditional and critical support, but support nonetheless, to the demands of the Human Rights Commission that the government grant it the power to impose affirmative action programs. It is clear however, that for unions the fight will not be won through the amendments to the Charter and the adoption of strong regulations. These will only give the union movement a tool to wage a long battle against the many complex forms of discrimination. But discrimination cannot be fought in isolation and cannot be separated from the struggle against the exploitation of men and women workers as a whole.

A SWORD, BUT A TWO-EDGED ONE

It is clear that the means currently available to combat discrimination against women are few and weak. The union movement needs strong laws that they can count on to bring about major changes in working conditions already the subject of negotiations (such as seniority rules, classifications and salaries) because it is clear that the employer will not accept such changes unless forced. Furthermore, imposing affirmative action programs on companies found guilty of discrimination would allow corrective measures to be imposed in areas the union currently has virtually no control over, such as recruitment, selection, hiring and training. The u.s. experience has amply demonstrated that personnel policies, while appearing to be neutral, often are discriminatory in practice.[15]

This is also true with respect to the organization of work itself, which must be changed to avoid a phenomenon where only "superwomen" are able to get the more interesting and well-paying jobs. The aspects of the organization of work that need changing may include the physical requirements of a job – often assessed in terms of the "average man," who is a little bigger, a little heavier and a little wider than the "average woman." This alone may render a suitable job completely unbearable for a woman, requiring her to perform a range of compensatory efforts just to do it. Modifications in the way the work is done, the instruments and tools used and even in the type of product produced may also be called for. For example, in tasks requiring handling without technical tools, the *shape* of the boxes to be lifted and stacked and the *height of the shelves* on which they are placed may constitute sufficient obstacles to prevent a woman from taking a job because she is smaller and her arms shorter than those of the men on whom the norms are standardized.

However, in spite of the need to turn to means other than those currently used to combat discrimination, recourse to affirmative action carries its own risks. These risks are related to the conditions of implementation of affirmative action programs as well as to the way the trade union movement will coordinate its action on this and other priorities. Affirmative action works best in a context of economic expansion where it permits women and/or other minorities to get a better share of existing conditions. However, in no way does it address issues related to the effects of the economic crisis, such as the rising rate of unemployment, the increasing number of unstable jobs with bad working conditions that make up the secondary labour market, or the effects of technological change, such as unemployment and deskilling of jobs.

That is why the following points must be kept in mind in the struggles for the affirmative action.

1. If the trade union movement does not take the lead in a struggle against unemployment and for control of technological change at the same time as it is getting involved in the establishment of affirmative action programs, such programs run the risk of becoming a struggle for jobs between women and men at a time when there are already too few jobs to go around. Such a situation, which would pit female workers and male workers against each other, would make it much more difficult to achieve a unified mobilization around global issues such as full employment. As far as technological change is concerned, not only may the number of available jobs be reduced, but women will be affected first. In a very short time, technological change could wipe out all the effects of an affirmative action program by promoting the disappearance of entire job classifications to which women have just gained access.[16]

2. If there is no breakthrough in the struggle for the improvement of working conditions of the least protected workers and for access to unionization for all those who are presently unable to join unions, the numbers of temporary and unstable jobs will soar. Thus affirmative action programs will bring improvements for only a tiny proportion of women relative to the growing number of superexploited and underpaid women.[17]

3. The trade union movement must be involved in the process of establishment and negotiation of the content of affirmative action programs. Otherwise, as has been the case in the United States, negotiations will take place between a para-governmental body and employers; the provisions of the contract negotiated by the union, especially

those bearing on seniority rights, may come to be seen as obstacles to the employment rights of minorities, such as women. American tribunals have, by and large, given support to the interpretation defended by employers and even, occasionally, by the u.s. Equal Opportunity Commission. Decisions handed down pit the unionized workers and their organizations against minority rights.[18]

4. Finally, there is one point that must be mentioned that is not often a concern of trade unions. In the labour movement, although there sometimes is resistance at the beginning, a great number of men come to support the demands of women. However, attempts to improve women's working conditions, to raise salaries and to assure women access to positions previously monopolized by men have met with extremely strong opposition. This does not come as a surprise: much resistance arises from men's fears of job insecurity and the personal threat men may feel about women's access to jobs considered "masculine."[19] If unions involved in the establishment of affirmative action programs in the workplace do not take care to bring their attitudes up to date, they may find themselves short-circuiting the goals they have set. Expressions of overt or covert hostility towards women taking over jobs men alone had access to or towards working side by side with women, may come out — and this makes life difficult for women who change jobs.[20]

The foregoing observations bring out the thorny and complex issue of the place of women in the labour movement. Within the movement, the issue has been raised first from the perspective of the proportional under-representation of women at all levels within unions. But as women have achieved greater involvement, through activity in their unions or in their women's committees, they have come to relate their under-representation as much to priorities for action as to the inner workings of the trade union movement.[21]

Unless unions take the steps necessary to ensure that women are allowed to take their rightful place in the labour movement, women will see it as just another manifestation of a chauvinistic and sexist society, and may give up on it as a means of struggle against their oppression. If, on the other hand, the union movement becomes the bearer of demands to end the discrimination of women, women's contribution will become a powerful lever in the struggles of all workers. This is because the double oppression women experience makes them more sensitive to the links between exploitation in the workplace and the oppression present in all aspects of social life. And as they join the trade union movement, this heightened consciousness will lead them to pursue the issues of working and employment conditions even further.[22] Thus, the issue of affirmative action brings to light other issues that far exceed the scope of one law to affect the fundamental way that trade unions function.

Translated by Daina Z. Green

NOTES

This article is based on research completed by the author at the Institut de recherche appliquée sur le travail. It will be published by the Institute in 1983 in a longer piece dealing with equal employment opportunities for women in industry.

1 The Canadian Human Rights Act has the same provisions in its articles 15(1) and 41. However, since the adoption of the Act in 1977, the Canadian Human Rights Commission has never made any recommendations to this effect. There might very soon be a landmark decision if the Human Rights Tribunal gives way to "Action-Travail des femmes" demands. In 1978, the Montreal-based group lodged a complaint against Canadian National Railways for discriminatory hiring practices and asked the Commission to impose an affirmative action program on the CN.

2 See Lorna R. Marsden, "The Role of the National Action Committee on the Status of Women in Facilitating Equal Pay Policy in Canada," in Ronnie Ratner Steinberg, *Equal Employment Policy for Women* (Philadelphia: Temple Univ. Press, 1980) pp. 250-55.

3 Commission des droits de la personne du Québec, *L'action positive et la Charte des droits et libertés de la personne*, Dec. 1980, pp. 44-45.

4 Quebec Employer's Council, Brief to the Parliamentary Justice Commission on amendments to the Quebec Charter of Human Rights and Freedoms, Sept. 1981, p. 5. (In the notes that follow, all briefs to this Commission will be cited as "Brief to the PJC on QCHRF.")

5 Quebec Teachers' Federation (CEQ), Brief to the PJC on the QCHRF, Oct. 1981, pp. 95-96.

6 Quebec Council of the Canadian Union of Public Employees (CUPE), to the PJC on the QCHRE, Oct. 1981, pp. 1, 5.

7 Confederation of National Trade Unions (CSN), Brief to the PJC on the QCHRF, Oct. 1981, pp. 4-5.

8 Rank and File, Brief to the PJC on the QCHRF, Sept. 1981, pp. 42, 47-52.

9 Quebec Federation of Labour (QFL/FTQ), Brief to the PJC on the QCHRF, Oct. 1981, pp. 4,6.

10 In particular, see *Les travailleuses et l'accès à la syndicalisation,* produced by the Action Committee of the Etats généraux of salaried Quebec women, CSN, Montréal, 1980, and *Dossier-garderies: pour un réseau universel et gratuit,* CSN, CEQ, SCFP, Montréal 1981.

11 See the briefs cited above.

12 SPGQ, *Mémoire,* p. 3.

13 The muscular ability needed to carry out heavy tasks is often a bit better developed in men, among other reasons, because the process of socialization leads boys and girls to develop different skills. Although boys learn to develop their physical strength and motor skills, girls learn to be meticulous, precise and quick. The differences are usually discussed in terms of the difficulties women face in taking on jobs previously reserved for men, but a similar situation is also faced by men who undertake jobs usually held by women. However, since these "women's" jobs are underpaid and not highly valued, it rarely occurs to one to ask whether or not men are able to meet the requirements of the jobs.

14 Confederation of National Trade Unions, *Mémoire,* pp. 1-3.

15 See, for example, Phyllis A. Wallace, *Equal Employment Opportunity and the* AT&T Case, (Cambridge: MIT Press, 1976).

16 Sally Hacker asserts this on the basis of a detailed study of the results of the affirmative action program imposed on AT&T in 1973 by the Equal Employment Opportunity Commission. See "Sex Stratification, Technology and Organizational Change: A Longitudinal Case Study of AT&T," *Social Problems,* Vol. 26, No. 5 (June 1979). See also Brigid O'Farrell and Sharon Harlan, *Job Integration Strategies: Today's Programs and Tomorrow's Needs,* Working Paper for the Committee on Women's Employment and Related Social Issues, National Research Council Center for Research on Women, Wellesley College, Wellesley, 1982.

17 In the U.S., for instance, the unions which have been fighting discrimination most actively through recourse to Title VII of the Civil Rights Act (which authorizes affirmative action programs), now feel that they must carry on a simultaneous battle for equal pay for work of equal value; see Winn Newman (General Counsel, 'UE and CLUW), "The New Concept

(sic) Equal Pay for Work of Equal Value," Paper presented at the annual
conference of the American Bar Association, 1980. Among advanced
capitalist nations, the country having the least spread between men's and
women's salaries is the only one without anti-discrimination legislation
as known elsewhere: the wage gap was diminished through national
negotiations between the labour movement and management on the basis
of demands for a more egalitarian society. The country is Sweden, where
a social-democratic government has been in power for almost forty
years; see Alice H. Cook, "Collective Bargaining as a Strategy for
Achieving Equal Opportunity and Equal Pay: Sweden and Germany" in
Steinberg, *Equal Employment Policy, op.cit.* pp. 53-78. A recent study
into the differences between employers who hire mainly women and
those hiring mainly men for similar accounting office jobs, concludes that
unionization and the improvement of working conditions through
negotiations for collective bargaining would be of greater value than
anti-discrimination legislation in creating equal employment opportunities for women.

18 This situation is amply documented in a statement to the Equal Opportu-
nity Employment Commission Task Force on Collective Bargaining by
the International Union of Electrical, Radio and Machine Workers and
Coalition of Labour Union Women, June 1979. See also Winn Newman
and Carole W. Wilson, "The Union Role in Affirmative Action," *Labor
Law Journal*, Vol. 32, No. 6 (June 1981); Brigid O'Farrell, "Women's Job
Choices, Barriers, and the Role of a Union Local," *The New England
Sociologist* Vol. 3, No. 1 (1981) and *Women and Non-traditional Blue
Collar Jobs: A Case Study of Local I,* Center for Research on Women,
Wellesley College, Wellesley, 1980.

19 This point was explained by Judith Long-Laws at the AT&T hearing. She
also suggested some simple and effective solutions to improve the situation. See "Psychological Dimensions of Labour Force Participation on
Women" and "The Bell Telephone System: A Case Study," chs. 6 and 7 in
Wallace, *Equal Employment, op.cit.* Brigid O'Farrell and Sharon L. Harlan have also commented on the importance of the behaviour of male
co-workers for women in non-traditional jobs in "Craftworkers and
Clerks: The Effect of Male Co-workers' Hostility on Women's Satisfaction with Non-traditional Jobs," *Social Problems,* Feb. 1982.

20 To see a union's handling of an affirmative action program at the local
level, see Brigid O'Farrell, *Women and Non-traditional Blue Collar Jobs,
op.cit.*

21 See the fourth report of the Committee on the Status of Women, Confederation of National Trade Unions, *In the* CSN *Women Cannot Go Backwards Anymore* (1982).

22 See Margaret Maruani, *Les syndicats à l'épreuve du féminisme (Paris: Syros,* 1979) *and Anni Borzeix, "Luttes des femmes, luttes d'*O.S.*," in Syndicalisme et organisaton du travail* (Paris: CNAM, 1980).

UNDER ATTACK: WOMEN, UNIONS AND MICROTECHNOLOGY

Marion Pollock

The Eighties are the computer decade, one in which so television and magazine advertising promises us our lives will be vastly improved by the new technology. If the present trends continue, however, the Computer Age may become the Decade of Despair, as employer-introduced computers in the workplace drastically change women's lives. One major aspect of this transformation will be a displacement of women from the work force. Other probable effects include deskilling, an increase in monitoring by supervisors, more shift and part-time work, increased isolation, and a growing gap between men's and women's wages. The trade union movement will face a critical challenge from employers in the years ahead; only through foresight and strong action can unions hope to ameliorate the most negative effects of new technology, much less establish the worker control over technological change that could ensure positive changes in our work and leisure lives.

This new technology, variously called microchip, microelectronic, or informatics, is made possible through the use of a fingernail-sized piece of material called a silicon chip, which contains all the circuitry of a modern computer. These computers are indeed minuscule, especially when compared with their forerunners. In 1946, the first modern computer, called ENIAC, weighed more than 30 tons and occupied a very large area. Today, these same functions and more can easily be performed by a desk-top computer. The main advantage of such miniaturization lies in the reduced cost of the technology. Microprocessors have lessened computing costs 100,000 times since 1960, making computerized systems both widely available and profitable.

Historically, large corporations have instituted technological change at a rapid pace during recessions in order to lower labour costs while maintaining or increasing profit levels. In times of relative economic equilibrium, large corporations can expand their markets rather than impose technological change. But corporations today are using microtechnology both to boost output and to sharply reduce wage payouts.

By increasing productivity, microchip technology allows more work to be done by the same or fewer numbers of people. Therefore, employers are most eager to introduce technological change in areas that have low productivity per worker and growing employment rates, for example, clerical work, banking and retail salessectors of the labour force where the majority of women are concentrated. The report of the 1982 Canada Task Force on Microelectronics and Employment has forecast the possible disappearance or modification of jobs due to microelectronics.[1] It cites the elimination of clerical positions, reductions in typing and secretarial jobs, a significant drop in the numbers of telephone operators, and a substantial cutback of bank tellers.

This trend has already begun. In 1969, Bell Canada employed 13,600 operators and by 1979 there were only 7,400.[2] In 1976, the first computerized switchboard was introduced into Vancouver by BC Tel; it requires 22% fewer operators. At the Carleton University Library in Ottawa, a computerized cataloguing system introduced in 1978 eliminated 10 out of 14 jobs. In the 15 years since automation was introduced in the Sigmund Samuel Library at the University of Toronto, 20% of the staff has been eliminated. The workers there predict another 25% staff decrease over the next few years.

Women who aren't displaced by new technology may yet find their jobs affected, since the implementation of technological change usually involves major changes in the nature and organization of work. One major change, the deskilling of workers, will have far-reaching implications for women's job satisfaction, promotional opportunities, and wage levels relative to men.

Deskilling occurs when skills and knowledge previously held by workers are transferred to machines. For example, point-of-sale terminals in supermarkets can read, record and print out food prices. The cashier is no longer required to know prices or even recognize products her job has been transformed into running the groceries over an electronic scanner and bagging them.

Jobs that might have been somewhat interesting prior to automation become fragmented and mindless. As jobs are separated into different components, workers are increasingly alienated both from each other and from the work process. At the post office, it is common to see a row of coders sitting side by side, each tuned into her or his own radio headset. For many people, it is the music alone that makes the job tolerable. With the introduction of new technology, management has made a choice: rather than enriching jobs or lessening hours of work, they use automation in order to deskill jobs, which are therefore more boring.

These boring, routine jobs can then be filled by workers with less training or skill, who can be paid less. In some cases, jobs previously held by men are transferred to lower-paid women workers when computerizaton reduces the skill and training required. Clearly, the new technology threatens any prospects of achieving equal pay for work of equal value. Section 11 of the Canadian Human Rights Code defines the criteria for assessing equal value as the "skill, effort, and responsibility required in the performance of work and the conditions under which work is performed." Technological change removes decision making from workers and decreases the skills used in the performance of job-related duties. And since it is women whose traditional jobs are being affected in this way, the real and perceived skill gaps between men and women will continue to widen.

Because new technology requires programmers, designers and other skilled personnel, government and business propaganda would have us believe that women will benefit from the creation of well-paying, challenging jobs. However, that is not likely. Currently, women are only about 19% of computer specialists, and are concentrated in the lowest skill and pay levels of computer jobs. The majority of women do not have the backgrounds that would qualify them for retraining programs, if such were even available to them. And as women's jobs become even more routinized, women workers will not be acquiring the kinds of job skills that could put them on promotional ladders. Women will be even more ghettoized in dead-end jobs.

Microchip technology threatens classification security. Since classification determines wage levels, fair wages are at risk. Jan Zimmerman in "How to Control the New Technology Before it Controls You" states that "many large banks and insurance companies ... have downgraded clerical jobs from secretary to word processor, from file clerk to data-entry technician."[3]

This threat to classification security also leads to attempts to classify people out of the bargaining unit. In the BC Tel computer centre, the ratio of non-union to union members is 50 to 1. In all other areas, the ratio is 1 to 3.7. These non-union members form a permanent strike-breaking force. Any threat to classification security, real or implied will lead to an increase in management control. Trade unions must fight not only for classification security but also for clauses that guarantee that no job duties can be added or transferred to other classifications without union approval.

Computerization also speeds up the trend towards a part-time work force. Employers hire part-time workers either to take on peak loads created by technological change or because computerization allows the employer to cut back on full-time workers. Shift work also increases with the introduction of automation because employers want to get the most out of their computer time when it is the cheapest. In Canada Post for example, the production emphasis switched from days to afternoon and graveyard (night) shifts after technological change. In addition to the health problems, such as sleep and digestive disorders, engendered by shift work, women workers face one more problem — the lack of adequate child care. In B.C., as in most provinces, there are no 24-hour child care centres. Women who are required to work graveyard shifts are faced with the additional burden of making inadequate or makeshift provisions for the care and safety of their children. When microchip technology is brought into the workplace, unions must not only bargain for strict limits on afternoon and graveyard shift work but also for some form of child care provisions.

The question of day care arises in another form through the introduction of the new technology since the technology allows the employer to develop a computer cottage industry. This mode of work enables companies to lend or lease computers to employees to perform work at home, increasing the employers' profits because it reduces overhead costs. *Business Week* estimates that by 1992, five million American workers are expected to be working in the home.[4] Most of these workers will be women.

Again, this aspect of the new technology has serious implications for the unions. It is difficult to maintain or organize unions when workers are isolated in their home. And the fact that employers can hire women to work cheaply at home means that these women will be forced to look after their children at the same time. Thus the bosses can avoid their social responsibilities and cut back on funding to child care centres. At the same time, if the work is based in the home, clauses such as paid maternity leave and sick leave can be dismantled. Women's organizations and trade unions must lead the fight against cottage industry at the same time as struggling to achieve 24-hour child care.

"Contracting out" computers has other advantages for employers. The development of large, centralized data banks means that large corporations can lend out communicating word processors to other large corporations. In so doing, they can bypass workers in the originating company. CP Airlines has leased out such equipment to large transnationals such as MacMillan Blodell and Cominco. Companies are now able to make airline reservations without using Brotherhood of Railway and Airline Clerks (BRAC) workers, whose job security is thereby threatened.

Another area of involvement for the labour movement is combating the effects of electronic scabbing during a strike. This modern twist on an old problem can be achieved in several ways. The software now available makes it possible for the employers to electronically transfer information and funds away from the struck workplace and carry on business as usual. In some cases, the technology can operate for the duration of a short strike without workers. Employer-introduced technology creates a permanent set of strikebreakers. In order to address this serious threat, it is necessary to develop new methods and strategies to prevent strikes from being undermined.

In addition to enabling employers to get more work out of the same or fewer workers while paying them lower wages for being less skilled, microtechnology dramatically increases the control employers have over workers. Word processors and point-of-sale terminals allow the employer to constantly monitor the pace of work, number of errors, keystrokes per hour, and the amount and length of breaks of all kinds. At BC Tel for example, a computer keeps track of what every operator is doing. When one call is finished, the next one instantly appears. A "calls waiting" button is always on. The machine paces the operator rather than the operator, her or himself, controlling the work flow. Each operator is expected to process at least 120 calls per hour. Operators who do not meet the company-set pace are reprimanded.

A brief presented by the Brotherhood of Railway and Airline Clerks (BRAC) to the Labour Canada Task Force on Microtechnology discussed the situation at CP Air:

> Employees must sign in and out of the telephone system, not just at the beginning and end of the shift but also for all breaks taken. As well, reservation agents also sign into their VDTs. The computer retains a daily record of each person's activities.

A complete record of an employee includes revenue protection and a complexity of statistics relating to telephone calls handled. As well, there is a sales programme and employees are exhorted to follow the format to the letter.

Deviation from the format has resulted in harassment and intimidation.[5]

Data entry operators in some Ontario Hospital Insurance Program offices work under a production quota. The speed of the keystroking is used to maintain their classification levels. In other workplaces data entry operators are paid piecework rates on the basis of the number of keystrokes per hour. Piecework not only undercuts wages; in the long run, it also decreases union consciousness. In response, unions must negotiate strict prohibitions against piecework.

Monitoring has other far more insidious effects. It is a form of union busting because it subtly pressures workers not to take advantage of their negotiated rights and benefits. For instance, if a worker observes certain contractual health and safety provisions, it may result in a minimally slower work output. Any such change will be duly recorded. If a worker wishes to leave her or his work area to speak to a shop steward, the absence will be noted. Although contract language exists to ensure that a worker has certain legal rights, monitoring can discourage the acquisition and/or implementation of them.

Some unions have been successful in opposing monitoring. CUPW has a clause in its collective agreement prohibiting any form of electronic surveillance or individual work measurement. Supermarket clerks in Denmark refused to work on point-of-sale terminals until the monitoring device was removed. At BC Tel, operators successfully struggled against the employer's attempt to bring in an even more draconian monitoring system than that which already exists.

The health hazards associated with microtechnology, particularly VDTs, have begun to receive attention from unions, media and government. Documented hazards include: eyestrain, loss of visual acuity, dizziness, postural problems and stress. New evidence suggests that the low level of radiation emitted by VDTs can cause eye cataracts and birth defects. Unions must negotiate strong clauses mitigating the physical effects of VDTs, ensuring medical tests *before* workers are assigned to VDTs, and protecting the right of pregnant women to transfer off potentially hazardous equipment.

New workplace technology presents a series of challenges to the labour movement. In order to adequately address the full range of problems created for working people by technological change, unions must begin to work in four areas: collective bargaining, education, legislation and long-term political action. Work has already begun, and this is particularly true in the area of health and safety as it relates to new technology. In virtually every set of negotiations involving B.C. unions that have a sizable membership of women, VDT protection has been raised as an issue. When the B.C. Government Employees' Union (BCGEU) carried out their strike action in the summer of 1982, one of their picket signs read, "On Strike for VDT Protecton for Pregnant Workers." The Communication Workers of Canada (CWC) broke ground on this issue by negotiating a clause allowing pregnant women to transfer to a job not involving VDT use.

But there is still much to do. Business and governments have resisted union demands for worker safety and control by refusing to negotiate and by denying that there is any real cause for concern.

In 1982, Labour Canada prepared a study of technological change provisions in various collective agreements.[6] What stands out about this study is the number of contracts that have no protection or wording on this issue:

No advance notice and/or consultation prior to the introduction of the technological change	72.2%
No training or retraining due to technological change	81.7%
No relocation allowance due to technological change	95.6%
No employment security due to technological change	87.8%
No notice of layoff due to technological change	92.5%
No reopener clause due to technological change	98.8%
No provision for worksharing techniques due to technological change	99.9%

The lack of these provisions is devastating for workers.

In "The Attitude of Trade Unions to Technological Change," S. Peitchinis comments on this lack of protective clauses.[7] He notes that technology provisions are not given priority by unions until the technology has been introduced. Unions end up fighting sporadic and rear-guard actions. Hindsight, however, is completely useless in dealing with technological change.

The attached appendix includes some sample clauses on technological change and some suggestions on how to implement them. It is important to realize that this is a long, hard fight. The experience of CUPW is a good example. In 1972, the union embarked on a "Boycott the Postal Code" campaign. In 1974, union members struck illegally for two weeks to prevent declassification of clerks who were working on the new machines. In 1975, postal workers struck for six weeks to gain a very strong technological change clause. The next year there were a series of illegal strikes to force the employer to adhere to that very clause. The liberal government, in 1978, declared a legal CUPW strike to be illegal. The result of this repression was a collective agreement that weakened some technological change provisions. In 1980, the union won a shorter work week. Many gains, including filling vacant positions, stronger prohibitions against both electronic surveillance and contracting out, improved health and safety clauses, and paid maternity leave were won as a result of their 1981 strike. This year, the employer is introducing a new program of technological change. Yet while CUPW has one of the strongest and most comprehensive clauses on technological change it is now inadequate to protect the long-term interests of postal workers.

The CUPW lesson is twofold. First, it points to the necessity of bargaining for very strong wording vis à vis technological change. Secondly, it shows that in order for any union to win strong collective agreements, the entire labour movement must be supportive.

Union consciousness, however, can be adversely affected by the new technology. It decreases the amount of interaction between co-workers and replaces it with a person-machine interface. Traditional work groups, which provide a basis for workplace solidarity, are broken up as workers become socially and physically isolated from each other. In addition, the psychological mind-set of workers can also be undermined by technological change. Many workers feel that automation is inevitable and feel powerless and negative about fightback campaigns.

This does not have to be the case. In February 1981, we saw a spectacular departure from technological determinism. For a five-day period in various B.C. cities, telephone workers occupied their employers' premises and maintained service. In many locations, especially in Vancouver, the telephone operators, who are among the most isolated of the BC Tel workers and usually hooked into their VDTs, formed the majority of occupiers. For many workers, it was a short but important lesson about control. The telephone operators found that their work was less alienating and stressful when they controlled their own work environment.

Education programs lie at the crux of attempts to gain some control over this technology and to combat technological literacy. Parent labour bodies in B.C. have developed an excellent program on the impact of technological change. Weekend schools, jointly run by local labour councils and the CLC, offer a two-day course on technology and systems change. This course covers the whole range of issues involved. An expanded version of this course is offered at the CLC/BC Federation of Labour (BCFL) residential winter school. The Metropolitan Toronto Labour Council has an active committee on the health hazards of VDTs. And one of the best debates at the 1983 CLC convention centred on technological change. The program adopted by that convention included legislative strategy (see below) as well as a call for new government policies and programs. Such policies include "full employment," taxation changes, a levy-grant system for training, and more research into health and safety aspects of the new technology. In addition, the CLC Standing Committee on Technological Change is still active. It has published several articles in the CLC's *Canadian Labour* magazine and is making plans to cover the next several-year period. This committee has broken down into three sub-committees on education, legislation and collective bargaining.

Other groups are also involved in educational work on technological change. In B.C., the NDP has a very active sub-committee that has widely distributed a questionnaire and presented policy papers to provincial NDP conventions. The Women's Action of Occupational Health Committee in Vancouver has a sub-committee on VDTs that has given many classes on the health hazards of VDTs, and is generally an excellent resource. *Kinesis,* the monthly newspaper of the Vancouver Status of Women, has published a number of articles on tech change.

Protection through legislation must be central to any comprehensive strategy. The 1982 CLC convention passed the following goals for legislation on technological change:

- advance notice of change
- immediate disclosure of plans
- full consultation on the introduction of new equipment or processes
- no change until an agreement has been reached with the bargaining agent
- training and retraining programs

The fight for legislation must be waged on several fronts. However, the federal government is not prepared to adopt these minimal standards without a major, protracted fight. In the current economic climate, governments are attacking workers' rights as a way to increase corporate profits. Yet history has shown us that legislation extending workers' rights usually follows breakthroughs in collective bargaining. The labour movement must embark on a committed struggle to achieve such legislation. The process of this fight can be used not only to educate but to mobilize and unite diverse groups of people.

The labour movement must also undertake a number of broad political struggles around the different issues related to technological change. The trade union movement has had policy calling for the shorter work week for years. But policy is not enough. We must begin a real fight involving mass mobilization for thirty hours of work for forty hours of pay with no loss of pay or benefits. The fight for the eight-hour day was bitter and long and it was also activist in nature. We must adopt similar strategies. The shorter work week would allow workers to benefit from the increased productivity brought about by automation and could be used to reduce unemployment.

At the same time the union must play a key role in organizing the unemployed. If the trade union movement fails to address unemployment and assist the unemployed, then we are giving employers a pool of strikebreakers and workers eager to accept any job. More than that, if unions default on organizing the unemployed, we are creating an atmosphere of despair and hopelessness that will seriously impair our struggle to gain control of this technology.

The majority of the office workers presently being faced with automation are unorganized women. This weakens the ability of unions to control the effects of technology on their members. Unionized employers will point out that the existence of VDTs elsewhere means that they, too, will have to automate in order to stay competitive. As long as the majority of women workers remain unorganized, the wages of all women will be held down.

Organizing the unorganized must be a priority for the labour movement. But there is a Catch-22 here. The introduction of microtechnology into offices can result in smaller workplaces, which are more difficult to organize than large job sites. The labour movement must stop being reluctant to organize small offices and embark on an aggressive campaign to unionize women office workers. In this instance, the union movement will have to reach beyond its traditional basis of support and ally itself with women's and citizen's groups.

The fight for women's rights, both from within and outside of the paid labour force, is critical to counter the effects of automation. This new technology threatens the gains that women have made. Not fighting back now would destroy any hope for equal pay for work of equal value, for access to non-traditional jobs, and for social benefits. These are the areas where the women's movement has played a leading role and it is important that this trend continue. The trade union movement must also give its full support and strength to this struggle. Joint community, women's movement, and union campaigns such as Women Back Into Stelco will have to be the rule rather than the exception. At the same time we have to remember that microtechnology and the use of robots also affects those areas where men are concentrated, such as the skilled trades, manufacturing and primary industry. It is no longer enough to want access to these jobs, because they too will be eliminated. When we discuss non-traditional jobs we have to expand our categories to include jobs such as systems analyst, computer programmer, graphics specialist and office technician.

The issue of microchip technology puts the labour movement at a crossroads. Are we going to allow the bosses to implement technological change at our expense? Are we going to develop new methods for organizing or are we going to be weakened and fragmented? Are we going to develop a unified fightback campaign or are we going to watch as unions get defeated, one by one? And finally, are we going to mount a campaign to ensure that women remain in the work force or are we going to sit by and watch while women get eased out of their jobs?

Jean Claude Parrot, National President of cupw, addressed these issues when he spoke at a January 27, 1983 session on Labour Issues for Public Policy at McMaster University in Hamilton, Ontario. He said:

> Employers are aware of our weaknesses and they are also aware that technological change protection may not be the highest priority for many unions at the present time.
>
> But the fact is that, for us we have no choice but to continue to fight this rear-guard battle to protect the membership in every way possible.
>
> We recognize that under the present system, the purpose of techno-logical change is to reduce labour costs and weaken unions. But does this mean we should accept it?
>
> We also recognize that our individual protections may be under-mined by technology. Does this mean we should give up the fight to maintain these protections? Should we accept defeat or fight even harder to achieve better protection?
>
> I think we have to recognize that there is something fundamentally wrong with a society in which advances in science and technology are in direct conflict with the interests of the majority of the population. A society where the benefits are not shared, where more and more research is devoted to weapons of mass destruction while health research is being cut back. Where new technology increases injuries instead of decreasing them ....
>
> So, when we talk of technological change, we should ask our-selves, "in the present system, is it possible to redirect science and tech-nology to resolve human needs even if this means higher labour costs?"
>
> Is this possible? Or is it a basic rule that in a society in which invest-ment depends on profits instead of human welfare, that workplace technology will be used to reduce labour costs instead of benefiting workers?
>
> If this is so, then it is necessary to do much more than change our collective agreements and legislation.

Microchip technology also challenges the structure of the trade union movement. The new technologies affect more than one trade union and unions struggling alone will be left far behind. For example, more and more mail is being electronically transmitted over telephone wires, thereby affecting postal workers, secretaries, telephone oper-ators, bank tellers, etc. A struggle for control of this technology will require a council of all unions touched by it. The increasing use of Telidon is another example. This technology will potentially affect all information and clerical workers, from journalists and librarians to directory assistance operators and mail sorters. One union cannot take on the fight alone. Unions will have to join together to fight the adverse effects of technological change.

The issue is not whether the technology is good or bad. It is too late to have those arguments. The question is one of control. If microchip technology is controlled by the workers, then we can benefit with shorter work weeks and less alienating jobs. However, when employers control this technology, they use it to make maximum profits at our expense. As women and as workers, we have to fight for control of this technology. It is our future.

APPENDIX

One of the most effective ways for unions to gain both protections and benefits from technological change is through contract clauses. It is crucial that unions bargain for such clauses in their collective agreements. However, an effective contract cannot limit technological change issues to one article. Protections and benefits from technological change have to be inserted in all articles of the collective agreement, ranging from hours of work to health and safety to staffing. In addition to this, separate articles also have to be negotiated to deal with some of the specifics of workplace automation.

The following are either suggestions for or examples of important contract clauses on the issue of technological change.

Definition: A good clause on this issue should include a comprehensive definition of what exactly constitutes technological change.

Advance Notice: This clause should require that management inform the union prior to ordering the new equipment. The employer must be required to disclose the full information about this change, including nature of equipment or system, anticipated changes in staffing levels, working hours, etc.

Consultation / Veto: It is crucial that unions negotiate a procedure to negotiate or consult on technological changes. If no agreement is reached, these differences could either be sent to arbitration *before* the change occurs, or give the union the right to strike over technological change. Some unions have opted for permanent Joint Union-Management Committees to receive and consult on all issues and information regarding technological change.

Technological Change Participating Fund: This is a new concept, whereby upon giving notice of technological change, the employer would be obligated to pay a certain amount of money into a proposed fund. The union would retain sole control over this fund. Payments would go for purposes relating to technological change, such as the hiring of special consultants, production of educational materials, or payment of registration and wages for employees participating in union-approved courses on technological change.

Eliminating Adverse Effects: Some unions have opted for clauses requiring the employer to eliminate all adverse effects on the employees as a result of technological change. This clause is advantageous because it covers adverse effects that cannot be forseen at the time of negotiations.

Job Security: There are several approaches to this issue. One of the most successful is the following clause between Suburban Press Limited and Vancouver New Westminster Newspaper Guild Local 115:

> No employee shall be dismissed as a result of the introduction of new or modified equipment, machines, apparatus or processes and any employee whose displacement may be agreed to shall be retrained at the expense and on the time of the company, and continue in the employ of the company in a suitable job, at no reduction in salary or impairment of benefits.

This clause could be strengthened by adding "or have her / his hours reduced." Other unions have opted for clauses guaranteeing no layoffs for employees who have accrued a certain amount of seniority.

Hours of Work: It is essential that unions negotiate a clause stating that there will be no changes or reductions in working hours without the full prior agreement of the union. However, workers should benefit from the increases in productivity brought about by technological change; one way is by negotiating for reduced working hours with *no loss of pay or benefits.*

Increased holidays, and all forms of paid leave (sick, parental, etc.) also allow workers to benefit from increased productivity.

Classification / Reclassification: A clause on this issue should include several items. First, there should be wording that provides that any new positions introduced as a result of technological change will automatically be included in the bargaining unit, unless mutually decided otherwise by both the union and the employer. Provisions should also be included to protect workers from the addition of new duties with no upgrading in pay, and to prevent the deskilling of jobs that is often accompanied by a decrease in pay. The union should also attempt to negotiate a clause stating that all reclassification must be mutually agreed upon by both the unon and the employer.

Monitoring: It is crucial that unions negotiate prohibitions on monitoring. These clauses should state that no monitoring shall be introduced or continued without the full knowledge and consent of the union.

Pace of Work: Although difficult to achieve, it is important that unions try to negotiate clauses that ensure that the worker, rather than the machine, will control the pace of work.

Rotation of Duties: Often the jobs created by technological change are very boring. A clause on rotation of duties will allow workers more variety in their jobs and could counteract some of the boredom.

Part-time Workers: Unions have to ensure that all part-timers receive fully pro-rated benefits. In addition, unions should negotiate a ratio between part-time and full-time employees.

Filling of Vacant Positions: Employer-introduced technological change allows employers to reduce the bargaining unit through attrition. A clause requiring them to fill all vacant positions would mean that people presently out of the work force would have a chance of being employed.

Training: Technological change in the workplace often requires new skills. Unions must negotiate clauses allowing workers access to retraining so they can acquire these skills.

Transfer: When jobs are eliminated by technological change it is important that employees who are affected retain the right to transfer into other jobs in the bargaining unit. This transfer must be voluntary.

Contracting Out: This is a real danger with the introduction of technological change. Unions should negotiate clauses prohibiting contracting out, as well as piecework.

Health and Safety: Unions must negotiate clauses setting standards relating to all aspects of VDTs: brightness, matrix size, refresher rate, radiation, heat, noise, glare, etc. Lighting, seating, positioning of screen, keyboard and paperwork must be worker-adjustable.

Eye tests should be available to all VDT operators. There have been notable victories giving pregnant women, and women trying to become pregnant, the right not to operate VDTs, to be transferred to other jobs within the plant, or to take a leave of absence.

Unions should also try to negotiate limits on the time workers spend at VDTs. Four to five hours a day is one recommended maximum.

During the current economic crisis many of these clauses may be difficult to attain. Employers seem intent on stripping away our hard-won rights. However, the union movement must not give up this fight. Achieving any protection on technological change, no matter how small, is a gain for all workers.

NOTES

I would like to thank Joan Meister, without whose invaluable assistance this article would never have been completed.

1 Labour Canada, "In the Chips: Opportunities, People, Partnerships," Ottawa, 1982.

2 C. Moorehouse, "Technological and Systems Change," CLC B.C. Regional Education Department, Vancouver, 1980, p. 37.

3 Jan Zimmerman, "How to Control the New Technology Before it Controls You," *Ms.,* Jan. 1981, p.83.

4 "If Home Is Where the Worker Is," *Business Week,* May 3, 1982.

5 Cited in F. Pomerg, "Technological Change: It's Coming to Your Workplace, Ready or Not," *Canadian Labour* (Oct. 1982), p. 18.

6 Labour Canada, *op. cit.,* pp. 77-78.

7 S. Peitchinis, "The Attitude of Trade Unions Towards Technological Change," Department of Industry, Trade and Commerce, Ottawa, 1980.

PART-TIME WORK AND UNIONS

Julie White

Part-time work* is a controversial issue within the trade union movement. Unlike other matters of significance to women, such as child care, equal pay and maternity leave, which have received growing support from unions, part-time work is commonly opposed by them, or at best considered a necessary evil. Few unions express active support for part-time work. However, this attitude is beginning to change. Unions have been forced to take more serious account of women's domestic responsibilities, and as it becomes clear that part-time work is an ever more integral part of the labour force, they begin to recognize the need for policies and practices to deal satisfactorily with the problems posed by part-time work.

This article outlines some of the problems and contradictions unions face in trying to deal with part-time work and details examples of the advances that have been made in negotiating protection for part-time workers.

PROBLEMS POSED BY PART-TIME WORK

Part-time workers occupy a secondary status within the labour force with lower pay, fewer benefits and less security than full-time workers. In 1981 almost half (49%) of all part-time jobs earned less than $5.00 an hour, compared to 21% of full-time jobs.[1] Part-time workers receive few non-wage benefits, such as health and welfare plans and pensions, particularly if their work is temporary.[2] It has been estimated that between two-thirds and three-quarters of all part-time jobs are temporary or casual in nature.[3] In these jobs part-time workers have no security and are not assured of regular days or hours of work. Many are on "call-in" lists, and contacted with little notice to meet a peak business period or to cover the absence of regular workers.

Employers' use of part-time work as a source of cheap labour is a concern by unionists and one reason for union opposition to part-time work. Part-time workers are not only cheap labour because of their low pay and benefits, but also because of their flexibility in covering

---

* For the purposes of this paper, part-time refers to part-week work, including both regular and casual work of less than the usual full-time weekly hours of work.

peak period work when and as it occurs, and their higher productivity as a result of fewer hours of work. Thus even where equal pay and benefit coverage are obtained by unions, part-time workers may still be cheaper than full-time workers. In the current economic climate of recession and high unemployment, it is feared that the pressure on employers to cut costs will make part-time work yet more attractive and lead to its further expansion.

Since 1953, when information on part-time work was first collected, part-time work has expanded from 3.7% of the labour force to 13.5% in 1981.[4] A special work history survey for 1981 conducted by Statistics Canada puts the percentage of part-time work even higher, at 20%.[5] This shift from full-time to part-time work is opposed by many unions because of the loss of full-time jobs. It is argued that workers need full-time jobs and full-time pay, and are being forced unwillingly into part-time work. Indeed it is the case that the number of part-time workers who said they worked part-time because they were unable to find full-time work rose from 11% to 18% between 1975 and 1981. Seventy percent of these involuntary workers are women.[6]

Part-time workers are less often unionized than full-time workers, making it difficult for unions to exercise control over the use and conditions of part-time workers. Of all part-time jobs held in 1981 only 15% were unionized, compared to 35% of full-time jobs.[7] There were several reasons for this low rate of unionizaton. A large proportion of part-time workers are employed on a casual basis, making them hard to contact in an organizing campaign. Moreover, in many jurisdictions, labour relations law and practice excludes casual workers from newly formed bargaining units, thereby denying them union representation. Legislation affecting certain government workers directly prohibits the unionization of casual workers and also of part-time workers employed for less than one-third the usual number of full-time hours. Part-time workers are also highly concentrated into small workplaces with few workers, which are difficult to unionize. For example, the retail trade employs 28% of all part-time workers, compared to 11% of full-time workers and each retail outlet employs 8 workers on average.[8] By comparison, manufacturing employs only 5% of all part-time workers, but 22% of full-time workers, and each manufacturing workplace employs 41 workers on average. Small workplaces are expensive and time-consuming to unionize, in part because of the complex legislative conditions and requirements for certification.

The use of part-time work as cheap labour, the consequent shift away from full-time work and the difficulty of unionizing part-time workers are the major, though not the only, reasons for union opposition to part-time work. This opposition has taken various forms — arguing against the expansion of part-time work in briefs and policy documents, organizing to prevent the introduction or expansion of part-time work and in a few cases negotiating restrictions on the use of part-time work into collective agreements. In Quebec, union opposition to part-time work is particularly strong, in part as a reaction against the provincial government's announcement of support for expanding part-time work. A coalition of unions and women's organizations formed in 1981 to oppose part-time work began its initial press release as follows:

> Part-time work is just another means by which women are kept in job ghettos where they are badly paid, where chances of unionization are limited and where they are subjected to indecent work conditions. We refuse to accept the fact that the future of women is restrained within the framework of part-time work and we denounce its use.[9]

PART-TIME WORK AND WOMEN

Part-time work is an issue of particular concern to women. Of all women in the labour force, 25% work part-time, and most of these are married and over the age of 25. By comparison, only 6% of employed men work part-time and they are predominantly young (under 25) and single.[10] For men, part-time work is most often a transitory phase from which they move on to full-time work, but for many women part-time work plays an integral role throughout their years in the labour force. Of all part-time workers almost three-quarters (72%) are women.[11]

Why do women work part-time? Do they do it because they want to? For many women part-time work is a compromise between the conflicting pressures they experience in their lives. While high rates of inflation and the consequent financial need pull women towards paid work, other factors work as disincentives. These include the high cost and lack of day care, inconvenient school hours, the stress of responsibility for both home and job, the absence of shared household work, and the still strong ideology of this society that mothers need and want to stay home with their children. Part-time work brings in some extra income while avoiding the full load of the double burden and at the same time enables mothers to spend time with their young children.

There is no doubt that a section of women in the labour force wants and needs part-time work. Asked why they work part-time, 43% of women part-time workers said they preferred part-time to full-time work, while a further 17% cite family responsibilities as the reason.[12] Twenty percent of unemployed women said that they are seeking part-time rather than full-time jobs.[13] More than one study has found that some women in full-time jobs would prefer to work part-time.[14]

The fact that some women want to work part-time raises questions about unions' protection of full-time jobs at the expense of part-time opportunities. The opposition of unions to part-time work would be entirely appropriate if all workers wanted full-time jobs, but this is not the case. In the current situation, part-time work continues to expand, most workers want full-time jobs and some workers want part-time jobs. The real question is just what the right mix of full and part-time work in any particular workplace or industry is – and the answer varies from one situation to another. Opposition to the introduction of part-time workers or restrictions on their use might be appropriate in some instances, particularly where workers are forced unwillingly into part-time jobs. Elsewhere it is possible that part-time work would be appreciated by workers who currently have no access to part-time hours, and should be negotiated as an option by unions.

It has been argued that improved day care services, shorter working hours for all and equal sharing of housework, rather than part-time work, are needed by women.[15] While these are certainly necessary elements in women's progress towards equality, it is not clear that the realization of such advances would make part-time work unnecessary. Some women do part-time work because they want to spend time with their children and improved day care would not alter this. Although shorter full-time hours are desirable, even if working hours were dramatically reduced, to say, 30 hours a week, this would be many more hours than those worked by the majority of part-time workers, who, on average, work only 15 hours a week.[16]

Concerning the equal sharing of housework and child care, the situation might be one where both mothers and fathers of young children would regard part-time work as a reasonable compromise during this period of greatly increased domestic responsibility. Whatever the future may hold, more immediately the situation is that good, low-cost day care is largely unavailable, that full-time hours for women average 38 per week, and that women continue to be responsible for domestic work.[17] Part-time work is a response to these realities and to work for its elimination or drastic reduction given current conditions is likely to cause further hardship to women.

The other arguments that trade unions have given for their opposition to part-time work, that it is cheap labour and hard to unionize, are also not convincing. Part-time workers are not the only workers who are underpaid and used as a source of cheap labour. Immigrant workers and women are two other sectors of the labour force that have been subject to secondary working conditions and remuneration. In fact, it is interesting to note that in the past, trade unions have supported policies to exclude both immigrants and women from the labour force, opposing them on the basis of their use as cheap labour and consequent threat to other workers.[18] While immigrants and women are still exploited as cheap labour, it is no longer acceptable to oppose their participation in the labour force. Unions now support the position that they must be protected and provided with equal pay, benefits and opportunities like other workers. The same policy would seem to be appropriate for the problem of exploitation of part-time workers.

The difficulty in unionizing part-time work, due to legislation and employer practices, is no reason to oppose it. Certainly, part-time work is not the only tactic used to inhibit the organization of unions. Employers may fire, transfer, demote and otherwise intimidate workers, may withhold benefits or suddenly provide good pay increases, to mention just a few of the methods used to prevent unionization. Unions do not generally oppose the labour force participation of workers who are difficult to organize because of the employer's anti-union practices.

A perspective is needed which does not see part-time work as undesirable in itself, but understands that its use can be detrimental for women workers. A consistent and cogent position would be to oppose the exploitation of part-time workers, rather than to oppose part-time work itself. Such a position does not entail approval of the uncontrolled expansion of part-time work, but takes specific circumstances into account. In assessing the impact of part-time work it is necessary to consider such factors as the economic climate, the industry, legisla-tion, the proportion of full- to part-time work and the needs of the workers. For example, it would be appropriate to oppose the expan-sion of part-time work if it was introduced as a scheme to deal with unemployment and created involuntary part-time work, or where pay and conditions were unequal. However, in workplaces where women want access to part-time work, and where remuneration and condi-tions are equal, then the introduction of part-time work would satisfy the needs of the workers.

While many unions continue to maintain a position of opposition to part-time work, the realities and complexities of the workplace have led to various ways of handling the issue in practice. As the number of part-time workers has expanded, some unions have moved to fully incorporate them and protect their interests. The following sections consider three ways in which unions have responded to the increase in part-time work: unionization, bargaining equal pay and benefits, and bargaining controls on part-time work.

UNIONIZATION[19]

In the past trade unions have not enthusiastically unionized part-time workers. They were often simply ignored and thereby excluded, while some unions formally prohibited their participation. This situation has changed. The United Food and Commercial Workers International Union (UFCW) represents workers in the large supermarket chain stores and made its first application for a local with part-time workers in Ontario in 1959, but in other provinces organizing part-time work-ers came much later. For example, the first UFCW local in New Brunswick to include part-time workers was not certified until 1972. Now, this union represents 50,000 part-time workers, one-third of the total Canadian membership of the union.

The Canadian Union of Postal Workers (CUPW), which represents inside workers in the post office, also has a large proportion of part-time members (25%). However, this has not always been the case. Until the post office became a crown corporation in 1981, the union negotiated under the Public Service Staff Relations Act, which pro-hibits the unionization of casual workers employed for less than six months. This meant that all casual workers, whether full- or part-time, could not belong to the union. Bitter conflicts resulted from the extensive use of casuals in the post office, a source of labour that could not be protected by unionization. When regular part-time workers were first introduced into the post office in the 1960s their position was not dissimilar to that of the casual, being called in as needed with little or no notice, paid less than the full-time workers and ineligible for benefits – "cheap labour pure and simple."[20] Influenced by the vehement opposition that had developed over the casual workers, the union at first refused to accept part-time workers as members, what Joe Davidson calls "the ostrich approach," in his frank description of the period.[21] Davidson also points out that the union's reluctance was not unrelated to the fact that all the part-time workers were women. CUPW was moved to action when the part-time workers started to join another union, and the constitution was amended to permit an associate status for part-time workers in 1966. It was not until 1975 that part-time workers obtained equal footing with full-time workers in the union.

Until recently substitute teachers were only admitted to the British Columbia Teachers' Federation (BCTF) as associate members, without the right to vote or hold office within the union. Since the mid-1970s the union has represented the interests of substitute teachers and in 1980 they were admitted to full status membership within the union, largely the result of agitation by the substitutes themselves.

In other unions part-time and casual workers have always been included as members, while in some this has yet to be achieved. For example, the Ontario Public Service Employees Union (OPSEU) has recently organized a local of substitute teachers, who were not accepted by the union representing the regularly employed teaching staff. However, the trend is undoubtedly towards increased unionization of part-time workers in sectors where full-time workers are already organized, and their inclusion in the formation of new locals. This trend also involves the equalization of the role of part-time workers within unions, and some unions have made special arrangements to encourage the participation of part-time workers. For example, OPSEU had nine wage negotiating committees, each of which sent representatives to negotiations. In 1981 a tenth committee was established to represent those workers defined by legislation as "unclassified," which covers all part-time and temporary workers employed

by the Ontario government. This committee also sends a representative to the negotiations.

The payment of union dues is another in which unions have to
accommodate part-time workers. Some unions – including the
Ontario Nurses Association, the Alberta Teachers' Association, the
Service Employees International Union, and many locals of the Canadian Union of Public Employees and the United Food and Commercial Workers Union – have a different, lower rate or system for part-
time workers. In general there is a clear trend towards a dues system
based upon a percentage of the members' income, which automatically
provides for lower dues for part-time workers. In most unions a percentage payment is considered a more progressive system, from which
all lower income workers benefit. Unions that have thus far retained a
single flat rate dues payment for all include the Public Service Alliance
of Canada (PSAC), CUPW and the Hotel and Restaurant Employees'
and Bartenders' International Union (HREBIU).

PAY AND BENEFITS

Once unionized, the pay and conditions of part-time workers have
become an increasingly important factor in union negotiations.
Whether the intention is to protect full-time jobs from a source of
cheap labour, to lessen the exploitation of part-time workers, or both,
some unions have successfully negotiated important improvements for
part-time workers. The United Food and Commercial Workers Union
has been largely successful in eliminating lower pay rates for students
and is progressing in its negotiations to equalize the starting pay rates
for full and part-time workers. Equal wages for part-time workers
have been obtained by the union in British Columbia and will be
equalized by 1983 in Quebec, while in other provinces differential rates
still apply. In fact most unions have negotiated equal starting rates and
pay increments for regular part-time workers. However, casual part-
time workers are often excluded from pay increments, and occasionally even from equal starting pay rates. In the teachers' unions, for
example, substitutes commonly receive a lower rate than regular
teachers, at least for an initial period of up to 20 days.

Arrangements to provide benefits for part-time workers and especially casual part-time workers, are technically complex as well as
difficult to negotiate because of employer resistance. Contract clauses

negotiated with full-time workers in mind cannot easily be directly applied to part-time workers. Union locals with a catch-all phrase stating that part-time workers are covered by the contract have found themselves dealing with complex grievances, as the part-time labour force expands and the contracts are found lacking.

Statutory holidays are one example of the many possible complications. Most contracts now provide a minimum of ten statutory holidays, the equivalent to two weeks of work, and a substantial benefit. When the holiday is worked, as is necessary in hospitals and other continuous-operation workplaces, the workers usually receive additional pay as recompense, and this may be easily applied to both full- and part-time workers. Problems arise in the more common situation where workers are taking time off for statutory holidays. For full-time workers the holidays are taken as days with pay, and often it is agreed that where the holiday falls on a weekend an alternative day of leave or an additional day's pay is provided. Regular part-time workers who work the same hours every day and spread over five days a week, may take holidays in the same way as full-time workers. However, as soon as there are changes in pattern, there are complications. For example, if someone works three full days per week, Thursday to Saturday, and the holiday falls on Monday, how should it be accounted for? Irregular hours or days of work that change from week to week are common for casual part-time workers and unless some provision is made they do not receive the benefit of statutory holidays.

It is not necessarily obvious how this problem should be handled, and indeed unions have negotiated a wide variety of different clauses on the issue. The United Food and Commercial Workers and Retail, Wholesale and Department Store Union have contracts in which part-time workers are eligible for holidays after three calendar months of employment and provided they have worked 12 days in the four weeks prior to the holidays, as well as their scheduled days of work both before and after the holidays. The Public Service Alliance of Canada has an arrangement whereby part-time workers must be working both the day before and the day after a statutory holiday in order to qualify for pay, an arbitrary situation whereby some would and some would not be eligible. The Ontario Nurses' Association, sections of the Canadian Union of Public Employees, and the Service Employees International Union, have negotiated for at least part of their membership, a payment-in-lieu package, which covers several benefits, including statutory holidays. However, in no case is the applied percentage sufficient to compensate for the benefits available to full-time workers.

The most advantageous arrangement has been negotiated by the Common Front Unions in Quebec.[22] As a percentage, the statutory holidays amount to 5.3% of the work year. This percentage is then applied to the part-time worker's annual wage and the resulting amount added to the regular wage. In any situation where part-time workers are employed in a irregular or casual basis this arrangement equalizes the benefit for the workers and the cost to employers.

Wage-related benefits, such as long-term disability, pensions and some life insurance plans, present difficulties because the reduced hours of employment of part-time workers means that their income is low. As a result the final benefits from the insurance plan may be no higher than government social security payments, and these will be reduced as a result of the insurance benefits. As well, because many part-time workers are employed on a casual basis and have a higher turnover rate than full-time workers, they would pay contributions into such plans, but leave before receiving the benefits. Thus, it is by no means clear that it is advantageous to negotiate part-time workers into these plans. It should be noted that many unions in the public sector are legally prohibited form negotiating pensions, and that much of the legislation governing pension plans for the public sector excludes part-time workers.

For readers interested in the details of how to bargain pay and benefits for part-time workers, good contracts on these issues include those negotiated by the Common Front Unions in Quebec, the Hospital Employees Union in British Columbia and CUPW. While most unionized part-time workers employed on a regular basis are paid the same as full-time workers, pay rates for casuals and benefits for all part-time workers are still far from equal in most unions. On the positive side, this situation is recognized as a problem by the majority of unions, which are moving to negotiate improvements.

One crucial issue, which directly affects the pay and benefits received by part-time workers, has been largely ignored by trade unions — and this is the ghettoization of part-time workers. To a greater extent even than full-time women workers, part-time workers are segregated into a limited number of industries and occupations. Eighty percent of women part-time workers are employed in just two industries, service and trade, while 72% are employed in only three occupations, as clerical, service and sales workers.[23] Part-time workers are often hired to perform the most menial and repetitive tasks with no training opportunities and even less chance of promotion. The ghettoization of part-time workers is not only an important factor in their relatively low pay rates, but also helps explain why part-time work is unavailable in some industries and occupations despite a need for it, while in others there is little but part-time work available.

BARGAINING CONTROLS

Negotiating controls on the number of part-time workers or their hours of work has been interpreted as a negative approach indicating that unions oppose part-time work and are seeking to protect full-time jobs.[24] Certainly such controls may be used to automatically protect full-time over part-time work, but in fact this is rarely the case. Contract clauses may in fact be restrictions upon the employer's use and misuse of part-time work and therefore be of advantage to part-tme workers.

For example, it seems that controls are necessary on the excessive use of casual part-time work. While most part-time jobs are temporary in nature, of unemployed women seeking part-time work only 25% of those under 25, and 13% of those married and over 25 wanted temporary work.[25] The Federation of Social Affairs in Quebec has a clause stating that casuals are to be hired only to temporarily replace the usual workers and not on a regular basis. This union has also negotiated that where possible, hospitals will establish mobile unions of permanent workers prepared to move from one department to another as required. Several hospitals have established such units, thus reducing the need for casual workers.

Controls on the scheduled hours of work may be desirable where employers reduce or extend the hours of work for part-time workers with little advance notice or regard for the needs of the workers. The Hospital Employees Union, the Ontario Nurses' Association, the B.C. Nurses Union and the Hotel and Restaurant Employees and Bartenders International Union have all negotiated a minimum number of hours of between 15 and 20 hours per week. In addition, the Hospital Employees Union has negotiated a clause that part-time workers may refuse to work more than 20 hours per week, thus protecting them from an involuntary extension of hours.

A minority of unions have bargained for controls on the number and proportion of part-time workers. In order to assess the impact of such controls it is necessary to consider the context in which they have been negotiated. Both the United Food and Commercial Workers and the Retail, Wholesale and Department Store Union have negotiated contract clauses placing ratios upon the number of part-time to full-time employed in retail stores. Thirty percent of workers in the retail trade are part-time, far above the national average of 13.5%, and 60% of the unions' members in the retail trade are part-time.[26] The questions raised here concern the appropriate mix of full- and part-time workers and the control the union has over this mix. There may be situations where full-time jobs are in need of protection, and restrictions on the number of part-time workers help ensure a reasonable balance of full- and part-time work. Answering this question in any particular workplace is no easy matter, but with 60% of union members part-time, some controls do not seem unreasonable. Also, given such a high proportion of part-time workers, it is apparent that the controls were hardly designed to drastically restrict the number of part-time jobs. To give an example, the Retail, Wholesale and Department Store Union has negotiated a ratio of one full-time to one part-time worker, rising to one full-time to four part-time workers at peak periods.

A few unions have negotiated controls of a more general nature. Contract clauses that do not allow the hiring of part-time workers to replace full-time workers are examples. The Hospital Employees Union has a far stronger clause, which states: "The employer shall eliminate, as far as possible, all part-time employees." Such clauses are not related to striking some reasonable balance between full- and part-time work, but serve to automatically protect full-time jobs. In these few cases it seems that the general opposition of the unions to part-time work has indeed been implemented through contract negotiations.

One further type of control is possible, though rare, through which the workers maintain control over when they undertake part-time work and for how long. The Quebec Teaching Congress negotiated a clause whereby any teacher may request a part-time position for a year, which may be extended to any number of years. Thus far, no one been denied such a request, though the union is intending to negotiate it as a right in the future. During the part-time period, the worker is paid on a pro-rated basis and retains all benefits and seniority rights, calculated on a half-time basis. All such part-time workers are guaranteed a return to a full-time position upon their request at the start of the following school year. Thus, these part-time positions cannot be used as cheap labour and the worker is able to move back into full-time work.

CONCLUSION

In general there are four areas in which improved conditions for part-time workers are necessary, and where unions have been or should be active.

1. *Organizing the Unorganized.* Since few part-time workers belong to unions a commitment of time and money to broad unionization campaigns is the first step to ensure protection for most part-time workers. Many aspects of the current labour relations laws inhibit the unionization of part-time workers; therefore action to change this legislation is also necessary.

2. *Bargaining for Control.* The excessive use of casual part-time work and the large proportion of involuntary part-time workers indicate that control of part-time work is necessary if it is to serve the needs of workers, and particularly women workers. Such controls might include:

- reducing casual work in favour of more regular part-time work
- guaranteeing certain minimum hours of work for part-time workers, with the right to refuse overtime
- ensuring job security for part-time workers
- providing the right to transfer from full- to part-time, and from part- to full-time jobs according to seniority, with the right to refuse such transfers without penalty
- the right to transfer to part-time work for a specified period with a guarantee of returning to a full-time position
- taking parental leave on a part-time basis
- monitoring the quantity of part-time work in relation to the needs of workers in order to appropriately oppose or support the introduction or expansion of part-time work.

3. *Equal Pay and Benefits.* In order to inhibit the use of part-time workers as a source of cheap labour and end their unequal treatment, continued efforts are necessary to obtain equal pay and benefits. The principle should be to work towards the reduction or elimination of

distinctions between workers, so that all are covered by the same pay and benefits regardless of the hours worked per week or the length of employment. This is especially important for casual part-time workers, who are subject to lower pay and benefits more often than regular part-time workers.

4. *Affirmative Action.* With women, and as women, part-time workers are confined to certain industrial and occupational ghettos. Since little if any attempt has been made to break down this ghettoization, employers have been free to hire part-time workers at their convenience and without regard to the needs of workers. Consequently, some full-time workers interested in part-time work have no access to reduced hours, while a proportion of part-time workers in fact need full-time work. Rectifying this imbalance involves, in part, breaking down the ghettoization of part-time workers and enabling broader access to controlled, equally remunerated and protected part-time work, with some guarantee of priority in returning to full-time work.

While opposition to part-time work continues to predominate in trade unions, this has not prevented real changes in the treatment of part-time workers. In the last ten years part-time workers have been increasingly accepted as full members within trade unions and improved pay and benefits have been obtained through collective bargaining. Only rarely has a union's stated position of opposition to part-time work translated into automatic and one-sided protection of full-time jobs in collective agreements.

Moreover, with the expansion of part-time work and the increasing recognition of women's particular relationship to the labour force, opposition to part-time work has in some unions given way to ambivalence, while a minority are prepared to support part-time work if it is properly remunerated and desired by the workers. Several unions have undertaken research on the issue in order to reach or clarify policy decisions, including the British Columbia Teachers' Federation, the Confederation of National Trade Unions, the Public Service Alliance of Canada and the Quebec Teachers' Corporation.

Like the entry of women into the labour force, the expansion of part-time work has thrown up new challenges to the trade union movement. For the future, a better understanding of the role of part-time work in women's lives is necessary, combined with the flexibility to deal with specific situations, and to avoid the blanket approval or disapproval of part-time work. In order to have any impact upon the lives of the one and a half million part-time workers in Canada there is first and foremost the overwhelming need to unionize the vast majority who remain unorganized.

NOTES

1 Statistics Canada, Labour Force Activity Section, "Survey of 1981 Work History," unpublished data.

2 See Gord Robertson, *Part-time Work in Ontario: 1966 to 1978*, Employment Information Series No. 20, Research Branch, Ontario Ministry of Labour, Aug. 1976; Wendy Weeks, "The Extent and Nature of Part-time Work in Hamilton, Survey Results of Selected Hamilton Businesses – 1978," prepared for the Community Permanent Part-time Work Committee, Hamilton, Sept. 1980, Table 29; Saskatchewan Department of Labour, *A Comparative Study of the Provision of Selected Non-Wage Benefits to Part-time and Full-time Employees in Rural Saskatchewan, April-June, 1978,* Oct. 1975.

3 Canadian Advisory Council on the Status of Women, *Part-time Work: A Review of the Issues,* a brief to the Advisory Council of Employment and Immigration Canada, Nov. 1980, p. 5; Weeks, "Part-time Work in Hamilton," tables 7 and 8.

4 Calculated from Statistics Canada, *Historical Labour Force Statistics,* Cat. No. 71-201, 1974-75, pp. 101-104; Statistics Canada, *The Labour Force,* Cat. No. 71-001, Dec. 1981, p. 110, table 85.

5 Statistics Canada, "Survey of 1981 Work History."

6 Statistics Canada, *Labour Force Annual Averages 1975-1978,* Cat. No. 71-529, p. 111, table 25; Statistics Canada, *The Labour Force,* Dec. 1981, p. 113, table 88.

7 Statistics Canada, "Survey of 1981 Work History."

8 Statistics Canada, *The Labour Force,* Dec. 1981, p. 112, table 87; Retail Council of Canada, "Part-Time Employment," submission to the Canada Employment and Immigration Advisory Council Task-Force on Part-Time Work, Sept. 1980, p. 2.

9 La Coalition (CSN, SFPQ, SPGQ, FQII, FSPIIQ, Action-travail des femmes, Ligue des femmes du Québec, Au bas de l'échelle, Carrefour des associations de familles monoparentales du Québec press release, "200,000 femmes dénoncent le piège du temps partiel" Dec. 8, 1981, p. 1.

10 Statistics Canada, *The Labour Force,* Dec. 1981, p. 110, table 85.

11 *Ibid.*

12 *Ibid.,* p. 113, table 88.

13 *Ibid.,* p. 123, table 98.

14 Carol Reich, "A Study of Interest in Part-Time Employment Among Non-Teaching Employees of the Board," Research Dept., Toronto Board of Education, Toronto, Sept. 1975; Michèle de Sève and Simon Langlois, "Les hommes et les femmes dans la Fonction publique Québécoise," Sept. 1977, p. 450.

15 The Public Service Alliance of Canada, "Part-Time Employment," Discussion Paper, mimeograph, Oct.1981; Gouvernement du Québec, Conseil du status de la femme, "Le travail à temps partiel: une mésure d'égalité en emploi ou d'inégalité en emploi," Sept. 1982.

16 The 13.5% of the labour force considered to be part-time by Statistics Canada are defined as such by the fact that they work less than 30 hours per week. In 1981 part-time workers were employed on average for 15 hours per week. See Statistics Canada, *The Labour Force,* Dec. 1981, p. 109, table 84.

17 *Ibid.*

18 Harold A. Logan, *The History of Trade Union Organization in Canada* (Chicago: Univ. of Chicago Press,1928), p. 189; Alice Kessler-Harris, "Where are the Organized Women Workers?", *Feminist Studies,* Vol. 2, No. 1/2 (Fall 1975), p. 97; Ruth Frager's article in this book.

19 The examples from specific unions mentioned in the following discussion were obtained from interviews with representatives of the 18 unions, carried out between Nov. 1981 and Feb. 1982. For a complete review of the results of these interviews see Julie White, *Women and Part-Time Work* (Ottawa: Canadian Advisory Council on the Status of Women, 1983).

20 Joe Davidson and John Deverell, *Joe Davidson* (Toronto: James Lorimer, 1978), p. 85.

21 *Ibid.,* p. 86.

22 The Common Front unions include all unions representing public sector workers employed by the government of Quebec.

23 Statistics Canada, *The Labour Force,* Dec. 1981, p. 112, table 87.

24 Marianne Bossen, *Part-Time Work in the Canadian Economy,* Labour Canada, Oct. 1975, p. 82; Joan McFarland, "Women and Unions: Help or Hindrance," *Atlantis,* Vol. 4, No.2 (Spring 1979), p. 57.

25 Statistics Canada, *The Labour Force,* Dec. 1981, p. 123, table 87.
26 Statistics Canada, Labour Force Survey Division, unpublished data, 1981.

SEXUAL HARASSMENT: AN ISSUE FOR UNIONS

Susan Attenborough

Sexual harassment is a serious and widespread problem affecting women in the workplace. It is not a new problem for women workers, yet it is only recently that sexual harassment has been openly confronted. Unions have been among the most active in seeking solutions to the problem of sexual harassment. The increase in the number and involvement of women members has prompted this activity. Women have organized within their unions to ensure their concerns on issues such as sexual harassment are dealt with. Particularly in the public sector, unions have responded by taking up the issue and seeking solutions through education and the collective bargaining process.

WHAT IS SEXUAL HARASSMENT?

Sexual harassment is any sexual advance that threatens a worker's job or well-being. It is usually an expression of power made by someone in authority. Most victims of sexual harassment are women, primarily because most people in powerful or authoritative positions in our society are men. They are able to use their authority to take sexual advantage of their female employees.

Sexual harassment can be expressed in a number of ways: unnecessary touching or patting, suggestive remarks or other verbal abuse, leering, demands for sexual favours, compromising invitations, and physical assault. All of these may or may not be accompanied by direct or implied threats to the victim's job or career.

Two factors ensure the perpetuation of sexual harassment. First, women are second-class citizens in the labour force. Concentrated into only a few occupations (mainly clerical, sales and service), where wages and status are low, women still earn only 57 percent of what men earn — and this gap is widening. And, once unemployed, women tend to stay out of the labour force longer because of the limited job opportunities available to them.

Secondly, traditional gender roles socialize women to be sexually passive and to want to appear attractive to men. At the same time, women are taught that they are responsible for controlling sexual situations. Men, on the other hand, are taught that their role is to be an economic provider and to be sexually aggressive, and that women often don't mean it when they say "no."

High unemployment rates, a widening gap and limited labour force opportunities keep women in an inferior and vulnerable position in the labour force. Combined with stereotypes of women's traditional role, they serve to maintain the conditions that perpetuate sexual harassment.

UNIONS AND SEXUAL HARASSMENT

Unions have historically been agents of social change. They have been at the forefront of struggles for decent working conditions, adequate pensions and medicare. Sexual harassment is a union issue because it is a social problem – a product of the inequality that exists in our society.

Unions are committed to protecting their members' health and safety on the job. Because sexual harassment has such a potentially hazardous effect on workers' health and safety, it has become a union issue. Victims of sexual harassment suffer anger, fear and frustration, feelings that often result in physical ailments such as headaches, loss of concentration and other nervous disorders. These psychological and physical symptoms are not imagined, and have negative effects on a victim's job peformance and personal life.

Unions are also committed to resolving the inequalities that contribute to the persistence of sexual harassment – high unemployment, unequal wages, limited labour force opportunities. This is an ongoing challenge. But unions recognize that victims of sexual harassment need prompt assistance. Although the long-term fight for equal opportunities may eventually equalize the workplace so that fewer women will be victims of sexual harassment, those women being victimized *now* need immediate solutions.

Many unions have recently adopted policies that recognize sexual harassment as a problem in the workplace. Unions are educating their members by publishing articles about sexual harassment in their monthly publications, sponsoring seminars, and including the topic in conferences and workshops. Many unions devote a session to discussing sexual harassment in their steward training courses. Educating stewards to the problem not only brings the issue directly to the membership but also aids stewards in dealing with sexual harassment cases at work.

Several recent breakthroughs have been made by unions negotiating sexual harassment clauses in their collective agreements. Initially, progress was made in small bargaining units. Gradually however, larger groups in the federal and provincial public service have successfully negotiated protective clauses. For example, the Manitoba Government Employees Association, which represents over 15,000 provincial employees, negotiated a sexual harassment clause in June 1982. In October 1982, the B.C. Government Employees' Union (BCGEU) negotiated a sexual harassment clause in their Master Agreement, which covers over 40,000 workers. Here is an example of a good clause negotiated in April 1981 with the Open Learning Institute, a small BCGEU bargaining unit.

1.08 SEXUAL HARASSMENT

a) The Union and the Employer recognize the right of the employees to work in an environment free from sexual harassment, and the Employer undertakes to discipline an employee engaging in sexual harassment.

b) Sexual harassment shall be defined as:

— persistent sexual solicitation or advance made by a person of authority who knows, or ought to know, it is unwelcome, or,

— a reprisal (or threat of a reprisal) by someone in authority after a sexual advance is rejected.

c) In cases of sexual harassment, the employee being harassed has the right to discontinue contact with the harasser without incurring any penalty. In cases where sexual harassment may result in the transfer of an employee, where possible it shall be the harasser who is transferred. The employee who is harassed shall not be transferred against the employee's will.

d) An employee may initiate a grievance under this clause at any step of the grievance procedure. Grievances under this clause will be handled with all possible confidentiality.

e) An alleged offender under this clause shall be entitled

i) to be given notice of the substance of a grievance under this clause,

ii) to be given notice and to attend, participate in and be represented in any arbitration hearing which is held as a result of a grievance under this clause.

This is considered to be a good clause because:

• It places the onus on the employer to discipline the harasser. In cases of co-worker harassment, the union can grieve the employer's inaction instead of pitting one member against another.

• It provides a broad definition of sexual harassment. Including the provision "knows or ought to know" prevents unjust use of the plea of ignorance.

• It provides for separation of the victim and the harasser to avoid unpleasant confrontations or further incidents. Although vague, "without penalty" presumably means without loss of pay or benefits.

• It states that where transfer is required it should be the harasser, not the victim, thus preventing any further disruption for the victim.

• It ensures that grievances will be handled with confidentiality and dispatch, although specific time limits would be better.

• It ensures that the alleged harasser is aware of the grievance and party to any hearings. The clause in the BCGEU Master Agreement goes further and prohibits the harasser from grieving disciplinary action.

It should be remembered that this clause is a product of the negotiating process. That is, there has been a lot of give and take on both sides. In preparing a clause for negotiations, consideration should be given to the criticisms noted here and to including provisions for penalties that may be invoked against the harasser (i.e., fines).

Unions are finding that protective clauses in collective agreements act as deterrents to potential harassers, as well as provide access to the grievance process for victims. Unions that have not yet negotiated such clauses have been trying other strategies − for example, using the non-discrimination, or health and safety clauses, to grieve sexual harassment. Often sexual harassment grievances are settled informally or at the first level of the grievance procedure. Management tends toward the quick resolution of this type of complaint. This is probably partly due to the sensitive nature of the issue and to the fact that in several cases in the United States the courts have ordered employers to pay large sums of money as part of settlement claims for sexual harassment victims.

The Canadian Labour Congress is lobbying for specific legislation to protect all workers from sexual harassment. For example, they have recommended to the federal government that it amend the Canadian Labour Code to include a section on sexual harassment. As well as this direct pressure, the fact that sexual harassment is an issue at many bargaining tables puts indirect pressure on legislators. Historically, trade union gains in the areas of medical insurance and pensions brought pressure on legislators to provide these benefits to all workers.

The fact that federal, Alberta and Ontario human rights legislation now refer specifically to sexual harassment is in part due to this kind of pressure.

CO-WORKER HARASSMENT

Sexual harassment is a power relationship and therefore often occurs between supervisors and employees. However, there are other sources of power that enable harassment to occur between co-workers. Men, by virtue of their size and strength, have a physical power over women. Although it may never be used, the threat of superior physical strength is very intimidating. Also, simply being a male in our society means having a certain perceived superiority over women. This stems from the traditional value society places on the male-dominated, paid labour force and the corresponding undervaluation of women's unpaid work in the home.

Occupations in construction, trades, machinery and heavy equipment are still considered to be "men's jobs." When women do break into these jobs, co-worker sexual harassment may be prevalent. Co-workers may use sexual harassment as an intimidation tactic to discourage women from applying for and working in traditionally male bastions. When women quit it is often not because they cannot handle the job, but because they are subject to the constant pressure and harassment that goes with being the only female in a male-dominated workplace.

Many men find it difficult to differentiate between workplace flirtation and sexual harassment. Workplace flirtation is based on mutual attraction and consent. Sexual harassment is coercive and may be accompanied by threats, promises or abuse. Once the differentiation is clear, men's behaviour often changes. Some women report that when their co-workers understand what sexual harassment is (and understand that women do not like it), much of the harassment disappears.

Dealing with sexual harassment by co-workers is a sensitive issue with unions. Union education attempts to discuss and clarify sexual harassment in the hopes of reducing its incidence among union members. However, attitudes are hard to change and there are usually some men who continue to harass even when told their behaviour is offensive. When co-worker harassment persists, there are two options the union may consider. One is to take the position that the onus should be on management to maintain a workplace free of harassment and discrimination. Unions can demand that management adopt a policy against sexual harassment. Where such a policy existed, and sexual harassment continued, the union would be able to grieve management's failure to comply with its policy. However, if the employer took disciplinary action against the harasser, the union might find itself in the incongruous position of defending the harasser in a grievance against the discipline because of the union's legal obligation to provide "fair representation" to all its members. Some unions with policies against sexual harassment have taken the position of not defending "convicted" harassers. This places the union in a conflict over defending a policy or a member – a position no union wants to find itself in.

The other option is for the union to use internal disciplinary procedures against members who harass other union members. Most union constitutions contain a clause specifying that union members must respect each other's rights. The union could take the position that a member who sexually harasses another member is violating that clause. The union would then have to discipline within its own structure. An example along this line is the Ontario Public Service Employees Union, which at its 1982 convention amended its constitution to prohibit sexual harassment. This amendment, a major step forward for the union movement, covers sexual harassment at the workplace as well as at union functions.

The difficulty with taking the internal approach to disciplinary co-worker harassment is that it has the potential to be very divisive. It is the union's objective to build solidarity among its members, not to destroy it. However, the existence of sexual harassment among co-members is a divisive factor itself.

There is no easy answer to the issue of co-worker harassment. But sensitive issues, like alcohol and drug abuse and even marital problems, have been tackled by unions before. Regardless of the approach a union chooses, the solution to co-worker harassment requires the hard work of activists, the commitment of the union leadership and a sensitization of the membership to the problem.

WHAT WOMEN CAN DO

Women in unions have a number of avenues open to them in promoting solutions to sexual harassment:

• Lobby elected officers to make them aware of the problem. They are elected by you to be responsive to your concerns.

• Let your steward know there's a problem with sexual harassment at your workplace. She or he may have some ideas on how to solve it at the workplace level.

• Talk to your staff representative about the problem. She or he may be able to help you get in touch with the other women in the union with the same problem.

• Form a women's committee or become active where one already exists.

• Raise the issue at coffee breaks; hold lunch-hour meetings for discussion or show a film (such as *The Workplace Hustle*) on the issue.

• Take a resolution to your union's convention that includes some direction on how the union should act on the problem. Try and seek support for the resolution before as well as at the convention. Select supporters to speak to the resolution on the convention floor. When the resolution is passed, follow up to make sure the action is taken.

• Get elected to the bargaining team or propose a protective clause for inclusion in demands. Priorities attached to demands during bargaining are often based on perceived membership support. Make sure the support is there and that it is vocal.

• Get the support of your male and female co-workers and fellow union members. It is important not to isolate sexual harassment as "just a woman's problem." Many men are concerned, and not just in an empathetic sense. They also have wives, daughters and mothers in the labour force.

• Contact other union women through organizations structured along the lines of Ontario's Organized Working Women or Saskatchewan Working Women.

There are other solutions available outside the union structure. Increasingly, human rights commissions are becoming aware of the issue and taking up cases. However, this can be a long, drawn-out process. The legal route (i.e., suing for the physical assault or defamation of character) is also time-consuming and often expensive.

As women's labour force participation increases, so does their role in unions. Union executives, especially in the public sector, are beginning to reflect this, both in the structure and in the priority women's issues receive. Despite problems such as male domination and the bureaucratic structure inherent in many unions, unions still provide some of the best ways for women to solve their workplace problems. Steady pressure by women activists will ensure that unions continue to confront issues like sexual harassment.

COERCION OR MALE CULTURE: A NEW LOOK AT CO-WORKER HARASSMENT

Debbie Field

> A pinch. A look. Pin-ups hung around the workplace. Ultimatums and threats. Economic blackmail. Offensive anti-women language. Physical violence. A grab. A leer. Jokes about what women are "good for."

An important focus of the women's movement in the last ten years has been the analysis of sexual harassment. Feminists have drawn attention to the widespread existence of sexual harassment, stressed the similarities between its many diverse forms and proposed initial tactics to combat it. The apparently isolated experience of individuals has been revealed as a problem shared by all working women. By pointing to the connection between various types of sexual harassment, from anti-women language to physical violence, the women's movement has deepened our understanding of women's oppression and men's economic, social and physical power over women. By breaking the silence traditionally surrounding sexual harassment and organizing collectively against it, women have laid the basis for successfully fighting sexual harassment. At times we have been able to stop the harassing behaviour, have the harasser fired or receive financial compensation for the suffering caused by harassment. The record of the women's movement has been positive, with specific campaigns and a deepening awareness among women of the severity of workplace sexual harassment.

Yet for all these strengths, there are problems with the women's movement's analysis of sexual harassment and the tactics developed to combat it. As with much of the analysis of the women's movement, we began by stressing that which was hidden – the general oppression of women throughout society; in this case, women's shared experience of sexual harassment. But in the same way that feminists have developed the analysis of women's shared oppression by investigating the particular ways class differences form and change that oppression, the analysis of sexual harassment could benefit by looking at the effects of class relations in the workplace. This means differentiating between co-worker and employer-initiated harassment.

The tactics developed in recent years suffer too from the tendency to lump all sexual harassment together. For example, lodging a human rights commission complaint may be successful in stopping a fore-man's coercive behaviour, but would be ineffective in preventing men harassing female co-workers with their sexist graffiti. Differentiating between types of harassment may thus help us to develop more effec-tive tactics.

We live in a society in which men of all classes engage in violence against women, and sexism is widespread. In a broad sense all forms of sexual harassment share common features. They all involve men view-ing women as sexual objects available for male pleasure. All forms of sexual harassment contain the threat, however implicit, of male vio-lence if women do not behave as men wish us to. The fact that women are regularly beaten up and raped by men, even men who are sup-posedly friends or lovers, serves as a constant reminder that apparently friendly male sexist behaviour from bosses or co-workers can turn into violence against women.

However, while all men have social and physical power over women, the direct economic power of employers intensifies their abil-ity to coerce women on the job. A class line tends to divide sexual harassment in the workplace. The more intense forms – physical vio-lence, sexual ultimatums and threats – are primarily perpetrated by men who have direct authority to hire and fire, promote and demote.[1] Employer-initiated harassment usually occurs in secret, one employer to one employee, under circumstances that make it extremely difficult for a women to complain or let anyone know what has happened to her.[2]

By the very definition of their "relationship" to employees, employ-ers can and often do behave in an arbitrary and harassing manner. Particularly in non-union situations, employers can manipulate those who work for them by using the threat of job discipline. Even where a union exists they can make life difficult for employees who do not act as the employer or manager feels they should. The step from random general workplace harassment to sexual harassment is not large, given the limited rights of workers and the pervasive sexism of male-female interaction. Sexual coercion by employers thus flows directly from the unequal workplace relations between employers and employees. Most cases of sexual harassment that have received publicity or been taken to court in recent years are examples of employer-initiated coercion in which the male in a position of direct economic authority uses his power to gain sexual favours from a woman employee.

In contrast to these forms of coercion, sexual harassment among co-workers most often consists of sexist language, sexual remarks, jokes, pin-ups and a work environment that women find offensive and which thereby limits our ability to survive on the job. Whether we work with many other women or in non-traditional areas where we are a minority, most women can recall instances of male group behaviour that we found upsetting or harassing. Men stand around the coffee machine ogling women, making embarrassing references to the shapes and sizes of our bodies. Some men ask whether we had enough sex the night before or leave gross drawings or jokes on our desks or workbenches.

What is critical to our understanding of male group behaviour is that it also occurs when women are absent. In fact, men are more sexist when there are no women around. It is common for men in all-male work areas to call a machine that is malfunctioning, or a co-worker they want to put down, a "bitch" or a "cunt." The fact that graffiti on the job site that says, "women belong on their back," is written by men for men does not lessen its damaging impact on women. It is also frightening because of the implicit threat that a man may forcibly put us on our backs.

Co-worker harassment in the form of graffiti or offensive language, though no more defensible than employer-initiated harassment, expresses a significantly different power relationship than that between employers and employees. Co-workers do not have direct economic power over us, nor is their behaviour usually geared towards eliciting sexual favours. In this sense it is not directly coercive.

Much of what women experience as workplace sexual harassment relates to very way men behave and particularly to male workplace culture. Co-worker sexual harassment occurs daily in thousands of different ways as men, consciously or not, turn women into sexual objects, put us down, joke about our bodies and our brains. Frustrated and angry at their general economic and political powerlessness, male co-workers engage in a classic scapegoating pattern. They harass women co-workers to make them feel better about themselves. By putting women down they attempt to forget their own limited power, and reinforce in their minds and in reality, that women's powerlessness is even deeper than their own. Sometimes male co-workers do use sexist behaviour to try and drive women out of the workplace, forcing women to quit or have such difficulty coping that they are fired. And there are instances of co-worker-initiated harassment in which a man explicitly demands sexual contact from a female co-worker — "Sleep with me ... or I will sabotage your work and you will be fired." When these types of behaviour occur, co-worker harassment becomes coercive, taking on qualities similar to that of harassment initiated by employers. Co-worker-initiated coercion is most likely to take place when there is unequal power between co-workers. For example, this might happen when a male clerk has secretarial tasks done by a lower-paid female clerk whose job evaluations are prepared by him.

However, I believe that the likelihood of extreme sexual coercion from co-workers is small in comparison to that from employers. Catherine McKinnon in her book, *Sexual Harassment of Working Women*,[3] cites many examples of grotesque coercion initiated by employers, and only one case in which co-workers were involved. Some male co-workers may have the desire to coerce, but the vast majority simply do not have the individual direct economic power to pull it off. What they have is the male social power to physically and sexually intimidate women, and the collective power as a group to drive women out of the workplace by persistent harassment.

The use of this collective power for harassing is limited by the shared job experience of female and male co-workers. Simultaneous with women's experience of male culture as offensive, men and women co-workers share common workplace conditions, problems and often general harassment initiated by employers and foremen. Even men inclined to view their interests as divergent from women's, particularly when the feel threatened by women's entry into so-called men's jobs, are affected by this fact.

It is therefore possible to speak of two patterns of sexual harassment, with some incidents falling between: first, employer-related harassment, which like other forms of employer behaviour, is coercive and directly threatening to a woman's job; and second, co-worker-initiated harassment, which is rarely coercive and which is connected to the sexist nature of male workplace culture.

I have not differentiated between these two patterns in order to justify or excuse co-worker harassment. Co-worker harassment, like that initiated by employers, can be devastating, and needs to be fought against. Rather I have made the distinction because I think it will help women understand and combat sexual harassment. The importance of making the distinction between employer and co-worker-initiated harassment was stressed for me while I was working in a non-traditional job at Stelco.*

RIPPING DOWN PIN-UPS ISN'T VERY USEFUL

In March 1980, along with one other woman, I began working as a labourer in the coke ovens of the Steel Company of Canada's (Stelco's) Hamilton plant. In the months previous I had participated with other women and the union representing the workers at Stelco (United Steelworkers Local 1005) in a campaign that forced the company to start hiring women. The majority of men were in favour of women's entry into the plant and during our early days and weeks at work demonstrated their support. Some wrote WELCOME in large letters on the door to our change trailer in the coke ovens. Men waved victory signs and solidarity fists. Others came up to us, and to the 120 other women who began work in departments throughout the 13,000 worker-plant,[5] and congratulated us on winning a battle against a large and usually unresponsive company like Stelco.

Alongside this support, the sexist nature of workplace culture made life difficult for the new women. Anti-women drawings and graffiti, many drawn years before we arrived, were common on the walls of the bathroom that Stelco forced us to share with men at the worksite.[6]

---

*The difficulties of lumping all types of sexual harassment together are evident in recent publications on sexual harassment that reveal that 80 to 90 percent of all working women have experienced some type of sexual harassment.[4] These otherwise excellent studies do not distinguish clearly between types of harassment, or whether its source is an employer, a co-worker, or a group of co-workers. Considering the sexist nature of our society and of male workplace culture, I suspect that close to 100 percent of women who work with men have encountered male co-worker behaviour that they found offensive and harassing . But how often does coercive harassment occur? Do co-workers as well as employers engage in threatening or intimidating behaviour? If so, does it take place as often? Do women distinguish between incidents in which the harasser wants something from them, and other behaviour that is related to male culture? Does it make any difference to women if the harassment is employer- or co-worker-initiated? Do the solutions to different types of harassment vary? Future studies of women's experience of sexual harassment could benefit by these types of questions.

Large nude pin-ups of women, often in violent and demeaning poses, appeared in the lunchroom. In the middle of night shift, to keep themselves (and the rest of the shift) awake, some of the younger men sang loud songs, which contained grotesquely anti-women images. The coke ovens are a dirty, brutal, unsafe place to work. One of the ways men have learned to survive conditions there, and in many other traditional male workplaces, is by affirming their maleness, their difference from women.[7] Men would often say to me, "We're tough, we can stand these conditions, we aren't complainers like women. This may be a terrible place, but at least here we can be real men, use the language we want, say what we want about women."

A minority of men, including those who never liked the raunchiness of daily workplace culture, understood that women found the graffiti and pin-ups a problem and urged changes in male behaviour.[8] But many others, including those who supported women's entry into the plant, held the view that "if a women wants a male job and a male wage, she better get used to a male atmosphere." It was as if our very presence in a traditional male workplace raised threatening questions. What did it mean to a male self-conception and identity that women could do the same job? Would industrial competition increase, making it harder for men to get higher-paying jobs? Would things change at home? Would wives, girlfriends, daughters want to work at Stelco too? If they did, who would make dinner, pack lunches, wash workclothes and do the necessary domestic tasks? Would the workplace be completely changed, as women nagged men to take their feet off the table? In response to these usually unspoken questions, a sizable minority of men felt the need to strengthen and reassert male culture by bringing in more nude pictures, writing more graffiti, intensifying sexist songs and jokes. It was as if they wanted to let us know, and reassure themselves, that the coke ovens were still a male domain.

I found the graffiti, the pictures, the jokes and unspoken solidarity of men against *all* women offensive. It made it difficult for me to cope with my work situation. It scared and unnerved me. I fought back, but unfortunately my tactics were not very effective and backfired against me, creating an intensification of those aspects of male culture that were upsetting to me. When particularly gross pin-ups went up in great numbers, I tore them down. When men wrote graffiti about the new women to see how we would react, I washed it off or responded with intense feminist messages.[9] When "A woman's place is at home with her legs spread unless she's prepared to do the same here" appeared on the bathroom wall, my blood boiled and I immediately reponded with a "A woman's place is anywhere she wants to be." After that the graffiti war was off and running. Rather than convincing my co-workers to change, my behaviour resulted in an escalation of the problem.

I was tremendously affected by the discussion in the women's movement that stressed the need for women to get angry as a first step in our efforts to combat sexual harassment. I understood that my initial reaction to sexism or sexual harassment, like that of most women, was to repress my anger, turning it inward on myself, blaming myself for the situation and becoming passive or depressed.[10] I didn't want to "understand" the pin-ups, I wanted to make it clear to my co-workers that I had a right to be comfortable at work. My anger was justified and I am glad I was able to feel and express it. But getting angry does not in and of itself ensure success.[11] I was in a very isolated situation. Though eight women worked in the coke ovens, we were usually on different shifts, with different days off. We rarely saw each other, let alone worked together. Though the other women I worked with were not happy about eating lunch eye-level with a picture of a naked crotch, they were not convinced there was anything we could do.

Had all eight of us been on the same shift we may have developed a plan to change the workplace atmosphere. In fact, during the one week we were, we noticed positive adjustments in the mood of the lunchroom. When we were eight out of fifty employees, we no longer felt that we were "visiting" and we could assert our needs more clearly. However, in the absence of a coordinated campaign, an individual woman has to pick her tactics carefully.

One successful example comes from a woman who worked in another department at Stelco. When she began work, the men in her area, realizing the potential irritation of nude pin-ups, stopped plastering the lunchroom with centerspreads. Several months later a huge pin-up appeared. It was a particularly gross one and bothered her as she ate her lunch. She left the lunchroom, deciding to stay out as long as it remained up. Word spread and a debate developed among her co-workers. Several men eventually went and took the pin-up down and asked her to return. Enough trust had been built between this woman and her co-workers that they did not want to offend her. Had she gone to the foreman or ripped the pin-up down herself, she might have polarized opposition against her, resulting in more pin-ups. Instead, she was able to use her anger creatively to move her co-workers into action against male behaviour that was upsetting her. It could be argued that she was forced into a classic female role, manipulating the men into action rather than directly acting on her environment. But such an interpretation overlooks the power, assertiveness and success of her tactic.

Another Stelco example illustrates an alternative approach. A women was working in a control shed for the first time by herself on the night shift. An intercom connected her shed with the other sheds throughout the department. To stay awake and ease the passing of time, operators would call to another shed, screaming abusive sexual language and obnoxious sounds at the other operators. Imagine this woman's feelings as she sat alone hearing violent anti-woman comments that were particularly intense that night because her reaction was being tested. She talked to her union chief steward during her break and he subsequently explained to the men why their behaviour disturbed her and why they should stop. The steward's intervention was successful. Had she gone to the foreman, the results would certainly been negative because her co-workers would have seen her as a "rat," someone who broke ranks and tattled on fellow workers.

Several suggestions for dealing with male co-worker harassment emerge from these examples. It is important that women proceed slowly, waiting until male and particularly female co-workers trust and agree with us before we propose sweeping changes in workplace atmosphere. As material on sexual harassment has stressed, talking to other women is the first step in fighting sexual harassment. When faced with offensive graffiti, we can only put forward changes when co-workers are prepared to listen, because we want co-workers to voluntarily change workplace atmosphere. Eliminating workplace sexual harassment requires an attitudinal change on the part of men. As such it cannot be legislated but must come about through pressure on men and our ability to force them to change.

In most work situations, either industrial or office, new employees go through a testing period while co-workers evaluate whether they can be trusted. During this time, which may last six months to several years, the new employee's attitudes towards management are of crucial importance. If they are seen to be siding with management against fellow workers, or running to management with problems instead of taking them to the union or dealing with them among the employees, their loyalties will be suspect. This does not mean that we should repress our anger and accept sexual harassment while we are waiting.

Women can meet with women co-workers to let out their anger. When that is not possible, women should find other avenues for venting anger – from joining women's groups outside the workplace to being supported by friends. It is absolutely crucial that we not blame ourselves for workplace male culture that upsets us. But there is a difference expressing outrage, letting male co-workers know how displeased and angry we are at their behaviour, and assuming that randomly expressed anger will automatically result in the changes we want. Releasing unmediated anger is personally vital to our sanity, but by itself will not change our situation.

It is outrageous that women may have to suffer while we await the formation of an offensive organized by a group of women, or in extreme cases, quit our jobs when such organization does not seem possible. There are, however, no individual solutions or magic tactics for combatting something as deeply rooted as the sexism of male co-workers. Changes in male behaviour can be achieved, but for our own sanity, women need to have a realistic appraisal of our specific situation.

Secondly, where they exist, women should seek out official union structures.[12] Other women in the union and women's committees can be a further source of support. Unfortunately, women often find that union officials are too much a part of the problem to be any help. Shocked by the sexism at union meetings many women find themselves organizing to change the set-up of union mettings and co-unionists' attitudes before they can begin to talk about the union fighting workplace sexual harassment.

Finally, differentiating between types of harassment can be crucial for the daily survival of a women experiencing co-worker harassment. This is particularly true for women in non-traditional jobs or other areas where women are a minority. Using tactics developed to fight employer-initiated harassment to combat co-worker harassment often backfires against the women being harassed.

Distinguishing between types of harassment helps women develop a long-term strategy for eliminating co-worker harassment. Such a strategy combines an organized and angry confrontation by some women of those aspects of male culture that make it difficult for us to survive at work, and proposals for an alternative workplace culture in which both women and men are comfortable. By making it clear that we understand the power differences between employers and co-workers, women lay the basis for a debate with male co-workers about the kind of workplace culture we want. Differentiating between employer and co-worker harassment makes it easier to unify male and female co-workers against harassment initiated by employers, and convinces men of the need for unions to lead a campaign in the workplace and in the union to change the sexism of male culture.

WHEN WORKING CLASS MEN GET FINGERED, LOOK WHO'S POINTING

Mass culture portrays working-class men as uncouth animals ready to molest women at the drop of a hat. From Archie Bunker and the daily newspaper cartoons to professional sociological analyses of sexual harassment, working-class men are portrayed as highly sexist, incapable of controlling their sexual urges and dangerous to women. Women are supposedly safe in offices or banks, but not in factories or mines. Contrary to the media portrayal, recent studies of sexual harassment have revealed many incidents of extreme coercion in government, law offices, banks, hospitals, universities and business.[13] Male construction workers may whistle and cat call as women pass by on the street in an attempt to confirm themselves as powerful physically and sexually. Meanwhile, the owner of the construction company, who finds it too crude to whistle, may be back at the office, sexually coercing female secretaries and exercising his substantial economic power over them.[14]

Flowing from the assumption that women have the most to fear from working-class men, from their co-workers, is the view that women in non-traditional jobs, where the majority of co-workers are men, will suffer a high, if not higher incidence of sexual harassment than other women. It is true that women in non-traditional jobs, surrounded by men, must cope with daily examples of sexist male culture. However I believe women in these jobs are safer from the extreme forms of sexual coercion from both co-workers, as I have argued, and from supervisors.

A high percentage of non-traditional areas are unionized, and where a union exists it is extremely difficult for employers to fire or demote women who refuse sexual contact. Though foremen and supervisors sometimes find ways to allocate more popular work within the same job class to favourites, in union workplaces jobs are distributed by seniority. As well, the group solidarity of industrial worksites hinders male employers' ability to coerce women. Though not adverse to engaging in mild forms of sexual harassment themselves, male workers have been known to defend women co-workers from management harassment. Most traditional male areas involve a team effort and women quickly become part of the team to be protected from management's efforts to harass team members. Finally, the passivity forced on women in traditional female areas where so many women's jobs are connected to "servicing" our employers, is absent when we work in male areas. In secretarial work, waitressing and nursing, women provide traditional female services to men. We help them get organized, we feed them, we take care of them. While we're fulfilling these classic roles, we are compelled to dress the part and act sweetly. In nontraditional areas we are completing tasks that do not directly service our foremen or our employers. Dressed in hard hat and boots, standing next to men similarly clad, our shovels in our hands, we're in a better position to resist pinches and sexual ultimatums.

Without romanticizing or justifying the behaviour of male co-workers, it is important for feminists to be aware of our society's pervasive anti-working-class bias and to differentiate our fight with co-worker harassment from media, government and employer attacks on working-class men.

While working at Stelco I had an experience which reinforced this need. Ten months after I began work at Stelco, during the height of the graffiti war, I attended a meeting on sexual harassment sponsored by a tripartite labour / business / union organization at McMaster University. Two executive members of my local, including Cec Taylor, local president, were going and suggested that I attend as well. The majority of the audience were government or business representatives. Although the presentations were interesting, in retrospect I think they suffered from lumping all sexual harassment together as a problem of male power over women. Several speakers stressed their concern that women in non-traditional jobs were facing extra harassment.

I rose in the discussion period to say that I did not believe that women in non-traditional jobs had it any worse. Men were men all over, and their sexism harassed women everywhere. I wanted to dispel the impression created at the meeting that male workers were the main danger, and the unspoken assumption that women may want to stay away from non-traditional jobs because of severe harassment. At the time I did not see the distinction I make in this article and my comments were not particularly clear. Though I argued that harassment was no worse in the coke ovens than in offices where I had worked, I was not able to cut through the anti-working-class bias in the meeting. Many people chose to hear my description of the problem of male culture at Stelco as a confirmation that male workers were a serious problem to women. One business representative said that he could see that workers harassed females, but men like him never did.

Here was a group of people with the time and the training to attend meetings in the Faculty Club of McMaster University, passing judgment on the kind of harassment that goes on in factories, clucking their tongues at the sexism of male workers and anxious to locate the source outside themselves.

The next day an article with my picture appeared in the *Hamilton Spectator*. The male reporter, picking up on the anti-working-class sentiment, and not understanding anything about sexual harassment, wrote an article that made Stelco workers look bad. He managed to get my main point upside down, reporting that I said there was *more* sexual harassment at Stelco. He quoted my comments about male industrial culture out of context, implying that Stelco workers were extreme harassers. There was no mention of Cec Taylor's comments that men, including himself, often harassed women without even realizing it because of their socialization as men. I tried to force a retraction and the paper printed another article which quoted my claim that I had been misquoted, but did not let me say anything else. It served only to make things more confused.

The two articles had a negative impact on male / female workplace relations at Stelco. Throughout the plant men reacted in anger to being described as harassers, when so many had been trying to welcome women into the plant. Wives, girlfriends and mothers wanted to know what the men were doing to us. No extreme incidents of sexual harassment had occurred anywhere in the plant. Though there were problems of graffiti and pin-ups in some areas, the men felt justifiably that any complaints should have been taken up inside the union before the whole community discussed their behaviour.

Through the newspaper fiasco I began to see the need to make clear distinctions between employer and co-worker harassment, to always discuss co-worker harassment internal to the union and workplace first. It also confirmed the need to be very cautious in speaking on controversial issues where the media is present.

THE DEBATE INSIDE THE UNIONS

Though many unions have taken strong positions against employer-initiated sexual harassment they have tended to avoid co-worker harassment. Male unionists' reluctance to look at problems in male behaviour has been further hindered by the confusion created when all types of harassment are lumped together. Differentiating between types of harassment lays the basis for successfully convincing unions to fight employer harassment with one set of tactics, and launching an educational campaign internal to the unions to fight co-worker harassment by transforming the workplace culture.

Prior to my experiences at Stelco I participated in an attempt to get an all-encompassing resolution on sexual harassment passed at the 1979 Ontario Public Service Employers Union (OSPEU) convention. We talked about different types of sexual harassment in the same breath. We were not prepared when male union members used the differences between management coercion and worker harassment to defeat us. Male delegates stood up to make fun of us, using the red herring argument that "women's libbers" were against human contact in the office. Nothing justifies the gross sexism of their comments, but our lack of clarity meant we were unable to effectively counter them.

The following year OSPEU Women's Caucus members developed an alternative strategy, which involved introducing two proposals, the first a strong resolution urging locals to negotiate for contract protection from employer-initiated harassment. This resolution passed easily. The second, an amendment to the union constitution that would have made it possible for members to charge co-members with sexual harassment, was defeated. But after a year's educational campaign, a constitutional amendment was passed at the 1982 OSPEU convention that included freedom "from sexual harassment" as a right of all members.

Most unionists, like most people, understand sexual harassment to mean sexual coercion, physical violence, rape of some kind. They are opposed to employers using their power to sexually coerce, and will vote in favour of motions that commit unions to fighting this harassment. Male unionists are not as clear about co-worker harassment, which they often say is mostly harmless workplace flirtation. In order to get resolutions adopted women have avoided raising the issue of co-worker harassment. This is as much a mistake as lumping all harassments together, since co-worker harassment is a serious concern. The OSPEU example demonstrates that separating employer and co-worker harassment is a useful strategy.

Though the constitutional amendment worked in OSPEU it may not be the only route. It views co-worker harassment as a problem of one member (male) who harasses another (female) rather than as the oppressive way men in general treat women in general. Charging a male co-worker with "foul language" would probably only produce more "foul language" and lots of "foul feelings" without changing the general way men in that area behave.[15]

CHANGING THE WORKPLACE

The best way of talking about sexual harassment inside unions is in terms of developing an environment acceptable to both male and female workers. This can be done in the following way:

Some of you may think that there's no such thing as co-worker sexual harassment. You're entitled to that opinion. But if so many women in our union say it is a problem for them, we have to listen. It's in our interests to pay attention to their concerns if we want to achieve a united work force capable of resisting the current employer offensive on our bargaining rights, living standards and working conditions. It's our job as a union to organize discussions about workplace atmosphere so that men and women can develop a mutually acceptable standard for workplace behaviour. If we don't take the responsibility, women will be forced to go to management or the human rights commissions, both options that make life more difficult for all of us. It is our job as a union to organize campaigns which clarify to men why women need workplace changes. As individual union activists and leaders, particularly those of us who are men, we can play an important role in finding out how women feel about potentially offending aspects of male behaviour and transmitting these opinions to men. Men's concerns are central in developing a new workplace culture too, but given the historic absence of women's input and the fact that so much of male workplace behaviour is offensive to women, men should give extra weight to the needs of women co-workers.

As long as workers do not have meaningful input into the structure and organization of our workplace, talking about a completely positive working environment is a bit unrealistic. But even now, within the limitations of our current society and its crisis, we can struggle for modifications in male culture and pose our vision of the future. We want a workplace in which everyone is comfortable, where physical greetings and expressions of affection are acceptable. We want a workplace in which a woman or a man can say they don't like a certain type of co-worker behaviour, and they will be taken at their word.

Susan Attenborough's article in this book makes the argument for the necessity of unions fighting employer-initiated sexual harassment. But for unions to be strong in the fight against all kinds of employer harassment, they must be strong internally too. This involves unions addressing the divisions inside the work force, inside unions. If unions do not deal with co-worker harassment, how can they expect women to be full participants in the union? How can a group of workers at the department, office or factory level expect to accomplish their work-place goals when the behaviour of one component – men – alienates, angers and terrifies another part – women? How can a strike, a work stoppage or contract negotiation be successful if women don't come to union meetings because we experience sexism there too?

As competition for scarce jobs increases, as inflation cuts into living standards, as social services and benefits are reduced, putting additional burdens on the family, male-female working-class conflict may increase. In their attempts to deal with intensification of the social and economic crisis of the 1980s, male workers may engage in co-worker sexual harassment, flexing their cultural muscles and taking out some of their anger on women. Feminists and unionists, insofar as we are able, must block this potentially disastrous development. This means pointing out to male workers the danger of scapegoating women and the potential weakening of working-class ability to resist economic and political attacks if men and women are divided. It means arguing inside unions that co-worker sexual harassment, and a work environment that is acceptable to men and women, are important issues. It means stressing solutions to co-worker harassment that strengthen male-female solidarity. To do this it is important that women and men clearly differentiate between co-worker and employer harassment and realize that our most serious conflict is not with co-workers.

NOTES

Thanks to the many people who helped with this article: Linda Briskin, Jeanette Easson, Maggie Fishbuch, Maureen FitzGerald, Amy Gottlieb, David Kraft, Jackie Larkin, Briget Rivers-Moore, Joan Sangster, Joanne Santucci, Jane Springer, Myrna Wood, and the members of the Winter 1982 Political Economy of Adult Education class at OISE.

1 Professional women also report instances of extreme coercion from senior "colleagues" who have the power to ruin their careers, or to block them entry into a firm or professional organization, and use this power to blackmail women into sexual relationships. Though co-workers in the sense that they both may be lawyers, a man's ability to directly influence a woman's job prospects puts him in a semi-employer relationship to her.

2 In my original draft I called employer-initiated sexual harassment *overt* harassment, meaning that it was harsh and direct, while I considered co-worker-initiated harassment to be more *subtle*. This distinction is sometimes made in the discussion of sexual harassment. Linda Briskin pointed out correctly that the words need to be reversed. Employer initiatives, though often very extreme, are usually *covert*, done on the sly. They may be very subtle. Co-worker initiatives, on the other hand, are usually loud, public, *direct*, anything but subtle.

3 Catherine McKinnon, *Sexual Harassment of Working Women* (New York: Yale University Press, 1979).

4 Among others, the B.C. Federation of Labour Women's Rights Committee and the Vancouver Women's Research Centre, found in 1978-80 that 90% of women who responded to their questionnaire had experienced some form of sexual harassment. *Redbook,* an American magazine, found in 1976 that 88% of women who responded had.

5 Though the Women Back Into Stelco campaign was successful in forcing Stelco to start hiring women, the massive layoffs in the steel industry, beginning in the winter of 1981, have meant that all the women, except for one or two in skilled trades, have been laid off.

6 Though Stelco provided separate women's change trailers and showers, women in many areas of the plant were forced to use men's washrooms at the worksite. Stelco simply added partitions to the existing bathrooms and declared them unisex. This caused anger and confusion on the part of many men, particularly the older ones, who had to cope with the shock of stepping out of a bathroom cubicle and facing a women washing her hands. It also indicated clearly Stelco's belief that women were just a passing fad, soon to disappear from the plant.

7 For an excellent discussion of male workplace culture, see Paul Willis, "Shopfloor Culture, Masculinity and the Wage Form," in John Clarke *et al.*, eds., *Working Class Culture* (London: St. Martin's Press, 1980). Willis describes the development of rough male culture as a response to the brutality and toughness of many traditional male workplaces.

8 Some men thought women were most bothered by four-letter words, and I often pointed out that it was not swearing that was so upsetting, but language that contained constant abusive references to women.

9 Though the graffiti about women was more sexist, it was generally similar to that used to test new employees.

10 "It is documented in other areas that women have a tendency to get depressed more often than men because it represents the internalization of anger. They don't know how to express the anger, the hostility they feel and so they internalize it and what it turns into is depression." Lorenne Clark at the Sexual Harassment Conference in Halifax, Nova Scotia, March 7, 1981 (Unpublished report of the conference), p. 12.

11 This also holds true for confronting employers. In the heat of the moment we are not always as clear as we are when we have had a chance to both experience and think about our anger.

12 See Susan Attenborough's article in this book for ideas about using union structures to fight sexual harassment.

13 See Constance Backhouse and Leah Cohen's excellent book, *The Secret Oppression: Sexual Harassment of Working Women* (Toronto: Macmillan, 1978). Among other examples of employer-initiated harassment they cite evidence of ongoing sexual coercion on the part of management to women employees in the Ontario Human Rights Office!

14 During the Women Back Into Stelco campaign a Stelco executive confided to a Steelworker union official that women wouldn't be hired at Stelco because male workers could not be trusted with women; they would go wild and sexually harass them. This executive conveniently overlooked the fact that much violent coercion occurs in offices.

15 There is further the powerlessness of internal union discipline procedures. Unless fines accompanied conviction, being slapped on the hand by the union would not in most cases be sufficient deterrent to many members.

LESBIANS AND GAYS IN THE UNION MOVEMENT

Susan Genge

My companion recently had a child. When she was still pregnant, I was extremely shy about telling my co-workers about her pregnancy. Over the years I had talked to most of them about the fact that I am a lesbian, and many of them had met my lover. But I was afraid that they would find it hard to accept lesbians raising a child; that they would disapprove. When I finally got up my courage to talk to two of the women in my department about the impending birth, I was ashamed of myself. Not only were they fully supportive of us having a child; they said that they had noticed the pregnancy and their main concern had been that I had been replaced by a man.

Most people spend the majority of their waking hours at work. People make important friendships among co-workers and discuss the regular everyday occurences in their lives with those they work with. Consider what it means to be a lesbian who can't talk at work about the person she lives with, holidays with, fights with, celebrates with and loves. Imagine the series of lies or half-truths. Imagine the loneliness.

For years this was the working reality for practically all gay people. Fear of loss of employment, loss of respect, loss of friendship kept gay people in the closet. While many lesbians and gays remain in the closet at work, the situation has improved considerably over the past few years, particularly for those in unionized jobs. Two social movements have been responsible for this change: the gay movement and the trade union movement. Through its public actions, the gay movement has raised the consciousness of the whole society about the existence and the oppression of gay people. Lesbians and gay men have organized demonstrations, publicity campaigns, court actions, rallies and speeches. The issue of sexual orientation has been raised and debated in an unprecedented way at all levels of society. Because thousands of gays and lesbians have "come out" (that is, let their sexual orientation be known) in the course of the last decade, more people than ever before have come into contact with gay people. Many more can now identify with the aims of the gay movement on an individual level because the know a neighbour, a co-worker, a friend or family member who is gay. One result of all this individual and collective activity is that there is a greater awareness, tolerance – and yes – even acceptance of gay people.

The union movement has also played a role in raising the consciousness of its membership and of society regarding its oppression of gay people. While the response has not always been immediately positive, on the whole the union movement has taken the issue seriously and has been supportive of the concerns raised by gay unionists.

The reasons for this support are many. The labour movement has a long tradition of support for and commitment to the struggle for human rights. It sees itself as a fighter for the weaker sectors of society, a champion of the underdog. One might debate how well the labour movement has done its job, but this interpretation of its role has created the basis for raising the question of gay liberation within the unions.

Unionists in support of gay rights have been able to use arguments that have traditionally and correctly been used to counter discrimination of any kind. Divisions among workers, whether based on race, sex, religious affiliation, sexual orientation or any other difference, only create disunity and strengthen the position of the employers.

The union credo, "an injury to one is an injury to all," is also used to oppose the oppression of gay people and has become especially relevant with the rise of the right wing and the direct state harassment of gays. A growing number of unionists recognize that gays and lesbians are only the first target of the political right. With unemployment at a record high, inflation continuing to soar, with interest rates out of reach and the traditional family in shambles, the right wing appeals to people's insecurity and fears.

In a climate of economic crisis and uncertainty such as this, the right wing demands a return to an idealized past, when everything was in its place – "where men were men and women were women." In right-wing ideology, the family is a secure haven, the source of all that is good in society. For these conservative forces, the family is especially important because it is the central institution responsible for teaching children (and women) respect for authority, law and order. According to conservative doctrine, the disintegration of the family threatens the very foundation of society.

Gays and lesbians live outside of the traditional family. By choosing to relate sexually and emotionally to someone of the same sex, they reject the roles required by the traditional family structure. Gays pose a serious threat to the family and thus are denounced as sick by the right wing to ensure no one will be tempted to follow their example. The rationale is that gays must be attacked in order to guarantee the survival of the family.

In Canada, groups such as the League Against Homosexuals, Positive Parents and Renaissance International argue these positions. While their focus is concentrated on the "homosexual menace," the political connections between these groups and other organizations on the far right are not hard to see. Alliances have been built with groups such as the National Citizen's Coalition, which is most vehement in its attacks on unions, the right to strike and the right to bargain collectively; the so-called Right to Life, which aims to deny women the right to control their own bodies; and the racist Ku Klux Klan.

All these groups agree that the solution to society's crisis is a return to the good old days. Rather than blaming those who control society, running it to maximize profit while ignoring the needs of ordinary members of society, they target groups whose militancy or existence seems to threaten those in power. They agree that someone is to blame, whether it be gays, unionists, Jews, women, blacks, immigrants or any combination of the above.

The climate created by the economic crisis and the prattle of the right wing has encouraged more repressive government legislation and harassment of various minority groups. In the last couple of years, for example, we have seen the introduction of wage controls federally and in Ontario – because unionists are to blame for high inflation. Immigration laws have been tightened to restrict even further the number of immigrants allowed into Canada – because immigrants are to blame for unemployment. And we have witnessed the largest mass arrests in Canada since the War Measures Act in the 1981 raids on the gay steam baths in Toronto – because gay people are to blame for the disintegration of the family. The gay newspaper, *The Body Politic*, has been prosecuted endlessly through the courts by the Ontario attorney general's office, despite acquittals at each step, because gays are to blame for declining morals.

These attacks on the right to strike, on the right to bargain, on freedom of association and freedom of the press are creating a basis for alliances between the various groups being singled out. In fact, unionists are increasingly seeing the need to unite with the gay and women's movements, as well as black and immigrant groups, to respond to escalating anti-gay, anti-woman, anti-worker assaults.

Over the past few years, women unionists in particular have been quick to acknowledge the relationship between discrimination on the basis of sexual orientation and discrimination on the basis of sex. Resolutions supportive of gay rights have often come from union locals with a large percentage of women workers. Women's caucuses at labour conventions have always discussed and supported gay resolutions along with those resolutions of specific concern to women.

One of the major reasons women have adopted such positions is that both gay oppression and the oppression of women are rooted in the nuclear family. Arguments against women's rights and gay rights are astonishingly similar. Gay relationships threaten the family. Women working threaten the family. Child care threatens the family. Being gay threatens "morality." The women's movement threatens "morality." And so on. Both women and gays have been targeted by the new right for special attention. Their message to us is clear: for women, back into the home; for gays, back into the closet. Given the common attack, women in unions will no doubt continue to be the strongest supporters of the battle for gay rights.

For all of these reasons, not to mention the fact that a large minority of workers are gay, the fight to end the oppression of gays and lesbians is very much a union fight. The right to live, work and be active union members, regardless of sexual preference, has been addressed on several different levels by the union movement. On the most basic level, union constitutions locally, provincially and nationally have been amended to include "sexual orientation" in their no-discrimination clauses. The following resolution, passed in 1979 at the Ontario Division Convention of the Canadian Union of Public Employees, shows the basic argument used:

> WHEREAS: Lesbian and gay workers face discrimination both in the workplace and in society at large; and
>
> WHEREAS: Trade unionists have traditionally stood for equality for all working people;

> THEREFORE BE IT RESOLVED: That... the constitution be amended to include sexual orientation (in the no-discrimination clause).

In 1979, the Ontario Federation of Labour and in 1980 the Canadian Labour Congress adopted this type of change – to cite only two of the most notable examples.

Union conventions have also adopted resolutions condemning the discrimination facing gays and lesbians in society, resolutions urging their affiliates to support gay issues and resolutions asking that the unions take up the issue publically. The following resolution, passed at the 1980 Canadian Labour Congress convention, is an example of how various demands have been posed.

> WHEREAS: lesbian and gay workers face discrimination both in the workplace and in society at large; and
>
> WHEREAS: we oppose all forms of prejudicial discrimination; and
>
> WHEREAS: sexual orientation is included in the no-discrimination clause of the Quebec Human Rights Charter;
>
> THEREFORE BE IT RESOLVED: that the Canadian Labour Congress support the inclusion of sexual orientation in the no-discrimination clauses of provincial human rights codes and in both the Canadian Human Rights Act and the Canadian Bill of Rights; and
>
> BE IT FURTHER RESOLVED: that the Canadian Labour Congress will make this position known to both the government and the public at any time these laws are up for amendment; and
>
> BE IT FURTHER RESOLVED: that the Canadian Labour Congress will encourage its affiliates to bargain for the inclusion of sexual orientation in the no-discrimination clauses of their collective agreements.

While it would be overly optimistic to say that such resolutions have been received with open arms by delegates to labour conventions, it is fair to say that the reception has been relatively good and that in all cases such resolutions have passed with very substantial majorities. I know of no instance where a labour union convention has rejected a resolution in support of gay rights.

The following report, which appeared in *The London Free Press* in May 1979 under the title "CUPE Constitution altered to protect homosexuals' rights," gives an accurate report of both the arguments used by supporters, and of the atmosphere in which such debates occur.

The 100,000 member Ontario division of the Canadian Union of Public Employees decided Friday that if it can't stand up for lesbians and homosexuals in its own ranks, it can hardly demand equality for others.

But before CUPE passed a resolution to amend its Ontario division constitution to ensure equality for members regardless of sexual orientation, there was some short debate on the merits of the change, with some nervous groans of opposition in the background.

The preface to the resolution stated that lesbians and "gays" faced discrimination in the workplace and society. One man stood up and said in opposition: "If you are talking about lesbians and queers, I thought the correct grammar was lesbians and homosexuals."

Hugh English, a CUPE delegate from a Toronto public library board local, said that if a resolution dealt with blacks, he wouldn't expect delegates to refer to them as "niggers." And if it dealt with a women's committee, would they call it a "chicks' committee"?   One woman delegate said that some might consider the resolution a "laughable issue." Unfortunately, the words "lesbian" and "gay" frighten some.

Susan Genge from the library board local said there are some estimates that 10 per cent of the population is homosexual, which she described as a "large minority," and even the postal workers' union and the CUPE staff representatives have constitutions or contracts that recognize "sexual orientation."   One male delegate said the question of male or female homosexuality is not for organized labour to judge. The union's job is simply to make sure it recognized their worth as people and guarantees their rights as members.

Changes have also occurred at a local level in many unions. In particular, the question of amending no-discrimination clauses in union contracts has been the focus of much of the discussion around union protection for gay and lesbian workers. There have been numerous success stories so far – however, many union contracts still lack this basic protective clause. Because the Ontario government refused to include sexual orientation in the Ontario Human Rights Code, negotiating protection for gay workers remains a very important battle.

No-discrimination clauses can take several forms. Unions can list prohibited grounds of discrimination or design a general clause that is inclusive of matters considered to be unrelated to work. The following example, taken from the CUPE Standard Agreement (which is a guide used by CUPE local unions to aid in the formulation of contract proposals), lists all the prohibited grounds.

NO DISCRIMINATION

The Employer Shall Not Discriminate The employer agrees that there shall be no discrimination, interference, restriction, or coercion exercised or practised with respect to any employee in the matter of hiring, wage rates, training, upgrading, promotion, transfer, layoff, recall, discipline, classification, discharge, or otherwise by reason of age, race, creed, colour, national origin, political or religious affiliation, sex or marital status, sexual orientation, family relationship, place or residence, nor by reason of his [her] membership or activity in the union, or any other reason.

In general, gay unionists favour this type of clause because it specifies the prohibited basis for discrimination. There are two important reasons for this. First, if it is spelled out, then the union will not have to argue in each case that a worker's sexuality is not relevant — there will already be an agreement to that effect. Secondly, there is the educational factor within the union itself. In most unions, the negotiating process involves a great deal of discussion among the ranks about the issues being negotiated, why they are important and what opposition the employer is putting forward and why. There is also some value to having "sexual orientation" there in print in a collective agreement for years to come for all to see. Spelling out "no discrimination on the basis of sexual orientation" opens up the question for wide-ranging discussion in the local union, which is useful for winning support for gay issues though it is difficult because homophobia does exist.

Some unions, such as the Toronto Teachers' Federation, have relied on simple "just cause" protection, which they have been able to use to protect gay teachers. This type of clause basically argues that any type of discipline (including suspension or discharge, for example) must be based on a "just," that is, fair or relevant factor; and the union has argued that one's sexual orientation is not relevant or fairly at issue.

The following example of a general clause is from the contract between the Metro Toronto Library and CUPE Local 1582.

Article 6 – No Discrimination There shall be no discrimination, interference, restriction, or coercion exercised or practised by the Board or the Union for any reason or factor not pertinent to employment with MTLB, or by reason of membership or non-membership in a labour union with respect of any Employee who is or is not a member of CUPE Local 1582.

Amending no-discrimination clauses has been the first and most obvious battle in extending contract protection to gay and lesbian workers. There are many other areas that need improvement. For example, bereavement leave clauses customarily include only legal family ties. The death of a gay partner is not recognized and bereavement leave is therefore not guaranteed. Similarly, clauses granting leave for illness in the family or paternity leave do not recognize the relation that lesbians in particular may have to a companion's children or to the birth of a companion's child. As well, medical, dental and insurance benefits won through union contracts are only available to legally recognized spouses or the children of a legally recognized marriage. Although in Ontario, the Family Law Reform Act extends these benefits to the spouse and children of unmarried heterosexual couples, no such law exists to recognize homosexual couples.

In order for union contracts to provide these benefits for lesbian and gay workers, the language in these and related clauses would have to be renegotiated. So, for example, a bereavement leave clause could be amended to include either "heterosexual or homosexual partner" or simply "friend" rather than "spouse." "Paternity leave" could be negotiated to read "companion leave" or "parental leave," which would then include lesbian partners. Benefit plans could allow "single" workers to name whatever beneficiary they choose. While, to date, very few unions have even begun discussion of these questions, let alone the battle for change in these areas, there is at least one success story. A woman worker in a CUPE local in Saskatchewan has been awarded "parental leave" to share in the first weeks' care of her partner's new son.

Negotiating for benefits and protection for workers has been the traditional approach of unions. In recent years however, unions have assumed an educational function with their members. In the last decade unions have also begun to deal more directly with questions concerning relations among workers. For example, educational materials have been prepared and distributed on racism, sexism and the oppression of women. Educational courses for unionists have been designed to deal with "women's issues" and "equal opportunity issues." While not much has been directly focused on gay oppression, the question is addressed in other educationals — especially those related to equal opportunity debates. In my experience, the issue has usually been raised in a supportive way by some unionist who is not gay. Educational work is also carried on through the process of debate during negotiations, during discussion of resolutions for conventions, and at conventions themselves.

While it would be wrong to create the impression that the union movement has easily accepted supportive positions on the gay issue, much educational work has been accomplished in a few years and the atmosphere has improved considerably. This change has been aided by a responsible attitude on the part of the leadership of the union movement. For example, at the 1980 CLC convention, president Denis McDermott interrupted and called to order a speaker who had made fun of the gay resolution being debated. The most passionate speaker on the question at that convention was a leader of the Ontario division of CUPE. He explained to delegates that as a father of ten children he wanted to see positive gay role models in the schools since he thought the odds were good that at least one of his kids would be gay!

As a result of the work that has been done to date, many unions and labour bodies have taken positions against the discrimination of lesbians and gays in society at large. Such unions as the Canadian Labour Congress, the Communication Workers of Canada, various provincial federations of labour, the Ontario Secondary School Teachers' Federation, the Canadian Association of University Teachers, the Toronto Teachers' Federation, the Windsor and District Labour Council, the Metro Toronto Labour Council have gone on record as opposing discrimination on the basis on sexual orientation. Many of these and other unions have also accepted resolutions supporting the inclusion of sexual orientation in the Human Rights Code in Ontario and in The Canadian Bill of Rights and Freedoms. Similarly, many unions and prominent unionists have been vocal in their support of *The Body Politic* during its continued court battles. Metro Toronto Labour Council and its president, Wally Majesky, have strongly opposed the police raids on the Toronto gay baths. Majesky has spoken publically at gay rallies in opposition to the attack on the gay movement in Toronto.

Although the question of gay rights has only been raised in the last few years, a great deal of progress has already been made. Credit for the gains goes to a handful of gay unionists and to the work of the gay movement itself. Despite the opposition of a few individuals within the union movement, the response to gay issues has been positive. However, much remains to be done before equality for gay workers is achieved. With this in mind, then, perhaps the most important gain of the past few years is that the basis has been laid for greater unity between the gay and union movements. It is this unity and the support for each others' struggles that will eventually bring us success – as unionists and as lesbians and gays.

THE RIGHT TO STRIKE

Judy Darcy and Catherine Lauzon

It was after midnight when the phone rang at the Toronto hospital workers' strike headquarters. The woman caller, her voice shaking, asked: "What do I do? The sheriff's at the door with a paper in his hand. My lights are out so he can't see me. What should I do?"

It was day six of a nine-day strike that began on January 26, 1981. It involved 16,000 workers organized by the Canadian Union of Public Employees (CUPE) at 65 hospitals in 19 cities in Ontario. The strike, an illegal one, had been called as a last resort measure; hospital workers' wages, already low, were being badly eroded by inflation, and the employer, the Ontario Hospital Association, had refused for months to enter into serious negotiations. The midnight visit by the sheriff was one of scores of such visits taking place that night, part of a terror campaign organized by the Ontario Hospital Association, the Tory government and police to break the strike.

That day the courts had issued an injunction ordering the workers back to their jobs. To continue picketing meant possibly facing criminal charges. The woman who had called strike headquarters for advice was in her early fifties, a mother of two, and local union president for just a few short months. She succumbed to the intimidation tactics. Within a few hours, under her urging, the members of her local returned to work. Yet her cooperation with the authorities did not protect her from legal action. In the wake of the broken strike a total of 18 Ontario hospital workers were charged, 4,000 were suspended, 30 fired.

Why? The hospital workers had gone on strike "illegally," in defiance of a law that denies them the right to strike. The government set out to teach them a lesson so that this first mass defiance of anti-strike legislation in Ontario would not soon be followed by others.

ANTI-STRIKE LEGISLATION INCREASING

The right to strike is under heavy attack, particularly in the public sector. This is because governments are, directly or indirectly, the employers of public sector workers and they can do what employers in the private sector cannot do — create legislation prohibiting their employees from going on strike. In 1965 the Hospital Labour Disputes

Arbitration Act was passed, taking away the right to strike from Ontario health care workers. In 1972 the Ontario government passed the Crown Employees Collective Bargaining Act (CECBA), which denies the right to strike to the majority of provincial government employees. In 1982 the federal government passed Bill C-124, which limits wage increases for the 585,000 workers in the federal public service to 6% the first year and 5% the second year of a two-year control period. This legislation also deprives these workers of the right to strike during the period the law is in effect. A few months after this wage control legislation was passed, the Ontario government introduced wage control/anti-strike legislation that takes away the right to strike from 500,000 Ontario public sector workers not already covered by the CECBA. The Alberta Public Service Act denies the right to strike to approximately 35,000 Alberta government employees. Thirteen thousand provincial employees in Nova Scotia are covered by similar legislation.

All told, 1,133,000 public sector workers in Canada are presently denied the right to strike. In addition, public sector workers in Manitoba and Prince Edward Island are covered by legislation that states that all issues not resolved during negotiations must be settled by binding arbitration. Although these laws do not formally prohibit workers from going on strike, binding arbitration means that the public sector workers in these two provinces are effectively denied the right to strike.[1]

The attack on the right to strike, which is a reflection of the deepening economic crisis, is of central concern to the trade union movement as a whole. The only power workers have when they negotiate with their employers is the right to withhold their labour. Historically workers have had to strike to win wage gains, health and safety protection and benefits such as pensions or paid holidays. At present, with well over one million organized workers in Canada deprived of the right to strike, the Canadian labour movement is seriously hampered in its fight to defend workers' living standards in the face of high interest rates and rapidly escalating prices.

The right to strike is also a women's issue. In 1982 women's wages were just under 60% of men's wages. This should not be seen in isolation from the fact that only 27% of working women in Canada are unionized – or from the fact that organized working women are heavily concentrated in the public sector, where anti-strike legislation is directed. For instance, the six unions in Canada with the largest actual number of women members are public sector unions.

In Ontario, approximately 315,000 women are unionized. However, this includes, among others, the following groups of women who are legally prohibited from striking: about 29,000 women members of the Ontario Nurses' Association; roughly 25,000 women members of the Ontario Public Service Employees Union (OPSEU); 13,000 women health care workers organized by CUPE; another 10,000 health care workers organized by the Service Employees International Union (SEIU); and the predominantly female staff of the Workmen's Compensation Board. It also includes the female membership of the federal public service unions who work in Ontario. At most, half the organized women workers in Ontario enjoy the right to strike. And in Ontario only 20% of the female labour force is unionized – compared to 27% for Canada as a whole.

The number of women denied the right to strike Canada-wide can only be estimated. (Legislation changes rapidly – for example, as recently as November 1982 the Quebec government was threatening to take away the right to strike from Quebec hospital workers, teachers and other public employees.) It is evident, however, that only a small percentage of women workers in Canada can legally go on strike – and in many cases their right to strike is in jeopardy.

Moreover, anti-strike legislation hits women especially hard. In fact, the Public Service Alliance of Canada has described the federal government's wage control/anti-strike legislation as sexist. By limiting wage increases to a percentage of *existing* wages Bill C-124 perpetuates the disparities between men's and women's wages in the federal public service. This law therefore stands in opposition to women's fundamental right to equal pay for work of equal value.

Besides holding down wages, Bill C-124 imposes a freeze on working conditions and benefits for the two-year control period. It takes away from federal government employees the right to negotiate for such things as paid maternity leave, protection from sexual harassment, day care allowances, and protection from the effects of technological change – women's issues that were increasingly becoming priority bargaining issues in the period immediately prior to controls. Bill C-124 ensures that issues of vital importance to women will not be won by taking away from women workers in the federal public service their most powerful weapon to press for these demands – the right to strike.

The rise in anti-strike legislation is both a reflection of the economic crisis and of the developing militancy of the workers forced to negotiate with governments and their agencies in the face of government restraint programs. Increased rank and file militancy has transformed many organizations of public sector workers from inactive employees' associations into militant trade unions. The Public Service Alliance of Canada (PSAC), for example, did not organize its first country-wide strike until 1974. Since then there have been strikes by government clerks, primary products inspectors, mint workers and many other groups of PSAC members.

Governments have responded to increased worker militancy with increasingly repressive legislation. One of the first groups to feel the brunt of anti-strike legislation was the Ontario hospital workers. Their experience shows both the effect of anti-strike legislation on workers' wages and the power of the strike weapon.

The Hospital Labour Disputes Arbitration Act, passed in 1965, denies hospital workers in Ontario the right to strike, but does not explicitly control wages. Yet not long after the Act was passed, hospital workers' wages began to fall behind the wages of municipal employees organized by the same union who had not lost the right to strike. In 1974, when the official poverty line for a family of four was $6,400 a year, the average woman hospital worker was paid $5,200; many received as little as $3,800.[2]

That year the workers at 13 CUPE-organized hospitals in Toronto threatened an illegal strike if their demands for a sizable catch-up pay increase were not met. The general public and even the usually hostile media recognized the legitimacy of their demands; their employers quickly signed a contract that raised their pay by about 65% over the following two years.

Workers in other hospitals soon demanded the same pay and used the same tactic. A few staged actual strikes. By the end of 1974 most hospital workers in Ontario had achieved wage parity with the Toronto hospital workers. The effectiveness of the strike weapon was impressed upon hospital workers strongly that year. In 1981, when they tried to repeat their earlier success, they failed, because of intense government repression and vacillating leadership at higher levels of the union and insufficient strike preparations.

OTHER FORMS OF ATTACK

Not all of the attacks on women's right to strike have been legislative. More subtle forms of attack are used as well. Most women in the work force are crowded into job ghettos where the work they do is an extension of the traditional "women's work" they perform in the home. They care for the sick, keep hospitals and schools clean, serve food to customers, educate children, run errands for their bosses. Consequently, when they go on strike, especially an illegal strike, they are open to being depicted in the media as heartless and unfeeling. The big newspaper chains do their utmost to spread their own anti-union views. After all, many Canadian newspapers, such as the *Globe and Mail* and the Hamilton *Spectator,* have broken strikes and organizing attempts by their own employees. They also represent the views of their paying advertisers. They are extremely biased in the area of labour relations — playing up stories of nurses supposedly abandoning their patients, of day care workers walking out on their children, of teachers forcing their students to spend an extra year in school.

A particularly gross example was a cartoon that appeared in the Hamilton *Spectator* during the 1981 hospital workers' strike. It depicted two hospital workers carrying picket signs made from a pair of crutches. Lying on the ground nearby was a patient, obviously the owner of the crutches, unable to get up, his leg in a cast.

Women are trained to feel responsible for the people they care for, whether at home or on the job. Consequently, they can easily be made to feel guilty if they refuse to take care of patients or teach their students. Because their oppression is internalized they can be made to feel it is their fault if, in the course of a strike, the school they usually keep immaculate becomes dirty, or the hospital bedding they usually clean and press, piles up by the bagful in the laundry.

Realistically, it is the employer's fault if working conditions become unbearable or if wages drop below an acceptable level. Labour legislation is based on the premise that conditions of employment are determined by the employer and few unions in the public sector have the right to negotiate staff complement and working conditions. Public sector unions have organized campaigns against health care cutbacks and the deplorable conditions that exist in nursing homes, but they have been unsuccessful in preventing health care from deteriorating to dangerous levels.

Hospitals lay off workers and eliminate jobs every day, to the point where emergency rooms are filled with patients waiting to be taken care of and patients needing surgery sometimes wait for months. Yet when hospital workers walk out to protest these intolerable conditions the state declares these workers "essential" and the media attacks them mercilessly. The public, via the media, is conditioned to see public sector workers as the culprits in contract disputes. And women workers are understandably reluctant to stand up to the combined forces of the state, the media, public opinion, sometimes hostile husbands, and their own internalized feelings of guilt.

WOMEN STRIKE BACK

In spite of these deterrents women in increasing numbers *are* using the strike weapon, and using it effectively. They are discovering that it is a powerful weapon, both in the struggle for economic gains and against specific forms of women's oppression.

One group of women who received widespread attention was the workers at Fleck Manufacturing in Centralia, Ontario. In March 1978 11 men and 119 women, organized by the United Auto Workers (UAW), went on strike for a first contract and a small wage increase. For the next five months every road leading to the plant was lined with Ontario Provincial Police cruisers. Buses carried scabs through the picket line almost daily. Police in riot gear strong-armed the women strikers who blocked their path. After one confrontation three women laid charges of assault causing bodily harm against the police.

Fleck Manufacturing, which produces wire harnessing for the auto industry, is half owned by the family of James Fleck, who was in 1978 Ontario's deputy minister of industry, trade and tourism. Thanks to Fleck's government connections, the Ontario government kept nearly 500 police on standby during the strike – at a cost of more than half a million dollars for the first two months of the strike alone.

Yet the women strikers stood firm in spite of this massive show of force. After five months on the line they won their key demands of union recognition and a wage increase. The myth that women are a docile part of the work force, working for pin money, and afraid to stand up for their rights, received a rude jolt during the Fleck strike. It was similarly shaken during strikes at Radio Shack, Puretex, Sandra Coffee and Irwin Toys. Indeed, a large percentage of the hard-fought strikes of the 1970s and early 1980s – the strikes that featured professional strikebreakers, police violence and mass arrests – have been strikes in which the majority of the strikers were women.

Another significant aspect of these strikes is that to a surprising degree they have been successful. The 80 workers, most of them women, at the Royal Connaught Hotel in Hamilton, were fired and replaced with scabs when they went on strike in March 1982. They had no past experience at organizing a strike and received little assistance from the international union that represented them. Yet they built support through the labour council and women's movement and in July they won all their key demands. The scabs were fired and even the hotel's general manager found himself out on the street as a result of the strike.

WINNING WOMEN'S DEMANDS

The strike is a crucial weapon in the fight against women's oppression. Many of the central demands of the women's movement – equal pay, pensions, parental rights, benefits for part-time – equal pay, pensions, parental rights, benefits for part-time workers, health and safety protection – have only been won after hard-fought strikes. Indeed, that is the only way they could have been won.

Employers have a poor history of granting labour's demands voluntarily. And governments are reluctant to put pressure on the employers. On August 27, 1982, for instance, Ontario Labour Minister Russell Ramsay outraged working women when he declared that he opposed introducing legislation granting women equal pay for work of equal value. His reason? Equal pay legislation would place too heavy a burden on businesses and lead to some of them going bankrupt. The effect on women trying to make do on subsistence wages was a question he did not address.

Yet in numerous strikes the demand for equal pay has been put forward. In some cases, such as the 1981 strike by the Hamilton school cleaners, wage disparities have been at least reduced. In one landmark case, that of the workers at the Kenworth truck plant in Vancouver, British Columbia, the principle of equal pay for work of equal value was achieved in full – but only after a long tough strike in 1980. This strike involved 350 male production workers and seven female data processors, members of the Canadian Association of Industrial

Machinists and Allied Workers (CAIMAW). The workers remained on the picket line until the employer agreed to the union's demand for job parity for the female workers.

An important demand of the women's movement – the right to fully-paid maternity leave – was won in Quebec as a result of the 1979 Common Front strike. Public sector workers there achieved a 26-week fully-paid maternity leave with no loss of rights or benefits plus provisions for paternity and adoption leave. Postal workers won the right to a 93% paid maternity leave for a 17-week period after their strike in 1981. These two strikes forced governments to recognize that childbearing is an important *social* function, a contribution to society for which women should not be penalized. This precedent has opened the door for women in other public sector unions and in the private sector as well to press for paid maternity leave and other parental rights clauses.

Pensions is another issue. The women who clean the public schools in Hamilton tried for years to get pensions, a benefit their male co-workers had had for many years. After a strike by the men and women workers in the winter of 1981-82 the women gained a pension for the first time.

Through strikes, unionized women have also won protection against technological change. Among them are the postal workers, who won protection for their jobs when postal sorting machines were introduced. As a result of their strike in 1975 postal workers were able to force the employer to take problems created by technological changes introduced during the life of the collective agreement to a special adjudication committee. Other unionized women have also won strong clauses protecting them from adverse effects of technological change. The Telecommunication Workers at B.C. Telephone Co. made their case through strike action in 1977 and the CUPE workers at Metro Toronto Library succeeded just prior to a strike deadline in 1981.

Gains won through strikes at one workplace may spread to other workplaces and filter down to unorganized workers, but without a strike or other mass action there are few breakthroughs. And as long as the majority of the working women in Canada are denied the right to strike, the struggle to generalize the gains made at particular workplaces is seriously impeded.

STRIKES AND WOMEN'S CONSCIOUSNESS

Not only is the strike a powerful weapon in the fight for women's rights, the experience of going on strike is liberating in its own right. Women's oppression is in part experienced as a sense of powerlessness and of dependency on others. And women's isolation in the home and limited experience outside their workplaces creates the feeling that politics and economics are matters beyond their grasp. But a strike gives women a sense of their collective strength: a clearer understanding of the roots of their own oppression and a broader sense of the social, economic and political relationships of the society in which they live.

Grace Litwiller, for example, spent nearly a year on the picket line at Dare Foods in Kitchener in 1973. During that time she had stood up to the Kitchener police and a professional strikebreaking company, the Canadian Drivers Pool. The union was on the verge of a decertification bid by the company when she was interviewed by Deanna Kaufman.[3] She emphasized that one of the real gains of the strike was how it had given women a new confidence. "The strike has done something for some women," she said. "It's made them realize that they have rights. Now they speak up without being bossy. This is something wonderful to see and it's not just happening to young women, women are now just coming out of themselves."

Diane Proderer, another Dare striker, said that "[Before the strike] I was a union member because I had to be a union member." She had originally voted against the strike. Nearly a year later she admitted, "I've been wakened up a lot since then."[4] For one thing she had become active in the Dare boycott. She traveled from city to city addressing groups of trade unionists on the importance of the boycott. Before the strike she would never have dreamed of giving a public speech.

The changes these two women describe have also been noted by the women involved in other strikes — even when they were not the actual strikers.[5] The film *A Wives' Tale* offers an unforgettable portrait of the women who built support for their husbands during the 1978-79 Inco strike in Sudbury, Ontario — and who raised their own consciousness in the process. The Inco strikers won their strike that year in no small part due to the work of the Wives Supporting the Strike committee. Strike support is often the key to whether a strike is won or lost. And

women, once they get involved in a strike, tend to recognize the need
for their support and build it effectively.

Women strikers have received growing support from the women's
and trade union movements. The women in the Fleck strike gained
support from as far away as Kitchener. The Irwin Toy women in 1981
received picket line support at least once a week from members of
Steelworkers Local 1005 who were themselves on strike against Stelco
in Hamilton, and from women's groups in Toronto, Hamilton and
other southern Ontario cities. Trade union locals in Hamilton took
turns walking the picket line during the Royal Connaught Hotel strike
in Hamilton. Hamilton women's groups organized a Mother's Day
brunch on the picket line and were also active in picket line support.
These strikes were won by bringing together the women's movement
and labour movement around issues of mutual concern, and both
movements were strengthened in the process.

Within the trade union movement, women strikers have come to see
both the obstacles and the challenges that confront them in fighting to
make unions serve their needs. Women strikers, previously led — and
grossly underestimated — by their union brothers, have had to struggle
hard to prove their own worth to themselves. But once they asserted
themselves, they still faced tough battles with their co-workers to
convince them that women can be leaders, and sometimes better leaders.

Strikes involving large numbers of women, such as the postal workers' strikes, have propelled the trade union movement forward, forcing
the leadership to take a more militant stand than they would have
otherwise. Women's strikes during the past decade have begun to teach
male workers that women's issues are important to the working class as
a whole. These strikes, and the women involved in them, have put
pressure on the leadership of the trade union movement to begin to
take up women's issues. Hundreds and thousands of women on picket
lines have learned about the hypocrisy of a system that claims to hold
women sacred, yet clubs and beats them when they demand a decent
wage and the right to a collective voice. Women have seen that laws
protect the right to private property, not women's and workers' rights
to jobs; that the courts mete out a different sort of "justice" for workers
than for factory owners or their managers. They have also learned
firsthand the importance and necessity of unity with male co-workers
and unionists.

Women who have taken part in bitter strikes have been through an intense experience of personal change and inevitably they bring their newly developed political awareness back with them into their work-places, unions and women's organizations. Through their experience, women have deepened their understanding of women's oppression and as a result have contributed new insights for analysis, strategy and tactics in the fight against women's oppression. Many of these women have worked hard to broaden the sphere of action of both the women's and trade union movements and to strengthen the alliances between the two. By organizing together they have gained a sense of their potential power and collective strength. In the process they have pushed both these movements to better defend the interests of working women.

NOTES

1 Information on anti-strike legislation in the various provinces was provided by Derek Fudge, research officer of the National Union of Provincial Government Employees.

2 "Hospital Workers' Wages: 1965-74," CUPE brief to Ontario Hospital Inquiry Commission, 1974.

3 Deanna Kaufman, "Inside a Strike," *On the Line,* July 1973 (reprinted from the University of Waterloo student paper, *The Chevron*).

4 *Ibid.*

5 See Arja Lane's and Meg Luxton's articles in this book.

BARGAINING FOR EQUALITY

Jane Adams and Julie Griffin

In this period of economic crisis, the right of women to work with dignity, respect and for adequate remuneration is under fierce attack. As women workers, we not only have the right, but the obligation to control our working lives. Some recent struggles and victories show that one of the ways to ensure this control is through the collective bargaining process. The negotiation of paid maternity leave for postal workers who bargain collectively through their union, the Canadian Union of Postal Workers (CUPW), is one such victory. Partially as a result of this breakthrough, Bell Telephone workers and Ontario government employees have now also achieved this benefit.

As women workers, we can also identify with the struggles of our sisters for the right to union security at Fleck Manufacturing, Radio Shack and Blue Cross, for the struggle for dignity in the workplace and for the right not to be monitored by closed circuit television at Puretex. In this article, we will explain how the collective bargaining process works, discuss how women can participate in the process and examine what women can and have gained through it.

DEFINITION OF TERMS

The "collective" aspect of collective bargaining is the key to the process. Women and men in unions come together to act collectively for their common good. This is in direct contrast to what occurs when we try to bargain with employers as individuals. Rather than a commitment to other workers as equals, the individual is forced to set herself or himself against other workers, to bargain on the basis of discrimination and difference rather than equality — for example, "I should get paid more than you because I am younger, prettier or male." When we bargain as a group, our numbers make it difficult for the employer to easily replace us or to discriminate against us on the basis of age, appearance or sex.

"Bargaining" implies power. In our dealings with employers, we trade our labour for decent wages, working conditions, fringe benefits and job security. We bargain with our labour — and our power comes from our ability to withhold our labour if certain conditions are not met.

Collective bargaining usually results in a "contract," or, as it is some-times referred to, a "collective agreement." This contract is a legal document that is binding on the union, the employees and the employer. Although labour laws vary from province to province, the law ensures that every contract includes a grievance procedure, out-lines who is covered by the agreement and defines the minimum length of time the contract will be in force.

In its narrowest sense, collective bargaining is a face-to-face discus-sion between management and the union. In a larger sense, collective bargaining is a step taken by workers to gain greater control over our working lives. Over the long term this will involve the restructuring of power relationships in the workplace. When we act collectively, we begin to redress the traditional imbalance of power between workers and bosses.

The collective bargaining process doesn't always end up in victory for the workers; rather it's like building the pyramids – one brick at a time. Sometimes the employer is strong enough to defeat the union or take away previously won rights or benefits, which is why the strength of the collective is so important. As individuals, we are helpless to stop the employer from changing our working conditions and we have little to bargain with. However, when all the employees demand a change, our chances of success are much higher. Union gains should be meas-ured by remembering that for the employer any concession – no matter how small – is giving up a previously unilateral management right. Prior to the introduction of a collective agreement in their work-places, managements could, and often did, change personnel policies and establish rules and regulations with little or no concern for the workers. This shift of control or balancing of power explains in part management's hard-nosed attitude at the bargaining table.

RESTRICTIONS ON COLLECTIVE BARGAINING

A number of factors affect how successfully unions, and particularly women in unions, can negotiate wage gains and other benefits. The state of the national economy is crucial because recessions make it difficult for all workers, even those who are unionized, to bargain.

Inflation and the unemployment rate are major determining factors. If the political party in power adopts a tight monetary policy in an attempt to curb inflation, high unemployment will result, with a corresponding reduction in the bargaining power of unions. Workers are generally reluctant to strike in a time of high unemployment and this is when employers take advantage of the situation by seeking concessions. Since it has never been established that monetarism (cutbacks) brings down inflation, it is evident that conservative and liberal governments throughout the western world are using their "tight money policies" as a form of union busting.

Local wage rates and recent settlements in the same jurisdiction also influence our success at the bargaining table. Sometimes that influence crosses national borders. The auto industry in the U.S., for example, recently won major concessions from the United Auto Workers (UAW) and as a result, the Canadian auto industry was successful in forcing Canadian workers, who are also members of the UAW, to make concessions. Due to a more militant membership and a stronger leadership in the Canadian sector of the UAW, the concessions were not as great as in the U.S., but some were made just the same.

Labour legislation and court decisions affecting unions, especially wage controls and limits on the right to strike, also infringe on the so-called "free" collective bargaining process. For instance, legislation passed in Ontario in 1965 denies hospital workers the right to strike and forces them to submit their contract demands to a Board of Arbitration. As a result, Ontario hospital workers' wages are substantially behind their counterparts in the private sector who have the right to strike.

However, the doctors in Ontario, with an average wage of $80,000, are not restricted by legislation in their dealings with the government. They are considered to be individual contractors in spite of the fact that they bargain through the powerful Ontario Medical Association. They engaged in strike action the same year as the hospital workers, and although they provide essential services, they were not disciplined – in fact, they achieved an increase of $5.80 per hour over a one-year period! Compare this to the last arbitrated settlement of hospital workers, who were awarded an increase of $1.65 per hour in four steps over a two-year period.

Wage controls effectively negate the bargaining process, injuring all workers, especially women. Unions have often tried to achieve better working conditions in lieu of reasonable pay increases during wage control situations. However, in September 1982, the Ontario government introduced wage control legislation that forbids strikes and arbitration even on non-monetary items. Women workers, who on the average earn just over half of the average male wage, will be doubly hit. Five percent of $6 or $7 an hour is substantially less than 5 percent of $10 or $12 an hour and with a ceiling of 5 percent for all monetary items, the chances of negotiating such things as paid maternity leave disappear. As well, with no recourse to strike or arbitration as a way to settling disputes over contract language, other items, like sexual harassment protection, are unlikely to be negotiated.

THE COLLECTIVE BARGAINING PROCESS

Women who want to be active in the collective bargaining process should consider the following:

- What is the bargaining structure in your union?
- Is your local covered by its own individual contract or by a province-wide agreement?
- Are there any legislated limitations on bargaining in your union?
- How are bargaining demands decided in your union or local?

There are a number of ways to find these things out:

- Ask your steward or staff representative.
- Attend a collective bargaining course sponsored by your union.
- Read your union newsletter.
- Talk to a former member of the bargaining committee.
- Most importantly, attend union meetings.

For women's issues to be taken up, women need to play a more active role in their locals. However, union office, while stimulating and rewarding, is still, for the most part, a voluntary position. The business of the local usually has to be conducted after work or on the weekends. Women workers, as we are painfully aware, already have two jobs — at the workplace and in the home. It takes a good deal of commitment and support to voluntarily take on a third unpaid position. Sometimes this problem can be partially overcome by bargaining for paid time off during working hours for the union executive or fighting for the right to hold union meetings during working hours and on company premises. This at least ensures that the women who have day care problems or small children returning from school will have a chance to participate.

If women's concerns are to be addressed by the union, the development of a union local with a leadership committed to helping women identify the issues is essential. In an "open local," the leadership ensures that the meetings provide an atmosphere where everyone feels free to speak out. Elections are held in a democratic fashion and a wide ranging exchange of opinions, criticisms and praise is encouraged. Suggestions for bargaining proposals emerge out of the ongoing discussions.

As there can only be one set of proposals presented to the employer (no minority proposals or any additions allowed) the whole local must be prepared to live with the package. It cannot be overemphasized how important it is to take time to hear everyone out, and to allow for full expression of disappointments as well as appreciation. Merely following Roberts Rules of Order and getting majority decisions is not good enough. If time is allowed to find the wording and variations to make as many people as possible comfortable, there will be much more support behind the collective bargaining team as it works its long and weary way toward a contract.

It is also necessary to ensure that the proposals are stated correctly. The collective agreement is a binding legal document and needs to be worded as clearly and precisely as possible. The common practice is to have general ideas translated into contract language by a union representative. Her knowledge and expertise will help ensure that the language accurately reflects the intent of the proposals.

However, more than good contract language is needed when seeking support for women's issues. In unions made up of both sexes, the domination of women by men must be dealt with. Women's committees are a good vehicle for training women in the basics such as parliamentary procedure, and once women understand how the local union functions, they will be more willing to take responsibility. Women's committees can also help women in the local to formulate their demands and lobby and organize to ensure that these issues become part of the proposals to management.

In order for any issue to be a priority at the bargaining table, it must have membership support. Women should approach fellow union members and explain the importance of the issue. They can also speak to the editor of the local union newsletter and offer to write an article on the issue and ask women's groups in the community to supply pamphlets or resource persons for a meeting.

BARGAINING COMMITTEES (TEAMS)

One way to ensure that women's issues get taken seriously during the bargaining process is to elect women to the negotiating team. An active women's committee can seek good candidates and then help run a campaign to get them elected. Serving on a bargaining team is a unique opportunity, both personally and politically, and provides women with an opportunity to take some control over their working lives.

Some bargaining committees assign certain clauses or issues to each member of the team. That member is then responsible for doing the research and preparing the argument for that portion of the demands. The union staff person can oversee this process, make sure the argument is sound, assist in the research and encourage the members of the team. When women see that they can fulfill these responsibilities their ability and confidence to deal with the day-to-day struggle in the workplace will also improve.

NEGOTIATIONS

After deciding as a group what proposals to put forward to management and electing a negotiating team to represent the union, the formal process begins with the establishment of a date for the exchange of the proposals. At this initial meeting, subsequent dates will be set, prior to which both sides have time to study each other's proposals. From there on, the employer and the union attempt, through discussion, to understand each other and to satisfy each other's demands where possible. Where it isn't possible, they try to reach a compromise. This process involves a great deal of strategic thinking, and an ability to be patient and not lose sight of our goals.

The membership must be kept fully informed of what is happening through regular reports. Some unions conduct bargaining behind closed doors and don't report back until a settlement is reached. Experience has shown that a knowledgeable, informed membership is far better equipped to make the appropriate decisions and take action if a struggle develops. Reporting back allows for ongoing discussion of the issues and is one of the ways women workers can keep their issues alive. If women are present and vocal at the meetings called to discuss bargaining progress, then their issues are less likely to be traded away or dropped. And through this interaction, the bargaining committee will have a better sense of the commitment of the members to these issues.

PRESSURE

The need to exert pressure on the employer prior to and during negotiations goes without saying. Pressure tactics depend on the type of employer. Public sector employers are often concerned about adverse publicity and politicians are sensitive to public relations campaigns that might give them a bad name. A good example is the public relations campaign set up by the Ontario Public Service Employees Union in the fall of 1981. OPSEU knew that their office and clerical group, which is almost exclusively female, were badly underpaid. They were also facing losses of jobs and health and safety hazards because of the introduction of video display terminals. The union launched a province-wide campaign that made use of pamphlets, buttons, rallies and newspaper ads. It convinced the employer that the union was serious, and in the next round of bargaining, OPSEU achieved major gains in wages and protection against technological changes.

Some private industry employers are also sensitive about their public image. In late 1981, the United Steelworkers of America mounted a successful boycott campaign against Irwin Toy. The workers were mainly immigrant women who were paid little more than minimum wage and worked under very oppressive conditions. The USWA sent out hundreds of leaflets to union members in their own and other unions, and among other tactics, leafleted parking lots of shopping malls. The campaign helped the union to force the employer back to the negotiating table. Unfortunately, most private employers don't give a damn about their public image.

The media in Canada is generally not sympathetic to labour. An example of this bias of the capitalist press is the way in which the postal workers' union has been maligned. Postal workers are portrayed as fanatics who already make too much money, and the media never mentions the thousands of unresolved grievances in the postal system or the unfavourable working conditions that most postal workers face.

Contrary to the image in the press, most bargaining ends with a signed collective agreement. In Canada, approximately 98 percent of all contracts are settled without resorting to strike and the usual term of agreement is one or two years. Sometimes it is impossible to come to an agreement, however. In the U.S., workers have the right to strike on the day their contract expires, but labour legislation in Canada provides for a process of government intervention to encourage a last-ditch attempt to resolve the dispute before allowing a strike to take place.

BREAKDOWNS IN NEGOTIATIONS

If contract talks break down, the most effective weapon is first the threat of a strike, and ultimately the strike itself. Historically, women workers have not always found it easy to go on strike; but with women's increased participation in the labour force and in unions, there is an increase in the number of strikes involving women workers.

With the sharp rise in the inflation rate since 1972 and government and employer policies of cutbacks, takeaways and ceilings on spending, women workers have been forced to strike, sometimes just to retain existing conditions and benefits. The increase in the cost of living and the continuing trend to single-parent families has meant that women can no longer ignore their need to organize and to develop clout in the workplace and in the political arena.

Women have also started to push for the changes in the traditionally male-dominated trade union movement. As the male union leaders see the growth of the number of women workers, and as these workers raise their voices collectively to demand change, some interesting things have happened. For instance, unions dominated by women have recently been the recipients of substantial assistance from the Canadian Labour Congress (CLC) and its affiliates. Striking Bell Canada operators and cafeteria staff, members of the Communication Workers Union of Canada, received direct contributions of more than $1 million from the CLC and its affiliates. Blue Cross workers in Ontario, members of the UAW, received substantial assistance from CLC affiliates in their unsuccessful fight for a first agreement and union protection. The company lost millions of dollars as unions forced other employers to switch from Blue Cross medical insurance.

These examples show the potential of alliances within the trade union movement and demonstrate to union leaders that women workers are an untapped source of militancy. As workers, we need to see union organization as a vehicle for achieving goals. As woman workers, we must realize that the human and financial resources of unions are not unlimited and that we sometimes have to work with imperfect organizations. Only by being at the bargaining tables, taking part in the work of the unions, by attending conventions can we help to make the process work better for us. We must become allies in a united cause.

THE GRIEVANCE PROCEDURE

After a contract is settled, it is important to ensure that the employer keeps to the agreement. This is called "policing the contract" and is an important part of the collective bargaining process. If a dispute arises, the grievance procedure outlined in the contract can be used to attempt to resolve it.

In these situations clear and indisputable contract language is necessary to deal effectively with the problem. But unless the union is determined to fight for the issue, and put time and money into the winning of a grievance, mere language is not enough. Employers often try to ignore the provisions of the contract in the hope that the union will not notice, or care, or be too impotent to resist. Sometimes the union seems less energetic on women's issues. Therefore, having women as officers of the union, as stewards, executive members and negotiating team members is crucial to the full realization of women's rights through collective bargaining. Often the contract doesn't provide for the right to grieve some of the more serious problems experienced by women workers. But file a grievance anyway. Although the grievance may not succeed, by going through the steps, you have the chance to:

- put the boss on notice that this problem is a real issue
- raise the consciousness of your sisters about a serious problem in your workplace
- demonstrate to all members of your local that your contract is weak and that this issue will have to be addressed in the next round of bargaining

Women must fight as hard as they can with the contracts they have. For too long, women were hesitant to file grievances, especially ones they knew would fail. They now see that they have to voice their discontent in a number of ways and not confine themselves to the limits of the labour laws. For example, in the late 1970s, public health nurses at Toronto City Hall were making substantially less than public health inspectors. The nurses' fight for equal pay for equal work was with both City Hall and their own local union leadership in CUPE 79. The nurses constantly solicited support from male members of their local, their women's committee, the aldermen and finally, the mayor. They made deputations to city council, issued leaflets, used the press and finally proved their point and won. Struggle around health and safety issues can also go beyond the formal contract: bring in the government inspectors, raise the issue at the health and safety meetings with the employer, and file the grievances. All of this will help support demands in the next round of bargaining.

WHAT WE HAVE TO GAIN
Economic Security

Economic security is the key issue for all women, and has been since the earliest days of the Industrial Revolution, when women and child labourers were used by factory owners to undermine the wage demands of male labourers. Today, woman are still seen as a threat by male workers, and employers are still able to pay women less than 60 percent of the average male income. Unions are, in many cases, seeking to achieve equal pay for work of equal value through:

- negotiating across-the-board wage increases instead of percentage increases

- initiating affirmative action programs

- dealing with historical discrimination

- developing joint (union/management) job evaluation

- helping women organize around the equal pay issue in conjunction with the women's movement and coalitions such as the Ontario Equal Pay Coalition

CONSCIOUSNESS RAISING

Collective bargaining is a conflict situation and is a very useful instrument for allowing women workers to understand the power context and the political reality within which they work. As individuals our participation in the collective bargaining process can be an important part of our growth as women. We are able to gain a sense of our power and our ability to achieve goals unavailable to us in any of the other roles we play. The special genius of the labour movement is that its very existence implies action. As a result of women's participation in this action, our consciousness is changing. As women in this labour movement, we experience breaking out of our isolation and out of the ghetto and having a significant say in our lives. Through planning, strategizing and action, we become part of the decision-making process in our workplaces and unions and we take up our role as leaders within the union movement and in the political arena.

SOCIAL CHANGE

Through the collective bargaining process, we are able to raise the consciousness not only of our fellow unionists but also of the public and the politicians. The collective bargaining process provides opportunities to put forward issues of concern to all women and to present the image of the kind of world we live in – one that cares not only for the young and strong but also for the weak and the old, one that recognizes that women shouldn't be punished because of our ability to bear children or victimized through violence and sexual harassment. It is not possible to separate the confirmation of women's rights through the collective bargaining process from progressive social change.

COLLECTIVE BARGAINING ISSUES

Every decade brings new issues to the fore; each year there are new battles. The major struggles now are for decent salaries, job security, equal pay for work of equal value and union security. Women have also began to look for ways to protect themselves during technological change and against sexual harassment. They seek better maternity leave provisions that contribute both to the well-being of the mother and the child. They are demanding quality child care provisions, family leave and provision for holding union meetings on company premises and on company time. A brief discussion of some of these negotiable issues will serve to concretize the potential of the collective bargaining process.

EQUAL PAY FOR WORK OF EQUAL VALUE

While equal pay for equal work is enshrined in the law, equal pay for work of equal value is a lot harder to achieve. The refusal of employers to reimburse women equally is an expression of contempt for the value of women's labour, a way of denying economic power to women, a technique to divide the male and female labour force through competition and jealousy, a reproach to the labour movement for failure to eliminate this problem, and severe hardship to women who work to support themselves and very often their children.

Sample clause: Employees shall receive equal pay for equal value regardless of sex.

MATERNITY LEAVE

Maternity leave is a thorny issue for women unionists, especially those who see it as symbolic of the request and encouragement afforded (or not afforded) for the issue in the local. (This is one motherhood issue that has no automatic legitimacy!) As one woman sized up the situation in her local, "The older women think, 'Well, I raised my kids on my own. Why should I have to give up wages now? They have to be tough. I was tough.'"

The older men are not helpful either; and the younger men often want the maximum amount of money (rather than benefits) so they can pay their mortgages. The younger women, the women who are having children or may do so soon, have gotten used to the lack of support. They have made child care arrangements and are making do. A member of CUPE Local 2316 – the Metro Children's Aid Society, expressed the irony of her situation:

I work for a child welfare agency where they pay me to go out and speak to women clients on the wonders and joys of early childhood bonding and the importance of being at home with their children. But until last year, my employer only gave minimum maternity leave required by law. Now we've got an unpaid leave beyond that, but it is terribly inadequate.

Sample clause: The employer shall provide a 17-week paid maternity leave of 93% of full pay with continuation of employee benefits and accumulation of seniority during the period. The employee shall, upon two week's notice to the employer, be entitled to a further leave of absence of up to six months, without pay or employee benefits. When

the employee returns from the leave of absence, or any extension
thereto, she shall be returned to her former classification at the rate of
that classification as of that date.

FAMILY LEAVE

Some locals have been successful in negotiating clauses that allow
workers to use their own accumulated sick leave when members of
their family are ill. This is especially important to women workers and
single parents who have small children, as it protects their pay if they
have to stay at home and look after a sick child.

Sample Clause: Where no other than the employee can provide for the
needs during illness of an immediate member of her/his family, an
employee shall be entitled, after notifying her/his supervisor, to use a
maximum of five accumulated sick leave days per illness for this purpose.

CHILD CARE/PARENTAL LEAVE

It is important in collective bargaining to see the principles behind each
of the proposals. In some cases, if you can "win" a principle in one
area, you can build on it in another area. For example, some women
have found that they have little problem negotiating paternity leave – a
few days off for fathers when a child is born – because it is not seen as
an expensive item for the employer. However, the acceptance of this
clause by the employer is also an acceptance of the fact that parenting
serves society and the employer has some responsibility in this area.
Having made this inroad into employer consciousness about the social
aspect of parenting, a later presentation of child care provisions will be
more easily made.

Women unionists debate how best to include child care provisions in
collective bargaining. In some instances women have won day care
centres in the workplace. Others feel that most worksites are terrible
places for workers, let alone for little children. They also point out that
many employers set up day care centres (in most cases of poorer
quality than public ones) in order to lower the absentee rate and
decrease worker mobility. This motivation does not suggest optimum
child care. Some unions have won subsidies for child care expenses that
give women with children in day care in the community x number of
dollars to help offset expenses.

Sample Clause: The employer shall pay to each employee who has one or more children under the age of nine a total of $30 each month to help defray the cost of child care. These sums shall be added to the employee's monthly pay.

This clause was originally negotiated in 1976 by the workers at the Metro Toronto YMCA, at that time, Federation of Community Agency Staffs (FOCAS) Local 75, now CUPE Local 2189. Their collective agreement was also one of the first to win union meetings on work time.

UNION MEETINGS ON WORK TIME

It takes a very special set of circumstances to win a provision for union meetings on work time or unpaid time during work hours. In the case of women working in any one of a thousand industrial settings, where their every move to the washroom is timed, it is highly unlikely the employer will give the union a chance to meet before quitting time. However, a few collective agreements do have the provision, and because it addresses a significant problem for women unionists, here is a sample clause.

The employer agrees that members of the bargaining unit may hold meetings on the premises of the employer other than during times when most of those attending would be scheduled for work, provided that there is adequate staff coverage which is approved by the management representative in the centre. The plan for providing such coverage must be submitted by the union steward in that centre to the management representative, in writing, and approved by the management representative at least twenty-four (24) hours in advance. Application for use of the meeting space must be submitted to the management representative and cleared by her at least twenty-four (24) hours in advance. Such clearance shall not be unreasonably withheld.

In addition to the foregoing, members of the bargaining unit may meet together at the employer's premises during work time, with no loss of pay, subject to the provisions for coverage and building use provided for in Clause x (above):

a) Bargaining unit members in each centre may meet five (5) times each calendar year for an extended lunch break, one (1) hour of which is the employee's regular lunch break and one (1) hour of which is work time taken consecutively at the time of day deemed most convenient for both employees and the management representative in the centre.

b) The total bargaining unit may meet three (3) times each calendar year for an extended lunch break, one (1) hour of which is work time taken consequently at the time of day deemed most convenient by both employees and the management representative in the centre. (This clause is presently in CUPE Local 2189's agreement.)

For sample clauses on sexual harassment and technological change, see Susan Attenborough's and Marion Pollock's articles, respectively, in this book.

BARGAINING FOR THE FUTURE

This article has considered women's use of collective bargaining to analyze the shared reality of their working lives and to gain power. Women unionists often feel that they are struggling in an uphill battle against sexism in their union and the exploitive practices on the job. However, these struggles and subsequent victories reverberate to an astonishing degree throughout the work force. A gain made by one local is quickly followed by another, which uses the original victory as a stepping stone. For example, only a few months after CUPW won 17 weeks maternity leave, the part-time workers at the University of Toronto Library, Local 1230 of CUPE, won 15 weeks paid maternity leave, the first part-time group to do so in Canada. As in the case of paid vacations, overtime work regulations, protection of women's jobs upon return from maternity leave, rights hard-won through collective bargaining gradually gain sufficient popular and political support to become legislation.

Health and safety legislation, a major benefit to women workers, is another example of the way union-initiated improvements become law. If such ground had not been broken, we would be in a much worse position to protest such immediate concerns as the introduction of inappropriate technological change.

Women have not stopped, and will not stop using the collective bargaining process to address the broad range of issues affecting women's health, happiness and welfare. Five years ago few people thought sexual harassment, paternity leave or paid child care were fit issues for collective bargaining. Now many people are looking at the whole range of seemingly "sacred" management rights. These issues will become increasingly subject to collective bargaining and women workers have only to gain from such challenges.

NOTES

The authors of this article were greatly assisted by Wendy Cuthbertson, Beverly Haitse, Sharon Taylor Henly, Joy Hodges, Laurell Ritchie, Barbara Waisberg and Pat Whealey.

III THE CHALLENGE
OF THE UNORGANIZED

WHY ARE SO MANY WOMEN UNORGANIZED?

Laurell Ritchie

When experts tell us the work force will have equal numbers of men and women by the year 2000, it does not surprise us, especially since in many areas of Canada women already make up well over forty percent of the labour force. However, dramatic changes in the size of the female labour force may give us a false sense of security. We assume that improvements in the lives of working women will flow naturally out of this change. But does our ever-increasing presence in the labour force mean we will be paid as much as a man for our job? Or that we will have pension schemes for our old age? That we will have coverage for benefits like dental care, which many unionized male workers now take for granted? That we will have full income protection and job security if we decide to become parents? That we will have stronger seniority rights to train and to develop new skills on the job? That we will enjoy some protection during times of technological change? Or that as women we will account for fewer among the unemployed?

Numbers themselves guarantee nothing. For example, although women increased their participation in the labour force at a startling rate after World War II, the influx had virtually no effect on the huge gap in earnings between men and women. Nor can we assume that great new vistas are opening up for women with the new office and factory technologies. In the long run, women are more likely to lose jobs as a result of these technologies because employers won't spend time and money on retraining. Most of those who remain will work on "deskilled" jobs. The same employers who argued five years ago that pay increases should only follow on productivity increases now argue that the increased productivity that comes with improved technology justifies downgrading because there is "less skill" required. Corporate Catch-22s like this one leave women on the short end of the stick either way.

Too often women have been the *victims* of change. For this reason union organization in the female job ghettos is absolutely essential. *We need the ability to control and influence changes that are taking place.* The Sun Life secretary, the Eaton's salesclerk, the Toronto-Dominion bank teller, the McDonald's cashier — they all have to organize. Without organization, they are doomed to job insecurity, inadequate pay and benefits, and working conditions that are dictated by management manoeuvrings to increase its profit margin. Unfair dismissals can take place, wage freezes can be instituted, hours of work can change. These women will only find a voice to challenge the work world around them through a union.

Since the earliest efforts to organize the skilled trades and craftsmen, the only two significant movements for unionization were those involving unskilled and semi-skilled industrial workers in the 1920s through to the 1940s and then those of public sector, semi-professional and professional workers in the 1960s and 1970s. There is no doubt that both efforts broadened the base of the labour movement and, in so doing, extended unionization to many women, especially the large numbers in the public sector. But almost two-thirds of the work force remain without a union and most of these workers are women. If these women succeed in organizing into unions where they are respected and their concerns are reflected in concrete actions, the Canadian labour movement will be fundamentally changed. At present, women's interests are not really integral to the trade union movement.

Seven out of ten working women are still unorganized. Only twenty-seven percent of women workers are unionized: for men the figure is forty-three percent. There are plenty of reasons why so many women remain unorganized. It is useful to look at some of these reasons, because we need a serious analysis of the stumbling blocks if we are going to effectively respond to the challenge.

Along with sophisticated employer opposition to unionization, we must confront the labour laws that hinder our best organizational efforts. And the union itself may not be responding to the needs of its women members. There are also the realities that exist beyond the workplace itself. Women continue to bear a double workload. They still bear major responsibility for home maintenance and child care. This limits the time they have to put into an organizing campaign. And, finally, we are still fighting the myth that women are "secondary" income earners and therefore secondary members of the paid labour force.

THE WORKPLACE

• Problems arise where the unorganized are in small workplaces of less than fifty workers. The workers often know the owner personally and are encouraged to feel they will be well provided for as part of "one big happy family." In spite of the fact that workers probably are not so well provided for, a paternalistic owner is sometimes successful in persuading employees that forming a union is akin to bringing a stranger into the family.

• Workers in smaller workplaces also tend to have less bargaining power, even when they are part of a larger business with multiple locations. If the workers decide to unionize and strike, the employer more readily considers replacing the small number of workers with strikebreakers or even closing the operation. Organizing in such situations must be geared to overcoming the physical isolation of smaller workplaces.

• Companies that employ large numbers of new immigrants sometimes segregate different nationalities by department or classification to minimize the physical contact between them. The communication needed for successful organizing is difficult when the Greek shipping department workers, for example, reach out, only to find they have no common language with the Portuguese finishers. This is especially true of women who have only limited opportunities to attend English classes (which are often held at night) and thus are less likely to speak English than men.

• Workplaces function with hierarchies — and it is always useful to appreciate the nature of that hierarchy, particularly when you are not at the top. The pyramid may be topped, for example, by male technicians or mechanics, reflecting the sex-typed job ghettos common in the labour force.

While there are many union-conscious tradesmen, it is wise to use caution when making contact with this group. There is a natural tendency for these men to "take charge" of the campaign and for others to accept their leadership, especially when it has been difficult finding volunteers. If the union leadership becomes concentrated in this elite, the union may be in a very vulnerable position with the employer. In a number of organizing campaigns, this elite has engaged in fair-weather alliances with other workers, only to be bought off at the end in a quick deal with an employer who is willing to pay extra for his hard-to-replace skilled workers. These workers then abandon the union. The resulting demoralization has destroyed more than one campaign. A widely based leadership is the best protection against these hierarchies.

• Historically, secretarial occupations have developed so as to foster a close relationship between individual secretaries and their bosses. Often, the secretary's boss and his rank, not the work she does, determines her pay. Thus secretaries can be doing the same work but receive different pay rates depending on their boss's position in the company. Advancement is not based on the seniority or abilities of the secretary: she gets a promotion when her boss gets one. This practice of "rug-ranking" privatizes the work experience and encourages secretaries to associate their future with their boss and not with their fellow workers.

• Three-quarters of the female labour force work in the "newer" industries of trade, finance, public administration, business and personal service — areas that do not have a long history of organization. The decline in Canadian manufacturing means that fewer women are working in the traditionally more organized sectors where there are some expectations about unionization. While 40.9 percent of the manufacturing industry is organized, only 22.5 percent of the service industry and 2.4 percent of the finance sector are organized.

• One in four working women is employed on a part-time basis, which minimizes workers' contact with one another. It also leaves these workers open to an employer's anti-union tactics. Part-time workers have fewer legal protections when organizing and fewer rights in labour standards legislation. They suffer too from the prevalent idea that part-time workers must be flexible to meet an employer's changing needs. Thus anti-union moves, such as changing the working hours of a union activist, will be disguised as "new production or service needs."

• High unemployment means there is heavy competition for the small number of "female" jobs and a tendency to say "I'm just glad I have a job." Unemployment is one of the key obstacles to unionization at this point in history.

EMPLOYER OPPOSITION

• The economic crisis is "milked" by employers to dissuade workers from organizing to make real gains. They argue that "This is a time for sacrifice, not expensive ideas like equal pay." And they have much of the machinery of government and the media supporting them.

• Workers have been organizing for many decades. For the large numbers of women who are making a "late start," organizing means confronting highly developed and sophisticated employer opposition. Management consultant firms now regularly sponsor seminars on "How to Keep Your Shop Union-Free" and many companies pay for the advice of lawyers who specialize in "labour relations," particularly during organizing campaigns.

Bank workers discovered the extent of their employers' sophistication when they faced the concerted counter-campaign of Canadian banks during recent organization attempts. A combination of "carrot and stick" tactics are used, alternating between giving extra pay increases to branches that stay clear of the union and discriminating against activists by transferring them to other locations.

• The organization of workspace is more sophisticated than ever and works to deter attempts to unionize. Workplace designs often take into account opportunities for surveillance of employees and the creation of isolated space with room dividers to prevent employees from having contact with one another. Video display terminals will also result in extreme isolation, especially if women eventually work on them in their homes.

• Employee associations and "company" unions have been developed to a fine art by employers. Companies encourage employees to view associations that work "in everyone's interest" as a "positive" alternative to unions.

• In the service, trade, finance and public administration industries, women work for private employers in greater numbers than men. Unlike the highly unionized public sector, private industry has fought hard against unionization. The anti-union campaign of Canadian banks is again a clear example of a well orchestrated and centralized opposition.

• The corporate lobby has been successful in winning laws that severely hinder organization. In Nova Scotia, in 1979, the government rammed through legislation popularly known as the "Michelin Bill," requiring the simultaneous organization of all locations of an integrated company. It was introduced to appease the Michelin Tire Company, which was setting up shop as a major employer in the province and had threatened to move elsewhere when union organizing campaigns began.

In Ontario, a 1981 amendment to the Ontario Labour Relations Act, Bill 89, allows an employer to force a vote of union members on the company's last contract offer at a time of his own choosing, thus undercutting the workers' control of their union bargaining and strike strategy. No parallel right exists for workers to intrude on an employer's internal deliberations with his management or board.

To add insult to injury, Bill 89 does not restrict strikebreakers from voting. A smart employer could pad his work force with pro-company hirings to get the vote results he wants prior to a strike. Or he could call for a vote after a strike has started and count on hand-picked strikebreakers to again carry the vote. The contract would then be considered ratified and any strike action thereafter would be illegal. Even where a company does not actually use this law, it can use its right to do so as a hammer over the heads of the union bargaining committee. This kind of legislation is frustrating for those involved in an organizing campaign. At the same time, it discourages unorganized workers about the possibilities of unionizing and bargaining for a collective agreement.

LABOUR LAWS

• There is still no effective method of preventing employers from firing or laying off workers who are organizing a union. Even if the workers are eventually reinstated, an employer gains through the delays and the demoralization that develops. New legislation for cases of "anti-union" discharge must ensure substantial fines to employers and the reinstatement of an employee until a hearing has occurred.

• When workers organize, the union applies to the Labour Relations Board, a government-appointed tribunal, for "certification." This gives the workers the right to bargain collectively and the right to strike. The certification process involves hearings of the Labour Relations Board where matters such as the union's evidence that a majority of workers wish to belong to a union are dealt with.

Workers are usually impatient from months of long, hard work convincing co-workers to join the union. They expect that the Board will process the application quickly and in a straightforward manner so that the union can get on with the job of negotiating a first contract. Instead, Labour Board hearings often stretch out over many months.

In part, this is the result of three-person panels juggling too many schedules, but it is also the result of the extensive role allowed company lawyers. Many hearings are monopolized by their technical and procedural arguments and other delaying tactics.

Needless to say, workers cannot interfere with a company's decision to join with other companies in a Chamber of Commerce. Why then should we tolerate their interference with a worker's decision to join a union? We must fight to limit the role of employers and their lawyers in certification proceedings to providing documentation on the union's proposed bargaining unit, for example, the names of all workers.

• Most Labour Relations Boards still allow anti-union petitions during certification proceedings, even though virtually all such petitions are inspired by management and rarely reflect a real "change of heart" on the part of workers. In 1977-78, the Ontario Labour Relations Board, for example, threw out forty-one of the fifty-five petitions they had entertained because the workers presenting the petition could not prove that they were free of management influence.

Usually management plants the idea of a petition opposing the union with a worker who believes the company will reward her in one way or another if the petition stops the union. The worker can count on management turning a blind eye while she collects signatures on the petition during working hours. Other workers, suspecting management's hand in the effort, often sign for fear the company will see the petition and discriminate against those whose names do not appear.

When an anti-union petition is presented at the certification hearings, there are inevitably days and days of examining witnesses. If the witnesses for the petition prove they have done this without management's direct or indirect assistance and if there is sufficient overlap of names with those of workers who also signed union cards, the Board may allow the petition and require a vote instead of giving an automatic certificate. This allows management time to launch a campaign of fear to prevent a union victory.

Even when a petition is eventually thrown out by the Board, the company succeeds in delaying proceedings, usually for months, and in creating chaos among employees, precisely when they should be working together to prepare for contract negotiations.

Petitions should not be allowed in certification proceedings. In Ontario, both the Liberal and NDP opposition parties have presented bills to try and end this outrageous Board practice.

• Most provinces, including Ontario, still do not provide for first contract arbitration at the request of the union. Quebec and B.C. on the other hand, are examples of provinces that provide for a government appointed arbitrator to set the terms and conditions of a first contract where the employer and union cannot agree on such terms and the union does not wish to exercise its right to strike when its members are so newly organized.

Many employers bargain in bad faith and then make totally unacceptable final offers, assuming that the workers will not strike. There is then no strike and no contract. This means that many certifications never result in a contract, the very point of organization. If a union does not make a contract within one year of its certification, the Ontario Labour Relations Act provides that any employee can ask the Board to declare that the union has lost its certification. An employer can always find at least one worker to make such a request. And so the workers lose their union.

• With the exception of the Federal Labour Relations Board, Labour Boards usually have a standing policy of excluding part-time workers from the bargaining unit at the request of either the company or the union. The company should not be allowed this option. This practice primarily affects women because it is mostly women who work part time. Office workers in a production plant are also often excluded. They aren't normally regarded as part of the larger unit because it is said they "do not share the same community of interest." But a separate office bargaining unit is small and less effective. Unions occasionally request the exclusion of office workers, not with the intention of preventing their unionization, but to protect their majority for certification if the sign-up in the office is low. Unions could be pushed harder to sign-up if the law did not give the company a veto.

• Restrictions on the organization of domestic and agricultural workers must be removed from offending legislation. The Ontario Labour Relations Act specifically excludes "domestics employed in a private home" and "persons employed in agriculture, hunting or trapping" from obtaining union certification.

UNIONS

• A number of unions do not take new organizing very seriously. They use the same cost-analysis that a profit-oriented employer uses, and apply it to union organization. Organizing a small or fragmented group or a new industry with a low rate of unionization is considered a bad "investment." These unions do not consider the time and money involved in organizing to be worth the small amount of union dues that will flow out of a successful campaign, even if they have enough funds to start with. This approach is part of what is referred to as "business unionism."

• Many unions, especially the American craft unions and some of the industrial unions, have a deep-rooted sexism within their leadership. And a lot of women know it. They worry that these unions will forget women's issues when they are behind closed doors during negotiations.

Generally, women have been better served and represented when they are in Canadian unions. The 1980 Corporations and Labour Unions Return Act Report shows that out of 160 women on union executive boards in Canada only four were in American-based unions, with the other 156 from Canadian national unions or Canadian government employees' organizations.

• Sometimes Canadian workers have little control over an American-based union's new organizing efforts. When Canadians are outnumbered at the American convention by ten to one, the dues money is more likely to be allocated to organizing in the southern United States than in Canada.

• The failure of two major white-collar organizing campaigns, that of SORWUC (Service, Office and Retail Workers Union of Canada) and ACTE (Association of Commercial and Technical Employees) to develop wide-scale organization has resulted in some discouragement. Misplaced feminist loyalty meant many women shied away from the

constructive criticism that should have been put forward when the
SORWUC leadership engaged in an organizing strategy that included
petitioning for assistance from the Canadian Labour Congress at the
same time that the Congress was opposing the independent union, and
in fact, running counter campaigns at the very bank branches that
SORWUC was organizing. SORWUC looked very silly and not just a
little naive. The CLC refused the request for assistance and continued its
attempt to defeat SORWUC and establish the CLC as the centre of bank
organizing.

In the case of ACTE, the CLC's white-collar campaign (remember the
ads for Mary, the Signed-Up Secretary?), the initial enthusiasm of
volunteer organizers died when they discovered ACTE would be set up
with each workplace as an individual local of the CLC. There was no
intention of connecting those locals in a national union, through which
the locals could have developed coordinated bargaining strategies and
lobbied for changes in Canadian law to make white-collar organizing
easier. They could have been in the forefront of the fight for decent
working conditions in the computerized office.

Instead, a deal had been struck whereby each ACTE local would be
pressed to feed into the American-based Office and Professional
Employees International Union (OPEIU) or, in a few cases, directed to
unions such as the United Steelworkers of America. While the publicity made it appear that a national organization had been set up, the CLC
had to go along with its own rules, which give the American-based
OPEIU the exclusive right to represent workers in the field of work,
even though OPEIU has not done much organizing in Canada.

The volunteer organizers were also not impressed by the ACTE litera-
ture, which promoted the idea that secretaries and clerks wanted to be
viewed as semi-professionals in an association rather than as workers
in a union. The publicity never mentioned the word "union" and
maintained instead that white-collar workers had a lot in common with
the medical and bar associations. The ACTE campaign never amounted
to much, bringing in a few locals across Canada.

THE ROAD AHEAD

We have yet to really find our voice among the unorganized. But it can
be developed. It must be. We can begin now by fighting on many
fronts. We need tougher labour laws to make union organizing easier

for those facing sophisticated employer opposition. We need an expanded community child care system to free women from their endless responsibilities at home and to allow them the time to organize with co-workers.

We need more English-as-a-second language programs to give the very large numbers of women who do not speak English the opportunity to participate more fully in the movement to assert our rights in the workplace. These programs should be set up at locations independent of the workplace, where management is prone to try and influence the curriculum and use withdrawal of the program as a form of blackmail.

We need equal pay for work of equal value, which would be one step towards relieving women of the stresses of inadequate income and would also have an important effect on the view of women as secondary income earners.

We need to lobby against wage controls whenever they are advanced by government and business. Such controls simply freeze women's inequality in the workplace and deny the right to bargain collectively for improved conditions. When wage controls are in effect, unorganized women ask themselves "Why bother with a union?"

We need laws that extend minimum standards legislation to fully cover part-time workers and Labour Board practices that assist such workers in organizing. We need laws to provide office workers with health and safety standards in the computerized office, especially where visual display terminals are in use.

These are some of the battlegrounds we must fight on. These are the kind of improvements that will allow organization to emerge in the unorganized sectors. In the end it will be the women in the job ghettos who must do their own organizing. Only then will their unions speak strongly and clearly about what must be changed in the workplace.

Women can start by talking to friends and co-workers they trust. They must choose a union carefully, to meet their needs and standards of democracy. In some fields, women may set up new unions. And then, women must get involved — as members of the organizing committee, the bargaining committee and eventually as stewards and convention delegates. The effort involved will be tremendous — but so too are the stakes.

NOTES

1 Anyone who wants to understand the problems of organization more fully should take a look at *Maria,* a National Film Board drama by Rick Salutin about immigrant women organizing in a textile plant. And Eileen Sufrin's book, *The Eaton Drive* (Toronto: Fitzhenry and Whiteside, 1982) realistically outlines the difficulties workers face in organizing, although she fails to critically examine the role of the unions involved in the 1948-52 campaign to organize the Toronto Eaton empire. See also Julie White's *Women and Unions* (Ottawa: Canadian Advisory Council on the Status of Women, 1980).

TRIPLE OPPRESSION: IMMIGRANT WOMEN IN THE LABOUR FORCE

Alejandra Cumsille, Carolyn Egan, Gladys Klestorny, Maria Terese Larrain

Immigrant women are the forgotten workers in Canadian society. We have no choice but to take the jobs that Canadian workers refuse; we earn the lowest wages of any sector of the working class and face the worst working conditions. As workers, as immigrants and as women we suffer a triple oppression, and the organizations that have been set up by and for working people in Canada are only beginning to take an interest in our concerns.

This article will examine first the three factors determining our position within the Canadian economy (class, race and sex), and second, the response of the trade union movement to our concerns. We will conclude by presenting some suggestions about how an improved response to immigrant women's concerns on the part of trade unions will help not only to solve our specific problems but to build a more democratic and militant union movement.

As a background to any discussion of the role of immigrant women in the work force, it is important to keep in mind that immigrants have a special role in the Canadian economy, and that immigration policies bear a direct relationship to the need for labour. Immigration does not occur in a steady flow but in waves. These waves are caused by the specific labour needs of each historical period, and the political and economic situations in our home countries that have forced so many of us to emigrate.

For example, during the Depression strict immigration laws were passed, severely restricting entry into Canada. Then during World War II, while Canadian men were overseas, women and immigrants were needed to work in the factories and immigration laws became more flexible. During the 1960s there was a shortage of unskilled labour and Canada opened its doors to thousands of immigrants fron the Third World, where many countries were in crisis. Today the economy is in trouble and the doors are once more being closed. Only workers filling very specific needs are being admitted. These include women who agree to work as domestic servants and people who are being brought into British Columbia as farm labourers because Canadian workers for the most part won't accept the harsh conditions and the low pay.

These are the hard political and economic realities faced by immigrant women and men, which have a direct bearing on where they find themselves, in the labour force and in society as a whole.

CLASS

It is important to realize that there are class differences between immigrants. Our class background determines in large part what our lives in Canada will be like. It defines the access we will have to education, training and jobs. A university education or access to capital can put us in a better position than Canadian-born working-class people.

Immigrants are allowed into Canada on the basis of a point system in which education and ownership of capital each count as one point. Professionals and highly skilled workers are encouraged to come to settle in Canada because it is cheaper and quicker to import our brains than to train Canadians. Thus, when the economy is in a downswing and ordinary workers are no longer needed, professionals, skilled workers and business people may still be allowed into the country.

Nevertheless, the majority of immigrants are working class and have been allowed entry to serve the needs of industry at particular times. In the 1960s and 1970s for example, the highly industrialized area of southern Ontario needed the cheap labour of thousands of immigrants.

The stories about poor immigrants rising from rags to riches are a thing of the past — if they were ever true. Most of us, especially those of us who are women, are permanent members of the working class of Canada.

RACE

Class is not the only basis for discrimination in Canadian society; race or ethnic origin is also a key issue in determining our position. Racism is an integral part of the society, and is institutionalized in Canadian immigration, labour and educational policies.

The desire to keep Canada as white and as British a possible has played an important role in setting immigration policies. Non-British immigrants, especially non-whites, have only been admitted into the country when the labour market has needed us, or when international pressure has been put upon the government. This policy is illustrated in a government promotional pamphlet from the turn of the century, quoted in *The Immigrant's Handbook,* by the Law Union of Ontario (Montreal: Black Rose, 1981):

> Canada is situated in the North Temperate Zone .... The climate is particularly suited to the white race. It is the land of homes — the new homelands of the British people.... British people soon find themselves at home in Canada. It is a British country, with British customs and ideas ...

Although some changes have been made since then, immigration policies continue to be racist. The distribution of Canadian immigration offices throughout the world is a case in point: there are five offices in the United Kingdom, and five offices for the whole of Africa; there are ten offices in the U.S., and only one for the whole of India.

When immigrants do get into Canada they find limited job opportunities. Certain types of jobs — for instance, seasonal farm work and domestic service — which are low-paying, low-status occupations, are virtual immigrant job ghettos. Canadian-born workers are reluctant to take these jobs, and immigrants are often allowed into the country only under the condition that they work in them. In other sectors, like the garment industry, employers make a point of hiring immigrant women because they will work for lower wages and because English is not needed to work on a sewing machine.

The ghettoization of immigrants is not a coincidence: it has the specific purpose of isolating us from Canadian workers. In this way we are less likely to organize a union or to demand the same wages and conditions as Canadian-born workers. Racism and antagonism between ethnic groups are also fostered by employers: for instance, in a factory outside Toronto, East Indian women were being paid substantially less than Italian women. When they protested, they were all fired, though eventually, due to public pressure, they were re-hired at the higher rate. Some employers consciously hire women from different ethnic groups to prevent workers from talking to one another about workplace concerns.

SEX

Immigrant women also face sexism. We experience the problems of sexism in our workplaces and in our daily lives, as well as in immigration policies and other Canadian institutions.

The sponsorship system is a clear example of the sexism of immigration policies. The majority of immigrant women enter the country not as independent immigrants, but sponsored by their husbands. If the marriage breaks down, they can lose their immigrant status because the sponsorship contract is no longer in force. Thus, husbands can use their sponsorship as a means of keeping their wives from leaving them. Also, important social services such as family benefits and welfare are not available to sponsored immigrants, unless they can prove that the sponsorship contract has indeed been broken. In many cases, men refuse to cooperate and say they are still supporting their wives and children, even when they are not, because they don't want their wives to become economically independent. The onus then falls on the woman to prove that her husband is not supporting her and that he has broken the sponsorship contract, which is difficult.

Immigrant women, like the majority of Canadian women, have jobs in predominantly female fields (as domestics, sewing machine operators, waitresses, cleaners), have few opportunities for training and education, are often unorganized and get low wages. This situation is all the more acute because of the language problem, racism and the general isolation we face. Our situation makes it very difficult for immigrant women to fight against sexist attitudes. For example, domestics are often sexually harassed by their male employers, but have little possibility of complaining if they don't want to lose their jobs. Also, because domestics are here on a work permit, they are afraid that if they are fired they will lose their visa and be forced to leave the country: they can't simply go and get another job. Farmworkers, who are also on work permits, are in the same situation. Factory workers, maids in hotels and waitresses in restaurants face sexual abuse by their employers or by the clients. Because of their lack of language, their unfamiliarity with existing legislation and their lack of access to support systems, immigrant women are not able to take action against this abuse.

One of the basic problems of any immigrant is learning the language of her/his new community. Immigrant women are at a disadvantage with respect to their husbands, because their access to free English classes is limited. English as a second language (ESL) classes are available either through the Employment and Immigration Department or through community agencies. Some community agencies do provide classes for women, though often women are unable to attend because no day care is provided, or, if the clases are in the evening, because their family responsibilities make it impossible.

The language classes provided by Employment and Immigration are subject to many restrictions, one of the chief ones being that free access to ESL classes is provided only for "heads of households," who are assumed to be male. Women are often told by Manpower officials that they don't need English classes because they don't need it for the kind of work they do! Thus, even if immigrant women overcome all the obstacles of finding out about classes, making arrangements for transportation and for child care, they often discover the door is closed to them.

Finally, the double day of labour – on the job and then at home, doing the housework – which is a burden for Canadian women, is even harder for immigrant women. Because they are in a new country, they often lack family support systems for child care. And all too often their husbands and children are reluctant to help with housework.

IMMIGRANT WOMEN IN THE CANADIAN LABOUR FORCE

Skilled and Professional Women

As we have noted, immigration policies are closely linked to the needs of the labour market. Many professionals and highly skilled immigrants were brought into the country in the 1950s and 1960s, when Canada needed them. Immigrant women in this category work mainly in the fields of health care, education and research. They are university teachers, engineers, doctors and scientists. Because of their skills, these women generally entered the country as independent applicants, not as sponsored immigrants. This puts them in a better position than immigrant women who are dependent on male sponsors.

The lives of these women are, generally speaking, much easier than the lives of their working-class counterparts. Their jobs are more meaningful, and they have better possibilities for developing themselves. They are often less isolated from Canadian society because they speak the language better and have access to educational and cultural privileges. Most professional immigrant women either speak English before they come or can learn it easily because training is available to them through their employers or through the government. These women do face some sexism and racism, but their class background helps to protect them from many of the problems confronting working-class immigrant women.

Clerical Workers

This has not been a traditional area for immigrant women, but more and more of us are now working as clerks, secretaries, stenographers, receptionists, bank tellers, bookkeepers, and data-processing and word-processing clerks. Immigrant women are being sought in large numbers to staff the new computerized offices that are run like assembly lines and no longer require secretarial and language skills. The federal government is currently putting money into training immigrant women to work in the lowest rungs of the clerical ladder. The Working Skills Centre in Toronto is one example and there are similar programs operating in most regions across the country.

Many immigrant women believe that a white collar job, no matter how badly paid, is a step up from being a peasant or a blue collar worker. They don't as yet realize how easily they can be laid off by automation, have wage controls imposed on them or their right to strike taken away.

Sales, Service and Manufacturing

These are the areas in which most immigrant women work. Typical sales and service occupations are: cleaner, maid, cafeteria worker, cashier. In manufacturing, the main areas are the textile and clothing industries, where immigrant women usually work as sewing machine operators. Next to farmworkers and domestics, these workers are the most exploited section of the Canadian work force. Many of these women are not covered by minimum wage legislation, and their working conditions are often deplorable. Language barriers prevent them from communicating with their employers or even their fellow workers. In fact, employers often hire women workers of different ethnic origins to prevent them from talking to one another and possibly organizing.

Domestics and Farmworkers

These workers are not protected by the minimum wage laws and other labour legislation that apply to most Canadian workers. They are often brought in from outside the country to do the kinds of jobs (fruit picking, domestic service, etc.) that Canadian workers are reluctant to do. Their work permits state, in most cases, the specific job they are allowed to do; if they attempt to move into other jobs they lose their status and can be deported. In the case of domestics, women are brought in by a sponsoring family, on whom they are completely dependent. Farmworkers, on the other hand, are usually brought in in groups by contractors or farmers. They have very little protection under the labour code and usually live on the farms where they work. There is a great need to organize both farmworkers and domestics, because of their vulnerability and extreme exploitation. Some union organizing is taking place – for example by the Canadian Farmworkers Union – but a great deal remains to be done.

WOMEN AND UNIONS IN CANADA

As we have pointed out, immigrant women face three levels of oppression in this society: oppression as women, as workers and as immigrants. When we examine our situation in relation to the trade union movement we must be aware of the impact and significance of all three. The trade union movement is, unfortunately, not immune to the sexism and the racism of our society, and it has been slow to take up the specific problems and needs of workers who are both women and immigrants.

Immigrant women have, for the most part, been excluded from active participation in unions. In the past, trade unions were developed to protect the skilled, native-born male workers in their fight for higher wages and better working conditions. As immigrants were brought in to match the needs of industry, and to keep wages low by increasing the number of workers available, unions sometimes perpetuated inequality and racism between ethnic groups. For instance, when the transcontinental railway was being built in the late nineteenth century, the doors were open to Chinese immigrants, but they were not allowed to bring their families and settle in Canada. After the economic collapse of 1929, many racist immigration laws were created and countless immigrants were deported in an effort to keep them out of the labour market. Though the labour movement was then not as large or as strong as today, it did not oppose these practices. It should have fought them by trying to eliminate the basis of competition between workers by making contract demands for equal pay for work of equal value, or for equal access to skilled jobs. Chinese workers were restricted in many instances to jobs that would not put them in competition with the white, male worker – for example, cooking and laundry work – which were generally viewed as women's tasks and therefore undervalued and underpaid.

Today we can see that although overt racism and sexism have declined, many union practices are still unsuited to the particular needs of immigrant women workers. For example, there are few translators and interpreters available during organizing and negotiations; union meetings are held at times that make it difficult for us to attend; day care is rarely available; and English as a second language classes are not a priority.

Unions must become more conscious of the needs of immigrant women. Only twenty-nine percent of working women are unionized, as opposed to forty-three percent of working men; and many of the unorganized women are immigrants. There is a prejudice that views immigrant women as uninterested in union activity, but many of the most militant strikes of the last few years (in Ontario at least) have involved immigrant women: Irwin Toy, CUPW, Puretex, Bell, CUPE hospital workers, etc. These strikes have been important not just for immigrant women, or even for working women in general, but for the whole labour movement. It is in the self-interest of the labour movement, for its growth and development to take up the tasks of organizing immigrant women.

Organizing is only the first step in a longer process of allowing and encouraging immigrant women to become active unionists fighting their own self-defined struggles. Too often union hierarchies, notably in the clothing trade unions, have been content to see us merely as a source of dues, and have made no effort to take the necessary steps to increase our involvement. Unions must begin by educating themselves about the objective conditions that have limited the involvement of the majority of immigrant women in union activity, and by developing strategies to overcome these conditions. Some of these are:

- lack of common language, a problem that is often exploited
- recent affiliation to the Canadian work force and lack of traditional support systems, both of which cause isolation
- a strong economic dependence on the husbands (because of sponsored

immigrant status), which often results in the husband limiting the wife's political activity

- fear of losing one's job as a result of union activity
- fear of deportation through involvement in political activity, a fear that is exploited by management
- the double day of labour, which leaves no time for outside activities
- a patriarchal family ideology, which stresses that women's primary loyalty is to homeland and family, not to our own jobs
- the fact that unions have not demonstrated much concern for the specific needs of immigrant women and have taken a narrow economic approach to unionism.

The result is that many women have not seen the benefits to be gained from unions. Unions must make the connection between our lives at work and our lives at home and in our communities.

A number of concrete steps could be taken: internal education and supportive skills development programs aimed especially at immigrant women; translation of contracts and basic labour legislation; interpreter services during and after the organizing drive; meetings held in times and places that will encourage attendance; day care. English language classes are a real priority; unions must recognize that this is a primary need for women, and take it up in a significant way. Many women have said that a major problem was the inability to speak English. The isolation that this produces is obvious; it divides workers and sets them in competition with one another. And it is the unions' responsibility to deal with this, either through collective bargaining or by setting up their own classes. Unions must also realize that most women have family responsibilities, and must alter their methods of functioning to take this into consideration by providing the necessary support services to allow for and promote involvement.

Some unions are beginning to break with the past, and are taking significant steps in addressing our concerns. The Canadian Union of Postal Workers has begun to pay particular attention to the needs of women, resulting in the increased participation of women members in the union. The Metro Toronto Labour Council has helped to set up a program of ESL classes, and some unions have started to organize restaurants and small factories that have a high proportion of immigrant workers. There is presently a drive to organize cleaning staff in downtown Toronto offices, involving Portuguese cleaners as organizers. The Confederation of Canadian Unions (CCU) offers translation and interpretation services in the garment trade as does the Canadian Farmworkers Union for farmworkers.

The broader issues of working women, such as the need to fight job ghettoization through affirmative action, and the lack of equal pay for work of equal value, will also have a tremendous impact on immigrant women, since we suffer so clearly from these. Some unions have taken up these issues but often in a hit-and-miss way. A coherent strategy must be developed with the active participation of immigrant women.

Unions must also understand that organizing immigrant women workers cannot be done in a vacuum: unions must take up social issues as well as economic ones. The labour movement has won higher wages, shorter hours, pensions and other benefits, but workers, particularly women workers, have needs that are greater than simply an increased wage package. In reality there is no sharp dividing line between fighting for workplace concerns and taking up broader social issues such as English as a second language or day care. And there are other issues, such as the impending transfer of Family Benefits to General Welfare by the Ontario government, or the need for free, accessible abortion services, that have a profound impact on the lives of working-class women, whether they are union members or not. Unions should make a commitment to these issues, and relate the specific struggles to the general problem of how the working class can maintain its gains and keep fighting in this time of economic recession.

Unions have the potential as workers' organizations to help solve many of the problems that we face, but they must recognize immigrants' special oppression on the basis not only of class, but of race and sex. If unions make a commitment to participate in a broader movement for change that is responsive to our needs as workers, immigrants and women, then it will encourage our wider participation in trade unions. Immigrant women will clearly benefit, and we will also have a stronger, more democratic, more militant trade union movement, which can take a leadership role in the struggle for political, social and economic change.

DOMESTIC WORKERS:
THE EXPERIENCE IN B.C.

Rachel Epstein

The employer I worked for when I first came here treated me as if I was a slave. I'm not speaking for myself alone as a matter of fact, it goes to all the women who come here on a work permit from the Caribbean. Some of them talk about the treatment they get, and some just suck it in, you know what I mean? Well, last August I noticed things were getting too heavy for me to handle, lots of work and less pay, so I just packed my things and left the job, but I had to check with the Immigration Department and they gave me two weeks to find another job. I did, this one is a little better than the first. So I am just trying to stick around a little longer, because when I leave Vancouver I am not sure I'll get to come back, because I made myself a promise. I am not going to leave my country on a work permit to go to another country, not ever again.

This statement is from a West Indian woman who has been in Canada since 1975 working as a live-in domestic in a private home. She has four children in the West Indies whom she is trying to support and keep in school. She hasn't seen them since she left. When she first came to Canada she was earning $200 a month plus room and board and had one day off per week. "Room" consisted of a small room she shared with one of the children she was taking care of. Currently she is earning $300 a month and has two days (but no evenings) off. She is responsible for the entire running and maintenance of a household of two adults and three children. She shops, cooks, washes and cleans up for five people. She is frequently asked to babysit in the evenings and occasionally to do the gardening. Her friends can not visit her and her phone calls and mail are closely watched. She is one of approximately 15,000 women who come to Canada each year on temporary employment visas to work as domestics.

This article describes some of the experiences of these women and the attempts they have made to take control of their lives and to demand the right to decent working and living conditions. All of the quotes in this article are taken from interviews with West Indian domestic workers. The latter part of the article focuses particularly on the achievements and difficulties encountered by domestic worker organizations in British Columbia. Similar groups exist all across the country.[1]

DOMESTIC WORKER SHORTAGE

Domestic jobs are characterized by low pay and hard work, as well as the degradation that has come to be associated with domestic work. It is not seen as "real" work, nor are the people who do it seen as "real" workers. This lack of status is an extension of the general devaluation of household maintenance in North American society.

The combination of substandard working conditions and low status has resulted in the need to import workers from other countries to do domestic work. The recruitment of labour has been used to maintain a supply of domestic servants, particularly since the 1900s, when as a result of industrialization women were entering occupations other than service. It has long been the concern of the Department of Immigration and employers of domestic servants that the women who enter the country to take domestic jobs will leave these jobs at the first opportunity to work at other employment. Various schemes have been used over the years to keep domestic servants doing domestic work. In the early 1970s, the government extended the employment visa system to domestic workers and stopped allowing these people in as landed immigrants. This system serves the double function of providing a reliable source of domestic labour and limiting the numbers of working-class people entering Canada as landed immigrants.

EMPLOYMENT VISAS

Employment visas are temporary visas that allow a worker to come to Canada to work in a particular job for a specific amount of time. The stated purpose of these visas is to fill temporary labour shortages in specific kinds of jobs, but in fact most visas have been used to fill jobs such as domestic, farm, and non-union hotel and restaurant work, jobs characterized by extremely low wages and poor working conditions. Instead of taking steps to improve the conditions of these jobs and thereby eliminate the labour shortage, the government relies heavily on the use of employment visas to fill the least desirable jobs. In 1974 the number of landed immigrants admitted to Canada was two and a half times as great as the number of employment visas issued. In 1978 the balance was reversed and there were more visas issued than landed immigrants admitted. Although in 1981 the numbers were almost equal, this represented a substantial increase in the numbers of people entering the country on employment visas and a decrease in the numbers of landed immigrants from previous years.[2]

Clearly the government is favouring employment visas over landed immigrant status and working-class people who formerly would have come to Canada as landed immigrants with the right to remain here permanently are, more and more, coming to work on temporary visas. This policy benefits the government and employers in that they receive a supply of workers who fill otherwise unfilled jobs, who will accept whatever wages and working conditions they are offered, and who need not be provided with the benefits that accompany landed immigrant status. The effect is to further reinforce the low wages and poor working conditions in these jobs, and to severely jeopardize attempts to organize trade unions or other protective organizations in those areas where visa workers are employed.

LIVING AND WORKING CONDITIONS

The number of employment visas issued annually to domestic workers has increased each year since 1979 with more than 15,000 issued in 1982.[3] These figures have consistently increased despite drastically rising unemployment rates. This is because Canadian workers are extremely reluctant to take jobs that require living-in and that offer such poor wages and working conditions.

The largest number of visas are issued in Ontario, with smaller numbers in British Columbia, Quebec, Alberta and other provinces.[4] The majority are issued to women from "Third World" countries where western imperialism has created widespread unemployment and poverty. Large numbers of women come from the West Indies and the Philippines to escape the hardship and poverty of their home countries. Many were unemployed before they came, or working for extremely low wages as domestics or in factories. Many have children back home who are looked after by a relative or friend while they are in Canada. These women come to Canada with the hopes of making enough money to feed, clothe, house and educate their children and other family members in their home countries.

> In St. Vincent it could be really rough, because as I said, there is not much job down there to do. And the few people that are there they pays nothing, you know, they don't pay no good salary and most of them do their household work themselves. That's domestic work. There is other

jobs, like mending the roads, and that kind of job, it's the kind of job that you have to sleep with the supervisor and then you might get a job.

I'm not looking for a lump sum of money to go back into my country. All I want is just to get a home for my kids, and get some furniture in it.

The high hopes that people have about Canada are fed by advertisements from domestic employment agencies and word-of-mouth stories about Canadian riches. Most women are shocked to discover that their promised salary, which initially seemed so high, is hard to live on, let alone save or support families with. As well, many women must borrow money in order to get to Canada and this has to be paid back.

Well, when I was on my first job I couldn't do much saving, right, because the salary was so small, right, and then you had to pay $80 each month until you finished paying off the passage. So from $200 (per month) you had to pay $80 for the passage. And the passage was $396. Then you have to save your passage to go back.

When a woman is in Canada on an employment visa her legal status is dependent on having a job. If she loses her job she risks being sent out of the country. This means visa workers are forced to accept the conditions offered by their employers for fear of losing their jobs. The Employment and Immigration Commission has set some minimum standards for wages and working conditions in domestic employment, but in many cases these standards are violated by employers and the Commission refuses to put itself in the role of "enforcement" agency.

She knew exactly what I supposed to get, right, but she never paid it. When I had the second extension, I said to her, 'How come you never mention to me about the salary at the Manpower Department?' and she said, 'Well, they don't care about what you pay once you put what they want on the form.'

Who are the employers? For the most part they are upper middle-class professionals (doctors, lawyers, university professors) and business people. A 1980 study conducted by the Canada Employment and Immigration Commission[5] indicates that the most common reason (71.4%) for employing a live-in domestic worker is to free both spouses for the labour market. The most common family composition is a husband and wife, age 30 to 40, with 1 to 3 children, ages 0 to 10. Sixty-seven percent of employers have an annual income over $40,000.

Despite the wealth of their employers, many domestics are vastly underpaid, some making as little as $150 per month plus room and board, although $350 is the current rate set by Employment and Immigration. Employment visa workers are required to pay Unemployment Insurance and Canada Pension Plan premiums but they can never benefit from these programs. It is estimated that Revenue Canada takes in almost $2 million each year from UIC and CPP premiums paid by domestics and their employers.[6] Most domestics work in excess of a 40-hour week. Some regularly work 15- to 16-hour days and are on call 24 hours a day. Job descriptions are rare – most domestics do the regular household work plus a multitude of extra tasks.

> Oh, I do anything in the house. The cleaning, the laundry, the cooking, right, look after the kids, like have their lunch ready for school, and stuff like that, everything.

> Well ... I go outside and do all the garden, water the lawn and sweep the back porch and sweep the front porch, take up all the garbage and take them outside. Do her garden, do her friend's garden, and, you know, everything. One day she took me to her friend's boat and I went there and washed that boat, it was very cold, cause there was not hot and cold water at the marina, and I got to use the cold water. My hand was frozen. It was very hard for me. Then when I came back I make supper.

> You know if they said, 'Well, okay we have to go out and can you stay with the kids and we'll pay you, right, for stayin' in.' But they don't say that, which mean you have to do that extra work and then no pay, right, just the same salary.

Domestics are supposed to get two days off per week. Many don't. Some employers give their domestic statutory holidays off, but often these are times when the domestic's services are even more in demand because of school holidays and entertaining. Some domestics get an annual holiday, others must take their holidays when their employers take theirs, often without pay.

> I said, 'What about the days off?' She said, 'Well, you have Sunday off and some of the evenings off, and either Wednesday or Thursday during the week.' But I never got that, I just had Sunday off.

Many domestics complain about a lack of privacy in the homes they both live and work in – employers and their children come in and out of their rooms, phone calls are not private and in some cases mail is read. The quality of room and board varies tremendously. Sometimes it is adequate, other times the domestic must share a room with the children, or have her room serve also as family, sewing or TV room. In one case, a domestic had a piano moved in for the children to practice on! Some women also complain of not being given enough food. There is no sick leave when you are a domestic. You simply must work or risk losing your job and your immigration status.

> I'm lying here thinking that I have to go and push a vacuum tomorrow and my chest is hurting me, it's really hurting me. I have a bad cold. Tomorrow I have to go and stick my head into the fridge and put my hand into some water or do the washing or go and iron, because I've got to iron every day, wash every day. And I can't make it, I just can't take that on.

If she is unhappy with her work situation a domestic can complain to an immigration officer, who can decide whether or not to allow her to look for a new job. If she is allowed to do this there is a great deal of pressure on her to find another job quickly, meaning the woman often takes the first job that comes along, and ends up in a situation no better than the first. Many women would rather stay in an oppressive situation than risk an encounter with the Immigration Department.

Besides the racism implicit in a system that brings women of colour from the "Third World" countries to Canada to work in the homes of wealthy, white Canadians, these women must deal with overt racism in their daily lives. One woman was told not to visit her friends because she returned smelling of curry; several women say they are told regularly they stink and asked if they have showered that day; another woman had her employer's child spit in her face and call her " a dirty Negro." Most domestics link the abuse they are subjected to with the fact that they are not white.

> This employer wanted me to come in and take the job the next day. She wanted me to come in and meet the lady who was leaving, to show me what to do. She told me that the last domestic, who was a white lady, didn't want to stay in the basement, so her son gave her his room upstairs on the first floor and the son took the basement. Well, if I take the job, I will have to go in the basement and give back her son his first floor. So I said, if I was white, I could have continued with the upstairs room, but because I am black I have to go down in the basement.

> Canada was different than I expected. I know I heard about the ice, but I thought I was coming to meet even more people of my colour, you know, and sometimes I sit on the bus and I am the only black person and I feel so worried. I say 'What am I doing in this place?', but then I travel and I meet other people and you know, they talk to me, and once I meet some black people and then I knew well, I wasn't the only black person in the country.

ORGANIZING

Organizing attempts by domestic workers go back a long way in B.C. history. The primary demands of the Home and Domestic Employees' Union, formed in 1913, were a nine-hour day and a minimum wage. In 1936 the Domestic Workers' Union Local 91 was formed. Both of these unions were shortlived for the same reasons that make it difficult for domestics to organize today: long hours of work, isolation from other domestic workers, lack of privacy in the homes of employers, the difficulties of a one-to-one employer-worker relationship, and the fact that many domestics do not see themselves as "workers."

There are other domestic workers besides those who live-in on employment visas. Some are employed through multinationally-controlled employment agencies that take a percentage (usually about 25%) of each worker's hourly wage. Other domestics are employed either directly or indirectly by the government, providing "home-making" services to the aged and handicapped. Others work for private individuals doing "day work." On the whole, the women who do all these jobs are working-class Canadians or landed immigrants.

The most successful recent organizing by domestic workers in B.C. has been done by "homemakers" working for agencies funded by the government. The Service, Office and Retail Workers' Union (SORWUC) has been certified and signed a contract for a bargaining unit in Powell River. This organizing, though a difficult struggle for the women involved, was possible because the workers have a common employer and opportunity to meet and talk with each other. They also have secure immigration status in Canada.

For temporary visa workers the obstacles are greater and the risks more severe. Nevertheless, over the past eight years four major groups have formed to organize domestics, including the Labour Advocacy and Research Association (LARA), which focused on research, education and advocacy; the British Columbia Domestics' Association (BCDA), which concerned itself with provincial legislative reform; the Committee for the Advancement of the Rights of Domestic Workers (CARDWO), which centred on federal immigration reform and the building of a domestic worker organization; and the Domestic Workers' Union (DWU), which set up a trade union. They arose at different times to meet the needs of different groups of domestics, and their work, as well as that of other domestic worker groups across the country, has significantly added to the visibility and the strength of the domestic workers' struggle.

LARA was formed in Vancouver in 1975 to assist employment visa workers to take steps to improve their situation. (It was also set up to do advocacy work for farmworkers and developed into the Farmworkers' Organizing Committee, the forerunner of the Canadian Farmworkers' Union.) A group of domestics, mainly from Jamaica and other West Indian islands, began by getting together on Sunday afternoons to talk about their work. LARA provided information on the legal rights (or lack of them) of visa workers and the social services available to them. The first meetings were dynamic and angry: as people described the often horrendous stories of their treatment in Canada, they were exhilarated to find other people with similar anecdotes and experiences. People also began to learn about the few rights they do have and in some instances started to deal individually with their exploitation. Several women made formal complaints about their jobs to the Immigration Department and were able to find new jobs and were granted new visas.

In general, however, the exploitation continued. From the LARA discussions the basic problem of organizing employment visa workers became clear: most of these women are in Canada out of desperation. For these women the most important thing is to keep their jobs in order to make *some* money to help their families back home. Complaining about treatment on the job is a sure-fire way to lose that job and thus jeopardize the right to stay in Canada. For most people it is not worth the risk, especially when complaints do not guarantee results. Also, most hope to return to Canada eventually as landed immigrants and hesitate to alienate an employer from whom they might want to obtain a job offer. The employment visa system thus creates a work force of people so vulnerable and insecure that they are guaranteed not to make waves.

Other major, though secondary, problems for this group of workers are relatively small numbers and, as mentioned above, the problem of dealing with a one-to-one employer-worker relationship. It is difficult for a domestic to confront an employer when she is alone, and when she eats, breathes and sleeps under the same roof. "Living-in" also means that it is difficult to find meeting places and to get the privacy, time and resources necessary to do the organizational work.

Because of the vulnerability and subsequent fear among the women, collective organizing did not progress. Individual women continued to fight back, however. One woman went so far as to sue her employer for back wages after almost a year of receiving $150 a month less than her employer had agreed to pay. After a time-consuming and emotionally exhausting process, she settled out of court for a third of what she was owed.

LARA continued to do support work – assisting individuals, producing audiovisual and written materials about the conditions of domestic workers, and speaking wherever possible about the situation. As well, LARA joined with SORWUC to lobby the provincial government for the labour standards protection that domestic workers, along with farmworkers, have historically been excluded from – including minimum wage, hours of work and holiday requirements. LARA continues to exist as a back-up resource for specific campaigns and projects.

In 1979 a new organization of domestic workers, the British Columbia Domestics' Association was formed. It was made up of women on employment visas but in a somewhat different situation. Most of the women came from the United Kingdom, Australia and New Zealand; they were white, single, younger and for the most part without dependents. They had come to Canada as "nannies" more out of interest than economic desperation. Still, many of the exploitive practices of employers were the same and BCDA was organized out of a need to improve their conditions of work. These women were less hesitant to speak out because they had less at stake.

Soon after its inception, BCDA joined with LARA and SORWUC to put pressure on the provincial government regarding labour standards legislation. As a result of these efforts, domestic workers were included in the new Employment Standards Act, which means they are covered by basic provincial labour laws regarding minimum wage, annual and general holidays, and maternity leave, etc. However, they are explicitly excluded from some crucial provisions of this Act which render the change less than effective. Domestics are not covered by the hours of work and overtime provisions in the new Act. Although the minimum wage set for the live-in domestics is $29.20 per day, this is somewhat meaningless considering there is no limit to the number of hours domestics can be made to work and no guarantee of payment for these hours.

Following the lobby, interest in the BCDA gradually waned. Some of the women who were most involved left the country when their visas expired; others knew they were here only temporarily and did not want to spend all their time struggling with employers and the government. For these women, the temporary nature of their employment visa rather than their vulnerability kept them from organizing.

It became clear from these experiences in B.C. that the only way to fundamentally change the conditions of visa workers was to change the employment visa system itself. The system is set up to create a form of bonded slavery under which workers have no power to demand decent working conditions. Similar conclusions were arrived at by domestic worker organizations across the country and in 1980 a campaign was begun to secure landed immigrant status for women coming to Canada as domestics. "Good enough to work, good enough to stay" was the slogan. The campaign was coordinated by International Coalition to End Domestics' Exploitation (INTERCEDE) in Toronto and supported by groups in Montreal, Toronto, Ottawa and LARA in Vancouver. It was a time-consuming process. Months were spent writing briefs, meeting and lobbying the government.

In the meantime another group of domestic workers got together in Vancouver. This group was initiated by some Filipino domestics who approached the International Association of Filipino Patriots (IAFP, an anti-Marcos organization) for assistance in organizing.[7] After the first meeting, the Committee for the Advancement of the Rights of Domestic Workers was set up. Although CARDWO began as a Filipino organization, it soon expanded to include West Indian and European domestics.

The domestic workers who came to the initial CARDWO meetings identified the immigration problem as their major concern. These women wanted the security of permanent status in Canada. As a result, CARDWO became active in the national campaign for landed status and did not focus immediately on the formation of a long-term association or union. CARDWO members wrote briefs and organized public meetings and demonstrations. Other activities included bi-monthly meetings for domestic workers, the publication of a newsletter, social events, production of a skit about the plight of domestic workers, fundraising events, and the handling of individual cases, which usually involved a combination of immigration and labour standard problems. Committees were formed to carry out most tasks and women who had never done organizational work before learned to participate in and chair meetings, to write articles and speeches, to speak publicly and to take on the responsibilities of an organization.

At the same time, through the initiative of the International Committee Against Racism (INCAR), another organization – which began as the Domestic Workers' Association and then became the Domestic Workers' Union (DWU) – was created. The DWU developed a constitution and bylaws and was set up as a trade union. Because at this time most activity among domestic workers was focused on the landed status campaign, the union participated in these activities as well as providing advocacy services similar to those offered by CARDWO. Although the DWU had a more specific goal than CARDWO, which acted more in response to the immediate needs of its members, their work was very similar.

The country-wide organizing paid off. The campaign had been organized tightly and effectively and therefore could not be ignored. After much politicking and many delays the federal government issued a new immigration policy in November 1981. The fact that the government had been forced to listen to domestic workers and to take what they were saying seriously enough to develop a new policy was a victory. Unfortunately, like most legislative concessions, the policy does not clearly meet the needs of the people it affects.

The new immigration policy gives domestic workers who have been in Canada for two years or more on employment visas the right to apply for landed immigrant status from within the country. The regular "point system" supposedly is waived and the criteria for admittance is the domestic's ability to be "self-sufficient." Ability to be "self-sufficient" is assessed using a number of criteria, an important one being the kind of skills "upgrading" a woman has done or is doing while in Canada. Employers are required to provide $20 a month and three hours a week off towards this upgrading.

While on the surface this policy sounds beneficial to some women, there are a number of areas of concern. First, it follows the tradition of Canadian immigration laws in leaving a great deal of discretion in the hands of individual immigration officers. Terms like "personal suitability," "aptitude for learning" and "adapted to Canadian lifestyle" are left to immigration officers to define. This can and has led to highly discriminatory application of policies.

Many employers are not providing the financial assistance and the time off they are required to contribute towards the domestic's "upgrading." And it is not clear what sort of courses or training are considered adequate. Already one CARDWO member has been told she cannot demonstrate "self-sufficiency," even though she has worked in Canada for seven years and has been taking courses to upgrade her skills for at least five of these seven years.

Women are also afraid that the fact that they have children in their home countries whom they would like to bring to Canada will be a negative factor in determining ability to be "self-sufficient." The CARDWO member mentioned above has four children in Jamaica. There is also a fear that because people coming in as domestics have the potential to be landed immigrants, the criteria for initially entering Canada as a domestic worker will favour those who are young, without families, educated and financially secure. This could mean that women who formerly would have qualified to come to Canada as domestic workers, no longer will. Moreover, women who are turned down in their applications for landed immigrant status have no right to an appeal of any sort, and the Immigration Department continues to harass and intimidate many of the women it sees.

The new policy has been in effect for almost two years, but it is still difficult to assess its full effect. As of July 1, 1981, 2,004 women had applied for landed status. Of these, 660 had been accepted, 687 were referred for training and 657 had applications still pending.[8] INTER-CEDE is organizing a country-wide assessment of the policy. It is hoped that the same forces that secured the new policy will be brought into action again to ensure that it is administered equitably and, if need be, changed to guarantee non-discrimination.

In B.C., both CARDWO and the DWU were very active in the period right after the new policy was introduced. Unfortunately, the level of activity has not been sustained in CARDWO, and since my experience is with that organization, I can comment more fully on what happened there. Women came to meetings eager for information on the policy and how it would affect them. Concrete information was slow in coming from the Immigration Department, but whatever was available was immediately shared and discussed. This period was followed by a lull, as people waited to see how the policy would work. At the same time, the IAFP, which had been taking an active leadership role in CARDWO, was forced to limit its involvement due to a shortage of resources and new work priorities. Both of these developments raised some important questions about methods of organizing.

The relative inactivity of CARDWO after the introduction of the new policy raises the question of whether it was a mistake for it to emphasize the landed status campaign rather than more long-term organizing. Did focusing on legislative reform take away from the building of a solid organization? Is it possible to form a solid organization without specific concrete issues to organize around? Does the trade union structure of the DWU allow for the building of an organization at the same time as dealing with specific issues? Clearly, neither CARDWO nor the DWU would have achieved as much as they have if it had not been for the landed status campaign, which spoke directly to the needs of domestic workers, and brought people to meetings and out onto the streets. But the campaign became the major focus, landed status the goal. Structural questions and long-term planning were secondary.

CARDWO's experience also raises important questions about leadership – questions faced by all organizations. When live-in domestic workers decide to organize they require assistance, at least initially, from people who have more time and freedom of movement than they do, and who also have the experience of organizing in Canada. This leadership must take its direction from domestic workers and be committed to sharing knowledge and skills so that more and more of its role is taken over by domestics themselves. This process was slowly occurring in CARDWO but was not complete when the IAFP pulled out. As a result, when the landed status campaign ended, there was not sufficient leadership in place to determine how to move the organization forward. This experience emphasizes how crucial it is for organizations and individuals to think ahead carefully before taking on a leadership role in a particular struggle or organization. Leadership withdrawn at the wrong time can set work back, perhaps even further than if it had not been provided in the first place.

While CARDWO has become less active, the DWU has continued its work. Membership in the union has grown to 75, and attendance at meetings is steadily increasing. The union continues to provide information and advocacy to its members as more and more domestic workers come forward with problems. As well, they are considering filing a class action against the B.C. government on the grounds that the exclusion of domestic workers from the hours of work and overtime provisions of the Employment Standards Act is discriminatory on the basis of sex and country of origin. The union is also considering a court action to challenge the federal Human Rights Act, which does not recognize workers in Canada on employment visas as "individuals," and subsequently denies them access to documents under the "Access to Information" provisions.

The DWU has also been focusing more on its development as a trade union. They have established a basic contract for domestic workers that was recently ratified by the membership. They are working on a "hiring hall" model for the union and seeking a first contract. The union is also going through the process of shifting its leadership from non-domestic workers to domestic workers themselves.

The success of the DWU or any organization of domestic workers is dependent upon not only day-to-day organizational assistance but solid and consistent support from the trade union movement and other progressive organizations. In order for this support to be forthcoming, there needs to be a change in the way unions and other groups view domestic work.

In 1975-76 when LARA was trying to secure funds to set up legal advocacy programs for domestics and farmworkers, there was a noticeable difference in the ways the two groups of workers were perceived. In spite of the multitude of extremely difficult obstacles to their organizing confronted by farmworkers, they were at least given some credibility as workers. But when LARA approached funding sources on behalf of domestics, it was hard for many people to think of domestic workers as needing that kind of assistance. A typical response was that: "Domestic work is something women do on the side for extra money or for free because they like doing it and it comes naturally."

Domestic workers encounter this same attitude today, not only from the government and their employers but from other workers and workers' organizations. The DWU has repeatedly approached the trade union movement for financial assistance, and has obtained some help from Canadian unions and unions not affiliated with the B.C. Federation of Labour. But to date, the DWU has received only $4,000 from union donations. The predominant unofficial attitude appears to be one of skepticism and "we'll help you when you prove you can survive."

It is not uncommon for previously unorganized workers to meet skepticism when they begin to organize. But the reaction is heightened for domestic workers because they are women, because they are non-white, and because they are doing work that is not recognized as having value. But despite this, domestic workers *are* organizing. They are demanding basic rights that workers in other areas have long taken for granted. It is time they were given not just token assistance, but sustained and solid support for their very "real" and very courageous struggle.

NOTES

1 The following are either domestic worker organizations or organizations that do advocacy on behalf of domestics:

Household Workers' Association (HWA)
445 St. Francois-Xavier
Montreal, Quebec
H2Y 2T1

Labour Rights for Domestic Servants (LRDS)
82 Warren Road, Apt. 704
Toronto, Ontario
M4V 2R7

International Coalition to End Domestics' Exploitation
(INTERCEDE)
348 College Street
Toronto, Ontario
M5T 1S4

Ottawa-Carleton Immigrant Services Organization
425 Gloucester
Ottawa, Ontario

Committee for the Advancement of the Rights of Domestic
Workers (CARDWO)
2520 Triumph Street
Vancouver, B.C.
V5K 1S8

Domestic Workers' Union
1992 West 1st Avenue
Vancouver, B.C.
V6J 1G6

2 The figures are: 1974 – 218,465 landed immigrants, 87,353 employment visas; 1978 – 72,475 landed immigrants, 83,497 employment visas; 1981 – 128,618 landed immigrants, 126,575 employment visas. These and subsequent immigration statistics were obtained from Employment and Immigration Canada.

3 The figures are: 1979 – 10,255 visas; 1980 – 11,820 visas; 1981 – 14,787 visas; 1982 – 15,514 visas.

4 In 1982 the breakdown by province of employment visas issued for domestic work was: Ontario – 9,377; B.C. – 2,070; Quebec – 1,991; Alberta – 1,463; Manitoba – 277; Nova Scotia – 118; Saskatchewan – 102; New Brunswick – 54; Newfoundland – 16; Northwest Territories – 12; Prince Edward Island – 4; not known – 30.

5 Robert Dubois, *Profile of Employers of Domestics and Babysitters on Employment Visas* (Economic Services Branch, Canada Employment and Immigration, Quebec Region, July 1980).

6 This figure was obtained from the brief presented by INTERCEDE, the IAFP, LARA and the Household Workers' Association (HWA) to the Task Force on Immigration Practices and Procedures, January 1981.

7 The number of Filipino domestics coming to Canada has substantially increased in recent years, while the number of West Indian women has decreased. The government favours the Filipino women, who tend to be from a slightly higher class background and have more education and training.

8 These figures were obtained from the Annual Report to Parliament on Immigration Levels, 1983, Canada Employment and Immigration Commission.

ORGANIZING FREELANCERS IN THE ARTS

Joanne Kates and Jane Springer

Women who work freelance in the area of culture in Canada – as writers, artists, editors, poets, translators – face a unique set of problems. On the one hand, they have a valuable skill and considerable control over their working conditions. On the other hand, they are seldom paid for each hour they work, and because they work alone, they lack the benefits of a collective work space. Although some artists and writers achieve a measure of artistic autonomy, most work under the constraints of having to produce what will sell. They confront the same problems of low wages and low status as women in other areas of the labour force, but the freelance nature of their work has meant they have rarely been a target of unionizing attempts.

In this article we look at people, particularly women, who freelance in the arts, examine the organizations they have formed to protect their interests, and make suggestions for new directions both within and outside these organizations. The discussion focuses on what we see to be two key areas: efforts to improve wages and working conditions (sometimes through collective bargaining), and attempts to organize around political issues that are related to culture. Our interest in this arises out of our own experiences organizing freelance writers and freelance editors.

Joanne was the first president of the Periodical Writers' Association of Canada (PWAC), which was established in May 1976. Sixty people joined PWAC at its founding meeting and by 1980 there were two hundred members. Membership was based on a point system that demonstrated a person's experience in writing for financial remuneration for mass market Canadian magazines and newspapers. From the beginning PWAC brought together the majority of Canada's successful freelance writers.

PWAC's goal was to create better working conditions for freelance writers. They wrote a contract to govern the transactions between writers and magazine and newspaper editors that included a number of strong protections for writers: a fifty percent "kill fee" (to be paid if an assigned article is not used), the right to see all edited copy and negotiate edits while there is still time to make changes, payment within two weeks of acceptance, and no major rewrites that deviate from the initial outline unless an extra fee is paid. The PWAC contract was an excellent one; it included unheard of protection for writers. The kill fee clause for example, was completely new in Canada at the time. PWAC negotiated the contract with editors and nineteen Canadian magazines signed it. The commitment to the collective bargaining process was so strong that PWAC twice threatened strike action — once against *Weekend* magazine and then against *Chatelaine*. A strong grievance committee that supported writers who were being maltreated by magazines won most of its battles.

By 1980 the original leadership was tired, and most of the people in it stepped down. But it was more than fatigue that caused so many to retire. The *Body Politic,* a newspaper of gay liberation, was facing a trial on obscenity charges. Some people thought an organization of freelance writers should support a minority newspaper under attack, in the name of the fight against censorship. They were overruled by a majority who felt that taking a stand on an issue like censorship was too "political" for the organization.

As soon as the original executive retired from active participation, the character of PWAC changed. Now there is no talk of strikes at annual meetings. Buying computers is a hotter topic than bargaining collectively. The style of the organization is more service-oriented, with a stress on professional development seminars, Grand and Toy discounts for Toronto members and a group disability insurance plan. The goals of collective bargaining have ceased to be a priority. People had wanted better wages and working conditions and the contract that would ensure this, but they did not want to call the organization a union or to be identified with union practices.

The *Body Politic* incident also indicated that issues not directly related to the economic concerns of freelance writers are not part of PWAC's agenda. "Women's issues" are also concerns that are outside the organization's scope. Although women have always dominated the membership and are the majority on the executive of PWAC, there has never been a discussion of the disadvantaged position of women in the field.

Jane was a founding member of the Freelance Editors' Association of Canada (FEAC), which was set up in January 1979. Freelance editors work on a contract basis with publishers, sometimes at an hourly rate, sometimes per manuscript. Their job can include any or all of developmental work with authors, substantive editing, copyediting, rewriting and proofreading. Although in some of the work that freelance editors do they appear to be in a business relationship between two equals, much of it is for large, often multinational companies that view them as skilled workers, not professionals. Freelancers are cheaper than full-time in-house people who are paid for regular office hours and get benefits. They provide fast service and no overhead cost. They have some control over their time and working conditions, but essentially they do what publishers ask them to, when they're asked to do it. In other words, freelance editors are more often in an employer/employee relationship than in a professional/client one.

These conditions would seem to be more conducive to collective bargaining than those of PWAC, for example, because editors' work is less "creative" and there is less concern for artistic autonomy. But union-type organizing was even less in evidence than in PWAC.

Most of the editors who came to the initial meeting of FEAC welcomed the opportunity to talk to other freelancers about their problems with publishers and the isolation they experienced. Recognizing that other people were in the same position as themselves, many were soon confident enough to admit they were badly underpaid. But some of the editors, especially the older, more experienced ones, found the discussion of rates and conditions threatening. They did not want to be associated with newcomers to the field and were worried that sharing information would diminish their high status. And all of the editors feared that publishers would stop hiring them if they organized. In addition, there was concern that because many freelancers worked for small Canadian publishers, some of which were underfinanced and unprofitable, that they would be threatening the industry itself if they asked for more money.

At least two of the men were hesitant to associate themselves with women and "women's work."[1] Organizing with us, they feared, meant losing their status and consequent higher wages. On one memorable occasion the women booed down a man who suggested that most of the women freelance editors were "housewives" who were "doing a little editing on the side."

The obvious benefits of sharing information and setting "suggested" rates were enough to at least temporarily allay most of these fears. It soon became clear that, although some publishers complained, most were prepared to pay what FEAC was asking for – which helped the editors realize not only the importance of their role in the publishing process but the fact that up until then, they had been grossly under-paid. FEAC developed a constitution, a central aim of which was "to establish guidelines to assist members in securing equitable compensa-tion and good working relations." However, it did not attempt to develop a standard contract or to bargain collectively and has never been able to agree to defend its members against publishers who do not pay on time (or at all!), or who change the conditions of work midway through a project.

Once these initial gains were made, the emphasis shifted from a concern with wages and working conditions to professional develop-ment. The current *Directory of Members* describes as one of FEAC's "most important" goals, "to promote communication and cooperation between freelance editors and their clients." Freelance editors seem to be making a tradeoff: instead of the higher wages and improved work-ing conditions they could win through collective bargaining, they have elected "professional" status.

FEAC has anonymously investigated members' hourly and yearly earnings, but it has never conducted an inquiry on the basis of sex to compare the earnings of men and women in the area. It has never raised the problem of child care or asked its members if they had difficulty attending meetings because of their children. In a field where women are continually in a position of looking for new work and meeting with in-house editors and authors (chiefly male), there has never been a discussion of sexual harassment. Yet all of these issues are becoming common concerns in trade unions today.

Our experiences in PWAC and FEAC raised serious doubts about the possibility of organizing freelancers into unions. It became clear that the actual *organizing* into advocacy groups was possible, and that such groups could flourish as professional service organizations. But we were thwarted in our desire to build unions; by and large the members of both PWAC and FEAC were not willing to put their energies into collective bargaining, even in order to deal with the narrowest of work area concerns. Broader, more "political" concerns, like the issues raised elsewhere by feminists and those suggested by the publishing industry – like censorship or the "motherhood" issue of Canadian content – have scarcely been considered.

When we began to study the other freelancers' organizations, it was obvious that all of them shared the same difficulties in terms of organizing and political action. All of them also treat so-called "women's issues" similarly. In addition to PWAC and FEAC, there are five other organizations defined by their field or work area that represent freelance cultural workers in Canada.[2] They are, in the order of their founding, the League of Canadian Poets, Canadian Artists' Representation (CAR), The Writers' Union of Canada (TWUC), the Guild of Canadian Playwrights and the Literary Translators' Association (LTA). (See table for comparative statistics on all of the organizations.)

From the founding of the League of Canadian Poets in 1967 to FEAC's birth in 1979, the organizations have developed along similar lines. The only two of them that do not generate the majority of their operating funds from government grants are FEAC and LTA. For all the others, most income comes from government arts granting agencies like the Canada Council and provincial arts councils.

The government funding allows five of these organizations to run secretariats (offices with executive directors and clerical staff) that lobby and provide information to their members, but it also acts as a powerful constraint that imposes a certain structure on the organizations, forcing them to operate in set ways. In order to fit arts council criteria for funding, and also in order to avoid making funding bodies nervous, the organizations create programs of a *service* nature. To be more specific: the Canada Council, which supplies the majority of the organizations' income, is willing to pay for cultural events (like reading tours) and professional development events (like seminars) but will not fund a secretariat's general operating expenses. The result of these funding criteria is a hidden but powerful influence on the organizations. They unwittingly tailor their goals to meet funding criteria, making it difficult for them to put priority on collective bargaining, even if they wished to do so. Unlike most trade unions, which have the freedom to determine their own goals because they generate all their income through membership dues, these organizations are influenced by outside forces.

Another important reason why these organizations have resisted collective bargaining is the marginality of the Canadian culture industries. In some areas of Canadian cultural production so little money is being spent and earned that books, for example, might not get published if authors bargained for a living wage. If a few poets refused to publish with a certain company because of the company's refusal to negotiate a satisfactory contract, the company would either go elsewhere for its poetry or not publish poetry at all. Except in the case of extremely popular products, the production of culture is rarely very profitable, and that economic marginality makes it hard to pressure company owners for a better deal for workers – especially in Canada, where the small population makes culture even less profitable than in countries like the u.s.

The other kind of marginality that affects cultural workers and their organizations has to do with the idea (shared by them and the people who consume their work) that culture is not an essential product. Although the production of ideas has a powerful effect on people's lives, culture is not considered in the same way as cars or clothing. Even many cultural workers believe that the work they do is not important to anybody but themselves. This lack of awareness of how important they are makes them shrink from militance because, fundamentally, they don't think anybody would notice if they were to withdraw their services or use the other persuasive tools employed by trade unions.

And so these organizations function mostly as service groups to provide information and individual benefits to their members. Those benefits include paid reading tours for members, such as are run by the Writers' Union and the League of Poets. Most of the groups hold professional development seminars and publish newsletters that keep members up to date on developments in their work area, and work opportunities; many have implemented disability insurance and other similar benefit programs.

When it comes to collective bargaining, which is, after all, the foundation of a union, the organizations have a weak history. Only three of them have made serious attempts at collective bargaining. Of the three, one has failed completely, one, CAR, has signed contracts with only a few sympathetic employers and PWAC has seen its contracts fall into disuse.

In June 1982 the Ontario local of CAR succeeded in negotiating an artist / gallery agreement with all publicly funded galleries in Ontario. This is a major victory, and an international first for visual artists, but achieving the same conditions with private galleries will be much more difficult.

As for the other organizations, the collective bargaining story is even more disheartening. In the fall of 1982 the Guild of Canadian Playwrights presented a contract to theatres in Canada that would have granted playwrights a ten percent share of any weekly box office gross receipts and more control over artistic decisions, such as the choice of director, designer and cast. The contract was good but the theatres turned it down flat and the Guild membership was unwilling to strike to stand up for it. The experience of the Writers' Union in trying to bargain for a good author / publisher contract has been the same.

Although the Writers' Union calls itself a union, and all the organizations have as their stated goals the idea of improving the working lives of their members, not one of them is really a union. If it does nothing else, a union bargains collectively for its members, and uses (or threatens to use) the clout created by withdrawal of services to give that bargaining some power. These organizations do not bargain collectively; they do not go on strike or even threaten to strike those who pay them.* They have achieved a degree of control over their work process that they do not want to give up.

At first glance, another difference between these organizations and most Canadian unions is the heavy participation of women in them. The average female membership in the seven organizations is 47 percent, and the leadership is made up of an average of 48 percent women. That is a rare and impressive example of female participation and leadership, but women nonetheless suffer from many of the same problems in cultural organizing as in other kinds of organizing. As in other work areas, women are substantially economically disadvantaged in cultural work. According to a recent Canadian study, women full-time writers earn an average of 53 percent of what men full-time writers earn.[3] And yet the organizations have done nothing to combat this discrimination against women.

The same problem exists *inside* the organizations. It is true that women constitute almost half the leadership of most of the organiza-

---

*A recent Writers' Union resolution to withdraw from the reading tours program until non-fiction writers are included in it has so far not been acted on.

tions, but they tend to do most of the work, both on a paid and volunteer basis. The paid secretaries and directors who keep the offices running are mostly women, probably because men would refuse to work for such low pay. And the volunteers who keep the committees going, which in turn are the lifeblood of any such organization, are by and large women. That is a reflection of the volunteer syndrome we see so often in our society, in which women do essential work on a volunteer basis, because no one is willing to pay for it to be done and men won't work for free.

So here we have a work area like other work areas, where women work as hard as men (or harder) and earn less money. In the face of that obvious discrimination, women in trade unions have responded by creating women's caucuses to fight for a fair deal for women. And yet these organizations have on the whole chosen to ignore the discrimination. Of all seven organizations, only one, the League of Canadian Poets, has such a caucus; and when the League inaugurated its Feminist Caucus in 1982, some members resigned in outrage. They were furious because membership in the League (and the ability to publish poetry at all) is based on standards of artistic excellence, and they feared that programs like affirmative action for women would substitute quotas for standards of excellence as selection criteria.

In general, the reaction of some of the outraged members of the League of Poets to the Feminist Caucus has reflected more general attitudes in all the organizations. They are all hobbled in their ability to fight for women by this fear of an abandonment of standards of excellence. In a work area where women are still earning half of what men earn doing the same work, it is clear that the organizations need women's caucuses. The recent history in trade unions shows that initiatives to improve women's incomes come from women's caucuses, and that before such caucuses form, little is said or done about the oppression of women. It would be not only useful but possible for these organizations to create women's caucuses, but here too they are dragging their feet because of a reluctance to identify with the women's and / or union movements. They see women's caucuses as a threat to their professional status, and thus in conflict with who they are and what they do.

This notion of how freelancers *see* themselves is crucial. The problems of organizing them exist on this level, the level of their consciousness, as well as on the more concrete levels that we have already discussed.

*   *   *   *   *

In a plant, in an office, even in a farm field where crops are being harvested, a worker looks over her shoulder a hundred times a day and she knows: "these people are my co-workers." That realization may be entirely unconscious, but the *consciousness* is there: it is the consciousness of working in the same place, for the same company, alongside other people. In contrast, freelance writers, visual artists, translators, editors, playwrights and poets, because they work alone, completely separate from one another, don't have that chance to identify with each other. If one of us writes a book published by McClelland and Stewart, we do not think of ourselves as Pierre Berton's co-worker. The isolation that freelancers experience has a profound effect. The immediate physical conditions for identifying with each other as working people do not exist.

Part of what keeps cultural workers from fighting for what they could win is their *feeling* of marginality, and this is especially true of women. At least half of Canadian cultural workers are women. According to a recent Canadian study, 42 percent of all Canadian freelance writers are women. Given that Brian Harrison, author of the study, only polled members of writers' organizations (which charge an average $100 annual fee that many women can ill afford), we can safely assume that the proportion of women writers is even higher than he found.[4] So many women do freelance cultural work because of its very marginal nature: it's what they can get. No employer is bound to give them job security or benefits like health insurance, vacation pay, pension plans or unemployment insurance contributions, or even a desk in an office. The work takes place in one's home and it requires little support from the employer. These are qualities that cultural work shares with some female job ghettos: the sporadic, home-centred nature of the work makes it more difficult and yet also more possible for women with child care responsibilities.

The feeling of marginality is a powerful internalized weapon for keeping people from being active in their own interests, and that feeling is exacerbated among women cultural workers by their economic marginality. Recent figures show that women get 28 percent of Canada Council writing grants and 33 percent of theatre grants. From 1978 to 1981 only 29 percent of Canadian writers in residence at universities were women. Women account for 28 percent of publication space in Canadian literary magazines and 7 percent of the poems published in anthologies.[5]

The battle has yet to begin. Katherine Anne Porter, speaking on why it took her twenty years to write *Ship of Fools* when she could have done it in two, said she was "trying to get to that table, to that typewriter, away from my jobs of teaching and trooping this country and of keeping house."[6] Before a woman writes a play, a poem, or a book, or paints a picture or translates a novel, she must contend with a problem that few men face: the double day of labour. And that problem is as inextricably intertwined with her ability to organize as it is with her ability to create.

Writers and artists function as independent producers who must compete with each other in a tight economy to market their work. We've grown up with certain basic myths that obscure the collective nature of our lot as creative workers, and hence also of the potential for collective action. The main myth for a cultural worker is that you might Make It! The myth features the starving artist (or writer) in his (never her) Paris garret, sacrificing money and family in order to create. Finally, after much suffering and dues paying, there springs the Great Canadian Novel (or painting, or play or poem or article) for which one gets a $50 thousand paperback contract, serialization and a movie sale, and fame forever. Although cultural workers no longer move to Paris to find their garrets, the myth is very much alive, and it is an important impediment to organizing cultural workers. Anyone whose energy is fuelled by dreams of individual fame and fortune is reluctant to function collectively.

Another important myth that keeps freelancers from forming real unions is the myth of Professionalism. Freelance cultural workers are said to be professionals, who have a professional commitment to their work, a dedication that supercedes financial gain. Thus they are supposed to care more about the work than about money, and collective bargaining for better wages would be seen as lowly and unprofessional. The myth has a germ of truth: most of us *are* university educated and have middle-class choices about where and how to work. Our work lives are privileged compared to people who are trapped in repetitive assembly-line jobs. There aren't any bosses or foremen standing over us, and we control our own schedules. We enjoy the luxury of making something from start to finish and knowing it's ours: an article, a painting, a book.

There has always been a relationship of power between the people who produced culture and the people who paid for it. If a painter could not attract a wealthy patron and do work that pleased the patron, then woe betide the painter, for no matter how "good" a painter he was, there would be no bread on the table. The system of cultural patronage is now corporate and governmental but the relationships still exist.

Freelancers appear to be in the same social class as their editors (or gallery or theatre directors). A working relationship between, for example, a writer and an editor, does not have the worker / boss or worker/foreman appearance of more conventional working relationships: it looks like a producer / client relationship, one between equals. But that appearance is deceiving when the client has the power to determine the nature of the product and the producer has almost none.

In this way it is obvious that consciousness plays a major role in freelancers' approach to organizing and to union activity. But the importance of consciousness extends beyond the bounds of how these people see or do not see themselves as workers; for they are in the business of producing ideas, which are the stuff of which consciousness is made.

Cultural workers are different from other workers: as the producers of ideas, they are the gatekeepers of society's image of itself. In producing the words and pictures that describe the world to people, they are creating and re-creating ideology. According to Stuart Hall, a sociologist at England's Open University, ideology is

> any of the frameworks which groups of people use in order to understand or define for themselves what's going on. We look out on the world: we think we know what we know. But actually, of course, we are perceiving the events within a particular framework. That framework has limits; there are certain things about it we don't see, certain kinds of questions we don't ask ... certain frameworks become dominant at a certain period.[7]

The dominant ideology in this period and place is pro-capitalist, anti-trade union. Successful artists and writers have passed through a series of invisible gates that open into the world of the dominant ideology. Whether they are aware of it or not, they produce what they have been socialized to produce after years of lengthy training (both formal and informal). They are prevented from producing oppositional culture (work that takes a clear position against the dominant ideology), as much by their own conditioning as by the dictates of their bosses.

One of the ways the dominant ideology is reproduced in cultural workers is through a code of professional ethics. The code is largely unwritten but everyone is taught to internalize it as she or he rises through the ranks. One of its articles of faith is that taking action — such as struggling as a worker against management — is an inappropriate role for a writer or artist. As truth tellers who reveal society to itself, writers must be "objective" observers of events; artists must hover over society, unpolluted by its politics. To participate by fighting for themselves or anyone else is to sacrifice the essential distance from events that gives them their perspective. In this way writers and artists are forced to reproduce and strengthen existing values, not to challenge them.

As individuals it is almost impossible for us to rebel against the strictures that decide what we can and cannot write or speak or depict, if we want to be published or shown. And this is a major political reason for organizing. Collectively, it *is* possible to make inroads on the dominant ideology and to begin to change it. During the 1970s, printers in England refused to print racist cartoons in newspapers, and major newspapers were published with blanked-out areas. In South America, journalists insisted on large areas of newspapers being left blank where the censors had left their mark. In Canada, well-known writers and journalists added their names to a list of feminist, gay and lesbian activists in support of the *Body Politic* in a full-page advertisement in *The Globe and Mail*.

The work area organizations of writers and artists that we have been considering have tended to put more emphasis on owning their ideas, through individual copyright,[8] than on controlling their ideas, through collective political action. Nevertheless, there have been serious attempts by artists and writers who want to challenge the status quo to put the strength of their numbers to political use. The now defunct Cultural Workers' Alliance (CWA) was an attempt to do just that.

Unlike the groups discussed so far, the CWA was organized by socialist artists, writers and musicians, across workplace lines. At its founding conference in Peterborough in May 1980, the CWA adopted the following objectives: to foster solidarity and cooperation among cultural workers; to support the development of culture produced by groups excluded from or discriminated against by the dominant socio-economic and cultural order; to oppose the increasing monopolization of the culture and communication industries; to oppose racist, sexist and other reactionary cultural expression; and to support freedom from censorship.

In contrast to the experience in the work-related organizations, feminists "came out" and played a strong role in CWA. At its founding meeting a feminist caucus called for a more democratic structure, which was adopted by the meeting. Robin Endres explained later:

> ... we felt that we had evolved ways of thinking, styles of work and organizational forms in the women's movement which could be used and adapted to the benefit of the group as a whole.[9]

CWA locals were set up in Halifax, Peterborough, Montreal and Toronto. In Halifax, a group of radicals at the prestigious Nova Scotia College of Art and Design urged students to take up the region's historical and social problems and make links with existing left organizations and unions. This involved opposition to a Michelin plant that was opening up with the provincial government's (illegal) assurance that the workers could not unionize, investigation of Nova Scotia's labour history, participation in an anti-Ku Klux Klan group and the recognition of the function of the art college as a showpiece for the province. The group also worked to improve the position of clerical workers and models at the school, most of whom were women, and to encourage student participation in hiring and firing (one of the concerns was to hire more women to the school's studio division). In Montreal, CWA activists picketed the Beaux Arts performance of *Balconville* in solidarity with locked-out support staff, members of Le Syndicat des placeurs et ouvreuses (Ushers and Ticket Takers Union). In Toronto, central issues were questions of censorship, racism, public funding of the arts and the economic status of cultural workers. Both Toronto and Montreal also had active feminist groups within their locals.

In spite of these forceful initiatives, the CWA dissolved a year later. The group had generated a lot of needed interaction between socialists in the cultural community. But the lack of central organization (for example, someone who heard about CWA and wanted to form a Halifax branch did not know where to apply) and clear priorities, combined with the problem of diverse political ideologies, all worked against it. Another problem was one of trying to bring together an extremely fragmented community of people from different work areas. CWA had no funding and no people who could afford to work full time to keep it going. There were no strong contacts with labour unions, which might have been able to support it.

A more specific and perhaps for that reason more successful organizational venture is the Toronto Women's Cultural Building, which was formed in early 1982 to consider setting up a women's cultural centre. After some discussion, it seemed wiser and more practical to put the group's enthusiasm and commitment into expanding feminist culture all over the city – and the "building" in their name became a verb.

The Women's Cultural Building is a collective of about thirty women, all feminists. They are artists, video artists, writers, theatre people and arts administrators, some of whom were involved in the CWA. In just over a year they captured the imagination of the Toronto feminist, art and left communities. On International Women's Day in 1983, the WCB launched a series of poetry readings, video, performance art, dance and visual art exhibitions with a feminist extravaganza called the Five Minute Feminist Cabaret. An evening of skits, songs and dance, written, produced and performed by women is one thing: under the direction of the WCB the event transformed the stuff of feminist politics into art and entertainment. For women long used to noting the oppressive and numbing effects of the dominant ideology, the Five Minute Feminist Cabaret and the weeks of feminist cultural events that followed it, showed clearly how successful feminists can be in transcending the dominant ideology. In focusing on bringing out the *culture* rather than on the *conditions* of cultural workers, the WCB is not itself a body that aims to organize women in the arts. But it encourages and supports feminist culture and it is using the political potential of culture to affect people.

We can look to Quebec to see another successful organizational form. In English Canada, there are very few progressive collective cultural organizations (like the Development Education Centre, the Women's Press, Broadside or Press Gang), but in Quebec, there are hundreds of co-ops that organize cultural workers. They function as anti-establishment collectives designed to give artists and writers both the support they need to create and access to an audience. The sculptor's association provides equipment that individuals could not afford; the theatre collectives produce progressive plays; publishing collectives publish indigenous poetry and fiction; feminist art collectives support and show feminist art; Montreal has a feminist theatre building and a feminist collectively run magazine, *La Vie en Rose*. Although these collectives run largely on volunteer labour and do not therefore change people's paid working lives, they are important. They give cultural workers the experience of working together, the support to continue and the basis from which to challenge the dominant ideology.

In Quebec there have been three attempts to organize militant, political umbrella organizations of workers in the area of culture. The first two, in 1972 and 1977, fell apart through political splintering and sectarian squabbles, but the third, the Front des travailleurs et travailleuses culturelles (FTC) began in 1981 and is still strong. Its aims are to fight for Quebec content in big institutional cultural expenditures, for democratic control of the culture industry, for a minimum wage for cultural workers, for their job security and health and other benefits. The majority of groups forming the FTC are not trade unions but these cultural collectives that are so common in Quebec. Although the FTC shares with the CWA some of the inevitable problems of organizing outside of the workplace, it demonstrates the progressive possibilities for cultural workers.

A recent development in Toronto is the Labour Arts and Media Working Group, a committee made up of trade unionists and people from the arts community whose aim is to "encourage communication and cooperation ... on economic, political and cultural issues of common interest." So far this has involved discussion of how trade unions and artists, to some extent both outsiders in this society, can benefit each other. For example, progressive artists and writers could use union-made materials and printing facilities in their work. Trade unions could ask artists to design their leaflets, posters, stickers and buttons, and progressive writers and editors to help produce their written material. Unions are a large potential audience for the work of playwrights and performance artists. And these art works and performances in turn are of value to unionists because they reflect people's daily experiences at work and elsewhere.

There are many ways for women who work in the cultural area to put forward their demands for better wages and working conditions and for recognition of their particular needs as women. Collective bargaining, though it is difficult to achieve through the existing workplace organizations, is still a possibility and requires encouraging people working in the arts to recognize the conditions they share with other workers. At the same time, it is important to understand that the traditionally individual nature of producing art and the differences between producing art and producing other consumer goods — the fact that cultural workers produce ideology — means workers in this area have interests different from other workers.

The vision expressed by the Women's Cultural Building illustrates the political potential of collective cultural production. It is no accident that this is a feminist organization: progressive cultural workers can be inspired by this group to find their common ground in political struggles. It is clear that freelancers' organizations cannot be traditional trade unions, but nonetheless both the possibility and the necessity exist for them to continue organizing both in separate work areas and across work area boundaries.

NOTES

We would like to thank Linda Briskin for her detailed and insightful comments on earlier drafts of this article. Larry Lyons, Rosemary Donegan and Lynda Yanz also provided valuable comments.

1 There have always been a disproportionate number of women in publishing, except of course at the level of management, where they are still underrepresented. This may have been in the first instance a result of the large numbers of women with degrees in the humanities who needed work, who were "over-educated" for jobs as secretaries and clerks, and who were willing to accept low wages for more "meaningful" work. And because women have dominated the field for some time, it continues to be low paid, which means women continue to predominate in the area. In this way publishing is a typical female job ghetto.

2 We use the term "cultural worker" in a very broad sense, and with some reservations. We intend it to indicate the commonalities between people who work in the area of culture and those who work in other areas, like steelworkers and garment workers. But, as we point out, there are many differences between people who work freelance in the arts and other workers. This becomes clear when we realize that both the printers who

work in a print shop and the writers whose books they print are cultural workers according to this definition. Some of the people we call "cultural workers" may be more properly termed "cultural producers" because they have more than the usual degree of control over their working conditions and their product and come close to the traditional concept of the independent artist. As we note, however, these people are in the minority.

3 Brian R. Harrison, *Canadian Freelance Writers: Characteristics and Issues* (Ottawa: Minister of Supply and Services, 1982).

4 *Ibid.*

5 Sharon Nelson, *Women in Canadian Writing* (Ottawa: Advisory Council on the Status of Women, 1982). See also Rina Fraticelli's excellent study, "The Invisibility Factor: Status of Women in Canadian Theatre," *Fuse,* Vol. 6, No. 3 (Sept. 1982), pp. 112-124.

6 Katherine Anne Porter, quoted in *Silences,* by Tillie Olson (New York: Dell, 1978), p. 13.

7 Stuart Hall in an interview in Part I of the four-part CBC radio *Ideas* series, "The Politics of Information," broadcast March 1982.

8 Artists and writers have traditionally defended the ownership of their ideas and maintained their professional independence through copyright. Copyright in fact seems to be the basis for the type of work area organization we've been looking at. See Raymond Williams, *Culture* (Glasgow: Fontana, 1981), p. 62 for a discussion of this point.

   However poorly writers and poets are paid for their work, they nevertheless "own" it. The Writers' Union and the League of Poets have insisted on their members retaining the copyright of the books they publish, so that nowadays it is unusual for a publisher or someone other than the author to hold the copyright. These groups have been pushing with less success to expand the boundaries of this ownership through a payment to authors for books borrowed from public libraries and for photocopying of their work. Copyright was the impetus for CAR, which was founded when an outraged Jack Chambers discovered the National Gallery planned to market slides of artists' works without asking permission or offering any royalty (usually a percentage of the retail price of each piece sold). Copyright is also becoming an issue for translators, and is aiding a transition from a concept of them as skilled workers to one as creative artists — and it will undoubtedly arise as an issue for editors. Already, editors have voiced their concern over lack of recognition, and are talking, if not about actual copyright of their work, at least of being named as editor on the copyright page of a book.

9 Robin Endres, *Spleen: The Central Organ of the* CWA, Vol. 1, No. 1 (Dec. 1980).

SEVEN CULTURAL WORK AREA ORGANIZATIONS

Organization	Founded	Total Members	No. & % of Women Members	No. & % of Men Members	Percent of Women in Leadership	Annual Dues	% Self Funded	% Government Funded	Collective Bargaining	Sources of Income from Work Area	Average Earnings From Work
League of Poets	1967	240	91 38%	149 62%	25	$100	15-20	75-80	no	royalties, advances (rare), reading tours,	$2,500
CAR	1968	500-600	50%	50%	50	$ 40	20-30	70-80	yes	sales, commissions, exhibition fees, rentals, reproductions	$4,500
TWUC	1973	364	163 45%	201 55%	41	$150	49	51	no	royalties, advances, reading tours	median $7,000
ATL/LTA	1975	57	24 42%	33 58%	20	min. $25 max. $60	50	50	no	contract per book (based on Canada Council rates of $.08 a word)	?(negligible)
Guild of Playwrights	1976	95	25 26%	70 74%	50	min. $25 max. $150	12	88	yes	% of box office receipts of plays, commissions	$2,200
PWAC	1976	200	110 55%	90 45%	80	$115	30	70	yes	per article contract (based on No. of words)	$13,480
FEAC	1979	60	46 77%	14 23%	78	$ 75	100	0	no	contract per book (normally based on hourly rate)	$12,000
Total			48%	52%	49%						

IV INSIDE UNIONS

WOMEN'S CHALLENGE TO ORGANIZED LABOUR

Linda Briskin

The union movement is at a critical point in its history, facing increasingly systematic attacks from governments and employers. At the same time, unprecedented numbers of women are becoming active in unions. The inability of the labour movement to effectively respond to the attacks and to the challenge of women activists has highlighted the limitations of its policies and practices. This article will examine these limitations and situate the difficulties women experience in making unions responsive to their concerns within this larger framework. It will also explore the unique contribution of women activists to the process of overcoming these limitations and transforming unions into more effective vehicles for social change.

Women make up over forty percent of the work force yet they continue to confront discrimination in their wages, working conditions and choice of jobs. At the same time, the economic situation of the family is changing: most families depend on two incomes and an increasing number of women are heads of households. Changing family and work patterns confront women with the growing importance of their role as workers. In a situation where women can no longer afford to ignore discrimination in the work force, they begin to see unions as a necessity.

Women who are not organized in unions are turning to them to solve workplace concerns. In Ontario alone, there have been a growing number of struggles for first contracts: at Fleck Manufacturing, at Blue Cross, at Radio Shack and at Mini-Skools. Women workers already in unions are faced with their collective agreements' inadequate treatment of such issues as maternity leave, sexual harassment, equal pay, job classification and the introduction of new technology. In numbers greater than ever before, these women are turning to their unions.

The experience of union activity — on the picket line, in the workplace and inside the union — changes the way that women workers see their problems. Fighting for a decent salary forces them to confront the fact that they earn, on average, forty percent less than men. This focuses women's attention on those jobs, mostly unionized, that pay better wages but are traditionally defined as men's jobs. Women's struggle for workplace gains thus becomes a struggle for the rights of women as workers. This transformation in consciousness is facilitated by a strong women's movement outside the unions that has heightened social awareness of the problems women face.

One of the great disappointments for many women who become union activists is the discovery that the structure and attitudes of unions seem no different from those of other institutions where women have faced discrimination. Like most institutions in our society, unions are dominated and controlled by men who are not necessarily receptive to women's concerns. In addition, the structures of unions are not set up to integrate women or to deal with their particular problems. In the past, women have often despaired of changing unions and have therefore rejected them as a vehicle to improve their situation.

Regardless of their limitations, however, unions are one of the key avenues to workplace improvements. Legislative change has historically come as a response to a mass public movement, and the unions with their large and identifiable membership and access to resources of staff, money and publications, have the potential to organize such mass pressure. Therefore, rather than rejecting unions, many women unionists are trying to change the current structures and policies of the union movement and are challenging it to fulfill its mandate, which is to protect and defend the interests of workers – women and men.

Women are becoming active in unions at a time when the union movement is facing one of the most serious crises in its history. The economic recession has meant widespread layoffs and reductions in union membership, especially in the industrial unions. For example, the United Auto Workers' membership fell from 130,000 in 1980 to 98,000 in 1983.[1] Governments are instituting wage controls, suspending negotiating rights and placing other limits on free collective bargaining. Employees are hiring management consultants to sabotage the organization of unions as well as supporting the Right-to-Work movement. Ed Finn, public relations officer for the Canadian Union of Public Employees, says about the Right-to-Work movement: "Not content to control Canadian workers' wages and limit or abolish their rights to bargain and to strike, right wing employers are now pressing governments to enact legislation to outlaw 'union shop' and even Rand formula clauses in collective agreements.... Such laws are designed for one purpose – to discourage and destroy unions." If enacted, these laws would "enable employers to hire non-union and anti-union workers [in unionized workplaces] and gradually reduce the number of union members. Soon employers would be able to break all strikes and promote successful decertification bids."[2]

Employers' organizations, like the Canadian Construction Association and some provincial governments, such as the British Columbia Socreds and the Alberta and Saskatchewan Conservatives, have expressed interest in this approach to labour relations that has its roots in the southern United States.

Not only are unions under attack, but the composition of union membership is changing. Many of the jobs that have opened up in the last two decades in the service sector and in government civil services have been filled by women. As union organization has expanded in these sectors, the number of women unionists and the size of the non-industrial unions have increased.

The profile of public sector and service workers, and of women workers in general, has been accentuated by government and employer attacks, many of which have been aimed directly at these groups. At the same time, the unions' weak response to these attacks has exposed two key areas of concern: the role of unions and membership apathy.

One important problem in relationship to the role of unions centres around defining what constitutes a legitimate union issue. This question reemerges yearly at union conventions whenever international questions, disarmament resolutions and women's issues come to the floor. Two questions are posed: should the union movement have policies on these issues? and further, should it develop a strategy to deal with them?

The union movement has traditionally seen its role as dealing with "workplace" issues. However, there is a growing awareness that the work experience cannot be neatly compartmentalized and separated from the non-work experience of politics, family and leisure. Perhaps the day care issue most clearly demonstrates the arbitrary nature of this separation. Day care appears to be a private family issue. The traditional expectation that women are responsible for child care means that without adequate day care women find it difficult to work full time (even though they and their families depend on their income). But the prohibitive cost of quality day care means that many women, given their low wages, cannot afford it. At the same time, day care workers, most of whom are women, are scarcely earning the minimum wage. Day care is a workplace issue, a family issue, an issue of women's rights and most certainly a union issue. This may seem obvious but it was not recognized by the labour movement until 1980, when the Ontario Federation of Labour passed a trend-setting policy on day care, and this only after a long, hard battle on the part of women activists.[3]

Although we have made some gains in broadening the perimeters of union concern, the debate about what is a union issue continues. For example, the abortion issue is currently being discussed in Ontario unions. It will be a long process to persuade the majority of unionists that for women, control over our bodies is relevant to our workplace rights.

Once a union has established a policy on an issue, the next step is determining how to use the policy to shift public attitudes, to get legislated change or to make workplace gains. There are two possible routes: contract negotiations and/or the political process, neither of which is presently used by unions to its full potential.

When a union passes a policy at its convention, on day care for example, it often has no way of ensuring that this will be an issue at the bargaining table (and if it is, that it won't be traded away). In most unions, the policy-setting process and the establishment of bargaining demands are quite separate — bridging them depends on an effective educational process.

Using the political process to realize a policy may involve electing a new government, trying to influence the current government through conventional lobbying techniques or developing a campaign through the widespread mobilization of the union membership (and allies in the community) to change attitudes and to publically pressure the government. But too often unions rely on a pseudo-diplomatic process (where the "head men" from both sides [government and union] meet to "resolve" the issue), or on the NDP, the party with whom the trade union movement has official links. However, the NDP seems to be losing support federally and, with the exception of Manitoba, it is not in power in the provinces. In those provinces where the NDP has been in power they have seldom actively defended the rights of workers and unions and in some instances have treated them badly.

There is no evidence that women or working people have any champions in government. Unions are left to represent the interests of working people, not just at the bargaining table but in the political arena. A union strategy successful at representing the interests of the majority will not depend primarily on lobbying or any form of tripartism (joint government, business and union committees). Rather the union movement must organize the vast resources of its membership to pose a militant challenge to governments in the public arena, to employers at the bargaining table and to the NDP.

However, an underlying and perhaps more serious question is posed by a discussion of the role of unions: if the workplace is the legitimate concern of the unions, why have unions abdicated their responsibility for confronting the most fundamental of workplace issues — who controls the work process, who owns what is produced and how is what is produced distributed?

Unions have rarely seen their role as challenging the essential nature of capitalist society — the fundamental inequities of power and wealth, the private ownership of property, the class structure or even management prerogative. This perspective has its roots in the traditions of labour organizing in the United States and in Britain, which have strongly influenced the development of Canadian unionism.

In the early part of this century, the largest union organization in the U.S. was the American Federation of Labour (AFL), a federation of craft unions under the leadership of Samuel Gompers. The basic premise of the AFL was that in exchange for the employer accepting the union's right to exist and agreeing to bargain over wages and benefits, the unions would not contest the employer's right to manage. This was an implicit acceptance that the organization of work and the control of both products and profits were the right of the employer. This narrow definition of the concerns of the union came to be known as "business unionism."

There have been periods of intense struggle against this conception of unionism. During the upheavals surrounding World War 1 and the Russian Revolution, the International Workers of the World (IWW) and a similar organization in Canada, the One Big Union (OBU) argued that unions should challenge the fundamental relationship between workers and employers. During the Depression and in the 1930s and 1940s there was an upsurge of militant unionism with the organization of the Congress of Industrial Organizations (CIO) and the building of the large industrial unions. By the 1950s, however, in both Canada and the u.s., business unionism had become institutionalized, and only now, partially through the efforts of women activists, are these parameters being challenged.

The second serious problem for the union movement is the general apathy of its membership, in spite of the numbers of militants and the newly activated groups of women in the unions. A large part of the explanation for this apathy must be sought in the social organization of capitalism, which reinforces the powerlessness of the majority through the organization of work and through the powerful ideology of individualism. However, the way unions are structured contributes to this apathy, and this too has its roots in the past.

During the 1950s, a period of relative economic prosperity and industrial peace, union activity focused almost entirely on improving wages and fringe benefits. This was a result of both the limited conception of the role of the union – derived from business unionism – and the economic climate. During a time of economic growth, it was possible to negotiate fairly good wage settlements without having to resort to militant action. Increasingly there was an outright rejection of confrontational methods of negotiation such as wildcat strikes, walkouts and sitdowns. The process of bargaining came to be identified with face-to-face discussions between a few union leaders and management, usually in secrecy. Although it might make sense for unions to try to negotiate peacefully and in a spirit of compromise with employers, this form of closed-door negotiation all but eliminated the active participation of the membership. Yet union members appeared to be the winners as they watched their wages rise and their benefit packages improve. This lent credibility to business unionism, and to this method of bargaining as an effective approach to industrial relations.

But this organization of the bargaining process created a service mentality. The leadership was elected to service the membership; the only significant responsibility of the membership was to elect the leadership and occasionally ratify its decisions. Dependence on the leadership to act in their best interests resulted in a passive, disinterested attitude on the part of the rank and file. Union memberships lost faith in their own ability to act collectively to effect change in the workplace, a direction that was exacerbated by the times. Employers were able to give workers enough (usually money) to convince them that struggle was not important, and the ideology of individualism labelled collective action as "communist."

Rather than resisting this process of demobilization, the leadership of unions came to feel that they knew what was in the best interests of the memberships and that they had the right to make all the significant decisions. They replaced the collective strength of the membership with their own ability to negotiate with the government or the employer. In turning away from the collective power of the membership to act in their own interests, union leaders cut themselves off from their most powerful bargaining tool and were left to operate in a vacuum.

The internal organizational structures of unions mirrored these developments: centralized, with final control vested in the top leadership and bureaucratic, with hierarchies of decision making and reams of red tape. As unions became wealthier and larger, the leaderships developed a vested personal interest in maintaining political control of their unions and were less able to accurately assess the needs of their membership.

This process did not occur without some resistance. Along with the tendency to centralize the organization came pressure from union activists against it. The result is a group of active militants who want decentralization of power and increased democracy, a largely apathetic membership who have conservatized at least partially as a result of enforced passivity, and a leadership with an interest in maintaining the status quo.

The rigidifying of union structures has resulted in a recurring debate about democracy that is inherently linked to the problems of membership apathy and to the split between membership and leadership. At all levels — local, regional, provincial, federal — unions are organized as representative democracies, modelled on the parliamentary system. This means that a few representatives are elected by a large group of people to represent their interests for a set term. This may seem fair (and practical) yet there are two underlying weaknesses. First, mechanisms for accountability during the term of office of those elected are rarely established. For example, leaders may pay lip service to union women during an election campaign, but there is no assurance that any of the promised action will be taken.

The second problem with representative democracy is that the majority participates in decision making only indirectly, through the election process. Thus the lack of accountability undermines the purpose of the election process and the lack of significant input into decision making produces first a sense of powerlessness and ultimately apathy.

The electing of representatives is not enshrined in union structures. A debate on this issue has surfaced with regards to the organization of the Canadian Labour Congress (CLC) and union federation women's committees. At present, members of these committees are appointed by the union leadership, with the result that these committees are less responsive to the women in the union than to the leadership who appointed them. As a result, the direction of the women's committees, even with the best intentions of the women appointed to them, have often reflected the problems in the unions as a whole. And in most cases where a women's committee *has* managed to organize a useful program or develop a progressive policy, it has been less a result of it being able to mobilize women than of learning to successfully manipulate the structures.

This example highlights two issues. Beyond the obvious point that representatives should be elected, unions should be creating structures that facilitate the participation of large numbers in an ongoing way. Participatory democracy, which depends on decentralized decision making and control, mobilization of the membership and leadership accountability, would promote enthusiasm for and active commitment to the union. And if the majority were to collectively shape union policy, their awareness of their power to affect society as a whole and their willingness to act to this end would be strengthened.

Fundamentally the limitations of unions are connected not only to their own history but to the fact that they are a part of and a product of the society we live in — a capitalist society. Organizational and political developments inside the unions have paralleled those in other institutions: the government, the educational system and big business. In all capitalist institutions, there has been increasing centralization, bureaucratization and specialization. But given their mandate to defend the interests of workers, it is unfortunate that unions have so willingly accepted the constraints of business unionism and the status of being one of many capitalist institutions. It is not surprising that governments and employers support this approach to unionism, which rests on "peaceful" cooperation between business, labour and government as if each were an equal player and as if the interests of all three groups were the same.

Thus unions themselves serve to demobilize and regulate the anger of workers and to maintain the status quo, in part through the use of structures that increase apathy, in part by accepting "rules" set up by governments, often in conjunction with employers. For example, in many provinces labour legislation prevents strikes during the life of the contract, denies government workers the right to strike and provides a bureaucratic process of mediation and conciliation that disallows strikes for lengthy periods, even when contracts have expired.

In the 1980s the union movement is faced with an enormous dilemma. The unions are no longer able to ensure decent wage increases when contracts duly and legally signed with government workers are broken through the imposition of wage control legislation and salary rollbacks, when working conditions and wages are declining relative to the cost of living, when the numbers of unionized workers are decreasing because of layoffs and even the government is admitting that full employment is impossible; when employers demand concessions from workers but simultaneously spend thousands of dollars sabotaging unions and supporting right-wing groups like the Right To Work. The traditional policies and practice of the unions are no longer tenable and the very survival of the union movement is at stake.

Union leaderships are finding it necessary to mobilize their memberships in defence of unionism. Mostly they are unsuccessful. Leaders are faced with union structures that militate against rank and file mobilization and with memberships disinterested or even hostile to the union. Union leaders have publically perpetrated and have come to believe the illusion that the membership is on standby – like a military regiment – ready to act when the leaders tell them to. The leaderships are now surprised and disheartened to find that this is not the case. They are also faced with union militants, many of whom have a long-standing critique of the organization of unions who are pressuring them to act.

What is the leaderships' response to the economic collapse, to attacks from government and employers, to declining memberships and pressure from activists? In 1983, the Canadian Labour Congress (CLC) launched the Economic Recovery Alternative (ERA) program, outlining steps the government should take to improve the economic situation, including major public investment in housing, transit systems and reforestation; personal income tax cuts; extension of unemployment insurance benefits for "exhaustees"; a "made in Canada" interest rate policy; and the scrapping of the six and five program. Although this does not go far enough, and its lack of explicit attention to the concerns of women workers is an insult, the more serious problem is the absence of a strategy for winning these demands.

Denis McDermott, president of the CLC, has promoted the ERA by saying, "The problem is economic; the solution is "political." Unfortunately, he explains that what he means by "political" is that workers should vote for the NDP. What McDermott is really telling workers, with his exhortation to vote for the NDP, is that workers themselves can do nothing.

This narrow conception of the political process relegates all political control to political parties and limits workers' participation to casting a ballot – implying that all that is needed is a change in leadership. This strategy has often backfired inside the union movement when militants were elected to top positions, only to find themselves coopted by the structures of the unions, with no organized or mobilizable base of support. Not even a progressive leadership can substitute itself for the organization of the membership.

The first part of this article situated unions within the larger framework of capitalist society and attempted to expose the limitations that arise as a result. This explanation dispels any illusions that transforming unions to meet the needs of women workers will be easy. In their struggle to make unions responsive to their concerns, women activists face a formidable task: legitimizing women's issues as union issues, broadening the conception of what is acceptable strategy for the union movement and challenging an undemocratic bureaucratic structure that reproduces membership apathy and powerlessness.

Women activists face two kinds of resistance in the union movement. One is resistance to us as women, a reflection of the patriarchal norms and values implicit in part of every institution in capitalist society. We expect this kind of resistance. The other form of resistance is not a particular resistance to us as women. It is a resistance to our militancy: to our challenge to the leadership, to our demand that the union movement take up issues outside the narrow framework of business unionism and that it operate with more democratic and accountable structures. Simply electing women, even if they have rank and file and feminist politics, will not solve the larger problems facing women unionists and the union movement.

Women activists have a unique perspective on the role of unions, as direct victims of the lack of democracy and accountability in governments, of male-dominated education and corporate institutions and of discrimination in the workplace. Out of our clearly felt needs arise our demands on the union movement to act. Women's experience of discrimination lays the basis for a committed rejection of the functioning of capitalist institutions, of which the union is one.

Many women activists have also been strongly influenced by the women's liberation movement. Not only does the women's movement provide an analysis of women's experience in the work force, but because the women's movement is situated outside of any large social institutions (the government, the unions, the schools) and outside of access to any identifiable source of power in the conventional sense, it has developed methods of grass roots organizing and a new conception of politics, democracy and organization that have been taken up by union women and transformed to meet the needs of their struggle.

The ideas, analysis and forms of organizing of the women's movement have influenced the movement of union women, but so have the successes of union women changed the attitude of the women's movement towards unions. Parts of the women's movement have turned to the union movement to make alliances in the struggle for women's liberation. Thus the union movement has been pressured both from within by union women and from without by the women's movement to take up issues of concern to women in a serious way. These alliances between trade union women and the women's movement have built the strength of both (though not without some problems) and point out the potential of coalition politics for the union movement as a whole.

In bringing forward such issues as day care, sexual harassment and abortion, union women have challenged traditional conceptions of what constitutes a union issue. Unions are now coming forward with broad policies outlining needed legislative and political change. These policy discussions have also generated intensive debate inside the union movement on women's issues, and usually result in winning the support of wider and wider layers of union members. Although passing these policies and having unions take public positions on women's issues is critical, it is not enough. Women's ability to make long-term gains in the workplace will depend not only on good union policies and education but also on the mobilization of large numbers of women and men to win them. Women activists have understood that the successful mobilization of large numbers depends in part upon the development of small group networks. So on the one hand, women unionists have pushed for and succeeded in getting the unions to endorse and partici- pate in International Women's Day activities; on the other hand, women have created new union structures in the form of women's committees and caucuses that have tried to avoid the pitfalls of tradi- tional union structures, which tend to reinforce apathy. In their emphasis on participatory decision making, flexible organization of leadership tasks and collective support, training and education, women's committees have been remarkably successful in influencing the direction of union conventions. In fact, the organization and politicization of union women will make it increasingly difficult for union leaders to sell out women's issues. The success of union women has rested on the belief that women must act in their own interests — and that means going on the offensive against the government, against the employer and, if need be, against the union establishment itself.

It is a victory when we convince the leadership to take up women's issues, when we organize a women's committee, when we speak at conventions, when we win protection against sexual harassment or technological change in our contracts. Each step broadens the periph- ery of interested and committed women, each step changes the attitudes of some brothers in the union, each step publically persuades women that unions have something to offer them.

In the last ten years, women's activity in unions has had a tremen- dous impact: policies have been passed, education programs under- taken, progressive demands for women have been brought to the bar- gaining table. But in spite of a few important breakthroughs — such as the Canadian Union of Postal Workers' success at negotiating paid maternity leave following a cross-country strike — the situation that women face in the work force has not improved significantly.

As women activists we recognize the potential of using unions to address women's concerns. Although we are, in this sense, pro-union, we do not idealize the current structures and policies of the union movement. We are critical of the continued dependence of the union movement on the theory and practice of business unionism and on a bureaucratic, highly centralized male-dominated structure. We know that to make significant gains for women in the workplace unions must be restructured.

We need a fighting union movement that will be a vehicle for social change because the discrimination that women face is deeply rooted, not only in the workplace but in the organization of the family. Whether or not our vision of new directions will be taken up will depend on the continued activity and leadership of women unionists, the mobilization of large numbers in a public and political way and the rejection of the limited perspective of business unionism.

NOTES

This article owes a great deal to many discussions with Debbie Field. I would also like to thank Sue Colley, Jane Springer and Lynda Yanz for their criticisms and their support.

1 Labour Canada, *Directory of Labour Organizations in Canada* (Ottawa: Minister of Supply and Services, 1980).

2 Ed Finn, "The Right to Work Threat," CUPE: *The Facts*, Vol. 5, No. 3 (April 1983), pp. 13-15.

3 See Susan Colley's article, "Free Universal Day Care: The OFL Takes a Stand" in this book.

4 *The Economic Recovery Alternative*, National Economic Conference, Canadian Labour Congress, March 1983.

WORKING, MOTHERING AND MILITANCY: WOMEN IN THE CNTU

Nancy Guberman

In the Confederation of National Trade Unions, one of the three major union federations in Quebec, women account for only 18% of the CNTU's Conseil confédéral, the highest body to meet between bi-annual conventions. At the 1982 convention no women were elected to the national executive. And yet, 44% of the CNTU's 225,000 members are women.

What do these figures tell us about women's place in the trade union movement — in the CNTU and elsewhere? Why is it that women are so underrepresented in decision-making bodies of a movement that is supposed to defend their interests as workers and as women? The Comité de la condition féminine (women's committee) of the CNTU has recently begun work not only to answer these questions but to initiate the struggles necessary to overcome the barriers that keep women out of the movement and its power structures.

THE CNTU AND ITS WOMEN'S COMMITTEE

The CNTU is composed mainly of public sector unions, with 61% of its membership working in the tertiary sector (social affairs, education, transportation and communication, commerce). However, 35.7% of the members are in manufacturing and construction industries and another 3.3% are in mining, fishing and forestry.

The CNTU is generally considered to be one of the most left-wing, militant and democratic federations in Quebec and Canada. Politically, the CNTU is left of the Parti Québécois on both social and national questions. Since the early Seventies its leaders have maintained an official stand calling for Quebec's independence and socialism, denouncing the Quebec and Canadian states, and generally applying a class analysis to Quebec. In 1971 it took an official anti-capitalist stand in its document "Il n'y a plus d'avenir pour le Québec dans le système économique actuel" (There is no future for Quebec in the current economic system).

THE DECISION-MAKING STRUCTURES OF THE CNTU

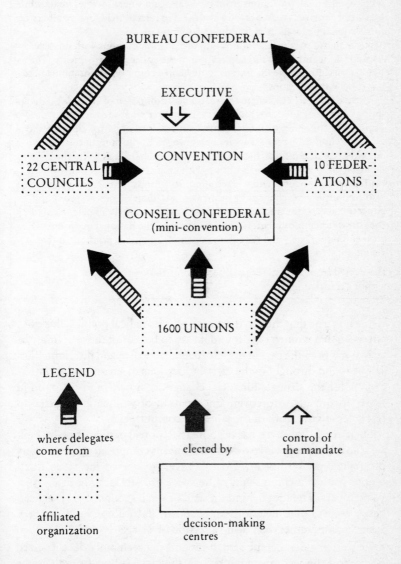

BUREAU CONFEDERAL

EXECUTIVE

22 CENTRAL COUNCILS

CONVENTION

10 FEDER-ATIONS

CONSEIL CONFEDERAL
(mini-convention)

1600 UNIONS

LEGEND

where delegates come from

elected by

control of the mandate

affiliated organization

decision-making centres

The CNTU is composed of *nine sectorial federations,* which bring together all the locals in the same sector. For example, the Federation of Social Affairs is composed of all the unions from the health and social services fields while unions of construction workers or workers in related fields are members of the National Federation of Building and Wood unions.

The main role of the federations is to provide their unions with the services needed for negotiations and application of the collective agreements. The federations also enable the unions to develop a common orientation and to coordinate their actions.

CNTU unions also belong to *central councils* composed of all the local CNTU unions of a particular geographic area, no matter what their federative affiliation. The chief role of the central council is to organize, develop and promote support for the struggles being waged by workers in the region — not only labour conflicts, but social and political battles as well. The central councils often work in collaboration with unions affiliated to other union centres (QFL, CEQ, etc.) and with community groups. The central councils are also responsible for channeling information to their members, providing educational sessions, regionally organizing the national campaigns voted by the CNTU (unemployment, factory shutdowns, the national question, women's issues, etc.) and organizing the non-unionized workers of the region.

(Extracted from *La* CSN: *mouvement et organisation,* 1981, pp. 44-51 — author's translation)

While it is true that the CNTU is unique for its radical politics, this does not mean that women have found it easy to be part of those politics. In fact, as has been the case in the left generally, sexism and discrimination can be found throughout the CNTU. Questions of sexism and its implications for the struggle for social change are nowhere to be found in CNTU documents. Moreover, any mention of women is relegated to references to the work of the women's committee.

Structurally, the CNTU has the potential for real participation by rank and file members — it is based on local unions composed of the workers of a single establishment. Thus the average size of the 1,600 CNTU unions was 148 members in 1979, and 60% of all its locals have less than 50 members. The idea behind this is that small groups of workers can better control their decisions and actions. Each union holds its own accreditation, rather than being a section of a larger body.[1]

Despite the democratic structures and the seemingly decentralized power (see the accompanying boxes), the CNTU suffers from the same problems as the majority of unions. In most cases, union locals are run by a handful of activists. Members of executives have trouble getting themselves replaced at the end of their terms. One generally sees the same faces at educational sessions, conventions and other decision-making meetings. Nowhere in the structures do we see the very real power that the CNTU employees (union organizers, strike advisors, etc.) hold. And, of course, the few hundred people who hold or are close to the reins of power are nearly all men.

Despite its militant stands, democratic structures and the fact that almost half of its membership is women, the CNTU has been slow in picking up women's issues and concerns. In fact, not until 1964 did the CNTU clearly state that it was not opposed to the idea of women working! And even then it took a protectionist stand, calling for special status for women because of their family responsibilities. A women's committee formed in 1953 was dissolved at its own request in 1966, stating that since women had equal rights there were no fundamental differences between male and female members and thus no need for a women's committee.[2] Even so, the period following this dissolution was one in which strikes and union drives involving women mushroomed throughout the province. Women began to play an increasingly militant role in these struggles.

The 1974 convention set up a second women's committee with the mandate to study the working conditions of women at home and in the workplace and to organize a debate throughout the CNTU in preparation for decisions to be taken at the 1976 convention. This was done and in 1976, the document "La lutte des femmes combat de tous les travaillers" (Women's struggles are workers' struggles) was presented to the convention. Thirty-eight resolutions proposed by the committee were adopted by the convention. These recognized first that there is a specific oppression of women and the struggle against this oppression is part of the working-class struggle against capitalism and for socialism. The resolutions also identified three major focuses for action by the CNTU – equal pay for work of equal value, fully paid maternity leave and comprehensive day care services.

Two years later, the committee proposed that the 1978 convention add a fourth major demand calling for the right to free and accessible contraception and abortion. It also called on the CNTU to reinforce its national and regional women's committees by hiring a full-time staff person and secretary to work with the committee. This was important; without the budget needed to hire a staff person and a secretary it would have been difficult for the committee to ensure continuity in its work. And of course, the budget was tangible evidence that the CNTU was beginning to be serious about its commitment to the women's question.

In 1980, the committee reiterated the four demands and the necessity to continue the struggle to attain them. It also proposed that the local CNTU unions begin to analyze their collective agreements to see how clauses were being applied. The intention was to eliminate all discriminatory clauses and at the same time avoid creating further inequality between men and women by not taking into account such things as differing work schedules and parental responsibilities. Local, regional and federation women's committees were called on to play an active role in stimulating debate around these issues.

In 1982, the committee's report to the convention "Les femmes à la CSN n'ont pas les moyens de reculer" (Women at the CNTU cannot afford to back down) focused on a new dimension of women's oppression. It took a closer look at the situation of CNTU women as union militants to show how oppression and discrimination exist within the CNTU itself. (This section of the report will be examined in detail later.) The report also contained recommendations linked to other issues the committee is involved in, including the question of technological change and its effect on workers, the fight against part-time jobs and the necessity to increase efforts to unionize women.

The women's committee, composed of fifteen women – twelve from the rank and file and three from the CNTU staff – does much more than write reports and recommendations for the conventions, however. Its work includes publishing information and organizing study sessions on health issues of concern to women, especially around "retrait préventif" (preventive job reassignments for pregnant women); research projects on women's health in the workplace; helping women and unions to deal with sexual harassment, including preparation of a model clause for collective agreements; participating in a day care coalition; developing an affirmative action campaign within the CNTU; continuing to fight for twenty weeks fully paid maternity leave for all women; supporting the national committee for free abortion on

demand; and organizing International Women's Day activities in collaboration with five other union federations and community and
women's groups.

Because of the gross underrepresentation of women within the CNTU
itself, the women's committee's current priority is to change the conditions of union militancy that stand as obstacles to their participation.
In the spring of 1980 the women's committee sent out an extensive
questionnaire to women who were members of local union executives.
Their aim was to begin documenting the situation of women activists:
who they were, where they worked and what was it that enabled them
to get involved in the union. Two hundred and forty-eight women out
of about one thousand answered.

In addition, questionnaires were answered by 175 women at the
Federation of Social Affairs 1981 annual convention and both men and
women on the CNTU staff. A shorter version was distributed to members of the Conseil confédéral and the Bureau fédéral, the two national
decision-making bodies that meet between conventions.

The women's committee did not expect to uncover much that it did
not already know about the concrete obstacles to women's militancy –
children, husbands, housework, meeting times and so on, but they felt
a "scientific" study would be more convincing to the men of the CNTU
than the "experimental" knowledge of the committee. In fact, the
committee learned a lot. Besides documenting what they already
knew, the study brought to light the scope of the problem and much
about how women activists perceived the CNTU.

Not surprisingly, the studies revealed that women are severely
underrepresented on elected bodies at all levels of the union hierarchy,
and that the higher up you go, the fewer women you find – from 33%
at the bi-annual convention to 17% at the national executive. In the
Social Affairs Federation, 75% of whose members are women, men
made up 75% of the 1980 negotiating team.

A second finding was that the women who do make it on to the
various leadership bodies are not representative of the average rank and
file woman. Women activists tend to be younger, have a higher income,
and more frequently live without a husband, male friend or children
than rank and file women. And again, the higher up you go in the union
hierarchy, the more striking the differences become. The final issue,
which is not disclosed by the figures, but which came up again and

again at educational sessions, meetings of women's committees and in the corridors, is that often women do not get involved in their unions because they reject the demands that union activism forces on their lives.

Male activists, who continue to function in the CNTU despite ulcers and heart attacks and what is said to be the highest divorce rate of any social group in Quebec, are generally married (for the second time), have children and tend to be slightly older than their rank and file counterparts. It is striking that male activists tend to be in relationships while women activists tend to be on their own. Let us look more closely at what it means to be a woman activist.

HAVING BABIES IS A FULL-TIME JOB

More than half of the women in the CNTU study do not have children. As the demands of militancy increase in the upper echelons of the hierarchy, the number of women with children significantly decreases. The opposite is true of men. Day care, of course, is not available in the evenings, overnight or on weekends. Two-thirds of the activists who do have children place them in day care five days a week, for six to ten hours a day, at an average daily cost of $45. An evening

PERCENTAGE OF ACTIVISTS WITHOUT CHILDREN
(1980-81)

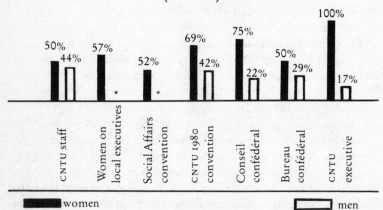

meeting means four or five more hours of babysitting and another $10, which more often than not the women have to pay themselves. In addition, many women want to spend more time with their families and feel guilty about subjecting their children to more babysitting in the evenings and on weekends.

All of the women in the study agreed that children and a family are major obstacles to participation in union activities. When we asked members "Do your children limit your involvement in your union?", 81.8% of the women and only 33.3% of the men said yes. The following statements by a rank and file militant eloquently demonstrate that children are still a woman's problem.

> I'm currently going through a separation, and it's going to put my involvement in the union into question because I will have total responsibility for our child. I don't want to have him babysat every evening after his father leaves.
>
> Before I had a child, being a union activist wasn't difficult. It was satisfying. But since I've had a child, I'm quite torn between the vital need to stay involved and all the other aspects of my life.
>
> I share child care with my ex, but it's not 50-50. I feel more responsible. Women are more attentive to the little things than men. When we have to go away for meetings, we plan things a long time in advance.
>
> We've changed child care arrangements four times because he wanted to try new sharing arrangements. I find it very difficult to adjust each time. When you get right down to it, it's always the women who assume the responsibility for the children.

IT'S ME OR THE UNION

Whereas 57% of working women in Quebec are married, less than half of CNTU activists are. As is the case with children, the percentage of married women decreases as the degree of responsibility increases. The following table also shows that there are marked differences between men and women activists in terms of their marital status.

Why is the presence of a husband or friend an obstacle to women's militancy? Discussions with rank and file women revealed that women are very hesitant about talking about the role played by their husband/friend. One mentioned that her divorce was speeded up by her participation on a picket line; another told of being thrown out of the house by her husband of fifteen years because she went to a meeting of her local union council's women's committee. But the camouflaged replies we usually heard show that resistance from husbands/friends usually takes less dramatic and more subtle forms. This constant psychological pressure is extremely wearing.

PERCENTAGE OF MARRIED ACTIVISTS IN DECISION-MAKING BODIES

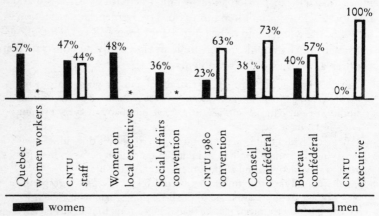

■ women   □ men

* no data available for men

Some husbands/friends hide their disapproval by claiming that it is not they but the children who are suffering. Other husbands adopt the tactic of ridiculing their wives' activities. "Why don't you work out our problems at home before solving those at the hospital?"

Even though they do not explicitly object to their wives' participation in the union, it is the rare husband who wouldn't be happy to see his wife spending less time in meetings and more time with him. As one woman stated, "My friend doesn't try and stop me from being active, but he'd be relieved if I'd stop travelling so much. When I get home he uses a bit of humoristic blackmail to make me feel guilty."

LET'S ALL GO FOR A BEER

Being a union activist can be an expensive undertaking. Meetings often involve eating at least one meal in a restaurant and going out for a beer with the gang. Conventions generally imply 24-hour child care expenses, many dollars in support of striking workers selling buttons and key rings, raffle tickets and the like, long distance phone calls to check on the children, and food and drink expenses – all in addition to the reimbursement paid by the local union. As the average wage of women attending the 1980 convention was $14,000, it is clear that these expenses are a real deterrent to union activism.

WHO'S GOING TO POLISH THE FLOOR?

Some of us would like to believe that with the growing consciousness in our society of the need to share housework and child care, these responsibilities are no longer an obstacle to women's participation in unions. Unfortunately, this is not the case. Women workers continue to put in a double day of work. If they are union activists, it becomes a triple day.

The average woman worker in Quebec who works 32 to 40 hours a week for a wage, works another 33.2 hours for free when she gets home. And this does not include shopping and transportation time, which add another six hours. This means that many put in a 75.2-hour work week before beginning any union activities. The questionnaire indicated, for example, that women holding positions on their local executives devote an average of 33.7 hours to domestic work. Women at the FAS convention averaged 28.7 hours.

The one study that questioned both men and women produced revealing results. When asked whether they were satisfied with the sharing of household tasks, 61.5% of the women and 88.8% of the men said yes. Hiding behind these replies is another figure that shows that the men (male staff members at the CNTU) spend an average of only 15.4 hours doing household work and child care, leaving them with between 13 and 18 hours more per week than the women for their union activities and recreation.

Some unsolicited comments on the question of time spent on domestic labour indicate aggressive attitudes on the part of some men:

I work outside the home. She works inside the home. It's a choice that each one has made.

None, my mother never taught me how to do housework. She said it was women's work.

None, the woman takes care of it.

And of course household tasks continue to exist even if you live alone, which is the case for many union activists:

> Even when you're single, it's not easy to be an activist. You become cut off from your social milieu. You're given more to do since you don't have children, and so of course are more available. The men at my local council don't understand how a single woman can have household responsibilities. But who else is going to do my washing or mow my lawn? When they travel to meetings, their wives pack their bags.

IF YOU WANT TO JOIN THE UNION, IT'S BETTER TO BE A MAN

Women activists are becoming increasingly vocal about the kind of unionism practised at the CNTU: a unionism they feel is organized for and by men. A woman interested in her union who only has a few hours a week to offer for union work does not feel very welcome. Meetings are rarely scheduled at fixed times. Long-term work plans are almost unknown as activists race from one emergency to another. And with her limited availability, she is never able to really feel part of the "gang," nor catch up to the subtleties of political power.

In addition, many women talk about their inability to master male ways of speaking. And many refuse to have to adapt their speaking style to a male model.

> For the men, unionism is like being part of a 'sect.' They all talk alike, in a very structured manner. They're always making high-powered global analyses. Women feel like they'll never be able to do that. And when a woman is able to overcome her feelings of inferiority, nothing is done to help her. No, instead they all judge her. When a new man arrives, he just plays along and accepts things as they are.

Those women who have succeeded in becoming part of this authoritarian, macho and sectarian world are often disillusioned and bitter. They feel they are being manipulated by the men. Over and over again women repeat the same story.

> There was a slate of men running for our union executive and at the last minute they decided they needed a woman for the job of secretary or for the women's committee. They first asked all the more docile women and they refused. Finally I said I'd run. But when I started to understand how things work and began giving my opinion, they quickly regretted having me on their team. After a while they began saying I was holding back the executive because I wasn't available often enough. Then they suggested I resign.

Women unionists are judged more harshly than their male counterparts, even when they are exemplary in their work. Most are not taken seriously. Women are often judged on the basis of their appearance, who their husbands or boyfriends are and whether or not they are available for sex at out-of-town meetings. They are not listened to and their ideas become important only when adopted by a man.

One woman who was on a negotiating committee with three men and a male union staff advisor spoke about her experience:

> During the month of heavy negotiations we were completely cut off from everybody. The four of us were always together. We'd go to negotiate in the morning, never knowing what time we'd be through. We never saw anyone else. Often at 3 AM we were still waiting for an answer from the bosses. If we decided to go home to sleep, it always took at least an hour to unwind, so I'd fall into bed around 5 AM and have to be back at the table at 10 AM. Should negotiations be based on your physical stamina, your capacity to tough it out until 3 AM? We often used this kind of tactic to try and wear the other side out. It's a very male way of doing things. It's like playing chess where you try and force your opponent into a position of weakness. But it shouldn't be like that. It becomes a confrontation between individuals. I'm not there to show off my physical stamina. I'm there to defend the group I represent. It's their strength, not mine, which should influence the negotiation. Unfortunately, I don't know any other models for negotiating.

IF WOMEN WERE TO TAKE OVER THE UNIONS ...

The women's committee report on militancy has sparked much interest and debate throughout the CNTU. More and more women are starting to speak out about their experiences as union militants. And there are a certain number of men who, having also been kept out of the power elite, are turning to the women's committees for leadership in the confrontations with male unionism, a style they too are uncomfortable with.

We hope the women's committees will be able to meet the challenge and develop new models of unionism. Without valid alternatives, criticism is easily countered with a haughty "Well, what do you propose instead?"

This is not an easy question. The recommendations proposed by the report and adopted by the convention are modest. They suggest such things as organizing widespread debate on the question; taking a few special measures to help women, like paying 24-hour babysitting for meetings of more than one day; and trying to fix meeting times that are more convenient to women with family responsibilities. These actions are certainly not to be scoffed at, but given the scope of the problem, they seem only to touch the surface.

What can we do about the organization of family life that leaves women responsible for the family and the home? What is a feminist model of negotiations when current public sector negotiations mean that more than 250 union activists have to move to Quebec City for anywhere from one to six months? What is a feminist model for a bi-annual convention that brings together 2,000 people and lasts a week? What changes can be made so that women attend and genuinely participate in such meetings?

An even more important question facing women activists is whether or not they can make these questions of women's participation in the union hierarchy and the very existence of such a centralized, elitist and male structure key questions for the whole labour movement. Can they make their voices heard? In recent years, women have thoroughly shaken up the Canadian left with their interrogations and demands around leadership, structures, work styles and rank and file participatory democracy. It remains to be seen if the women's committees can do the same in their unions.

NOTES

1 In comparison to CLC unions, unions affiliated with the CNTU are each separate legal entities. For example, a CNTU hospital union is accredited as the "Union of the Employees of Hospital x," whereas a CLC union would only be a local of an overall accredited body known as the "Hospital x Employees' Union" and would be known as local 123 of that body.

2 This is reported by Michèle Jean in "Histoire des luttes féministes au Québec," *Possibles*, Vol. 4, No. 1 (Fall 1979), pp.17-33.

WOMEN'S COMMITTEES:
THE QUEBEC EXPERIENCE

Francoise David

The Fédération des affaires sociales (FAS) / Social Affairs Federation is the largest federation in the Confédération des syndicats nationaux (CSN) / Confederation of National Trade Unions (CNTU). It is made up of 450 unions and has a membership of 80,000, 72 percent of whom are women. These women are nurses' aides, nurses, teachers, social workers, office clerks and technicians.

The setting up of a women's committee at the FAS Congress in 1980 was an important step for both the women in FAS and the CSN as a whole. Until a few years ago, there were at most twenty committees or caucuses at the local level and five or six in the central councils (regional groupings of CSN unions). This article tells the story of the FAS women's committee and outlines some of the issues we have had to confront so far.

FEMINISM AND UNIONISM

To be a woman and a worker is increasingly common. To be a woman and unionized is rarer, but our numbers are growing. But to be a woman and an active trade unionist – that is another story! There are still very few of us, although there are more than our numbers in union leaderships would indicate.

What specific qualities must a woman have who, suffering from a large dose of enthusiasm, decides to become involved in trade unionism? A great deal of energy, endurance and the ability to last through meetings three, four or five hours long. Time ... lots of time! A sense of humour, a dash of cynicism and tolerance for the rhetoric, actions and manners of male comrades. But most of all, she has an unshakable conviction that trade unionism is an essential tool in achieving the demands of women.

When unions decide to take on demands and struggles, there are few bosses and governments who are not forced to relinquish *some* control and give some concessions. Working women have been able to better their working and life conditions through trade unions. For example, unions have helped us win equal pay for equal work, maternity leave, preventive leave in case of health risk during pregnancy. But today, militant women are going much further: we want to bring about changes in everyday life. We want to discuss the sharing of housework, the question of abortion and affirmative action in union meetings. And more, we want to feminize the standard concepts of trade union militancy — the competition and grueling demands of activist life. We want to change the world, yes, but we do not have to be martyrs in order to do it.

GETTING STARTED

I don't know if we had all these considerations in mind when we worked to set up a FAS women's committee. What was clear at the 1980 congress was that women wanted to be heard: they wanted an autonomous and organized voice, a committee to deal with the conditions of women. There was no opposition to establishing a women's committee. Its mandate, agreed on with little debate at the congress, was as follows:

- to enforce the new parental rights (maternity leave) clause
- to analyze policies that discriminate against FAS workers, especially nursing attendants. (In fact, these workers had just achieved salary parity with their male counterparts, and this had led certain employers to assign female workers extra tasks without allowing any time for retraining)
- to work towards setting up child care centres in the workplace
- to establish concrete measures to increase the participation of women in trade unions.

Getting the committee accepted was easy, defining its mandate was no problem, but when we got down to discussing money, the "progressive discourse" cracked. We were told that $8,000 should be more than enough for the first two years for the eleven members of the committee to travel across the province to attend five to six meetings a year. We were finally given $16,000, thanks to the persistence of the women and the support of a few men. Our demand was for more than just the right to exist.

The members of the committee were to be elected from each of the eleven regions in Quebec. I was elected from the Montreal region, and then became chairperson of the committee. It took a year to fill the eleven positions. One of the paradoxes of a women's committee is that it adds time and travel demands to the all-too-busy schedules of women activists.

All the women representatives either held or had held positions on the executives of their local unions. Some had served on the executive committee of their central councils. All of us had a number of years of union experience and wanted to continue our activism by struggling against the oppression of women. The majority of the women on the committee had children and more than half were single parents.

The awareness of women's oppression was different for each woman on the committee. For some, it was simply a question of problems women face at work; their analysis did not extend to all the aspects of oppression in women's lives. For others, including myself, the struggle against oppression was an integral part of our everyday lives, and discussing our daily struggles was often stimulating to us. At other times it was the focus of despair.

We began our work by trying to meet the demands set out by the mandate. For many months our work consisted mainly of research and reflection on various topics. Among others, the problems facing nursing assistants led us to ask the following question: when women and men earn equal pay for equal work, work that is equivalent but not exactly the same, should we say that the jobs are in fact identical? Many unions within the FAS are hesitant to answer yes. We also distributed and compiled the responses to a questionnaire dealing with women's participation in union life and publicized issues like parental rights. We worked cautiously, diligently and efficiently, without making too many waves. There was a great feeling of solidarity among the women. During our first year, we didn't have to take a vote, everything — work strategies, division of tasks, demands — was decided through consensus. We also had communal dinners where we discussed our children, our loves and our failures ...

Our presence was appreciated by women, who showed strong support for our work. Some of them feared that the contradictions between men and women would eventually surface. The men were skeptical but curious; some were openly hostile, others sympathetic to our cause.

THE NEGOTIATING PROCESS

The negotiation of a contract for 80,000 union members is the most intense period in the life of a federation. The proposal for contract amendments is an amalgam of the demands deemed by the diverse groups of union members to be the most urgent. While we were preparing to negotiate for our upcoming collective agreement, things began to change – both within the committee and among the delegates to the federal councils, the highest bodies of the 450 affiliated unions of the FAS.

This period, starting with preparation of the contract amendments, and right up until the settlement (including strikes), is marked by much internal debate and tension. Each man and woman has his or her own priorities. Which priorities are the most important? What role should the negotiating committee play? On which demands should we unite with the other labour federations? What should our strategies be when facing the government?

The women's committee began to upset the union executive and staff as well as certain union delegates when it tried to change some of the rules of the negotiations game. First we asked for the right to have a woman from the women's committee sit on the negotiating committee. This committee is usually made up of delegates elected on the basis of type of work, region and sector, including fourteen members from the Federal Bureau (the governing body of the FAS). The role of our representative would be to ensure that women's demands were defended and not bargained away at the last moment.

At first the executive of the FAS was opposed to our demand. Some were disturbed at our lack of confidence in the negotiating committee. Others found our desire to get closer to the centres of power suspicious. After all, we were a committee – the same as any other. Who did we think we were?

We certainly understood the reluctance and even the hostility of certain delegates and leaders of the FAS when faced with women's demand to be present at this meeting of the "inner sanctum," voicing and defending our demands. The negotiating committee's privileged access to information, the nature of their debates, whether among themselves or with other federations, and the fact of their working on the definition of the new collective agreement, give their recommendations to the federal councils a lot of weight. In fact, a recommendation emanating from the negotiating committee is rarely defeated on the council floor.

When the Federal Council finally agreed to allow our committee a member on the negotiating committee, only one of us felt able to take on the task, which required complete availability for at least a year. Few mothers could afford such commitment.

At the same time, the women's committee submitted a document proposing that the issue of women be a priority in negotiations and emphasizing the importance of demands such as the protection of part-time workers and a platform of progressive elimination of part-time work. The proposal advocated full-time employment for all, with partial (part-time) leave for people in certain situations, such as health problems, family responsibilities and studies. The proposal also advocated:

- complete salary parity for women and men
- the establishment of equal opportunity programs (affirmative action) to maintain the proportion of women in the public sector
- improvements to the parental rights clause, including the establishment of a leave fund for parental responsibility
- The "de-sexing" of social service jobs where employers tend to hire men rather than women for certain tasks, in spite of women's greater seniority. The reasons usually given are: safety (from disturbed patients), physical strength (moving chronic-care patients), and the necessity to reproduce the "family image" (and therefore have equal numbers of male teachers in the newcomer reception centres).

Our brief was well received by the Federation, and was subsequently distributed to the unions. But the regional debates were not well organized. In some regions, the "issue of women" was adopted as a negotiating priority, but in others it was never even discussed. Then in the spring of 1982, at a meeting of a Federal Council, the negotiating committee set forward its priorities for the next contract. The "issue of women" was omitted. The reason given was that only two or three regions out of eleven had made the issue a priority in their demand-setting meetings, and others had put forward specific demands, such as child care centred in the workplace and leave for family responsibility. One priority, access to promotion, was adopted although it had been brought forward by only one region. The negotiating committee had ignored the fact that the provincial government was anxious to pass a law providing for the establishment of equal opportunity programs and that it was high time the labour movement came up with proposals of its own.

On the urging of several members of the women's committee, a women's caucus of fifty women was quickly set up and was able to bring the debate to the Council floor. After a full day of discussion, the vote was 155 to 153 in favour of our previous resolution that women's demands be a priority. Some delegates, displeased by the results of the vote, attempted to move reconsideration, but they were unsuccessful.

The result of the vote, though close, was received with great enthusiasm by the majority of women. Losing the vote would have meant putting most of our demands on the back burner. It also would have been proof to the provincial government that the unions were not yet ready to mobilize their efforts to improve women's working conditions. We were aware that the split vote showed a lack of understanding on the part of unions about many women's issues, especially affirmative action and part-time leave. We had a difficult task ahead of us: to get enough grass-roots support in the FAS to ensure our demands would be defended right down to the settlement of the contract.

However, this process caused us great difficulties within our committee. For the first time we were divided. The majority felt that we were right to challenge the negotiating committee's recommendations, but some members, including our representative on the negotiating committee, felt we had gone too far, too fast. They argued that the negotiating committee felt attacked by us (which was true) and that this might work against our future efforts. Our representative felt trapped between her solidarity with us and the solidarity she felt she owed to the negotiating committee. According to tradition, once elected from their trades, regions or sectors, the delegates put their constituency in second place to the collective body of the negotiating team.

For this reason our representative quickly found herself in a situation where she no longer represented our interests. She stopped coming to us for mandates and direction. Although she was still fundamentally in agreement with the principles of our committee, she didn't feel it necessary to consult with us about ways to apply these principles. In reality we no longer had a *representative* on the negotiating committee. Our committee was very critical of what had happened but we weren't able to find a replacement, since none of us was able to make the time commitment necessary to serve on the committee. In any case, the problem would not have been solved by replacing our representative because the structure and function of the negotiating process would not have been changed. It would have been idealistic to think that a single activist could work miracles!

THERE'S NO GOING BACK

The women's committee lived this first round of debate very intensively. All the debates (and they are far from over) have helped us realize that we cannot easily insert ourselves into trade union structures. Without meaning to, we raised questions about bureaucracy and traditional political perspectives. The most determined activists have lost a few illusions along the way, namely:

- the illusion of absolute unity among women, just by virtue of being women, workers, mothers, etc.
- the illusion of openness in the structure of the labour movement
- the illusion of autonomy for the women's movement within a given central council.

The minute we say "union committee" we are talking about control by the union structure. In our federation and the CSN, women certainly have significant weight, and their position is stronger day by day. In fact, many perceive us as a parallel "power." We are watched nervously; no one dares to oppose us systematically. If the union structure disagrees with us, it is always on "technical grounds," never for political reasons. Women and their situation are in fashion. The hitch comes when we try to take our place at the heart of the power structure. We are no longer asking for permission, we are making demands. This is profoundly disturbing to people who identify with the heavy-handed and hierarchical union structures.

Our problem is to be somewhat autonomous while at the same time assume a leadership role. This same contradiction often arises when women attempt to become active in left politics. We know that overall, we are making progress. Ideas change, mentalities evolve and more and more women claim an active role. But sometimes we become discouraged, faced with the long road ahead and the patience we need to explain and to convince men trade unionists to support our positions.

We must also convince many women that defending our rights won't increase the divisions that already exist. Our committee is now well established, and more and more women are looking to us for support and direction.

At a time when Quebec's unions are on the defensive against the attacks of government and the capitalists, women have the thankless task of convincing the membership about the correctness of our point of view and the absolute need to defend it. We will need to form a united front to face the skepticism and distrust from within the structure of the trade union movement. We have no choice. We will continue to struggle.

Translated by Francoise Pelletier and Daina Green

THE DILEMMA FACING WOMEN'S COMMITTEES

Debbie Field

Faced with the many inequalities women experience in the workplace, a growing number of women turn to unions as vehicles for solving job problems. But when we do, we often find that unions themselves are not immediately willing or able to aggressively fight for us. Women's committees form inside unions to pressure unions to become better fighters for women's rights.

As the number of women in unions has dramatically increased in the last fifteen years, union struggles involving women and the politicization of women workers has grown.[1] Working women have been both a part of and influenced by the women's movement of the 1960s and 1970s. Women's public questioning of the stereotyped and unequal roles assigned to us has led to a massive debate throughout North American society. The debate has raged inside the unions too. Radicalized by our growing recognition of job and social inequalities, women have looked to unions as collective institutions with the muscle, interests and progressive traditions to fight for and win changes in our situation.

In this process women and male supporters have come up against three problems. The first is the very nature of unions. For thirty years business unionism has dominated Canadian and Quebec unions. Business unionism sees the central focus of union activity as bargaining over narrow economic issues. Within the limited framework of collective bargaining, unions have been successful in securing economic gains for their members. However, far too often social and political questions, from the expansion of social services to electoral politics, have taken a backseat, as have the interests of non-unionized workers. Along with this narrow view of their function, from the 1950s on, unions became increasingly controlled by leaderships who acted on behalf of a largely passive membership to win contract demands through negotiations rather than membership mobilization and political campaigns.

Business unionism is particularly unsuited to winning the demands of women. Though higher wages and better job mobility can be negotiated for women through the contract process, simply adding women's demands to others without activating women and developing new negotiation tactics does not work. A broad political campaign is required to win any women's issues – from equal pay to equal job access. Such a campaign would include organizing drives to unionize women's job ghettos, contract demands for preferential adjustments in the wages of women, and political action to change laws, employer hiring practices and general social attitudes. Unfortunately this type of campaign is in contradiction with the practice of business unionism and outside the perceived scope of the union movement. The labour movement's efforts to defeat the wage controls introduced in 1975, and the plans for a one-day general work stoppage / strike on October 14, 1976, demonstrate the problem. The union movement was incapable of the political campaign and mobilization necessary to defeat controls or even to ensure the success of October 14th. As the economic crisis of the 1980s deepens, business unionism becomes less and less capable even of maintaining past wage gains. The need for political campaigns is ever more urgent.

Second, women come up against the sexism of capitalist society. Male unionists have been reluctant to see women's job demands, or the integration of women into the daily functioning and power structures of unions, as central priorities. Women have had to confront myths about working women, and sometimes male hostility and fear of women. The myths are many: "women working create unemployment and steal jobs away from the main breadwinners – men"; "children of working mothers become juvenile delinquents"; "women are not emotionally or physically capable of filling traditional male jobs"; "women are useless in a strike – they are scared of the picket line and always vote to return to work"; "women's contract demands come out of the pockets of men – if a union wins maternity leave, men will have to give up something else."

Finally, women come up against the reflection of this dominant ideology in ourselves and in the women around us. Though there are historical examples of women's thwarted attempts to get involved in unions, women have too often accepted the wages and jobs available to us, and the passive and secondary role relegated to women in unions. Before the reemergence of the women's movement in the 1960s women were not a significant force within unions. Not socialized to be active in the public realm, women internalize the view that we are less interested in politics than men, less able to speak at a meeting or demonstration, to write a leaflet, or to stand strong against employers.

Women's activity is hindered by more than personal doubts and social attitudes. We still have primary responsibility for preparing food, caring for children, doing the wash and cleaning the house. It is physically as well as emotionally more difficult for women to attend union meetings or run for union office when there are so few personal or social alternatives to performing these household tasks. For these reasons, women's participation in unions has been at a lower level than men's.

Women's committees have developed as an attempt to alleviate these three interrelated problems.[2] As subgroupings within unions, they bring women and male supporters together to develop strategies to make unions more responsive to women. They talk about ways to overcome the sexism of male unionists and combat the fears and concrete life problems that block women from participating in unions. Invariably, as women's committees pose demands and articulate strategies, there is a need to restructure the union movement away from business unionism.

Women's committees now exist inside unions across the country — at the local, city, regional and provincial levels, in all the provincial federations of labour, union centrals and in many city labour councils. The Canadian Labour Congress, through its women's conferences and Women's Bureau, coordinates information and fulfills some of the functions of a country-wide women's committee.

The development of women's committees is one of the most exciting movements within unions today and should be supported by feminists and unionists interested in making unions more democratic, more responsive to the needs of members and more militant. These committees represent an important example of the power of women's self-organization, and have been largely responsible for pressuring unions to struggle for women's rights.

However, the simple existence of women's committees does not guarantee the winning of women's demands. In what follows I look at the conditions that affect the success of a women's committee. My observations arise from my experience as a member of the Ontario Public Service Employees Union's (OPSEU's) Women's Caucus,

(1977-79), as OPSEU's Equal Opportunities Coordinator (1978-79), and as a member of the Women's Committee of Local 1005 of the United Steelworkers of America (USWA) (1980-81).

* * * * *

Women's committees often start by informal caucusing at the local, provincial or national level; the women's caucuses inside OPSEU began this way.[3] For several years women came together from across the province at convention time to ensure that the convention would discuss women's issues and to urge women to speak and run for leadership bodies. These meetings reduced our isolation and enhanced our intervention in the convention. They also enabled women from different cities and work areas to meet one another and discover shared problems. The informal caucusing led to the formation in 1977 of a women's caucus in the Toronto area that met on a monthly basis. There are now officially supported caucuses in several cities, as well as an elected provincial women's committee.

The caucuses draft convention resolutions and contract proposals; encourage women to become more active in local and regional union politics; train women in the functioning and structure of the union, in public speaking and in parliamentary procedure; provide a base for women to get integrated into the leadership of the union; and generally keep the attention of the union focused on women's concerns. Participation in a caucus also serves as a personal growth and learning experience for women. Women credit membership in a caucus as a significant step in becoming independent and articulate. Unlike many union structures, the caucuses, influenced by the conception of sisterhood in the women's movement, are warm and friendly meeting places.

Caucus members have raised the need for child care at union meetings and OPSEU was the first union in Ontario to provide free child care at conventions. Members also encourage the union to endorse women's movement activities such as International Women's Day and to support the strikes and struggles of other workers. During the Fleck strike, a strike of women for a first contract in southwestern Ontario, caucus members were influential in winning a donation of $10,000 from OPSEU.

OPSEU was also the first union in Canada to establish an Equal Opportunities Program with a full-time Equal Opportunities Coordinator. The number of women who are active in locals and conventions has grown significantly over the past five years and women's issues have a very high profile in the union.[4]

The OPSEU experience highlights three benefits of women's committees: the more active and organized women there are, the more unions will address our concerns; the more vocal a union's defence of women's rights, the more the union will attract women activists; and finally, the more active women are, the stronger unions become. Contrary to opponents who fear that women's committees divide the union, women's caucuses in OPSEU have brought increased energy to OPSEU and all its campaigns.

The development of women's caucuses in OPSEU has not been without problems. First, the caucuses have had their share of enemies. Some women active in the union prior to the development of caucuses are hostile to the concept of separate women's committees. Able to succeed on their own, these women insist they don't understand the need for support networks. Sometimes, these women team up with men in the union to red- or lesbian-bait caucus members. They suggest that caucus members are not representative of the majority of women, who, they say, are content with the way things are.

Others in the union have been angered by the caucuses' attempts to make the union more democratic, more involved in social issues and more accountable to the rank and file. A feature of the OPSEU caucuses has been their anti-status-quo stance. Its members have not necessarily articulated this philosophy, but in their efforts to defend the interests of women, they have come up against the status quo and the bureaucracy of the union.

Second, it is not easy to get large numbers of women involved in the caucus or the union. The caucuses are hindered in their development by the very problems they came into existence to combat: the nature of business unionism, of sexism, of the lives of working women. OPSEU's Equal Opportunities Program, adopted by its central leadership and annual conventions, supports the building and expansion of caucuses throughout the union. Nevertheless, it has still been very difficult for caucuses to gel.

As OPSEU's first Equal Opportunities Coordinator, a central mandate of my job was to help activate women and build caucuses across the province. Many people in the union, myself included, believed the success of the Toronto women's caucus could be reproduced in other cities through the initiative of the Equal Opportunities Coordinator. This strategy put the organizational form — the caucus — before the political development — women's expressed need for a caucus. But caucuses or committees are only successful if they arise, as the initial OPSEU Toronto area caucus did, out of the desire of women to meet together to pursue a common goal — for example, to make their union more accessible to women's participation, or to demand that the union negotiate a specific demand such as equal job access or pay rates. Without a concrete goal, consciousness of problems women face does not usually provide sufficient motivation for the formation of a caucus.

As the Equal Opportunity Coordinator I also faced problems as a union staff member. A staff person can play an important educational and resource role, clarifying issues and helping women structure a caucus once they have decided to form one, but cannot create sufficient interest where it has not yet coalesced. Frances Lankin, OPSEU's current Equal Opportunities Coordinator, has developed a sensible strategy in which she focuses on educational courses rather than caucus building, thereby laying the basis for caucuses but allowing the initiative to come from women themselves.

Those women already active in an OPSEU women's caucus face a complicated dilemma. While their efforts to activate broader layers of women often fail, and the expansion of new caucuses moves slowly, their activity in the caucus and in other union structures provides them with increased visibility in the union as a whole. They are increasingly able to confer directly with union leaders and to win acceptance of particular women's demands without relying on membership mobilization. Given the difficulties of organizing women in unions, it is no wonder that the focus of the caucus may move towards consolidating the influence and stucture of the caucus. There is no easy solution to this dilemma. However, it is important for women to recognize the tension between developing strategies to activate women and negotiating gains for women's rights. Though it may appear easier to strike an agreement with the leadership of a union on the need to negotiate workplace day care, for example, in the long run, it can never be effectively won without active support.

*   *   *   *   *

My experience in the women's committee of Local 1005 of the USWA confirmed the importance of discovering the needs of women before putting too much energy into building a committee. In 1979 I was one of a group of women who, working closely with Local 1005 of the steelworkers, organized a campaign to get women hired into Stelco's Hamilton plant. Though there had been thousands of female appli-·cants, Stelco had not hired any women production or trades workers in eighteen years. After six months of the campaign, Stelco backed down and hired the five of us who had laid complaints with the Ontario Human Rights Commission. Within a year of the successful Women Back Into Stelco campaign, there were over 200 women in a plant of 13,000.

Once inside Stelco, those of us who had been active in the campaign felt a need to get women together. We were very isolated: a few women on each shift, spread out in different departments, in different loca-tions. We needed to talk about inadequate washroom and change house facilities, about difficulties women faced getting into training pro-grams, and about how we were doing as the first women in a very male environment.

Stelco was using inadequate washroom facilities as a symbolic test for the women. By not providing permanent facilities, and by making many women in the plant share already limited facilities with men, Stelco was telling us they did not expect we would be staying in the plant long.[5] As the problems surrounding the washrooms became more urgent, we approached the union local for a list of the women in the plant. This request was denied because no formal female leadership list existed.

We then wrote to the local asking that a women's committee be formed. After much informal discussion with members of the local executive, a committee was voted in by the local in October 1980. Four women, myself included, and three male executive members were appointed to it.

Because of its birth as a component of the leadership of Local 1005 — its members all handpicked by the local president — the committee was from its beginning affected by the bureaucratic functioning of that leadership. Instead of trying to organize the women of the local, we were forced to spend time fighting for the survival of the committee. Our energies were sucked into the infighting that occupied the leadership.

Although we had anticipated some of the problems of an appointed committee, we felt trapped in it because it was the only form that was immediately attainable.[6] We accepted the appointed committee as an interim structure, hoping that regular open committee meetings would involve more women and provide the basis for a restructured committee proposal. At the time we were so unsure of ourselves — a few women in a predominantly male workplace and union — that we accepted the view that only formal structures would be allowed.

Unlike the OPSEU caucuses, the USWA Local 1005 women's committee did not develop as a result of women caucusing with each other over a long period of time. The committee was at the mercy of the leadership. If it suited their political goals, the leadership supported women's issues. OPSEU, a younger union with a less hardened leadership structure, allows members a greater range of ways to become active. In a local like USWA 1005, with a membership of 10,000 to 13,000 and strong traditions, activity can occur only in particular and long established ways.

The future of a USWA Local 1005 women's committee is uncertain, given the massive layoffs that have hit the local. Hundreds of men and all recently hired women have been laid off.

In hindsight, and from the vantage point of no longer working at Stelco, I believe we made a mistake forming a women's committee so closely tied to the leadership. It would have been better to spend time, even a year or two, getting to know women in the plant before moving to structure a formal committee. This approach would have involved experimenting with new forms of organizing. For example, we could have stood outside the plant gates, introducing ourselves to women leaving the plant, inviting them to a gathering at one of our homes, or out for a drink after work. Though a small number of women attended women's committee meetings, the majority did not.

Unions could generally strengthen membership involvement if more informal methods of meeting and transmitting information were developed. Particularly when trying to mobilize women or new union members, it is important to develop creative tactics to make the union more accessible.

*   *   *   *   *

Social change does not occur without an organized fight. Adopting positions in favour of change is insufficient; people have to fight for the change through daily discussions, through job resistance, demonstrations and mass meetings. Until the union movement is prepared to participate in the type of campaign that won the forty-hour work week, the yearly Canadian Labour Congress resolutions demanding the thirty-two-hour week are only paper, with minimal educational value. Likewise, although research on equal pay and child care can motivate people to fight for them, without mobilizations of large numbers, they will never be won.

To what extent do women's committees serve to mobilize women? In the first place, the very existence of a women's committee is a result of a crystalization of women's opinion, if not always their action. If there was no pressure from women demanding equal rights, unions would not be responding by setting up women's committees. A union's support of women's concerns, for whatever reason, unleashes a dynamic that activates women. The existence of articulate women leaders, even appointed ones, strengthens women's confidence and the possibility that other women will speak out. Even a small grouping of women can pressure their union to adopt positions that favour women and to publicize these positions using the resources of the union. A union's commitment to negotiate equal pay or to provide child care at conventions has an undeniably positive impact on the lives of women.

Although unions have tried to "accommodate" the demands of women, unions as they exist today cannot tolerate intense or prolonged mobilization, which in itself challenges the traditions of business unionism. As a result unions often try to incorporate, co-opt or control women's committees. Faced with resistance to membership involvement by the leadership and the difficulties of organizing a fairly passive rank and file, women's committees face a problem. Can we keep our focus on the mobilization of rank and file women and risk losing credibility with the leadership? Or, given the difficulties of membership mobilizations, should we focus energy on consolidating positions in the hope that we will be able to achieve changes that benefit women?

This is a difficult problem. As we did in Local 1005 USWA, women often choose to consolidate our positions, and that of our committee, because there seems to be no other alternative. But as women's committees become a fixed component of the union organization, their relationship with rank and file women inevitably becomes attenuated. The committee can lose touch with the immediate goals and struggles of women, and therefore be less able to win positions that favour women. Too often we spend our time researching the facts and figures of an issue, without meeting women to find our their opinions, and to convince them to be aggressive and active in supporting the issue. We then find ourselves with a beautifully worded resolution at a local meeting, convention or press conference, but without any troops to back us up. It is for these quite practical reasons that I keep returning to the mobilization of women as the key to winning women's job and social improvements.

Women's committees can play an important role in organizing women to fight, particularly in the difficult economic and social times to come. In this period of wage controls and high unemployment women's committees will need to defeat the arguments that this is not the time to fight for women's rights. The continuing self-organization of women in women's committees presents an alternative to the traditions of business unionism and challenges the union movement to take an aggressive and public stand on the basic job rights of all working people.

NOTES

Thanks to Linda Briskin and David Kraft for their patient advice, editing help and support. Thanks also to the women I worked with in OPSEU's women's caucuses and USWA Local 1005 women's committee. Their energy, optimism and political sense were a constant source of inspiration to me.

1 See Linda Briskin's statistical article in this book.

2 In some unions, women's formations are called women's caucuses, in others, women's committees. Sometimes the terms are used

interchangeably, but they have slightly different histories and characteristics. A women's committee is a formal structure set up by the leadership of the union. Its members are either appointed by the leadership or elected by the membership as a whole. A women's caucus usually begins with an informal meeting of women. Caucuses are open to all women (and sometimes all men) members of the union and have steering committees or executives elected by the caucus itself. In the OPSEU case, the women's caucus retains many caucus features, such as open membership, while at the same time it has moved to receive formal union recognition along the lines of a women's committee.

3 OPSEU is a large public sector union. The vast majority of its members work for the Ontario government and close to half of its members are women.

4 In 1976, 30.7% of all OPSEU local executive committee members were women; in 1981, 36.5% were. Interestingly, of the 816 new executive committee members between those years, 56.6% were women. In 1976, 21.1% of local executive presidents were women; in 1981 that figure had increased to 25.4% In 1976, 23.4% of OPSEU annual convention delegates were women, and by 1981 32.4% were women. In 1976, 35.5% of those attending union educational programs were women; by 1981 that figure had increased to 53.6%. (Figures from *Women in* OPSEU: *A Statistical Analysis of Participation by Women and Related Issues*, Feb. 15, 1982.)

5 Though women in the plant had private change and shower facilities in movable trailers, Stelco used recent changes in Ontario law as the basis for making women and men share washrooms at the worksite in certain areas of the plant. Rather than specifying private or separate washrooms, the new wording simply stated that employers need provide "discreet" facilities. So Stelco put up a partition around the urinals!

6 In Local 1005 there are only two kinds of committees — those whose members were appointed by the president or executive, and those elected by the membership at a plant-wide election. If a women's committee were elected by ballot at the plant gate at a time when women's presence in the plant was still a new event, the majority elected would probably have been men well-known in the plant, but not necessarily informed on women's concerns.

V THE POWER OF
ALLIANCES

FREE UNIVERSAL DAY CARE:
THE OFL TAKES A STAND

Susan Colley

During economic recessions grass roots movements often wither and die. Yet the day care movement in Ontario is flourishing. A handful of activists have managed to transform the disparate struggles around the issue of day care into a province-wide movement under the umbrella of the Ontario Coalition for Better Day Care. The involvement of the Ontario Federation of Labour (OFL) has been central to this transformation.

Activity at the workplace to improve the appallingly low salaries, status and working conditions of day care workers is at an all-time low, however. The Canadian Union of Public Employees (CUPE), the Ontario Public Service Employees Union (OPSEU) and the Service Employees International Union (SEIU) have flirted with the idea of organizing day care staff into a strong bargaining unit, but after early enthusiasm, these campaigns have been abandoned.

Most people are aware of the enormous problems facing the consumers and teachers of day care. It is estimated that in Ontario 355,000 children with working mothers need day care and yet there are only 47,000 full-time day care spaces to accommodate them.[1] Over half of these spaces must be paid for by the parents at a cost ranging from $300 to $650 per month.[2] The government's financial role in day care services is minimal. One-third of one percent of the provincial budget is spent on day care, amounting to a total of $36.29 per annum for every child in Ontario under 9.[3] The funding that does exist provides day care subsidies to only 19,000 children.[4] The consequence of high costs to parents and a low level of government subsidization is that the vast majority of parents cannot obtain a government subsidy and cannot afford fees.

Even though the present costs of day care are beyond most parent's pocketbooks, the cost of high quality day care would rise still further if day care staff did not subsidize the service with their low salaries. Average wages for qualified day care teachers are $10,000 per year with no benefits. Compare this to a registered nurse with roughly equivalent educational qualifications, in a unionized position, who receives between $22,800 and $26,000 per year plus a 14 percent benefit package.[5]

The day care system is in a Catch-22 situation: if teachers' salaries increase, then day care fees must rise. If fees rise, parents can no longer afford the service and therefore must seek cheaper arrangements. If there are day care spaces vacant, then the government screams, "What do you mean, you need more day care; there are hundreds of spaces sitting empty!" Meanwhile, over 300,000 children in Ontario alone are receiving day care in informal babysitting arrangements. This care may be excellent, but generally it is mediocre, and in some cases, it is so bad as to be harmful.[6]

The day care movement has been attempting to overcome this crisis for several years and this struggle has given birth to the demand for free universal quality day care. High quality day care and education for our young children means supervised, regulated care, rather than informal, unsupervised care. That care is already expensive and will become more so if we are to lower staff turnover and attract high quality, well-trained workers. If we want this care to be widely available, we will need at least a tenfold expansion. In order for it to be financially accessible to the children of working parents, where the biggest need exists, there will have to be a very high level of government subsidization. Therefore, the day care movement's strategy is to fight for complete public funding of day care programs.[7]

A radical and comprehensive day care policy was adopted by the Ontario Federation of Labour and its affiliates at its annual convention in 1980. This policy demanded that day care be free and universally accessible; that a variety of parent-worker controlled day care centres with a range of different types of day care (known as the neighbourhood hub model) be offered; that the Labour Code be reformed to extend maternity leave and grant paternity leave and that the exploitive nature of a system that condemns teachers in day care to poverty-level wages be recognized and rectified.[8]

The OFL's adoption of this policy marked the first time in Canada that the fundamental demand for a free universal day care system gained the support and influence of a major institution. And it was the first time that the trade union movement had embraced a central demand of the women's movement and agreed to act on it.

The Federation proposed a specific plan of action to implement the policy. At the union level, the OFL called for day care at union functions; contract negotiations for family-related provisions, such as job-sharing and part-time work, with the same benefits and pay; flexible working hours; allowances to cover day care costs; workplace day care where appropriate; and a limitation on voluntary overtime and shift work. On the political level, it called on all provincial candidates to support universal day care in their election campaigns; it also voted to organize a government lobby and to set up public forums across the province in order to ascertain regional problems and educate communities around the issue. In effect, the OFL was initiating a provincial day care coalition.

Forums across the province were quickly organized. A panel composed of leaders from the Ontario Federation of Labour, the Ontario Teachers' Federation, the Ontario Welfare Council, the Association for Early Childhood Education and Action Day Care toured the province hearing briefs from about 200 individuals and organizations. Media coverage was excellent, press conferences were well attended, there was both national and local television coverage and panelists participated in about a dozen radio talk shows.

The briefs concentrated on problems that were familiar to day care activists: the lack of day care spaces, the high cost of day care, the inadequacy of the subsidy system, the low wages of day care workers and, of course, insufficient government funding to provide high quality care. In addition, many workers stressed the need for 24-hour care. The emotional impact of these meetings was stunning. One woman came forward to explain how the lack of good day care had caused her a great deal of fear and guilt. One morning she had arrived at her babysitter's house to find that no one was home. The next-door neighbour excitedly told her that her babysitter had been arrested in a drug raid the night before. The mother was left with no day care and with a lot of questions in her head about what had been going on at that home when she was at work. At another forum, an older woman described her experiences organizing to maintain day care services at the end of the Second World War and her disillusionment 35 years later because very little had changed despite the enormous increase in need. The panelists also heard from a day care teacher at the People's Church in Welland who explained that her day care centre was in such financial difficulty that the staff had been working without pay for some time. Another woman, a mother of a two-year-old, said that lack of day care in Thunder Bay forced her to make inadequate private arrangements for her child.

> My son was fed starches and sugars because they keep children quiet and were cheaper than fruits and vegetables, and was plunked in front of a TV instead of being provided with stimulating play.[9]

Stories such as these convinced panelists of the need for a provincial day care coalition; and the interest and enthusiasm of the panelists convinced local day care activists, women's centres and trade unionists that continuing the struggle at the local level was worthwhile. The panelists returned to Toronto to summarize the results of the forum and to persuade other groups to join them in making a presentation to the provincial government. This idea was embraced by other key organizations in the spring of 1981: Action Day Care, the Association for Early Childhood Education, CUPE, all of the teachers' federations, the International Women's Day Committee, the National Action Committee on the Status of Women, the Ontario Committee on the Status of Women, the Ontario Federation of Students, OPSEU, the Ontario Welfare Council, the Ontario Association of Family Service Agencies and the Ontario Association of Professional Social Workers. Over the summer, representatives from these organizations met weekly to hash out the wording of the brief. To get support of the social service organizations, the group dropped the demand for free universal day care and substituted the more nebulous phrase, "universally-accessible." Nevertheless the final brief, entitled "Deadline Day Care 1990" called for a drastic overhaul of the day care system to make it publicly funded and universally accessible by 1990. Out of this process, the Ontario Coalition for Better Day Care was launched. The coalition demanded the immediate implementation of some short-term emergency measures:

> (a) a $5 per day grant for every child enrolled in a non-profit day care program in order to allow wages to rise and fees to remain stable

> (b) the creation of an additional 10,000 subsidized spaces to deal with the immediate crises

> (c) the creation of a task force to investigate means of upgrading the salaries, working conditions and training opportunities for day care workers, eliminating public funding of commercial day care centres,

and transferring the jurisdiction of day care from the realm of welfare to the realm of education, to ensure that the care and education of children under six would become a right in the same way that it is for children over six.

This brief was published and distributed across the province and a mass lobby day organized at Queen's Park in November 1981. The Cabinet faced 100 lobbyists from across the province demanding the changes specified in the coalition's brief. After the initial presentation, the lobbyists divided into groups of four or five and visited every MPP in the legislature. It was surprising how much pro-day care sentiment existed in the legislature that day — but that sentiment was never translated into dollars. Although this experience consolidated a broad layer of day care activists across the province, it also convinced them that lobbying alone would not achieve the aims of the coalition.

During the winter of 1981-82 members of the coalition were in constant demand to speak at day care meetings throughout the province. Activists from day care centres, women's centres, trade unions and social service agencies began to lobby their MPPs at the local level as a first step in creating strong local organizations. By mid-1982 local coalitions existed in Toronto, Oshawa, Hamilton, Kingston, Peterborough, Sudbury, Windsor, Sault Ste. Marie, Kitchener-Waterloo, Stratford and Glengary. The initial phase of organizing a province-wide coalition was well underway.

Without the leadership, commitment and resources of the trade union movement such an achievement would never have been possible. In an era when the issues of high unemployment, mass layoffs, double-digit inflation and erosion of real wages were dominating the concerns of Ontario workers, it is remarkable that the OFL made their day care campaign a priority. The idea of conducting forums across the province was not new for them. They had already put on a successful series of forums about unemployment and been satisfied by the response. But the success of the day care campaign was due to the fact that the labour movement had tapped into the resources of women's and community groups and begun the organization of a broad provincial coalition. This *was* new for the OFL.

How did it happen? Three major groups contributed to the development of trade union policy and strategy: the OFL Women's Committee, Action Day Care and the trade union movement itself. For an understanding of how the positions and activities of these groups intertwined and culminated in the formation of the Ontario Coalition for Better Day Care, we need to turn back the clock several years.

Agitation around the day care issue began in the late Sixties and coincided with the rise of the women's movement. Women's liberation groups in Toronto, Montreal and Vancouver developed manifestoes that included the recognition that adequate child care was a precondition to women's liberation. During this period the women's movement developed an excellent position on day care. However, it chose to move away from political campaigns such as the fight for free universal day care to focus on improving the quality of women's lives through information networks and support services. This often meant small groups of women setting up day care centres, rape crisis centres or bookstores. Although these services filled an important need, they consumed the energy of the women's movement, leaving political action to win legislative reform and social change on the back burner.

During the same period the day care movement was launched by groups of parents determined to set up community-controlled cooperative day care centres. The fight for Campus Co-op Community Day Care Centre in Toronto is a landmark in this stage of the struggle. Confronting a university administration that refused to provide day care for students and workers, a determined group of parents organized meetings, demonstrations and a month-long occupation of a university building before the university eventually surrendered to their demands. Community-controlled day care centres subsequently opened in Ottawa, Waterloo and Hamilton, and under the auspices of the Day Care Organizing Committee, day care centres continued to press for capital funding and government reform. However, the activists dedicated to the struggle for free universal day care were in the minority. The mainstream of the movement was dominated by day care owners, administrators and teachers, none of whom saw day care in a larger political context.

Generally the day care movement concentrated on a defensive campaign to maintain the quality of service and was unwilling to launch an active campaign for higher wages for day care workers or drastic government reform. When Margaret Birch, Ontario Minister of Social Development, introduced proposals (known as the "Birch proposals") in the legislature in 1974 that threatened to reduce the standards usually considered basic for providing quality day care, the entire day care community in Ontario united to fight them. It formed a strong political organization, the Day Care Reform Action Alliance, representing a variety of groups involved in day care, including parent groups, private day care operators, co-op centres, the Social Planning Council, YWCA and the Association of Early Childhood Education in Ontario. The Alliance's actions included briefs to the government, letter-writing campaigns, petitions, public meetings, media coverage, lobbying local municipal councils, a mass demonstration at Queen's Park and picketing Margaret Birch at her public appearances across the province. The enormous pressure forced the government to quietly drop the proposals, a resounding victory for the day care movement.

Although the Alliance had set a precedent for a strong, politically-oriented day care organization, the day care community had not yet reached the collective conclusion that a fight for quality also meant a fight for more funding and expansion. It was capable of organizing some parents and disgruntled teachers to defend the quality of the service, but it was unable to mobilize enough support, especially among the potential consumers of the service, to fight offensively for expansion. Consequently, during the period 1975-79, the day care movement resorted to the traditional tactics of individual lobbying and participation on government advisory committees. As a result of this weakness in strategy, the movement witnessed real cutbacks in service and felt a lot of despair.

The emergence of Action Day Care in 1979 broke with this traditional response and produced a new direction for the movement. Composed of parents, day care workers, representatives from community and women's groups and trade unionists, Action Day Care met initially to fight cutbacks in day care funding. In the course of establishing themselves, they made four strategic decisions that set the stage for subsequent events.

First they decided that the only route to improving day care service was to organize politically around a demand for free universal quality day care. After ten years of debate, the day care movement had finally come to realize that without a free universal system, day care would always be subject to cutbacks, or to needs of labour force participation, or to the whims of individual government ministers.

Secondly, Action Day Care decided not only to continue the defensive struggles around cutbacks, quality of service and subsidy arrangements but to take the offensive. Three hundred and fifty thousand spaces were needed, which would require a major shift in Ontario government policy and allocation of funds. For Action Day Care this meant the provincial government was to become the prime target of political pressure.

Thirdly, Action Day Care agreed that the day care movement would have to broaden its base to include the trade union movement, the women's movement and the NDP. And finally, Action Day Care decided that it was time to organize day care teachers and workers into trade unions, both as a means of improving their immediate situation and of building political clout for the ultimate conflict with the government.

Action Day Care undertook a series of open forums to develop a comprehensive platform, which was then distributed within the NDP, the OFL and women's organizations. This platform laid the basis for both NDP and OFL policy. Action Day Care ensured that the fight against the cutbacks in the summer of 1980 was clearly and militantly aimed at the provincial government. By occupying City Hall, pressure was put on Metro Toronto Council to throw its support behind the day care movement. A demonstration at Queen's Park in October 1980 resulted in day care becoming a very hot issue in the pre-election fall of 1980. In fact, this series of events forced the government to increase funding to day care by an additional $12 million. Not nearly enough, but it showed that such agitation could be effective.

During 1979-80, Action Day Care cultivated strong links with the OFL Women's Committee, laying the basis for the work of that committee in the trade union movement. In the summer of 1980 the OFL Women's Committee decided that day care was a critical issue for trade union women and that a comprehensive policy could successfully be presented to trade unionists. They knew it would not be easy. About six years earlier, the Day Care Reform Action Alliance had sent two women to the OFL convention in Niagara Falls to set up an information table on day care. They came back discouraged, having been bombarded with such witticisms as "Day care, eh, what I need is a little night care, baby." But attitudes seemed to be changing.

In October 1980, the OFL Women's Committee organized a Sharing the Caring conference to bring the issue of day care to trade unionists across the province. The conference drew 100 delegates, both women and men, who talked about the problems facing their membership and discussed the concrete recommendations contained in the OFL Women's Committee's policy paper. These recommendations were adopted at the conference, endorsed by the leadership of the OFL, and overwhelmingly passed by the delegates to the 1980 OFL convention; they then became the working program for trade unionists in Ontario.

The consciousness of the trade union membership was another factor, along with the work of Action Day Care and the OFL Women's Committee, that contributed to the adoption of the day care policy at the OFL. Ten years earlier it could not have happened. But there had been a perceptible change in consciousness concerning women's issues in the union movement. Increasingly, trade unionists, particularly women, were standing up at conventions urging the defence of women's right to work, support for demands for equal pay for work of equal value, affirmative action programs, and, of course, for more child care. Because these demands coincided with the needs and problems facing working women, they began to gain credibility.

By 1980 the trade union movement was ready to accept some of the demands of working women, especially their demand for the right to work. It had recognized that many of the demands put forward by the women's movement were important social and political issues. It was no surprise when applause swept the room at the OFL Day Care Conference in Toronto when Stew Cooke, a middle-aged steelworker union director, credited the women's movement for the current involvement of the unions in the day care issue. "Indeed, when the social history of the latter part of the century is written," he said, "the story of the women's movement will be properly underlined as a major step forward for humankind. No matter how often all of us rightly refer to day care as a 'people' issue, the women's movement deserves the political credit for transforming day care from a background issue into a central item on our social agenda."[10] Free universal quality child care had become a policy of the labour movement. And not only had the movement passed a convention resolution in favour of quality child care, it had also committed staff and financial resources to a campaign to win it.

Today, the Ontario Coalition for Better Day Care is an Ontario-wide coalition of major organizations and locally active coalition groups. Representatives from these local groups, together with representatives from the provincial organizations, met together for the first time at a conference, The Caring Future, in the fall of 1982. They were able to share experiences of their struggles in their respective communities and talk about a direction for the future. In the plenary sessions they endorsed the original demands of "Day Care: Deadline 1990" and generated renewed enthusiasm to return to their regions and continue to organize.

Success has not come so readily, however, to the attempts to organize day care workers into trade unions for higher wages and better conditions. Initial successes in Ottawa and Toronto have subsequently petered out, leaving day care workers in a weak position to face restraint-minded employers and governments.

In 1979, Ottawa day care workers from a number of day care centres were certified into one central bargaining unit in a CUPE local. They used the strength of their numbers to force the regional municipality to increase the subsidized day care fees in order to bring wages to parity with the better-paid municipal workers. Work to organize day care staff into trade unions in Toronto began in the fall of 1980. It was led by Action Day Care, who set up a series of workshops presenting Ottawa's successful drive as a model. High wage demands by day care staff cannot be granted without significant fee hikes. So, the idea was to persuade workers and parents to unite as a political force in a campaign aimed at winning a direct grant from the provincial government. Key to this strategy was organizing large numbers of day care workers quickly and using a joint bargaining committee to negotiate contracts. Seventeen day care centres were organized into a CUPE local by the end of 1981, but by the end of 1982, only a few contracts were signed, the concept of the "central bargaining table" had crumbled, day care centres were working on individual wage schedules, two of the centres were ready to decertify and day care workers were facing a new era of cutbacks and wage controls divided, demoralized and disarmed.

A number of factors led to this situation. The first involved day care workers and the nature of their workplaces. Few day care workers have any trade union or political experience. And there are special problems with organizing these workers. In a day care situation, relationships between workers, parents and administrators are often very personal. Day care workers are wary of organizing if it will bring them into conflict with the parents of children they know and love. The threat of conflict with a supervisor with whom they work closely is also very disconcerting. In this context, traditional forms of union organizing and strike tactics are inadequate. Many unions in public service industries have faced a similar dilemma. When they go on strike, they are said to be hurting the public rather than the boss. In day care this contradiction is multiplied because the strike immediately affects the children and their parents. Newspapers and other media delight in emphasizing the suffering the strike is causing, completely ignoring the plight of minimum wage day care workers. These relationships and the fear of going on strike lead day care workers to resist union organization.

Secondly, Action Day Care's unionization strategy, designed to overcome these problems, backfired. Action Day Care is a small organization, separate from the union movement. It does not have the political or organizational strength to influence the strategies of the unions. Action Day Care successfully launched the Direct Grant Campaign and carried it through the OFL Women's Committee, the NDP and the women's groups. But it did not develop a close working relationship with leaders, staff and committees of trade unions – particularly CUPE. Consequently, there was no organization able to bring together political and economic components of the strategy: the political strategy went in one direction and the economic strategy moved in another.

The third factor was a lack of strategy on the part of the trade unions. When CUPE began to organize day care workers in Toronto, it understood the economic reasons why day care workers should unionize. It had a mandate and a commitment to organize and support low-paid workers in women's job ghettos. But it did not understand the political implications of the struggle, and treated day care workers in the same way it did hospital, municipal and social service workers. Day care is not yet a universally funded service, so negotiations with employers meant negotiations with working-class as well as middle-class parents, and the impact of high wages resulted in fee hikes that forced many parents to withdraw their children from day care. The CUPE attempts at wage negotiations, in addition to being a threat to the parents, posed a threat to the job security of the workers.

CUPE did not commit the necessary resources to the organizing drive and never came to terms with the complicated day care funding structure. The CUPE staff did not understand that all day care budgets must be approved by Metro Community Services in October for the following year. When negotiations dragged on past October, day care directors had already submitted their budgets to Metro, and there was no mechanism for negotiating the budgets retroactively. Consequently, day care workers were left to the mercy of their day care directors. The concept of a political strategy for winning increased wages and benefits for day care workers was completely alien to CUPE. Staff representatives listened politely to Action Day Care's ideas, but then continued to organize in the same manner. In addition, CUPE played a minimal role in the Ontario Coalition for Better Day Care, where political ideas and strategies were being developed. There was no education campaign. Members were not informed about conferences, committees or union schools. They pleaded for an organizer, but were left to the resources of the overworked CUPE field worker — the sole organizer for Ontario. Demoralization set in. One centre closed down and set up elsewhere with a new name and no union, without being challenged by CUPE. Two bargaining units decertified, and others were considering it. Three management teams refused to negotiate acceptable terms and appeared before the Conciliation Board. Faced with a strike situation, the workers shuddered at the thought of an experience such as Mini-Skool workers were engaged in, and quickly backed down.

What is now needed is for the unions involved in day care — CUPE, OPSEU and the SEIU — to sit down with representatives from the day care movement and work out a new, creative strategy that combines the political struggle against the government with the economic struggle for higher wages and better working conditions.

APPENDIX

Resolutions from *Statement on Day Care*,
Ontario Federation of Labour, November 1980

To this end, the OFL proposes the following as a comprehensive child care plan:

1 Access to a free, universal publicly-funded quality service of care for children aged 0-12 be recognized as an essential social right of every family wishing to use the service.

2 Existing facilities should be developed into a pattern of local satellite child care centres which would fulfill the educational and developmental needs of young children in the community. Each centre would act as a training and resource point for registered private home care givers and playgroups in its area, and might also provide some child health services. Advantage should be taken of the falling numbers of school children caused by the drop in the birth rate to convert unused classrooms into centres. Provincial government funding must be made available to these.

3 Responsibility for the service should be removed from the Ministry of Community and Social Services where it will always be seen as a welfare service and not a universal right. An early childhood education division of the Ministry of Education must be established which ensures flexibility of approach combined with community control. We do not want day care services to be centrally controlled or become lost in a monolithic structure that parents cannot hope to influence. Day care must be responsive to the changing priorities of its users; it must also be available as a right to all. Only by creating an *autonomous* division of the Ministry of Education can we hope to combine these two principles.

4 The province be committed to fund and assist child care provision when 25 children within a school attendance area require care; such funding must be available only to non-profit and government-operated centres.

5 Private home day care could be organized as part of this system, with the neighbourhood group day care centre as the hub of the wheel, and the family homes as the spokes. Family caregivers would be registered as a condition of public funding.

6 The standards set down in the Day Nurseries Act should be regarded as the "minimum;" and persons with education and experience in early childhood education must continue to be the primary staff in day care centres.

7 Day care workers must receive salaries and benefits commensurate with the value of their work and on a par with workers in education, nursing and social work. Unions must make greater efforts to organize day care workers, and to this end, continue the fight for less restrictive labour laws.

8 The provision of day care facilities cannot be seen in isolation. Just as centres can offer parents the opportunity to return to work or education knowing their child is well looked after, it is equally necessary for society to offer a realistic opportunity to remain at home and care for their child at birth and for a reasonable period afterwards. Present leave provisions fail to acknowledge the wish and right of the father to be involved in child rearing and do not account for the severe stress for parents when children are sick. Legislative amendments should include:

a) Paid parental leave available to either parent for the care of a child up to a joint total of one year after birth, or adoption. (Entitlement to leave comes under The Employment Standards Act pay under the Unemployment Insurance Act.)

b) Employees receiving such leave will retain and accumulate seniority and have all benefits maintained during such leave.

c) Employees who have been employed with their employer for 6 months will be entitled to such leave.

d) Parents be guaranteed paid leave up to 10 days per year for the care of their children who are ill or who have special needs requiring parental attention.

NOTES

1 Estimate by the Ontario Women's Bureau, 1981.

2 The Day Care Research Group, *The Day Care Kit,* 1982, p. 7.

3 *Ibid.*

4 *Ibid.*

5 The lastest figures on salaries of day care teachers have been compiled by Action Day Care in a pamphlet, "For Universally Accessible, Non-compulsory Day Care in Canada," 1982. Nurses' salaries were provided by the Ontario Nurses' Association, based on 1982 wage scales.

6 For a further discussion of informal babysitting arrangements see Laura C. Johnson and Janice Dineen, *The Kin Trade* (Toronto: McGraw Hill Ryerson, 1981).

7 Resolutions passed at the Second National Day Care Conference in Winnipeg in Sept. 1982 support this program. Available from Canada, Health and Welfare, Day Care Information Service.

8 See Appendix for a list of OFL resolutions on day care.

9 A summary of the presentations to these province-wide forums, as well as the analysis and program, is contained in "Day Care Deadline, 1990: Brief to the Government of the Province of Ontario on the Future of Day Care Services in Ontario by the Ontario Coalition for Better Day Care," Nov. 1981. Available from the Ontario Coalition for Better Day Care, 1260 Bay Street, 7th Floor, Toronto, Ontario.

10 "Day Care: Deadline 1990."

WIVES SUPPORTING THE STRIKE

Arja Lane

Wives Supporting the Strike (wss) evolved during the 1978 strike by 12,000 members of Local 6500 of the United Steelworkers of America against International Nickel Company (Inco), a international company that has its greatest assets flowing out of Sudbury.

Inco has been Sudbury's main employer for a long time. Before a more modern smelting process was developed, Inco smelted the ore in huge open hearth fires, using up the trees surrounding the town as fuel. But now, with the Super Stack and refineries, the fumes blow out of Sudbury so the trees and people don't choke as much; and the fifty-year old furnaces are now inside the refineries and no longer blacken life quite so openly.

wss was a volunteer organization with about 200 women on its mailing list, and an active core of forty. Our ethnic backgrounds included Finnish, French, Indian, Italian, Polish and Ukrainian women. During the eight and a half month strike, we created a support system and a morale booster that helped the workers and their families stand firm until the terms of the contract were satisfactory to the majority.

The idea of forming a women's strike support group emerged during a meeting of Women Helping Women (whw) a political, action-oriented women's group that had been around Sudbury for seven years. whw had done some mildly militant community education work: the presentations of briefs to local health councils; production of videotapes dealing with women and our oppression. The women in whw varied in age and background, but we did have common interests — one of which was to vocalize the needs of women in Sudbury to the rest of the community. When the strike began, I was one of the few women in the group who was also the wife of a striker; and when I brought my newest dilemma of being on strike to a monthly meeting of whw, the group sought ways to do strike support work. We were aware that the homemaker bears the brunt of a strike because it is she who has to cope with running the household on less money; and that this pressure can be destructive to the individual woman and to the whole strike effort.

Our discussion generated a leaflet announcing a meeting for wives of strikers who were interested in learning more about the issues of the strike. We stood inside the Steelworkers' union hall and handed out leaflets to workers who were registering for strike assistance vouchers. Some of the leaflets were brought home and passed on to the women at home; some were thrown in the garbage as soon as the men noticed that they were addressed to the "women of the household." Some of the men told us to go home, that the union hall was no place for a woman. During those initial leafleting sessions, we began to get an idea of the many-faceted struggle we were going to face.

A meeting of interested women was held, despite the fact that many of our leaflets never reached their intended destination. Most of the women who came to that initial meeting had worked mainly as home-workers — that ever-challenging job of creating a mini-world of warmth and shelter. At this meeting and the ones that followed, I learned about the issues of the strike, and why the contract offer had been rejected: the poor pensions, wages that were not keeping up with the rate of inflation, the job insecurity with impending layoffs, unsafe working conditions. I realized that because I was living with a Steel-worker when his local decided to strike, my life as his partner was inextricably connected to the strike and its outcome.

The money he earned paid for the expenses of organizing and oper-ating a home. And the instabilities of his workplace, whether it be overtime or an accident, filtered into the home and changed my work patterns, my emotions and home life routines. I may not have had a union card in my wallet, or been the one who trudged off to spend eight hours in the copper refinery, but the quality of my life and work depended largely on how things went with him at work, what contract benefits he had and what happened during the strike. When he went on strike, he took me on strike too.

As homemakers, we had excellent organizational skills; and it didn't take long to begin applying these skills at meetings or to organize events or services that would help people cope. We knew where it was going to hurt when there was no paycheque coming in regularly. We also knew that in order to win this strike, we had to remain united with the union against Inco. To do that most effectively, we had to remain united within our own families which necessitated building support of the spouses.

In 1958, during a strike between workers and Inco, a painful point was proven — it was easy to manipulate the wives of strikers when they were uninformed. Back then, the wives were called together at the Sudbury arena by civic and church leaders and were encouraged to urge their husbands to return to work because of the hardships of the strike. Those women were used as pawns, and as a result, they were labeled strikebreakers. We did not want history to repeat itself!

So we formed a group and called ourselves Wives Supporting the Strike (wss) because that name best described our reason for organizing. Our goals were to provide moral support and practical assistance to families of strikers. We also wanted to stay informed about the issues concerning the strike so that we wouldn't feel so frightened about the future or so isolated in our struggle to survive. Once we learned the basic facts about the strike, we saw how wss could help build a stronger strike effort. The union executive board was involved in administering strike assistance pay, organizing picket lines and attending strike benefits. wss tried to plan events that shared information about the strike or provided some practical assistance to strikers' families.

One of our first big events was a Christmas party for the children of strikers. We knew there wasn't going to be money to buy toys and gifts after three months of strike, so we began an appeal for donations of toys and food to local businesses, most of whom responded positively. News of our plans to host a Christmas party for 10,000 children soon reached other cities, and truckloads of toys, new and old, began arriving at the union hall. To inform the children about what was going on in the strike, we produced a cartoon leaflet that explained the strike in terms they could understand and handed it out with their toys and treats.

In order to raise morale and educate the community about the issues of our strike, a group of us staged a theatrical performance that portrayed the directors of Inco on trial for their "crimes" against the community and the workers. Needless to say, the directors were found unanimously guilty by the audience-jury. To make a dramatic statement about how "Inco gets the gravy and we get the beans," we planned a free bean supper that fed over 5,000 strikers on Valentine's Day. In addition, a clothing depot was set up and operated by a few of the women for most of the duration of the strike. Later, as many women were having babies, a "baby depot," where strikers' wives could pick up formula, diapers and other baby accessories was created.

We held plantgate collections, requesting money from workers of other plants who weren't on strike. Normally, plantgating takes place at the gate of the plant where workers go in to their workplace. It is a common practice within the labour movement and it is an important survival tactic for those on strike. Plantgating also provides an opportunity to share information about the strike and to create a sense of solidarity. There were many plantgate collections organized by and for Local 6500 during the strike. Members went to cities across Canada to collect money and share information with union brothers and sisters, and some wives went along.

But the plantgating that wss initiated was quite controversial: at the same time as we played women's traditional role as peacemakers, we organized plantgate collections at Falconbridge Mines, in Sudbury, where members of Local 598 of the Mine, Mill and Smelter workers had not struck against a similar contract offer earlier that summer. Members of our local were hesitant to initiate these collections because they feared there would be hard feelings between the two locals. But our logic was different. wss had no hard feelings, the union needed money to operate the various crisis committees, and there were all these plants near Sudbury that were not being tapped for support.

At first, some of the wives felt that we were meddling with something potentially explosive. But the workers at Falconbridge donated generously, asked how things were going with our strike and congratulated us for organizing. Some were surprised to see women, and we explained that the guys were busy elsewhere so we were covering this ground. They gave us wishes of strength and solidarity with the dollars.

Our decision to plantgate Falcongate workers served a dual purpose: the money we collected provided practical assistance to strikers, and the action helped to clear the air between Local 6500 of USWA and Local 598 of Mine, Mill and Smelter Workers.

In order to organize these events efficiently, wss had to be structured to encourage the maximum participation of our members. A steering committee was elected every three months, and only wives of strikers qualified as voting members. The steering committee included a chairperson, a secretary, a treasurer, two spokespeople (one French-speaking and one English-speaking) and a union liaison officer. The spokespeople were the only two official media representatives of wss.

The union liaison officer was the woman who kept lines of communication open between the wss and the union executive board. All recommendations of the steering committee had to be ratified by the membership at a general membership meeting before action could be implemented. This way, a small group couldn't run the organization, which is what often happens with the traditional "union board" concept.

wss was made up of women of various ages and cultural backgrounds, and so our personal and political interests varied. Some of us were very traditional in our roles as women and activists within the strike; some of us were more politicized about the connections between our personal lives and the political arena and so tradition seemed a hindrance. Working together made us realize that our varying skills could complement each other. Some women were good at keeping records, so they took care of the bookkeeping, or recorded minutes of meetings; some were better at verbal communication, so they went to strike benefits to explain our cause to others; some were good on the telephone, so they did the calling to get other jobs done; some had connections with people in other sectors of the community, such as food stores or business, and they worked at organizing support from these sectors. By using the varying skills within the group to organize practical assistance as well as to politicize the public through intelligent information-sharing, the strike gained a kind of public support that would not have happened without our involvement.

One source of public support was the strike support benefits organized by activists in other union locals, women's groups or political groups around the country. The benefits were usually fun for the audience, who danced to the live music and listened to tales of striking workers. Wives' tales began to be heard at these strike support benefits as women from our group were invited to speak to them. It was amazing to get up in front of hundreds of people for the first time and speak into a microphone to tell a crowd about the strike, and it was even more amazing to feel the genuine interest of the crowd. The enthusiasm and energy generated at these benefits provided real solidarity for the strike.

But the same reasons that made wss a many-faceted and creative organization also caused difficulties. Some of us were feminists, and some of us weren't. Some of us were socialists and some of us weren't.

We had to deal continually with conflicts stemming from these personal and political differences. Those of us who were feminists wanted to expand our roles as activists in the strike. We didn't just want to make sandwiches for picketers, we wanted to picket. It was a constant effort to get the non-traditional activities like plantgating, public speaking, petitions, theatre and press releases approved and supported by the group. Some meetings dragged late into the night with nothing else resolved except that some of us were feminists or that some of us must be "commies" or that some of us were "just" housewives. One event that split the group into two factions was the way wss spent International Women's Day in 1979. We had been invited by the International Women's Day Committee in Toronto to sing and talk at their celebrations. The invitation excited enough of us to put together a chorus, practise some songs of solidarity and bus down to Toronto. Most of us had never been to a march of any kind, let alone one in Toronto. I knew that the celebration of International Women's Day originated in 1908 when women in New York City walked off their jobs as garment workers and stayed out until a first contract was negotiated. It was one of the pioneer organizing efforts against oppression, and it had come from women. And that was easy for wss to relate to mid-way through a strike.

But the march in Toronto showed how women's fight against oppression had grown to include lesbian mothers, punky dykes, pro-abortion groups and left activists. Some of the wss women were horrified to be associated in public with such "perverted, unchristian, communist hippies." I was amazed and relieved to learn that so much was happening in Toronto, but not all of us were as thrilled. Some thought it was "disgusting, family destroying and boring."

The arguing slowly made us realize that what each faction wanted to do did not have to interfere with the other's plans. To have a united strike effort, we needed both to "look after our own" through practical assistance, and to make "others" aware of our struggles in order in inspire broader solidarity. We agreed that those who didn't want to participate in an event didn't have to and that if there were enough people to get it done, then there was no reason why it shouldn't. We agreed that press releases had to be voted on, and the majority would rule the decision. Our differences ceased to be as threatening, even though they didn't melt away. We came to understand why there were such differences and this enabled us to respect each individual's contributions.

However, there were other problems beyond our internal group dynamics that weren't very easy to deal with – especially the all-male union board. The executive board is elected by the membership once a year, and consists of a president, vice-president, secretary and treasurer. Unfortunately, because of low membership participation, ignorant reactionaries can get elected to the executive board. At first WSS was able to operate fairly autonomously, although we always invited a member of the union executive board to our meetings to answer any questions about the strike. When the executive realized how effective we were, there was an immediate move to control our actions. This added to the tension inside WSS. The board's influence on the more traditional faction of WSS created a lot of antagonism within our group because many of the events that the less traditional faction planned were made difficult to organize due to the lack of support from the board.

There were other areas of conflict with the board. For example, once WSS established a bank account with donations from individuals and groups across Canada, the board wanted to have signing power on our cheques. We requested the same right on controlling their expenditures, but that didn't go over well. WSS used the union's duplicating equipment to print our publicity. When the board disagreed with an event they vetoed our access to this equipment, thereby slowing up our work tremendously and sometimes actually preventing us from organizing an event. We suggested that we be allowed to attend the union's membership meetings to improve the flow of information between WSS and the membership of Local 6500, but that didn't go over well either.

The executive board's reluctance to cooperate on several occasions indicated their desire to control, rather than to work with the WSS. It was infuriating to work with such a sexist group of men. One of their particularly exasperating attitudes was that "If there wasn't a strike, WSS wouldn't even be here now; so, we as leaders of this strike have the right to say no to your activities if we think they jeopardize the success of the strike." There were times when some of us questioned in whose interests they were running this strike: the company's, the union bureaucrats' or the rank and file workers'. WSS learned to work around the most offensive board members by networking more with the support staff at the union hall. But we also believed that this was not the time to sort out our differences — we were so busy organizing support for the strike that we did not have time. We felt that we couldn't change everything at once, and that if we tried to, the strike may have been lost and once again blamed on the women. As the wss union liaison officer for the duration of the strike, I would say that although the executive board and wss remained adversaries in private, we tolerated each other in public.

wss challenged yet another age-old tradition and as a result rocked the foundations of the community. Many of the husbands were very threatened by the element of "women's liberation" in wss. It threatened men that their wives were going to meetings where they themselves were not present, and were making decisions and planning actions about "their strike." Some of the men began to see another side of their women, a side that they had not realized existed and one that could grow out of their control. Allegations about women's liberation were quickly denied by many of the women themselves, who claimed that this strike was not a platform for feminism, but an attempt to secure a stable future.

Some of the husbands were upset that they were left to tend to the children. In other families, this was a welcome role reversal and gave fathers an opportunity to spend time with their kids — something they had little chance to do when working three shifts in the mines. During the strike, personal adjustments had to be made within the family unit, especially when the woman of the house was interested in something other than cooking and cleaning. The routine changed: she was out a lot more, at meetings, plantgate collections, strike benefits. She was feeling excited and productive in a different way while he was at home with the kids, cooking sometimes, or helping with the dishes, maybe cleaning up the house a bit, feeling baffled by the workload.

Many men weren't willing to try and adjust to any changes in routine and as a result, many women didn't get involved in wss. Even some of the women who were active in wss were harassed by husbands when the group made a decision contrary to their male philosophy. Women would come to meetings and say that their husbands had yelled at them for staying out so late or for the wording of a letter or a poster. Women would describe the complaints about how the kids had not eaten their supper or gone to sleep because she had not been there. Talking it over with women in the group gave many of us a chance to share how we coped with these problems, and often we'd go home with new ideas or ways to approach irate husbands.

We organized car pools and babysitting bees to help out with changes in our routines. As individuals we constantly worried about how to ward off the bill collector for a while longer, or how to budget for the next week's food. At times, the tension during our meetings grew to the point of cracking. Choir practices at the beginnings of meetings helped ease the stress. We learned songs like "Union Maid," "Solidarity For-ever" and "Bread and Roses," which made our hearts sing and reminded us of better times to come.

My partner was away for most of the first five months of the strike, working in Elliot Lake. Some strikers were "lucky" to get work else-where during the strike; but elsewhere usually meant out of town and that created involuntary separations within families. I avoided a lot of the isolation resulting from such separation by becoming involved with wss.

Working with wss was a politicizing experience. As women and wives of Inco workers we learned a lot about the external forces that affect and manipulate our personal realities as members of a commu-nity in a one-industry city. Realizing that the board of directors sat on the boards of banks we dealt with explained the added pressure on strikers about loans. The fact that cabinet ministers and members of parliament are often business partners with Inco officials, or are large shareholders of Inco stock, explains why multinational corporations get tax breaks while workers get laid off, or have to strike for job security and decent wages. Understanding that my contribution to Inco's profits was to help "my man" make it to work and to make babies so that "the family" would be more likely to stay while he ruined his health to support us, made me feel used in a worse way than any individual man had ever made me feel. As women, we began to see the long struggle ahead of us, one that will continue long after any strike, and for some of us this realization was painful.

But it wasn't a totally negative experience. As women we "came out" in many ways. We became more confident about our ability to use our homemaking skills to organize actions that effected change outside the home. We became less shy about speaking out about the way we saw issues. For many, it was our first time at meetings, and our first exposure to the how's, what's and why's of labour versus management. The information and skills that were shared at meetings and events enabled us to cope better with our everyday lives. The negotiating skills we polished up on at our meetings could be applied at home too. As wss, we realized how much stronger and more creative we were when we worked together.

Being part of the strike in this way changed many of our lives. Adjusting to "the way it is" after the strike was very difficult for me. It meant going back to a routine to fit his work routine: scheduling meals at different times, going to bed at different times, socializing mostly on his days off, with people who had the same day off as he. Too much happened to really go back to "the way it was." The strike had an impact on everybody in the community in one way or another. Citizens in Sudbury and around the country had their eyes opened to the arrogance of "our" multinational company, and so in many ways, community solidarity grew against Inco.

Since then, Sudbury has changed a lot. More citizens are active or at least aware of Inco's impact on the quality of life. With the continued shutdowns and layoffs of workers, a group calling itself the Laid-Off Inco Employees (LIES) is researching the effects and possible solutions to economic problems in Sudbury. An alliance of community groups is campaigning to nationalize the multinational culprit. Women workers at Inco have reactivated the Women's Committee of the union, and are challenging Inco from another perspective. A Women's Centre is now busy addressing the needs of women in Sudbury by helping women on mother's allowance to organize, setting up a rape crisis centre and organizing conferences on different issues. Women in the trades have formed a group ... and the list goes on.

Wives Supporting the Strike changed the status of women in Sudbury and provided a model for other groups. Wives' support groups around the country have formed to do similar work. Cape Breton coal miners were supported by a group of women who organized soon after their strike began in 1981. Steelworkers' wives formed a support group in Hamilton the same year when several Stelco plants were closed due to a strike. Women in Thompson, Manitoba backed the strike effort when workers there struck against another Inco operation during the fall and winter of 1981.

During the 1978 strike wss organized and left a mark. The effort was worth it because in 1982 when Local 6500 of the United Steelworkers of America was in a strike position again, wss was ready to swing into action. This time around, the union provided telephones and meetings rooms for wss use. Leaders of that union local have begun to realize that women can add needed strength to labour struggles.

The potential of this kind of alliance is enormous. At one point during the 1978 strike, wss suggested that we be allowed to attend union membership meetings to voice our opinion. At the time, the idea was rejected as ridiculous by the union executive board. Can you imagine how women's input would inspire and broaden the scope of issues that the labour movement is presently concerned with? Union meetings could become revolutionary if women attended and began discussing the effects of Inco operations on our lives. The effort to improve the quality of our lives, whether it be work life at Inco plants or at home would be that much stronger. This kind of unity would weaken the company's position because it could no longer use women or the rest of the community against the workers. But women would have to voice their own opinions and not just echo "their man's." This in itself would be a major hurdle because many men in the trade union movement don't realize or won't accept the contributions that women, as their wives, make to the whole effort of living. At best they reduce the role played by women to one of helper. This attitude has to change because we aren't just helpers, we are partners and co-workers. The experience of Wives Supporting the Strike has proven it.

FROM LADIES' AUXILIARIES TO WIVES' COMMITTEES

Meg Luxton

> I'm just a housewife. I've done that all my life and I ain't ever been a member of a union. But I figure that I'm really part of the United Mineworkers. My husband's a miner and a steward in the union but he couldn't do either without me. Without us wives, that union wouldn't amount to a hill of beans. Of course, the men will never admit it – but it's true.[1]

Vast numbers of Canadian women who have never been members of unions have nevertheless very significant relations with the trade union movement. Housewives who are married to trade union members find their daily lives profoundly affected by those unions and in turn, they often organize in support of the unions. Just as there is a tendency to ignore the activities and concerns of women workers in the trade union movement, the role of "union wives" in building and maintaining unions is often overlooked, or worse, denied.

> There was this guy came up from the International (union head office) to meet with the union to discuss negotiations. A bunch of us wives asked to meet with him. We wanted to tell him what we thought about the next contract. But he wouldn't see us – told [the local union representative] to tell us he was glad we were behind our husbands and not to worry! Well, I was just furious but what could I do? I mean, when our own union leaders don't think wives are part of all this ...

From the earliest days of union organizing in North America, wives of paid workers have been involved in their husband's unions. In the late nineteenth and early twentieth centuries, when the first major unionizing drives were fought, wives were often central to the struggles.[2] They helped to smuggle union organizers into their communities, protecting them from the company security guards. When the courts issued injunctions to prevent the men from picketing, wives took over for them. When scabs and police attacked the workers, the women joined in the fray as well. Mother Jones, a militant union organizer of mine workers in the United States, often drew on the strength and militancy of the women to mobilize pro-union forces. In one incident, she led a battalion of wives against the militia. Armed with mops and brooms, and beating on kitchen pots and pans, the wives marched through the night across a mountain pass to urge men from a nearby mine to join the union.[3]

In recent years in Canada, wives of male trade unionists have continued this tradition. During a ten-month strike against the International Nickel Company of Canada (Inco) in Sudbury in 1978, women formed a Wives Supporting the Strike committee and played a crucial role in the final union victory against a major multinational corporation. In Cape Breton in 1981 women formed the United Miners' Wives' Association and similarly played an essential role in helping the union win against the Cape Breton Development Corporation (Devco).

In Thompson, Flin Flon, Edmonton and Hamilton, similar committees have sprung up in recent years. The existence of such committees, the political issues they raise and the struggles they engage in all point to the fact that women, as wives of trade union men, have a relationship to the union and to the larger organized labour movement in Canada. What is that relationship? What are the implications for women of the links between wives and trade unions?

The answer to these questions is based on the family form that currently predominates in advanced capitalism; that is, a breadwinner husband and a relatively dependent wife. Because men regularly earn almost fifty percent more than women, even if women are themselves working for wages, they depend in part on their husbands' earnings.[4] For full-time housewives, dependence on the husbands' wages is absolute. As a result, in families with a male breadwinner, the wife has a vested interest in his wages.

On the basis of that dependency and vested interest, wives have a fundamental concern about the way their husbands organize to retain and, when possible, increase their earnings. Beyond these economic concerns, wives have an interest in what happens to their husbands at the workplace. If the man comes home regularly exhausted and irritable, growls at her and their children and falls asleep instead of spending time with the family, his work experiences are directly affecting her life. If he internalizes the poisons and filth of his workplace, she may have to care for him on inadequate disability pay and suffer with him as he dies from cancer or silicosis. On a more subtle yet all-pervasive level, to the extent that she and their children are dependent on his earnings, wife and husband both recognize that he is bound to his work in part because of their dependency.[5]

Out of this complex of material and emotional relations, the wife has both a direct personal interest in her husband's working conditions and level of pay and an indirect interest in his work-related experiences.[6] For the majority of people, these concerns are expressed only in private, if at all. However, when the men work in situations that are unionized or when the workers decide to try to unionize, an opportunity is created for the wives to organize their concerns and activities in a collective way, alongside and in support of the union.

Historically, however, the trade union movement has had a very ambivalent relationship to such women and their wives' groups. As other authors in this book demonstrate, the trade union movement has generally accepted the gendered division of labour, which assumes that women are first and foremost wives and mothers. In the early years of union organizing, unions defended male privilege and that legacy lingers today.[7] Unions are often reluctant to organize women workers and hesitant to fight for "women's issues" (so-called), such as parental (maternity) leave, day care and time off work to care for family members who are ill. The organized labour movement has been slow to fight for equal pay or for equal access to all jobs. Reflecting the sexism of Canadian society, the trade union movement tends to ignore the political potential of wives, paternalistically reminding them to stick by their husbands and not worry.

The trade union movement's relationship to wives of union members is further complicated by the structure of the union. Unions are designed to be collective defence organizations of the paid workers in a given work situation. The existence of the union requires a basic autonomy from any outside influence. As a result, there is no structure for including others who are not part of that work situation and non-union members have no place in the union.

Out of these conflicting interests and positions emerged, in the early twentieth century, the ladies' auxiliary. Found among unions, but particularly among the large, male-dominated industrial unions like Auto (UAW) and Steel (USWA), ladies' auxiliaries were union-recognized organizations designed for women who were related to union men. Modelled after similar ladies' auxiliaries of church groups or male voluntary associations, these groups were funded in part by the union. They were intended as a forum for wives to get together for social activities, fundraising, educationals and for organizing a variety of union-related social functions like Christmas parties or summer picnics.

In times of crisis such as organizing drives, plant occupations or strikes, these auxiliaries were mobilized to provide support for the union membership. Women in union auxiliaries traditionally collected and distributed clothes, supplies and toys for distressed union families. They cooked meals to feed picketing strikers and organized supplies for occupying workers. They held bake sales to raise money for the depleted union funds.

Inevitably tensions emerged both within the auxiliaries and between a specific auxiliary and the union with which it was affiliated, over the issue of what constitutes appropriate activities for the members of these ladies' auxiliaries. As long as the women stuck to activities traditionally defined as suitable for women, there was no problem. But many women wanted to do more than just service support.

They wanted to be involved in the actual picketing, in the fights with the police and the scabs, in the strategical and tactical debates of the organizers. Fundamentally they wanted to be part of the decision-making and political life of the union.

In the film, *With Babies and Banners,* about a plant occupation in the 1930s in Flint, Michigan, where autoworkers were trying to form a union, one wife expresses these views very succinctly. She described going down to union headquarters during the occupation.[8] Her offer of help was warmly received and she was directed to the kitchen to peel and cook potatoes. Pointing out that she did that kind of work at home all day, she refused, and instead (against the wishes of the strike organizers) organized a very effective children's picket, which won national publicity and much sympathy for the occupiers.

This tension between service work and political activity has been exacerbated in the last decade with the rise of the second wave of feminism. On the one hand, as more and more women have joined the paid labour force and the proportion of women in unions has increased, women inside trade unions have forced those organizations to become more sensitive to women's issues. On the other hand, as women generally have become more politically aware of their situation, more and more "ordinary" women have started challenging old notions of what constitutes appropriate activities for women. Specifically, many housewives have begun to rethink the parameters of their jobs and the nature of their relationships with their husbands.[9]

As a result, many ladies' auxiliaries have declined in membership and in activities over the last decade; some have even dissolved. However, a new organizational form has emerged that reflects the service-politics tension in new ways and is closely linked to the women's liberation movement. Usually referred to as "wives' committees," these are remarkably different from ladies' auxiliaries. Like traditional auxiliaries, their membership is comprised of women who are married to trade union members, and their activities are oriented to supporting the struggles of predominantly male trade unions. However, in sharp contrast with the auxiliaries, these committees prioritize the autonomy of the wives' committees, including the right to control funds and make political decisions apart from the union. Furthermore, these committees are action-oriented, developing their own political strategies and tactics on the picket line and in public relations.

So far, the wives' committees have all come into being in response to a specific strike situation. While they continue to do traditional service activities, these are largely viewed as part of a two-pronged strategy for winning the strike: as a means of helping workers and their families survive during the hardship of the strike period and as a way of educating other wives and members of the community who may be unfamiliar with the issues and hence reluctant to support the strike.

An important feature of any strike is the extent to which it tears apart families and disrupts marital relationships. There is a longstanding tradition that argues that wives are often opposed to strikes and that they drive their husbands back to work, forcing them to accept inadequate settlements against the advice of the union leadership. In numerous situations, management or other anti-strike forces have attempted to use wives to do just that. Management organizers and sympathisers meet with wives, warning them of the terrible consequences of a prolonged strike and playing on the understandable fears these women have of no income, hardship and perhaps permanent unemployment. When organized labour fails to address the specific situation of women whose livelihood depends on wages, they not only lose a potentially large and active group of supporters, they leave those women vulnerable to management manipulation.

It is ironic that management has often been quicker than trade union men to recognize the potential strength of mobilized wives. One of the motivating forces behind the growth of wives' committees is an attempt to resist just such pro-management manipulation. During the

1981 strike in the Cape Breton coal fields, the United Miners' Wives Association issued a warning to other wives:

> We are asking the women of striking families to please be aware of media manipulation. Some are trying to force our men back to work. The provincial election is now in full swing and pressure will be coming from both the provincial and federal levels of government. Ignore it. [10]

The history of the Sudbury Wives Supporting the Strike (wss) committee, its origins, its transformation from a ladies' auxiliary into a wives' committee, its activities during the 1978 strike and the follow-up activities after the strike was won, illustrate very clearly the character of the relationship between wives and their husbands' unions. It shows the potential for organizing women in such a position and reflects all the contradictions inherent in a union support group. [11]

The first union at Inco was the Mine, Mill and Smelter Workers, and wives were involved with it from the start. During the organizing drive, wives helped in a variety of ways to ensure the union's victory. When the union was finally recognized in 1944, the women formed a ladies' auxiliary, which continued to exist on and off until 1958.

The auxiliary maintained formal links with the union. Members went to union meetings regularly as observers, entitled to speak in the discussions although they had no vote. The union education officer worked with the auxiliary to plan regular educationals on a wide variety of topics. The Communist Party of Canada had a strong influence on Mine Mill and, as one of their policies was to include union members and their families in various campaigns they supported, the union periodically organized the women of the auxiliary to support drives like the International Peace Action.

For the most part, however, members of the auxiliary carried on activities well within traditional definitions of women's sphere. They catered for union functions, providing meals, organizing parties and cleaning up afterwards. They also played an important role in organizing and maintaining a whole range of services that helped to knit together the social fabric of Sudbury.

During the critical strike in 1958, the ladies' auxiliary, with about fifty or sixty regularly active members, worked very hard on a series of services and events. Opposition to that strike, occurring as it did at the height of the Cold War and organized by a union know to be favourable to the Communist Party, was particularly vicious. Inco manage-

ment, Sudbury civic officials and the provincial and federal governments coordinated their efforts, with the help of the police, in order to
smash the union.

In the second week of December 1958, the ladies' auxiliary called a
meeting to organize the wives in support of their striking husbands.
About nine hundred women are estimated to have attended that meeting and they agreed by straw vote to support the union demands. To
back up those demands, they decided to march the next Friday on City
Hall.

Realizing that a mobilization of the women of Sudbury would give a
great deal of weight to the union, the mayor attempted to co-opt the
women's initiative by announcing that he and other civic officials
would meet with all interested women in the city arena. The organizers
of the ladies' auxiliary decided that they wanted no part of such an
event and called off the march. The Sudbury newspaper however,
announced the meeting with the mayor in banner headlines and the
majority of women were confused, unsure which meeting was which.

> As I recall, it was all very unclear. One meeting had been planned by the
> wives. The mayor was holding a meeting. Some of us thought they were
> the same meeting. Others said they couldn't possibly be as the mayor
> wouldn't come to a ladies' auxiliary meeting. But we didn't know, so we
> went to the arena.

Over two thousand women turned up to meet with the mayor. The
meeting was brilliantly orchestrated by pro-Inco civic officials. The
mayor and several others spoke first, stressing the need to maintain
community unity.[12] Then the mayor asked if anyone had motions to
present.

Two women stepped forward and read their motions into a broadcast
system that did not work very well. The mayor then asked any people
who wanted to vote "no" to leave their seats and come down onto the
ice.

> Well, when he called for the vote it got really ridiculous. No one could
> hear the motions so everyone was really confused about what was
> happening. All those women had their children with them and it was
> freezing cold in that stupid arena. Then the mayor said that if women
> came down that meant they wanted to close Sudbury. Well, nobody
> wanted that, so most women stayed where they were, confused and
> frustrated by everything.

About one hundred and fifty women who had managed to follow the events actually climbed down onto the ice to indicate their disagreement with the motions but the mayor announced that the meeting was over.

The local papers ran banner headlines claiming that the wives had voted to settle at 1957 pay rates, that they wanted a quick settlement and were opposed to the men holding out for wage increases. The result was a very powerful tool for the pro-Inco forces. By seizing the propaganda initiative right from the start, they were able to swing behind them many people who otherwise would have supported the union position. These events further weakened the union. A week later, afraid that it would be thoroughly smashed, the union agreed to settle.

This defeat of both the ladies' auxiliary campaign and the union was a prelude to the subsequent smashing of Mine Mill at Inco. By 1961 Steelworker raids finally defeated Mine Mill and the United Steelworkers of America Local 6500 became the official union there. A result was that it became generally assumed in Sudbury that the miners' wives had been opposed to the 1958 strike. This generated a great deal of hostility towards those women and led many to assume that housewives are anti-union and conservative.

> In those few years after the strike it was just awful. Everyone kept saying, just as a matter of fact, that we had opposed the strike, that we lost the strike. I even heard men say stuff about how it was the wives who defeated Mine Mill by voting against the union. It wasn't true but they had said so in the newspaper so it became true.

Through the period of the raid and after Steel became the official union, there continued to be a ladies' auxiliary. Participation in its activities dwindled, though representatives from it walked the picket lines during the 1966 and 1969 strikes. Steel continued to support it until 1975 when it was disbanded because by that time it was very small and badly immobilized by internal conflicts.

While the ladies' auxiliary was slowly dissolving, other women's groups in Sudbury were springing up and growing. During the early 1970s, as a result of the spreading radicalization of the women's liberation movement, a group of women formed, calling themselves Women Helping Women. In 1978 when it became clear that the union was once again going to strike, this group began discussing the role of wives in strike. As one of them put it:

> At that time we didn't know the truth about the '58 strike. We just believed what they told us – that in '58 the wives forced their husbands to accept a really bad contract – that wives were really conservative and don't understand union policies and can't be trusted.

They were concerned that the same thing not happen again:

> Sudbury women don't want a repeat of the 1958 strike when church leaders and politicians brought thousands of strikers' wives to a "back-to-work" rally. Within a month, the strike had ended in humiliating defeat for the union just before Christmas.[13]

And so they called for the formation of a new group, one that was obviously related to the earlier ladies' auxiliary, but one that was fundamentally different as well. The result was Wives Supporting the Strike (wss).

Essentially this group began with a core of politically aware feminists who had heard anti-women stories of the '58 strike, who were pro-union and who wanted to draw Sudbury housewives into some form of political action. Some of these women had experience organizing feminist groups, activities and political events. Drawing on these skills, and on their intimate knowledge of the local community, they proposed a campaign that resonated with felt needs in Sudbury. Very rapidly, Wives Supporting the Strike grew into a large, significant organization involved in the strike.

wss had three basic tasks it hoped to carry out. The first continued an important tradition of auxiliaries – that of providing material and social support for the families of striking miners. Their second task involved educating wives about the union, and the third was to provide direct support for the striking union. As it did so, wss was forced to confront the political implications of its existence. It struggled constantly within itself and with the union in an attempt to define the group and its relationship to the union.

Another issue that generated stress within wss and between the committee and union members focused on the few women who were steelworkers. The tensions between women as wives of steelworkers and women as steelworkers clearly predated the strike and the formation of the Wives' Committee, but under the pressure of the political struggles, these tensions worsened. A number of wives were uncomfortable with the thought of their husbands working with women, and were upset when they saw their husbands with other women in the union offices or on the picket line.

> One woman actually said to me that why I was walking on the picket line was because I just liked to be around men. She told me I should stay away and stop pretending I cared about the union when it was really the men I wanted.

Some women who were full-time housewives maintained that the women who worked for Inco were violating traditional women's roles and therefore were untrustworthy.

> I work for the strike because I support my husband, not some other woman. I don't really think they should be working there. It isn't right.

In contrast, other wives were pleased that some of the union members were women. They felt it broke down some of the distance between the wives' group and the union membership.

> I was real glad to have [those women] around. There was so much tension between us and the union at times, that having a union member who was a woman and who could come to our meetings and help us really made a difference.

The most problematic tension, however, surfaced only after the strike was won. By the end of the strike wss had earned the respect of even the most chauvinistic of the union members. The executive had come around to a position of respect and support for them. They had proved their abilities and their usefulness. However, when the strike ended, their reason for existing also came to an end.

Initially many of the women insisted that they wanted to keep on meeting and "doing things" but there was no real basis for them to do so. Attendance at meetings dwindled and for a while, women who had been politically active retreated to their homes. Six months after the strike, one of the key organizers said despairingly:

> It's almost as if the strike never happened. It ended. Everyone went home. All that energy and excitement went away. The strike really changed me. I don't understand how it had no effect on anyone else.

Particularly for those women who had been involved in the initial organizing activities, who had dreamed of building a feminist organization that would have a long-term political impact on Sudbury, the dissolution of the group was a bitter disappointment. However, over the next year a number of events suggested that their hopes and vision had not been entirely in vain.

> At first the effects didn't show up. Everyone just went home and that was that. Or so it seemed. But gradually, the long-term effects started to

show up. Women who had been involved in the Wives' Committee will never be the same again.

On a personal level, it seems that most of the women who were involved in the committee were transformed by their experience. They gained a new perspective on their relationship with the world around them and found new sources of strength and power in themselves.

Well, my husband saw me in a new way after that strike. He saw me yelling at meetings and going by myself to Toronto to that rally and I realized I had more rights in this family. Some of it is small stuff like now he has to look after the kids once in a while if I want to go away for a weekend. But other stuff is bigger like I say what I think about family plans. And now he listens.

I had a fight with the bank manager the other day. He was being real ignorant and I got mad and started yelling at him that he couldn't treat me like that — right there in the bank with all those people around me! At the time I didn't think nothing of it. I just did it. When I got home I got real uptight and embarrassed like how did I ever get up the nerve? Then I realized I learned to stand up for myself during the strike.

On a wider scale, the Sudbury Wives' Committee had an impact that is still reverberating through women's movement and trade union circles. The film of their activities, *A Wives' Tale,* has been shown widely across the country. [14] Their format and activities have been an inspiration and in some cases a model for similar wives' groups in different locations.

In July 1981 in Cape Breton, Nova Scotia, miners voted to go on strike against Devco. A few weeks after the strike began, women were calling into a local radio station phone-in show to complain about miners' wages and how hard it was to raise a family on them.

I happened to wake up one morning and heard this woman on the talk-back show and she was bellyaching about the high cost of living and the low wages both she and her husband were given to live on. I said to myself, "What the hell is happening out here? Why doesn't she go out and do something instead of complaining?"

So I phoned the "talk-back" show and said: "Instead of that woman complaining, we (the women) should get a move on and get something going." That now was the time to do it. I said: "If women are interested in getting something organized, to give me a call." I gave my phone number over the air. About two seconds after I hung up, the phone started to ring and it is ringing yet. I guess I was disgusted and fed-up with my husband's pay cheque coming in every week and I knew I couldn't continue to look after six kids on it. I was never involved in anything like this before. I was just a housewife who minded her own business. But looking at those pay cheques over the years made me angrier and angrier.[15]

Women responded in all the small Cape Breton mining centres, and soon a United Miners' Wives' Association was established, with locals in each community and over three hundred active members. While the initial impetus to "get something going" came from the Cape Breton wives themselves, local Sydney feminists were instrumental in providing organizational expertise and in forging links between the indigenous Miners' Wives' Association and the Sudbury group.

At the Cape Breton Labour Day support rally, feminists from local women's groups and the regional NDP arranged for a showing of *A Wives' Tale* and brought one of the key women from Sudbury to speak at the rally. As a result, the Cape Breton women were able to draw on the experience of the Sudbury women.

We had been doing things about the strike but when we saw that film and heard Linda George talking about what those wives did in Sudbury, then we got a whole bunch of new ideas. We said, well they tried this and it didn't work so we won't bother trying it. They did this but things are different here so we think this is right here even if it wasn't in Sudbury and so on. It was like we had had our own idea and got going here but then we found out they had done it too. So we felt inspired and like we weren't all alone.

Following the Inco and Devco strikes, a Local 6500 union steward commented:

What the unions have learned from the wives' committees is that union strength can't lie just with union members. Of course, that is our main strength and always will be. But we need to join with other people and groups and the wives of union members, and the husbands too, of course, are one of our first allies.

There are other insights to be drawn from the Sudbury and Cape Breton experiences. First of all, both of these occurred in single industry communities where most of the men had the same employer and job opportunities for women were very limited. Because these were relatively isolated communities, the strikers and their families constituted the majority of the local population. A strike in such a community affects everyone directly and makes very obvious the way the whole community suffers when wages stop. Mobilizing the wives of trade unionists in larger urban centres where residences are widely dispersed and community relations are unlikely to overlap significantly with employment based relations is much more difficult.

Nevertheless, the mobilized force of the wives' committees has proved so important that some union officials have begun to be more receptive and more willing to cooperate with them. As long as women earn less than men, their economic dependency gives them a vested interest in their husbands' wages and working conditions. This interest can be mobilized, either for or against union politics, in any community, small or large. A Sudbury woman who moved to Toronto when her husband got a new job observed that:

> It's easier to organize the wives when you have a whole community organized but regardless of where people live, married men and women share concerns about each other's employment. After all, wages are designed to recognize families — we get health care and dental and pension if he dies and all. The bosses have had to deal with their workers' families for years. So it's time the unions did too. Just think how much stronger the unions would be with all those extra people behind them.

Her husband, a former union steward, commented:

> If unions did take up organizing the families of their members seriously, it would really change what the unions are. It's one thing for wives to hold parties and rummage sales, but if you start getting them involved in the political struggles of the union, then you start to have a different view of the union .... Of course, a few years ago, the labour movement got directly involved in politics by working with the NDP, so it's not like there is no precedent, but organizing rank and file wives — wow, that would be really different ... cause it wouldn't just change union priorities, but it would force the men to see that women can be political too.

For women involved with trade union men, the Sudbury and Cape Breton examples suggest that collective organizations of wives (or perhaps of spouses) can play a very important role in overcoming the personal hardships experienced by individual families and the social and political crises of labour/management confrontations. These experiences also show the importance of the women's movement both in providing expertise and in forging links between women in similar circumstances. Finally, there is something very important about groups of wives meeting independently of either the women's movement or trade unions to decide for themselves the issues that are important to them and how they are going to approach them.

> That seemed like a new thing, women holding a bake sale to raise money to send themselves, not their husbands, to the Labour Day rally in Sydney.

These wives' committees thus pose a number of serious challenges to the trade union movement. How the trade union movement responds in the next few years will have serious repercussions for the character of the unions and for trade union and feminist politics.

NOTES

1 This and all subsequent quotations are from interviews conducted with women from Sudbury, Cape Breton and Hamilton during 1982.

2 See Kathy Kahn, *Hillbilly Women* (New York: Avon Books, 1973), p. 39 and Elizabeth Jameson, "Imperfect Unions: Class and Gender in Cripple Creek 1895-1904," in Milton Cantor and Bruce Laurie, eds., *Class, Sex, and the Woman Worker* (Westport, Conn.: Greenwood Press, 1977), pp. 169-79.

3 Dale Fetherling, *Mother Jones, the Miners' Angel: A Portrait* (Carbondale: Southern Illinois Univ. Press, 1974), p.41.

4 The Women's Bureau, "Women in the Labour Force: Basic Facts" (Toronto: Ontario Ministry of Labour, 1982).

5 For more details on this interdependency and its impact on the individuals involved, see Meg Luxton, *More than a Labour of Love* (Toronto: Women's Press, 1980), pp. 48-70.

6 J. Paul Grayson, "The Effects of a Plant Closure on the Stress Levels and Health of Worker's Wives – A Preliminary Analysis" (Paper presented at the Ontario Association of Sociology and Anthropology meetings, Ottawa, Oct. 1982).

7 See for example, Ruth Frager's article in this book.

8 Ann Bohlen, Lyn Goldfarb and Lorraine Gray, *With Babies and Banners* (New Jersey, 1978). See the Cineography by Dinah Forbes in this book for more information.

9 See Meg Luxton, "Two Hands for the Clock: Changing Patterns in the Gendered Division of Labour in the Home," *Studies in Political Economy*, forthcoming 1983.

10 United Miners' Wives' Association Bulletin No. 1, Sept. 16, 1981.

11 Information for the following section on events in Sudbury was compiled from interviews; the newspaper archives of the *Sudbury Star;* Wallace Clement, *Hardrock Mining: Industrial Relations and Technological Change at Inco* (Toronto: McClelland and Stewart, 1981); and John Lang, "A Lion in a Den of Daniels: A History of the International Union of Mine, Mill and Smelter Workers in Sudbury, Ontario, 1942-1962" (Master's Thesis, University of Guelph, 1970). See also Arja Lane's article in this book.

12 "My Responsibility to Look After Interests of All – Mayor," *Sudbury Star*, Dec. 13, 1958.

13 From a leaflet handed out by the Wives Supporting the Strike group at the public rally held at the Ontario Institute for Studies in Education, Toronto, Dec. 8, 1978.

14 Sophie Bissonnette, Joyce Rock and Martin Duckworth, *A Wives' Tale* (Canada, 1980). See the Cineography in this book for more information.

15 Nova Scotia Labour Research and Support Centre, *Labour's Side,* Special Issue 25, Sept. 1981.

TRADE UNION WOMEN AND THE NDP

Janis Sarra

Women are often ambivalent about political parties or the value of political activism. Yet if we want to change the power structures, to make real social and economic gains, we must consider all avenues, all alliances that might help to make these changes a reality. Decisions of alliance are decisions of strategy, of applying our collective strength in any and all ways that will help our struggles for equal rights. As feminists and socialists, we wish to break down the power structures and male attitudes that have dominated for so long.

The NDP is one option to consider. There are important historical links between the trade union movement and the NDP. This article will explore what these links have given trade union women in the past and the potential for future alliance. Because my experience is in Ontario, where the NDP has always been in opposition, the Ontario NDP will be the main focus of the following discussion. However, I will briefly consider the Saskatchewan experience, where the NDP was in power for thirty of the last forty years.

Formal structural links between the NDP and the trade union movement have existed since the formation of the NDP. Union locals can affiliate directly with the NDP, so that in Ontario 250,000 trade unionists are NDP members through union affiliation. Affiliates have full membership and voting rights in the party. One delegate to the NDP convention is allowed for every 100 members or less of an affiliated union local. Trade unionists usually comprise one-quarter of the party's annual convention: at the 1982 convention, for example, there were over 500 trade union delegates. At the Provincial Council, the NDP's decision-making body that meets quarterly between conventions, trade unionists are represented by one delegate for every 300 members. This longstanding structural alliance has meant that NDP policies have been formulated with trade union participation. It has also allowed trade unionists to occupy key decision-making positions in the party. As a result, NDP policies, strategies and campaigns for new legislation have often been consistent with the economic and social demands made at the bargaining table.

WHAT CAN THE NDP OFFER WOMEN?

The structural ties outlined above are based on a commonality of interests on socioeconomic issues, which provide a strong basis for an alliance. Both the NDP and the trade union movement take a position in favour of equal pay for work of equal value, affirmative action, universal quality child care and other support services, for first contract legislation, layoff protection, and an end to sexual harassment and violence against women. Alliance on these specific issues could provide the framework for a broader political perspective that would include restructuring of the economy, full employment, and greater worker control over production and distribution of resources.

The NDP, as a political party, can also be used to directly confront provincial governments in the legislature on policies that adversely affect women. Because the media tends to confine its reporting on political questions to legislative debates, these issues gain wider public attention when raised by the NDP. As part of a strategy that included other forms of mobilizing such as demonstrations, this has been an effective means of winning some concessions. Finally, the NDP has access to a wide range of information and government statistics not readily available to the public, information that is useful to trade union women at the bargaining table.

In spite of the interests shared by women in the labour movement and the NDP, a brief analysis of Ontario voting patterns indicates that in 1979, for example, women made up only 38.5% of the NDP's electoral base.[1] Sylvia Bashevkin reports that in 1981 only 13.1% of women voters expressed "identification" with the ONDP, compared with 25.5% of the male voters.[2] In contrast, almost one-half of women voters expressed identification with the Conservative Party. She notes that while it is tempting to attribute these patterns to factors such as the low rate of unionization among women workers in Ontario, an analysis of trade union voting statistics shows the same pattern. In 1979, only 15.6% of the women trade unionists surveyed expressed identification with the NDP, compared to 31.7% of male unionists. Although the precise figures may have changed since then, it is a reasonable assumption that the increased activism of trade union women has not substantially altered voting patterns.

From these statistics it is clear that efforts by the New Democratic Party to communicate both its policies and its support of women's struggles and workers' struggles have not reached many rank and file unionists. This is largely a result of a media that has historically been anti-labour and anti-NDP, and that has greater access to women workers in this province than any political party or trade union.

However, the failure cannot be attributed entirely to the media. Too often the NDP consults only with the labour leadership, which continues to be male-dominated. Thus women and the rank and file membership have little influence on NDP policy. Few strategies that would affect the grass roots membership — such as on-the-job canvasses in female-oriented job ghettos, educationals, issue-oriented campaigns and broad-based coalitions — have been fully utilized.

Faced with limited financial resources, the NDP is often unable to effectively use the media, disseminate printed material or hire the staff necessary to reach out. For example, the loss of the 1981 election and the sweep to a Conservative majority meant twenty-two staff layoffs for the NDP caucus, including the newly appointed women's coordinator. A women's organizer scheduled to become full time in 1981 was also laid off in order to cope with the party's debt. Given these financial constraints, the NDP must develop more creative ways to use its most valuable and plentiful resource — its membership.

ONTARIO NDP WOMEN

The development of trade union women's consciousness and activism in the last few years coincides with the increased consciousness of women within the Ontario New Democratic Party. These are not two mutually exclusive groups of women; the development of activism in the labour movement has often resulted in increased political activism in the NDP, and the reverse holds true. They have both struggled against male-dominated decision-making structures in an attempt to become a vital part of that decision-making process *and* to get action on issues related to women.

The NDP Women's Executive Committee was established as a result of a resolution at the Ontario NDP's 1972 convention. In December 1973, a meeting of 100 women delegates elected a nine-woman executive plus one representative each for nine regions of the province. The purpose of the Women's Committee was to educate women, to increase the participation of women through the development of riding and regional committees, to monitor and influence legislation on women's issues and to undertake solidarity support work with women in the labour movement and in the community.

The structure quickly proved to be untenable for a political party with limited financial resources. The northern delegates were unable to actively participate on the Committee without monetary support for travel, paid time off or child care. To assist with cost barriers to travel, meetings were held coinciding with the Provincial Council meetings. However, this meant that many women activists were torn between their efforts to raise women's issues and their involvement with mainstream policy and organizing. Scarce resources both in time and money meant that only occasional newsletters were sent to the membership and that local women's committees failed to thrive.

In 1977 the Women's Committee was restructured, with each member responsible for a particular area of outreach, including one for trade unions. During the same period, several strong local women's committees in Kapuskasing, Waterloo, Thunder Bay and in several Toronto ridings were able to organize trade union solidarity work. Despite the establishment of a trade union liaison and the commitment of the local committees, the Women's Committee did not have an overall strategy for mobilizing rank and file women, either inside the party or in the labour movement.

Recent initiatives by the committee to involve both NDP and rank and file trade union women are encouraging. Sub-committees are now decentralizing both the work and the decision making and are becoming more active in newsletter production, conference organizing and outreach. The outreach committee is attempting not only to build formal links with trade unions, but to encourage alliances at the grass roots. A "how-to" kit has been developed, which includes material on establishing local NDP women's action committees, identifying trade union women's caucuses, obtaining films and visual resources, and the "how-to's" of trade union support work.

Beyond the growing emphasis on trade union work inside the Women's Committee, two events formalized the link between the ONDP and labour women. The first was the redrafting of the NDP women's policies in the summer of 1979. As part of a process of policy review, the ONDP Executive delegated the Women's Committee to reformulate all of the NDP's policies on women. A number of NDP women who were also trade union activists from the United Steelworkers of America USWA, the United Auto Workers (UAW), the Canadian Union of Public Employees (CUPE) and the Ontario Public Service Employees Union (OPSEU) came forward and offered to develop the policy, which was then discussed by the Women's Committee and at a women's conference held in Kitchener. This case is remarkable for the fact that trade union women took the initiative to participate in the formulation of an NDP policy that could have a direct impact on their working lives. The result was a more comprehensive statement on the development of links between trade union and NDP women, support of policies on skills training and equal pay, occupational health and affirmative action, a celebration of accomplishments of women in the NDP and labour movement, and demands for the future. This document became part of *Policies for Equality,* adopted by the party at its 1980 convention.[3] It has served as the framework for legislation proposed by the NDP and the basis for education of the membership on issues of importance to women.

The second significant change came with the appointment in 1980 of the NDP Women's Coordinator to the Ontario Federation of Labour (OFL) Women's Committee.[4] This was the first time in Canada that an NDP woman was given full participatory rights on a federation of labour committee. The British Columbia Federation of Labour had for some years allowed a member of the B.C. NDP Women's Committee observer status only, despite that committee's well-known activism and support for struggles of women in the labour movement. At the federal level the NDP women's organizer has historically attended Canadian Labour Congress Women's Committee meetings, but without voting rights. The OFL appointment marked the beginning of a more formal link, including increased cooperation on issues, strike support efforts and carrying the needs of labour women back to the NDP. Joint solidarity work has involved strike support around Fleck, Radio Shack, Blue Cross, Irwin Toy; efforts to get rights for domestic workers; protection against unjust dismissal and to eliminate practices such as washroom punch cards for women at Block Drug Company.

The OFL Women's Committee's attempts to democratize and decentralize that committee have included inviting local trade union women's committees to be active in the organizing of forums and pickets. The NDP Women's Committee has also been invited to partici-pate, bringing rank and file New Democrats together with rank and file trade union women. A recent cooperative effort that helped win back the jobs of twenty-three immigrant women workers at Canadian Pizza Crust in Mississauga is one illustration of the potential of such an alliance.

Labour laws in Ontario work against the organizing of workers into unions. This holds particularly true in female white collar ghettos. Trade union and NDP women are working together to support organiz-ing drives, first contract strikes and other campaigns to protect and promote equality in the workplace. Where trade union activists do not have access to unorganized workplaces, it may be that there are NDP women working there, able to provide the educating and organizing support from within. Such collective efforts need to be consciously pursued by both the NDP and the labour movement as a whole.

The OFL Women's Committee has encouraged increased contact with NDP women. A major step forward was the invitation to NDP women to be delegates to the OFL's policy conference on affirmative action in May 1982. This offered the opportunity not only for direct interaction between NDP and rank and file union women but a chance to contribute policy suggestions, information and strategies to the conference's key document *Our Fair Share,* which was subsequently adopted as policy at the 1982 OFL convention.

Increasingly women in the NDP and in trade unions are working together to apply pressure to the leaderships of both to give priority to women's issues. More visible support by NDP women and the party as a whole for the struggles of women for first contracts, in strike efforts and in organizing trade unions needs to be forthcoming in order for these links to be cemented.

LEGISLATION

In recent years the ONDP has tried to bring about legislative change favourable to women. Labour women have contributed their experi-ence and expertise to the formulation of this proposed legislation. In the following section I will examine four ONDP private members' bills: Equal Pay for Work of Equal Value (1979), The Women's Economic Equality Act (1980), the Act to Protect Video Display Terminal Oper-ators (1982) and an Affirmative Action Bill, which is presently in the draft stage. I will briefly describe the content of each bill, the way in which the policy was formulated and the attempts to build public support for the bill.

The Act to Provide Equal Pay for Work of Equal Value called for equal pay for work of equal value to be evaluated in terms of skill, effort, responsibility and working conditions. It provided a focused attack on the existing Employment Standards Act, which recognizes only equal pay for equal work and therefore gives no recourse to women who work in traditional "female ghettos" – office and clerical workers, restaurant, laundry and retail workers. It was first tabled in 1978 by Ted Bounsall, then NDP MPP for Windsor-Sandwich. It died on the legislative order paper.

Bounsall reintroduced the bill in March 1979. The Equal Pay Coalition and a number of unions organized active support for the bill. The highlight of this process took place when women packed the galleries

---

A Note on the Legislative Process in Ontario

A private member's bill is any bill introduced by a member of the opposition or backbencher of the ruling party. The first step is tabling the bill in the legislature, referred to as first reading; the bill is announced and becomes a matter of public record by being published. Thereafter it appears on the legislative order paper.

Private member's bills are heard only one afternoon per week, and because so little time is allocated for so many bills, they are selected on a lottery basis to be brought forward for debate. This debate of the bill "in principle" is called a second reading. After the debate, the government can usually defeat the bill by voting against it, or by having twenty members of the legislature stand up and block a vote. Only rarely in a majority government situation does a private member's bill pass a vote on second reading.

If it does pass second reading as the Equal Pay Bill did, it is referred to an all-party committee of the legislature, which *may* organize public hearings. It is at the committee stage that amendments may be made to the original bill.

After the committee makes its recommendations, the government may or may not choose to put the bill back on the legislative order paper, thereby calling it for third and final reading. At the end of a legislative session, any bills not brought forward automatically die, so that the government always controls the proceedings of the house. No matter how much public pressure is brought to bear on a government, the government can use procedures to stifle a bill.

in the legislature on the day of the debate. As a result of this public show of support and extensive lobbying of MPPs, the bill passed second reading in May 1979. This was an important precedent for a private member's bill and gave the public and trade union women in particular, access to the public hearings that must be conducted after a bill has passed second reading. Although the government chose not to bring the bill back for third reading and let it die, the bill, and especially the hearings held to discuss it, were a real victory – a result of a collective effort between the NDP, the trade union movement and the women's movement. The bill and the hearings were also a vehicle to educate women in the workplace about the value of their labour and the limits of their legislative rights.

The second bill, The Women's Economic Equality Act, was tabled by the NDP caucus in the fall of 1980. This act reflected the Policies for Equality drafted by trade union women and later debated and passed at the 1980 NDP Convention. The bill outlines five prerequisites for economic equality for women. The first was a mandatory affirmative action program, including targets and timetables, access to hiring and promotion information, and monetary and legal sanctions for non-compliance. Secondly, the act called for a comprehensive skills training and apprenticeship program geared to meet the occupational needs of our economy and ensuring women a fair share in training opportunities. Third, it demanded equal pay for work of equal value. The NDP bill proposed a public system of universally accessible quality child care to dismantle a major barrier to women's equal participation in the work force and finally, it called for an end to sexual harassment by including such a section in the Employment Standards Act.

The act was tabled with two others, in recognition that women's economic equality is not possible without other major legislative reform. The Full Employment Act and Job Security Act, with the Women's Economic Equality Act, called upon the government to take action on the economic issues of employment, and to provide vastly improved protection against layoffs. It offered a more comprehensive legislative initiative and attempted to link women's struggles with the broader needs of all workers. Termed a Bill of Economic Rights, the three acts served as educative tools in the labour movement, the media and the community at large.

The Women's Economic Equality Act differed from the Equal Pay Bill in two critical respects: on the one hand, rank and file women had direct input into it, both in the formulation of the policy and through debate on the convention floor, and secondly, women's economic concerns were placed in a larger economic and social context.

The third bill, an Act to Protect Video Display Terminal (VDT) Operators, introduced by Richard Johnston, NDP MPP Scarborough West, in the fall of 1981 was seen as a way to pull together and articulate the growing concerns, particularly of women in the labour movement, about the health effects and suspected reproductive hazards of VDTs. There are over 300,000 VDT operators in Canada, the majority of whom are women. Protection under existing occupational health and safety legislation in Ontario and in most North American jurisdictions is virtually non-existent.

The substance of the bill included radiation shielding and testing at the point of production, adjustable equipment, lighting of work areas, rest periods, proper ventilation, the right to opthalmological examinations, necessary preventive and corrective lenses, access to medical and technical information, worker control of the introduction of the technology into the workplace, protection against individual monitoring, and rights to work away from the VDT, at equal pay if an operator is pregnant. This act was drafted through the collective efforts of members of the Ad Hoc VDT Committee of the Metro Toronto Labour Council and members of the NDP. In particular, credit must be given to members and staff of OPSEU and Communication Workers of Canada (CWC) for providing technical expertise and political input. The extensive discussion and debate that preceded the bill's introduction meant it was the most comprehensive piece of VDT legislation drafted in North America to date. The bill came up for second reading in April 1982, and with support in the legislative gallery of sixty VDT operators (both organized and unorganized), and a number of trade union activists, primarily women, the NDP pressured the government to pass the bill or to bring in its own legislation. Unfortunately the bill was overwhelmingly defeated; in fact, Conservative government members came out in full force to vote against it. However, the campaign did put some pressure on the government as evidenced in an arbitration award in July 1982 affecting up to 60,000 Ontario civil servants, which gave

VDT operators rest periods, eye examinations and rights to alternative work when pregnant.

Finally, the fourth bill calls for mandatory affirmative action programs in all workplaces in Ontario where women are underrepresented, and for joint employer-union affirmative action committees. The development of this bill is a direct result of the close ties between the ONDP and women in the trade union movement. The OFL Affirmative Action policy was used as the basis for drafting the NDP Bill on Affirmative Action. Further, in support of affirmative action and the NDP Bill, the OFL Women's Committee is building a provincial coalition in which NDP women are committed to participate.

Most often, legislation that brings about social or economic gains for the working class follows gains that have been negotiated at the bargaining table. From the examples of this legislation, we can see that trade union women are providing leadership to which the NDP is responding. However, in a majority Conservative government situation any progressive legislative measures will come about only as a result of public pressure. This means continuing the struggle to build effective alliances.

THE NDP IN POWER

Although the NDP has never formed a government or had the opportunity to directly implement legislation in Ontario, the NDP has been in power provincially: in British Columbia from 1972-76, in Saskatchewan from 1944-64 and from 1971-81, and in Manitoba from 1969-77 and 1981 to the present. By examining the behaviour of the NDP in power, trade union women can better assess the commitment of the NDP to their concerns. There is no doubt that women have made some concrete gains. For example, in Saskatchewan during the twelve years of NDP government prior to the defeat of the Blakeney government, gains were made in affirmative action and in occupational health and safety, particularly in establishing workers' rights. That government was the only one in Canada to pass legislation giving workers the right to strike for health and safety reasons during the life of a contract. Stricter regulation of employers and greater worker control of health in the workplace are commendable accomplishments. The affirmative action plan has had a more sporadic career, with some substantial gains made in programs in crown corporations, but no fundamental restructuring of women's position in the corporate hierarchy.

The NDP government in Saskatchewan also substantially increased resources for support services, child care, drop-in centres and health clinics. It brought in publicly funded dental care as a major preventive health program. It created some good programs to encourage employment, which people in the community ran on a cooperative and nonprofit basis. However, during its tenure in Saskatchewan, the NDP failed to challenge the distribution of wealth in the province, poverty, or the existing class structure. Perhaps most disturbing was the inadequacy of the NDP's alliance with labour. Consider the 1979 strike of the Saskatchewan Government Employees Union (SGEU) (then Association) of 1979.

In autumn 1979, the outstanding issues in negotiations with SGEA were flex hours, the introduction of overtime pay and a limit to the number of hours of work expected. The demands were part of an effort to seek parity with employees of the crown corporations. In the late fall, the government was unmovable, and a strike vote was taken, with 67% of workers voting in favour. The union called the strike in November 1979. It lasted four weeks; 10,500 of 11,000 unionized workers went out. During the strike, a small group calling itself the SGEA Rights' Group took the union to court in order to have the strike declared illegal under the Trade Union Act, which specifies that a majority of eligible members of a bargaining unit must vote to strike. In December 1980, the court decided that abstentions were no votes, and since only 45% of the membership had voted, the strike was declared illegal. This decision failed to acknowledge the almost unanimous action of these workers, 95% of whom had gone out on strike.

The Saskatchewan and the federal Supreme Courts would not hear appeals. But the most significant factor was the government's silence on the issue of the strike's legality. It did not support SGEA in its appeal, thereby stripping away the rights of those workers to settle contract demands through the legitimate vehicle of work withdrawal.

This confrontation points to two important conclusions. The first is that the government had become complacent in its assurance of support by labour. Events such as this inevitably contributed to the erosion of working-class and organized labour support, which was reflected in the devastation of the Saskatchewan NDP in the 1982 election. Secondly, it points to the need for labour to have a clear perspective on cooperation with an NDP government. The primary role of any trade union is to represent its membership in contract negotiations, to ensure that the contract is enforced and to struggle for economic and social gains for labour. Trade unionists should attempt to influence NDP policy in these directions through cooperation where possible and through pressure tactics where necessary. An additional arena of conflict occurs because the NDP tends to relate to labour through the labour leadership, and the concerns of the rank and file may not be those articulated by the leadership. The rank and file have a responsibility to insist on accountability not only from their own leadership but from the NDP.

Although experience shows that the NDP will not automatically represent the interests of women or workers, there will never be a fundamental economic restructuring with a Conservative or Liberal government. We must take the responsibility to make our political demands known, to insist that political leaders be accountable and that political ideals not be sacrificed for the prospect of electoral gain. We must ultimately take responsibility to change the decision-making structure itself. When the NDP forms governments, workers have some opportunity to press for worker control of industry, for worker cooperatives, for guaranteed income programs and for creative delivery of health and social services that both meet the needs of people in the community and are controlled by them.

NOTES

1 Sylvia Bashevkin, *The Facts of Political Life in the* ONDP, 1981, p. 3.

2 *Ibid.*, p.2.

3 *Policies for Equality* is the NDP policy on women, passed at its 1980 convention, and includes sections on women in the labour force, sex stereotyping, the education system, health care, social services and social justice.

4 I was appointed to the OFL Women's Committee as the ONDP representative in August 1981 after the layoff of the full-time women's coordinator in the post-1981 election layoffs.

BUILDING LINKS: LABOUR AND THE WOMEN'S MOVEMENT

Carolyn Egan and Lynda Yanz

One of the most exciting trends in the women's movement in Toronto in the last few years has been the developing relationship between the women's and trade union movements. This is in large part a result of the increasing recognition by both movements of the other's importance as each battles an escalating economic crisis. That feminists in unions are insisting on support for issues like sexual harassment and abortion reflects a major change in orientation since the early 1970s. And in the women's movement more and more women are acknowledging that wage controls, union recognition, the right to strike and technological change are issues central to a discussion of women's liberation.

The most visible manifestation of this alliance has been the annual International Women's Day celebrations on March 8. In 1983 7000 women, men and children marched to demand jobs with full employment rights and no wage controls, women's right to choose whether or not to have children, and our right to peace, to a world free from the threat of nuclear war and where Third World countries like El Salvador and Nicaragua no longer have to fight the violence of imperialism. The demonstrators were active in unions, in peace, lesbian, gay, women's, community and Third World solidarity groups. Together we represented the strength and diversity of a growing women's movement.

Unionists' involvement in International Women's Day has been increasing steadily for the last five years. In 1983, over twenty percent of the demonstrators marched in the union contingent. But more important than numbers: unionists are now central to building March 8. They play a major role in defining the political issues to be highlighted, in the working committees and the day-to-day slogging needed to plan a successful March 8. Support from the union leadership and central bodies such as the Ontario Federation of Labour (OFL), the Canadian Labour Congress and local and regional labour councils has also grown. The OFL now passes resolutions supporting a coalition-sponsored International Women's Day and does an initial mailing to all affiliates. This support facilitates individual unions and locals' endorsing, distributing leaflets and posters, making financial contributions and urging their members to come out to the demonstration. For two months each year hundreds of feminists inside and outside unions work closely developing and putting forward an analysis of how the economic crisis affects women and stressing the importance of women's demands.

A few years ago it would not have been possible for representatives from each of the major political movements in Toronto to work together to plan an event like International Women's Day. It is especially unusual to find the trade union movement involved and lending the kind of official support it does, considering that it is the most institutionalized and structured of all our movements. Many people, and in particular women, have worked hard to build links between the women's and trade union movements. In that sense International Women's Day is a signpost for what goes on in the movements throughout the year and, not surprisingly, the relationships in the coalition often reflect the developments (and problems) of the previous year.

Our experience of the trade union-women's movement alliance is not as trade unionists, but as activists in the women's movement and members of the International Women's Day Committee (IWDC), a socialist feminist group in Toronto. IWDC initiates and plays a leading role in the March 8 coalition as well as working year round. IWDC has made working with the trade union movement a specific priority since it formed in 1978. This article describes the development of our trade union work in the context of changes taking place in both the women's and trade union movements. It also raises some of the difficulties we have encountered. It is important that together we begin to reflect on the working relationships that are being built, their strengths and weaknesses, in order to determine the direction we want to take these alliances in the future.

*   *   *   *   *

The links between the women's movement and labour are by no means limited to Toronto. The trend to a closer working relationship is visible across the country, although the form this takes is different in different cities. It is important for those of us in the women's movement and outside the trade union movement to recognize that the success of any alliance depends in the first place on the role of women in unions.

Women's activity within unions has increased dramatically in the past decade. Women have been at the forefront of major union battles for the right to join a union, for the right to strike, against wage controls and concessions and for landmark gains on issues like maternity leave. Women have organized and fought for women's committees and caucuses, for equal pay and maternity leave to be negotiating priorities, and for unions to take up new and often controversial issues like child care, affirmative action, sexual orientation, sexual harassment and abortion.

More and more union activists see themselves as *women* unionists, acting for women in the fight against women's inequality and oppression. Some of these women were first politicized in the women's movement and bring with them traditions of action that challenge present-day union priorities and norms. Others developed as feminists through their work as unionists. Each brings a different perspective to women's struggles; together they represent a growing movement of women within the union movement fighting for women on the job and challenging unions to better represent women. And in so doing they have challenged the union movement's generally narrow view of what is and is not a union issue and who is and is not an appropriate union movement ally.

As many of the other articles point out, women unionists are confronting the concrete limitations and contradictions posed by union structures and the union movement. Nevertheless, the demands of union women have already had a impact on the consciousness and structures of the trade union movement and have led to a much greater openness on the part of unions to the women's movement. Feminist unionists have also given important leadership to the women's movement. As union women began to claim the right to speak for themselves and from their experience they demanded that the women's movement take up issues that are not, strictly speaking, "women's issues" — issues like wage controls, the right to a union and the right to strike. They taught us that it makes no sense to separate "union" from "women's" issues, or to say that an issue like abortion is more inherently feminist than the whole range of issues at work: they are equally important for women's equality. Feminist unionists fought us when we seemed to be saying there was no room for their union brothers in "our" struggle. And they challenged us to be more relevant to working-class women.

Union women's increasing visibility coincided with important political changes in the women's movement that have resulted in parts of the feminist community actively seeking out new working relationships with the trade union movement. The setbacks women faced in the first few years of economic crisis had a profound effect on the women's movement. As we lost ground on equal pay and affirmative action, as funding to women's centres and services was cut back drastically and violence and harassment of women increased, many more of us became convinced of the limitations of traditional feminist strategies — which focused on changing attitudes or lobbying for legislative equality and protection or labelling all men as our enemy. In spite of the political differences that exist in the women's movement, by the mid-Seventies the majority of feminists were ready to at least consider new strategies.

Activists stressed the need to involve many more women and build a mass women's movement and to seek out new allies in the fight for women's liberation. Given the developing role of women in the union movement it is not surprising that feminists and women's groups looked to the potential strength of the trade union movement. The union movement was seen as a way of reaching new women, and, because of its large membership and available resources, as an important organizational base for feminist campaigns and as a vehicle for putting forward women's demands. The union movement was, of course, more relevant as an ally on some issues than others: affirmative action, equal pay and even day care rather than the struggle against violence or for women's right to control their bodies. Some of the early debates in the women's movement about the emphasis that should be put on union involvement divided along issue lines. Those involved in some aspect of the struggle against violence against women were often wary about being pressured to downplay their concerns in favour of more "important and acceptable" issues. This debate has arisen on different occasions in the March 8 coalition — regarding, for example, what priority to give lesbian rights as opposed to economic demands. This was to some extent a reflection of the reluctance on the part of many unions to deal with issues involving conflict between women and men and thus potentially between union members.

INTERNATIONAL WOMEN'S DAY COMMITTEE

IWDC came into being in 1978 in the midst of the kind of developments described above. Many long-time feminist activists across the country were stepping back to rethink how to involve more women in the women's movement. They were also questioning the kinds of alliances and organizational forms required to make gains for women. Unions were beginning to actively take up women's issues. The NDP was in power in three provinces and quickly made clear the gap that exists between strong party policy on women and government action. Single issue groups and services were making some gains but more often than not were reaching the limits imposed by government cutbacks. Of course, "stepping back" and "reflecting" did not mean stopping to organize. Study groups flourished and heated strategy discussions took place in after-meeting bars, at demonstrations and on picket lines.

In Toronto in the fall of 1977 a group of ten women active in different sections of the women's movement came together to discuss the possibility of organizing an event for International Women's Day 1978. These women reflected different political outlooks, and were active in different parts of the feminist community. Out of that group came the first IWD coalition in Toronto. The idea was to bring together all those committed to women's liberation in a show of strength and unity to counteract the media view that the women's movement was dead. Women were convinced of the need for the women's movement to revitalize, to reach out to new women and at the same time to become more activist-oriented. International Women's Day, with its militant history linked to the struggles of working trade union and socialist women, seemed a perfect occasion to begin.

It was a difficult coalition: some women felt they couldn't be part of the organizing because it was too oriented to trade union issues, others because it was overwhelmingly feminist. But for those of us who stuck it through, IWD 1978 was a victory. Women with different politics and representing different communities had worked hard together, and close to 2000 people came out on the day. The representation of trade union and immigrant women was low but women active in unions and the immigrant community played a strong and public role in the day's events. That in itself was a significant change.

The success of March 8, 1978 gave impetus to an ongoing organization, the International Women's Day Committee. IWDC soon became involved in trade union support work. Following from the work for International Women's Day IWDC was asked to organize a women's solidarity picket with Organized Working Women for the Fleck strikers. Fleck was a United Auto Workers (UAW) first contract strike at a small auto parts plant near Stratford, Ontario. It received a lot of publicity because of the heavy use of police force and violence. The strong role played by the women strikers became a cause célèbre and brought together the UAW and broad sections of both the women's and union movements in support of their struggle.

The connections made between the Fleck strikers, the women's movement and the UAW had a long-term impact. Two feminist filmmakers produced a videotape with the Fleck strikers that has been used as a tool to politicize both the women's movement and trade unionists about the experiences of women becoming trade union militants. IWDC showed that we could mobilize relatively large numbers of feminists in support of union struggles, that we were experienced organizers and that, although we were outside the union movement, we could be depended on not to cause problems. Our "strengths," combined with the commitment of women inside the union movement to working with groups like IWDC, meant that we would be called on again.

In the fall of 1978 Organized Working Women asked IWDC to help organize a benefit, one of many throughout the province, for the Inco strike in Sudbury, a single industry town in northern Ontario. This strike was very important. It was a time when concessions were becoming standard in contracts, and when many parts of the labour movement were taking a defensive stance. The Inco strikers went on the offensive, despite Inco's huge stockpiles, and their threat to move operations to Guatemala and Indonesia. Women were playing a key role through the wives' committee and our benefit aimed to highlight their work and determination. Over 500 people attended the benefit and it raised $14,000, again laying a basis for future work, this time with the Steelworkers.

The Inco benefit and Fleck solidarity pickets were significant in building the fledgling working relationship between the women's movement and women trade unionists. Many of the trade union women we worked with had had no previous contact with actual groups in the women's movement, and a number had no doubt been alienated by a media version of feminism. Through the concrete organizing work involved in the support pickets and rallies they more clearly began to see themselves as part of the women's movement. Many of us within the women's movement were pushed to broaden our notions of feminism to include women who might not call themselves feminists but who were waging important battles for women. This had a clear impact both on the kinds of issues that were taken up through International Women's Day coalitions and the number of unionists — both rank and file and staff — who got involved.

But working together also had its tensions. The woman-identified culture and highly vocal — and important — lesbian visibility within our movement was new to many trade union women. The cultural / political gaps between our different constituencies are perhaps most noticeable when all come together for International Women's Day. Arja Lane describes in her article what happened when women from Sudbury Wives Supporting the Strike (wss) came to take part in iwd and discovered they followed the lesbian speaker on the rally program. Confronted with "lesbian mothers, punk dykes, pro-abortion groups and left activists," wss was not so sure they wanted to be part of this "movement." Although they did perform, their experience at iwd added more fuel to the growing political differences within their group. For iwdc the experience highlighted the precarious and sometimes uncomfortable situation that can develop when the different sections of our movement come together. It made clear the importance of better groundwork in the trade union movement on the links between women's and lesbian issues but also on the connections between the whole range of issues that the women's movement has raised. With better political education we might have been able to avoid some of these problems.

By the end of our first year and after organizing the second coalition for March 8, iwdc had reached the point where we had to establish clearer priorities. We were involved in too many activities and because we were a very visible, albeit small group, every week we received new requests to become involved in other events. We decided to spend a period discussing our future work and priorities.

One question we had to settle was what emphasis to put on trade union work. From early on we had received criticism from sections of the women's movement about our concentration on "economic issues." Within IWDC the debate was posed in terms of our self-definition: were we a trade union support group, a left group or a feminist group? It seemed important to define our bottom-line allegiances because few believed we could balance ourselves equally between all three constituencies.

Early in September 1979 we decided officially to call ourselves socialist feminist and adopted a basis of unity that still defines our basic politics. We agree that women's oppression is integral to the capitalist patriarchal system in which we live and that women's liberation cannot be won by appealing to politicians, by changing legislation or by electing any existing political party. In our basis of unity we state:

> IWDC operates on the principle that mass actions are our most effective instruments of change. We believe that the oppression of women touches every aspect of our lives and that the liberation of women will require fundamental changes in the structure of society. We cannot see the Canadian government as a neutral bystander in our struggle. Government must be seen as part of the problem — not part of the solution. It is clear that we have little to gain by lobbying the government. Rather we must put our energies into building mass actions and a mass united women's movement which can begin to challenge the system in a more direct and serious way.

Women's liberation depends in the first place on women organizing themselves in a political movement. We also believe that it is essential that women organize with men and, that more broadly, the women's movement unite with other progressive movements. "We will need allies for our battle. Our primary allies are to be found in the women's movement, but we also want to work with all those who challenge the economic, social and governmental forces which promote our oppression."

The description of socialist feminist did not imply an attachment to any particular brand of socialism. What socialism is and how we will get there is something we in IWDC have never tried to agree on, although we would do well to have more discussions about our different views. Some of us work in the NDP, some in Marxist organizations, while others do not think that socialist party affiliation is important at this time. As a socialist feminist group IWDC is unique in Canada. Although groups have emerged in other cities, none has established an ongoing practice. Socialist feminism as a current in the Canadian women's movement, however, has grown quite dramatically in the last few years. Many women identify themselves as anti-capitalist, feminist and socialist, and in Toronto at least, socialist feminists provide leadership in International Women's Day activities, in the day care and abortion campaigns currently being waged, and, as well, many socialist feminists are active in the union movement.

Our basis of unity committed us to building working relations with the union movement and to continuing the kinds of work we had begun with Fleck, Inco and the two previous March 8 coalitions. We had a double role. One priority was to build support in the women's movement for union struggles. We wanted to politicize feminists about the importance of the trade union movement in the struggle for women's equality *and* mobilize feminists around trade union issues and women's struggles in unions. Secondly, we wanted to involve the trade union movement in issues like abortion, lesbian rights, day care and violence against women. This priority was more controversial. IWDC is outside the trade union movement and therefore has a very different relation to trade unions and trade unionists than we do to groups and individuals in the women's movement. How appropriate it is for IWDC to put forward political views about what the trade union movement should do is an ongoing debate in IWDC and with some of the trade unionists with whom we work.

Strike support continued to be a major aspect of our trade union work. In the fall of 1979 the Steelworkers asked us to help organize a women's solidarity picket for Radio Shack women who were on strike for a first contract in Barrie, Ontario. The support organized through the women's movement together with the boycott initiated by the Steelworkers were instrumental in developing public support for the strike and eventual victory. After Radio Shack IWDC was off and quite literally running. We became involved in support work for a whole series of women's strikes – the federal government clerks (PSAC), Bell Canada (CWC), Fotomat (USWA), Puretex Workers (CCU), Ontario hospital workers (CUPE), Postal Workers (CUPW), Tel-Air Answering Service (CWC), Irwin Toy (USWA), Blue Cross (UAW), and most recently at Mini-Skools (OPSEU).

In 1980 we set up an ongoing committee to coordinate our trade union activities. Until then we had survived with small ad hoc committees working on individual strikes or events. The trade union and education committees, each with about six members, became IWDC's first regular committees. Besides coordinating and doing a lot of the actual work, the trade union committee was to initiate discussions with IWDC.

As we developed better relations with unions and women's strikes became more prominent, our role began to expand beyond one rally or support picket per strike. At Irwin Toy, for example, IWDC took responsibility for being on the picket line one morning a week, at the same time as being involved in organizing larger solidarity pickets, and distributing materials advertising the strike to Christmas shoppers. On International Women's Day 1982, the women from Irwin Toy led the demonstration. This practice is almost a tradition: in 1980, Blue Cross and Radio Shack strikers led the march, in 1981 it was the Bell strikers, in 1982 Irwin Toy, and in 1983, the Mini-Skool strikers.

Our relationship with key members of the OFL women's committee has been particularly significant in opening up new options for us. In 1980 we started attending the OFL annual conventions, which attract over 1500 delegates from across the province. The first year we listened and offered support where we could, but weren't really visible as an organization. Since then we've become more active. For two years now we have staffed information tables where people can find out who we are and what we do, and distributed leaflets about International Women's Day and other issues and current campaigns. This past year we spoke on a panel on microtechnology at the women's forum and also participated in the women's caucus to help with strategizing for the convention resolutions on abortion.

Soon after we set up the trade union committee IWDC made a conscious decision to put forward our politics even in strike support work. We were there to help the strikers win their battle but we also wanted to share our political vision of how each individual battle fit into the general struggle for women's liberation. Through speeches, in leaflets, or just talking to people on picket lines, we share our own experiences and in so doing, raise issues that might not be union priorities. The leaflet we distributed during the CUPW strike in 1981 called for united action by the women's and union movements:

> The strike being waged by CUPW has implications for all of us. Certainly those of us active in the women's movement realize that in attacking unions the state is also attacking women's struggle for equality. We need to work together to fight this offensive by governments and

employers in this country. We in the women's movement and the trade union movement have to be ready and willing to take up each other's battle as our own.

The CUPW strike in 1981 was a public and national example of the political shifts that had taken place in both movements in the few years previous to the strike. CUPW had a clear perspective on the need and possibility of involving the women's movement in support of their struggle for new maternity leave provisions and set about actively recruiting that support. In response to a letter sent country-wide by leader Jean Claude Parrot, women's groups organized press conferences, wrote briefs and held demonstrations and rallies. It was particularly significant that this strike gained the support of many of the establishment women's groups in Canada, groups like the National Action Committee on the Status of Women and provincial Action Committees, many of whom had not been supportive of union battles in the past. The strike paved the way for institutionalizing better maternity leave benefits for both organized and unorganized women across Canada and demonstrated the strength of the united trade union and women's movements.

Although the women's movement mobilized support for CUPW, there were strong political differences on whether or not groups should support just the maternity leave issue or also oppose attempts by the federal government to limit CUPW's right to strike. These differences within the women's movement around how to work with unions and on which issues continue. More work still needs doing within the women's movement to gain a stronger foothold for more progressive political orientations. The debates around the issue of the right to strike during the CUPW strike prompted IWDC to write a leaflet on "the right to strike as a feminist issue."

By this time IWDC was playing a more active role in the trade union movement. Instead of limiting what we did to responding to requests from the trade union movement we felt we could begin initiating more activities, and had a number of discussions in the trade union committee and with trade union activists about the ways we might be most useful on issues like affirmative action, microtechnology and wage controls. We set up a mini-educational campaign on microtechnology for the fall of 1982.

Both the women's and trade union movements had begun to be very active on microtechnology but there was little overlap in terms of analysis or action. We thought IWDC could help build links between the individuals and groups working in this area. In leaflets, at union local educationals and on workshop panels we talked about the potentially devastating effects the new technology was likely to have on women's work lives and on our battles for affirmative action and equal pay. We also talked strategy. We wanted to echo the view of activists within the union movement that this issue cannot be won solely at the bargaining table or through legislation, but requires a coalition based in the unions, which includes women's, community, peace, unemployed and unorganized groups in developing a united and coordinated campaign.

In the short time we focused on microtechnology IWDC accomplished a lot. We talked to many unionists, facilitated links between groups in the women's and union movements, distributed close to 3000 leaflets and extended IWDC's visibility and credibility. But IWDC is not a single issue group and by the end of the fall it was clear we couldn't put the kind of energy into microtechnology that would be required if we were to make it a real priority. The Mini-Skool strike was in full swing and IWDC was on the picket line once a week. The OFL convention had passed a policy statement on affirmative action that included plans for a coalition to be launched early in the new year. And the preparatory work for International Women's Day 1983 had begun. As an activist group it was an important step to find a better balance between action and analysis.

IWDC has developed to the point where our involvement in union actions is no longer just tied to our personal relations with one or another trade unionist, although these continue to be very important. We have access to the trade union movement's structures in a way we didn't when we first started working in this area and this represents a real shift in the relationship between our two movements. The practical and personal links IWDC has established tend to be with union staff and through the structures like union offices, the Metro Labour Council and the OFL. These are absolutely essential for getting official endorsation, trade union speakers and resolutions of support. Links at this level have meant public support for the women's movement and have been a vehicle for reaching a broad number of trade unionists. But building them has also meant we haven't had the time to work regularly with rank and file women. This is a weakness. In the next phase of our work we must consciously aim to develop a stronger base and reference group among rank and file activists.

The most visible indication of the changed relation between our two movements is the increasing number of coalitions that have been set up by both the women's and union movements. The Ontario Coalition for Abortion Clinics is a good example. OCAC has a very specific goal, the establishment and legalization of free-standing abortion clinics in Ontario. The clinics are intended to provide more equitable access to abortion services and to ensure safer conditions for women who choose to have an abortion. The campaign is quickly becoming national in scope with coalitions also in B.C., Alberta, Saskatchewan and Manitoba. Clinics have already opened in Manitoba and Ontario.

The women's movement, through coalitions like OCAC, has initiated a major offensive with the first possibility of making gains on the abortion issue in a decade. In this sense it is similar to CUPW's precedent-setting strike for maternity leave. To win a pro-choice victory requires a broad-based movement willing to be vocal in its support and able to defend the clinics once they are in operation. In Ontario the trade union movement has provided the most significant and consistent support outside the women's movement. Representatives from major unions, the Ontario Federation of Labour and the Canadian Labour Congress spoke out publicly prior to the clinic opening and continued to do so (in spite of some hostile opposition within their ranks) even after the clinic was raided by police, in July 1983.

Developing a working relationship with the trade union movement has of course not been without its difficulties. Alliances are never smooth sailing. They are built around issues and political perspectives for which there are divergent opinions within as well as between movements. And working relationships are even more complicated when aimed at uniting movements as different in structure, organization and history as the women's and trade union movements.

Early on, during strikes at Fleck and Inco, IWDC was content to do mainly support work, mobilizing large numbers of people, often more than the union movement could, for specific events. At that point we weren't sure we had a right to raise political issues in the trade union movement and in any event were primarily concerned to get to know and work with different unions. But the connections between women's issues and trade union struggles usually did not get raised unless we had an opportunity to speak out. In not making a political input we came to feel more and more like a service group for the trade union movement.

IWDC's decision to be more public about our role was important, and one that has been, for the most part, supported by those we work with in the trade union movement. We wanted to be viewed not only as supporters, but as credible in our own right, able to speak publicly and share our general perspective on women's liberation and social change through mass mobilization and progressive alliances. We have no illusions about having answers but want to add our voice, insights and experience to those in the union movement challenging the leadership and bureaucracy to be a more effective vehicle for defending women's and workers' interests.

The issue about what is appropriate for IWDC to do and say still comes up. Recently we were asked to speak at a public forum and at the last moment were told that our speaker had to be a trade unionist. IWDC has always had members who are trade unionists and yet we have been hesitant to use them as our passports to legitimacy. In the short term it might have been more effective to base our trade union practice around their work but it would not have so directly built the acknowledged alliance between the women's and trade union movements that we think is essential. It is an achievement to be asked to speak at trade union events, but from our point of view it is equally important that IWDC publicly represent ourselves as who we are, a women's group *working with* the trade union movement. From the point of view of trade unionists who work hard just to get us included in events, no doubt the principle often seems insignificant. This is obviously something that needs discussion.

Another aspect that will have to be confronted more directly in the months to come is the role IWDC or the women's movement can or should have in debates on labour issues and strategy. If we are involved in strike support work is it appropriate for us to raise questions about the way a union is handling a strike? We are not familiar with all the workings of the union structure and could not tell unionists what they should be doing, but we have learned a lot from the support work we've done and could bring a different vantage point to building strike support. Until now our role has been consultative.

This is also an issue in campaigns initiated by the trade union movement, but which they have broadened to include women's groups. The current OFL campaign on affirmative action is an example. Although IWDC recognizes that getting the OFL to make affirmative action a priority at this point is a real victory for women in the union movement, it is not clear that the OFL's strategy of mandatory affirmative action legislation will be effective, given the economic crisis. This debate is going on inside the trade union movement itself and some unionists have reservations about the campaign. It remains to be seen whether those unionists instrumental in the coalition will be open to IWDC's raising questions about OFL policy and strategy. We hope this campaign will give us the opportunity to find ways of having political discussion, working together as equals *and* being responsive to the concerns of each other's constituency.

The March 8 Coalitions, OCAC, the Affirmative Action Campaign and the ongoing work of groups like IWDC and trade unionists are all part of building an active alliance between our two movements. Working together pushes our separate constituencies to take seriously a much wider range of issues and concerns and thus to incorporate a fuller analysis of the ways this society works to oppress women and working people. All our work is part of a long-term process of building a strong political movement with the capacity to change this society. The kinds of working relationships we build today will in part determine the strengths and weaknesses of that movement.

NOTES

Nancy Adamson, Linda Briskin, Leslie Cotter, Shelly Gordon, Tula Lindholm, David Kidd, Liza McCoy, David Smith and Jane Springer all helped in different ways. Thank you.

VI RESOURCES

WOMEN, WORK AND UNIONS – A CINEOGRAPHY

Dinah Forbes

The number of resources on the subject of women and work has expanded considerably in the last few years. Many are virtually unknown outside the organizations and communities that made them. Others are easily available from anywhere in Canada and are already relatively well used. This cineography includes not only resources that focus on women in unions, but those of interest to working women generally – those working in non-union jobs and women working in the home.

Few resources directly examine role of unions for women or the role of women in unions. Exceptions are a few excellent films such as *The Wilmar 8* and *Union Maids,* and videos like *The Fleck Women,* but by and large this topic has not had the treatment it deserves. Nevertheless, many of these tapes, films and slide-shows do confront the major concerns of working women.

Technical information on the resources includes the country where it was produced, the year, the producer, the medium (16mm film, slide-tape show or video, and the size of the video where available), the length and the distributor. Synopses for the Québec productions, which are listed after the English ones, have been translated from French material. Addresses and phone numbers for the distributors are appended to the list.

The list should be useful in the planning stages of film series, conferences, workshops and meetings, especially if you have a budget. Films from the National Film Board are free, but independent distributors charge both for the film and for the costs of getting it to you and back. Rental cost varies with the running time of the film. Some distributors charge union locals or community groups less than they would national union offices or universities. Remember, when you're shocked by a quoted rental price, that a hefty portion of it (in DEC Films, it's fifty percent) goes to the filmmaker, who very likely is in debt after making the film.

I would like to thank all of the women working in distribution, production and programming who have helped me to make this list a comprehensive one.

Account Overdue (Canada, 13 mm, video. CLC Labour Education and Studies Centre)
> The story of the CLC bank workers' organizing campaign with the Union of Bank Employees.

After the Difficulties (Canada 1982, Souad Sharabani, Helene Klodowski and DEC. 20 min., slide-tape show. DEC Films)
> At once a personal and political document on the social upheaval faced by thousands of young women in Southeast Asia. From village girls growing up in protective families they become factory girls in the rapidly expanding garment and electronic sweatshops. The slide show depicts the social and emotional dislocation and the penalties these women pay with their health and reputations.

The Amazing Equal Pay Show (Britain 1974, London Women's Film Group. 50 min, colour, 16mm. DEC Films)
> A film about the British Equal Pay Act. It portrays the stereotypical situations women find themselves in at work, at home and in the union through a series of sketches which incorporate elements from musicals, horror films and slapstick comedy.

Are Unions An Alternative? (Focus Manitoba. 1 inch reel-to-reel video. Red River Community College)
> What do labour organizations mean to women? This tape explores the reasons for the lack of strength and support given to the organization of women into unions. Two women are interviewed — Patrice Pratt of the MGEA and Susan Robinson of the SEIU.

Backwards, Forwards, Upside Down (Canada 1978, NFB. 27 min., colour, ¼ inch video. NFB/DEC Films)
> Women in unions discuss their problems in the work force.

Breaking Through (Canada 1981, Women's Workshop. 27 min., colour, 16mm. Women's Workshop)
> A sensitive docudrama that shows the challenges facing women in training for trade work. The film profiles three women and their reactions to the breakdown of old socialized fears of tackling "men's work."

CUPW *1981: Mother's Rights, Union Rights* (Canada 1981, Amelia Productions. 27 min., colour, ¼ inch videocassette. DEC Films and Amelia Productions)
> Deals with the rights of women who work outside the home to be

mothers. It explains the successful fight for the right to paid maternity leave by the Canadian Union of Postal Workers who went on strike over this issue.

Don't Call Me Baby (Canada 1975, Margo Trevelyan. 28 min., colour, 16mm. CUPE)
A look at how some women members of CUPE feel about and view their work, their union and their role in society.

The Double Day (Latin America/USA 1975, International Women's Film Project. 56 min., colour, 16mm. DEC Films)
An excellent documentary on working women in Latin America. The issues – relations within the family, the undervaluing of housework, discrimination in the workplace – are ones we are familiar with as Canadian women. The film shows the increasing social and political awareness of Latin American women and their struggles against female socialization, oppressive traditions and institutions, and the exploitive economic system.

The Emerging Woman (USA 1974, Women's Film Project. 40 min., b/w, 16mm. DEC)
A carefully researched documentary on the history of American women, which deals in part with the situation of working women and how we have been used as a reserve army of labour to be exploited when needed by the economy.

An Equal Opportunity (Canada 1982, NFB. 12 min., colour, 16mm. NFB)
An open-ended drama intended to trigger discussions on the subject of equal opportunities for women in the workplace, and on the role of unions and of the "sisterhood" in securing such opportunities.

The Fleck Women (Canada 1978, Kem Murch, Women's Workshop. 24 min., colour, ¼ inch videocassette. DEC Films)
In March 1978 the women at Fleck Manufacturing went out on strike. This video traces the personal and political struggles of the women during this bitter and protracted strike, exploring the growing solidarity between them and the strength they found in collective action. This tape is an important document on Canadian women's labour history.

Good Day Care (Canada 1978, Barbara Martineau and Lorna Rasmussen. 30 min., colour, 16mm. DEC Films)
This film shows the benefits of good day care and suggests why day care is at the bottom of the educational heap. Footage from three day care centres in Toronto shows different approaches to good day care and the positive picture they present contrasts sharply with the footage on the history of day care in Canada.

Good Monday Morning (Canada 1982, Sky Works 30 min., colour, 16mm. Sky Works)
The office is the setting, and women are the "stars" as they talk candidly and movingly about their work and how it affects every facet of their lives. In this white-collar ghetto of shiny, bright machines women are beginning to feel as if they are on factory assembly lines. But while they are losing their skills, their earning power and their opportunities, they are not losing their fight. The spirit of the women infuses the film with optimism.

The Hidden Price (Canada 1980, Women's Committee, B.C. Federation of Labour Education and Studies Centre. 25 min., Video CLC Labour)
A dramatization of the problems of sexual harassment in the workplace and the ways it can be fought.

How They Saw Us
A package of eight films available from the National Film Board. They were made in the 1940s and 1950s and have been re-released as examples of propaganda about women's roles at home and at work.

It's Not Enough (Canada 1974, NFB. 15 min., colour, 16mm. NFB)
A general discussion about why most women work outside their homes and the kinds of jobs available to us.

It's Not Your Imagination (Canada 1980, Women in Focus. ¼ inch videocassette. Women in Focus)
Six women relate their experiences of sexual harassment in the workplace. The video shows that sexual harassment is less an issue of sexuality than one of power, domination and socially accepted norms of behaviour.

Job Search — The Interview (Canada 1980, Cross Cultural Communications Centre. 23 min., colour, ¼ inch videocassette. CCCC)
Job search is a dramatization of what happens to three women from different backgrounds when they look for work in three different fields. A panel discussion of the issues raised follows an enactment of three job interviews.

Just A Minute (Canada 1976, NFB. Part 1, 7 min., Part 2, 6 min., colour, 16mm. NFB)
A series of film clips that highlight some of the problems and attitudes facing women in our work at home and outside.

The Labour Movement and Women (Video. Vancouver Status of Women)
The director of Women's Programs for the B.C. Federation of Labour discusses her job and the necessity of organizing women.

Looking For A Job? (Canada 1976, Women in Focus. 30 min., colour, ¼ inch videocassette. Women in Focus)
A video offering practical advice to assist women in getting a job. It particularly encourages women to consider non-traditional jobs.

Maria (Canada 1977, screenplay by Rick Salutin, CBC. 46 min., b/w, 16mm. NFB)

The story of Maria, a young immigrant garment worker, and her struggle to organize her factory. The film shows both the problems she faces at work in the long process of unionizing, and her problems at home when she takes on this enormous task. A strong and moving film.

A Matter of Life (Canada 1970, NFB. 65 min., b/w, 16mm. NFB)

The story of a young Montréal woman, deserted by her husband, working in a clothing factory to support her three children.

Mother's Day, 1980 (Canada 1980, Amelia Productions. 30 min., colour, ¼ inch videocassette. Amelia Productions)

Women gathered to celebrate Mother's Day 1980 under the banner, "every mother is a working mother" in a community park in the east end of Vancouver. The program includes feminist songs, a skit and a variety of speakers from feminist and community organizations.

Moving Mountains (Canada 1981, Laura Sky. 30 min., colour, 16mm. Skyworks and Steelworkers National Office)

Alongside 1,042 men in an open pit coal mine in B.C., 80 women work at jobs usually held only by men. This film shows their work, and their capabilities in drilling, blasting and driving gigantic machinery.

Nine To Five (USA 1980. Colour, 35mm/16mm. Bellevue for the 16mm print)

A very successful feature film starring Jane Fonda, Dolly Parton and Lily Tomlin. The solidarity of three office workers against their boss is the base for a hilarious flight of fantasy. The film offers a real and valuable outlet for frustrations of women office workers but in the end offers no suggestions for organizing for change,

No Life For A Women (Canada 1979, Bonnie Kreps. Colour, 16mm. NFB)

This film describes through interviews what is like for women to live in single-industry towns. The women talk about how they have learned to cope in a town that was designed without any consideration for the needs of women at home.

Norma Rae (USA 1979, 20th Century Fox. 115 min., colour, 35mm/16mm. Bellevue for 16mm print)

A feature movie based loosely on the story of Crystal Lee Sutton. Sally Fields stars as a garment worker in the Southern USA struggling to unionize the plant in which she works. A popular movie, it was one of the first Hollywood films to show unions and the situation of working women with sympathy.

On the Bias (Canada 1980, Women's Group, DEC. 28 min., colour, slide-tape show. DEC Films)

Focuses on the situation of women workers in the garment and retail industries and at home. It looks at the role of fashion and advertising in the manipulation of women's self image and at the history of women's work and women's clothing, as changes in fashion styles have matched changes in women's roles at work and in society. A provocative and useful resource.

Operation Finger Pinky (Canada 1978, NFB. 35 min., colour, 16 mm. NFB/DEC Films)
After help from employment counselors and a course in welding, Lynn...
A fictionalized account of the three-year struggle waged by the office staff at York University in their attempt to unionize.

Part of the Union (BBC)
Although women are now joining unions in greater numbers then men, many still feel that unions are a man's concern. Women are poorly represented in unions. This film looks at women's role in three British unions.

Pretend You're Wearing A Barrel (Canada 1978, NFB. 9 min., colour, 16mm. NFB)
After help from employment counselors and a course in welding, Lynn Ryan at 35 has a job as an apprentice engineer in a Vancouver shipyard.

Rights of Working Women (Canada 1980, Cross Cultural Communications Centre. 28 min., colour, ¼ inch videocassette. CCCC)
This video discusses most of the major legislation affecting working women: sex and racial discrimination, wages and hours of work, vacation and maternity leave, working conditions, compensation and unionization. Areas where legislation is lacking are identified.

Rising Up Strong: Women in the '80s (Canada 1981, Linda Briskin / Lorna Weir in cooperation with Rogers Cable TV. Part 1 – At Work and At Home, 30 min. Part 2 – Control of our Bodies, 30 min., colour, ¼ inch video cassette. DEC Films)
Examines the problems women face: low wages, job ghettos, responsibility for housework, inadequate child care, violence against women, persecution of lesbians, attacks on reproductive rights. This program is unique in its focus on the individual and collective struggles of Ontario women.

Role Of Woman As Worker (Focus Manitoba. 1 inch reel-to-reel video. Red River Community College)
Deals with work in capitalist society with particular relevance to women. It explores the questions, "who has control over the ways in which women work?" and "who has control over the ways in which work is organized?"

Roll Over (USA 1974, Marian Hunter. 10 min., colour, 16 mm. Women in Focus)
A film about women working in both typical and atypical jobs that exposes the discrimination inherent in the notion of "women's work."

Rosie The Riveter (USA 1980, Connie Field. 60 min., colour, 16mm. DEC Films)
An excellent documentary on women workers in the USA during World

War II based on interviews with five "Rosies" and the use of war-time propaganda films. At the outbreak of war women moved en masse into men's jobs, and they successfully performed skilled work after minimal training. They discovered dignity in their work, camaraderie on the job and pride in unionization. At the end of the war the women were sent home. *Rosie the Riveter* is a warm, personal and important film.

Sexual Harassment (Canada 1980, CLC. 10 min., video. CLC Labour Education and Studies Centre)
The debate on a resolution against sexual harassment in the workplace that focuses on the speech of Sylvia Porter of the B.C. Government Employees Union. An excellent description of the problem and what one union did about it.

She's A Railroader (Canada 1978, NFB. 9 min., colour, 16 mm. NFB)
Karen Zaitchik works on the trains. This short film shows how she manages in a traditionally male world.

Shirts and Songs(France 1972, Paul Bourron, Iskra. 15 min., colour, 16mm. DEC Films)
Responding to the arbitrary firing of one of their fellow workers, the women featured in this film walk out of the plant and set up production on their own. They mobilize support from the local community, who buy the shirts the strikers make themselves. The film documents the ways in which the women's growing self-confidence and assertiveness transform their relationships with one another.

Starting From Nina (Canada 1978, DEC 30 min., colour, 16mm. DEC Films)
Documents some experiences of consciousness-raising among working people in Ontario: immigrant workers, school children in a working-class neighbourhood and clerical workers. In the section with clerical workers they discuss the nature and pressure of their work and decide to form a staff association with a view to unionizing.

Striptease (Canada 1980, Kay Armitage. 25 min. Lauron Films)
Examines an aspect of the role of working women and raises questions of sexuality and society's notion of the human body. This film is an examination of the world of the stripper – as a human being and as a worker. The dancers discuss their lives as entertainers and the feelings of friends and audiences towards their chosen profession.

Taken For Granted (Canada 1980, Labour Advocacy and Research Association. 34 min., colour, slide-tape show in two carousels. Labour Advocacy and Research Association)
A two-part slide show on farm and domestic workers in B.C. Part 1 shows the history of these workers in B.C. Part 2 focuses on the current working conditions and organizing attempts. A kit of background readings is included with the show.

They Always Take Me For Granted (Canada 1981, NFB. 18 min., colour, sound
filmstrip. McIntrye Educational Media)
Examines the role of women in the workplace from late 19th century to
the present day. This filmstrip focuses on the sectors of the economy
where women worked and details the problems they encountered, including Eileen Tallman-Suffin's attempt to organize women workers at
Eaton's. The contemporary scene, including the Fleck strike and continuing struggles such as equal pay for work of equal value, are touched upon.

They Appreciate You More (Canada 1974, NFB. 14 min., colour, 16mm. NFB)
A film about the impact on her husband, her children and the division of
housework that occurs when a Montréal women, Aliette, starts a paid job.

This Line Is Not In Service (Canada 1981, Amelia Productions and Cable 10
Vancouver. 28 min., colour, ¼ inch videocassette. Amelia Productions)
In February 1981, workers at BC Tel occupied their workplaces in strike
against the company. This video was shot at that time on the floors of the
Seymour St. building where the operators work. We are shown the ways
their consciousness as workers developed through the occupation and
how they felt having control over their own work for the first time.

A Time To Rise (Canada 1981, Jim Munro and Anand Patwardhan. 40 min.,
colour, 16mm. NFB)
A moving and well-crafted account of B.C. farmworkers' struggle to
unionize. Many of the farmworkers are immigrant women. The film
documents the conditions that provoked the formation of the union as
well as the opposition — sometimes violent, sometimes racist — from
growers and labour contractors. Not only does the film provide us with
stirring examples of dignity and determination, it also suggests that our
society benefits from the underpaid and undervalued labour of many
people.

TWU *Tel* (Canada 1981, Amelia Productions. 9 min., colour, ¼ inch
videocassette. Amelia Productions)
A brief look at the issues of the strike and occupation at B.C. Tel in 1981.

The UIC *And You: Benefit Control* (Canada 1980, Victor Schwartzman. 21
min., colour, ¼ inch videocassette. DEC Films)
Produced for claimants and legal aid workers, this video is geared to help
the unemployed deal with the Unemployment Insurance Commission
and get the benefits to which they are entitled.

Union Maids (USA 1977, Julia Reichart and James Klein. 40 min., b/w, 16mm.
DEC Films)
The personal histories of three women union organizers in Chicago in the
1930s. The women, a laundry worker, a stockyard worker and a factory
worker, relate their own experiences — the strikes, the union meetings, the
sitdowns. They recall the growth of their awareness of working-class

oppression, of women's oppression and of the clear need for collective action to win change. An inspiring film.

Up From The Bargain Basement (Canada 1979, Film League. 30 min., colour, 16mm. DEC Films)
A look at the situation of workers in service industries that concentrates on the history of Eaton's and its employees. The film uses a docudrama technique to demolish the Eaton image and to demonstrate contradictions in the relationship between workers and the boss.

Video Display Terminals (Very Dangerous Technology) (Canada 1981, Amelia Productions. 31 min., colour, ¼ inch videocassette. Amelia Productions)
A video of a Vancouver Newspaper Guild workshop that explains radiation and other hazards of VDTS. It outlines actions that unions and working women can take to protect themselves.

We Women Workers (Canada 1979, Working Women's Centre. 20 min., colour, slide-tape show. Working Women's Centre)
Three immigrant women from different backgrounds tell their stories and the problems in the work world. The show points out that regardless of ethnic background, immigrant women face the same problems. The importance of learning English, of unionization and of community agencies are emphasized.

We Won't Live Like That (Canada 1980, Steelworkers. 18 min., colour, 16mm. Steelworkers National Office)
A film about the strike of women workers against Radio Shack. It shows the difficulties of negotiating a first contract and the strains of a long strike. The women talk about their new understanding of the role of the police, who intervened constantly in the picket line. It also shows the support the strikers got from women in the community.

Who's Ripping Off Whom? (Canada 1980, Victor Schwartzman. 25 min., colour, ¼ inch videocassette. DEC Films)
This tape provides a history of the UIC and its role in the current crisis. At a time when unemployment is high, the Commission, instead of helping, arbitrarily cuts back on the number of recipients, particularly women, immigrants and youth, knowing full well that even if every job vacancy in the country were filled, 16 out of 17 of those currently unemployed would still be out of work.

Why Aren't You Smiling? (USA 1980, Community Media Productions. 20 min., colour, slide-tape show. DEC Films)
Looks at the situation of women office workers in the US. It traces the history of women's work in the office, shows the problems faced by black women, the impact of new office technologies on women's work, and ends with a powerful call for women to organize. A useful and important resource.

The Wilmar 8 (USA 1980, Mary Beth Yarrow and Julie Thompson. 55 min.,
colour, 16mm. IDERA Films)
In a small midwestern town, eight women working in a bank go on strike
against low wages, poor working conditions and sexual discrimination in
job promotion. *The Wilmar 8* tells the story of the women's struggle for
a contract, a struggle which placed them in the forefront of the fight for
working women's rights.

With Babies and Banners (USA 1978, Anne Bohlen, Lyn Goldfarb and Lorraine
Gray. 45 min., colour, 16mm. DEC Films)
On December 30, 1936, autoworkers at the GM plant in Flint, Michigan
struck and occupied the factories. The strikers won 44 days later and their
victory became the turning point in the CIO's drive for unionization. The
women, organized into the Women's Emergency Brigade, played a critical
role in the strike and this film tells their story. It shows the changes in their
lives as they emerged from the isolation of their own homes and joined in
collective action. The film also points out that all the issues raised in 1936
still face working women today.

A Wives' Tale (Canada 1980, Sophie Bissonnette, Joyce Rock and Martin
Duckworth. 73 min., colour, 16mm. DEC Films)
The powerful and emotional story of Sudbury women who organized to
support the Steelworkers at Inco during their ten-month strike in 1979.
The film's power is rooted in its meticulous recording of the personal and
collective struggles of these women, who hang together despite company
intimidation, the strikers' lack of trust at critical moments, and internal
differences. It shows the pain, the fears, the solidarity and the incredible
strength developed by the process of collective organizing. A superb
feminist film.

A Woman's Work (Canada 1976, Gail McClurg. 20 min., 16mm. Canadian
Filmmakers Distribution Centre)
This film investigates the widening wage gap between men and women.
Interviews with working women, lawyers and unionists bring to light
some of the difficulties with current legislation in Canada.

Women and the Economy (Focus Manitoba. 1 inch reel-to-reel video. Red
River College)
Talks about the present situation of women in the Canadian labour force.
A working woman presents her analysis of the problems of working
women, focusing on the powerlessness that comes from the kind of work
women do.

Women at Work: Employment Discrimination (USA 1978, Seattle Feminist
Video. 30 min., b/w, ¼ inch videocassette. Women in Focus)
This video examines employment discrimination against women in both
traditional and non-traditional jobs.

Women in New Employment (Focus Manitoba. 1 inch reel-to-reel video. Red
   River Community College)
   An interview with a group of women in Winnipeg who are running a
   unique employment agency that deals specifically with women in the
   labour force, especially those trying to go back to work.

Women in the Labour Force (Focus Manitoba. 1 inch reel-to-reel. Red River
   Community College)
   An interview with Madeline Parent of the Canadian Textile and Chemical
   Union about women in the labour force. Topics discussed include an
   historical look at women as workers, some current issues (equal pay for
   work of equal value), organizing and unions.

Women in the Trades (Pre-Trades Program) (Canada 1977, Georgette Ganne. 25
   min., b/w, ¼ inch videocassette. Women in Focus)
   Features the Pre-Trades Program for women in Winnipeg. Women
   involved in the course share their ideas and enthusiasm, and discuss their
   problems on entering and working within the male-dominated trades.

Women in Trades (Canada 1980, Saskatchewan Women in Trades. 57 min.,
   colour, ¼ inch videocassette, Women in Focus)
   Women from eight different skilled trades demonstrate their jobs, talk
   about different aspects of their work and comment on some of the advantages and disadvantages of employment in the trades.

Women Want (Canada 1975, NFB. 25 min., colour, 16mm. NFB)
   Touches on some of the major issues affecting women: equal pay for work
   of equal value, property rights, day care and the problems facing women
   re-entering the work force.

Women's Work (Canada 1977, E & A Productions. 20 min., colour, 16mm. DEC)
   Critiques the Equal Pay Act and its implementation in the workplace. The
   film calls for broader action on equal pay for work of equal value. Presented in a TV interview style.

Working For Your Life (USA 1980, Charles Light. 57 min., colour, 16mm. DEC
   Films)
   This film, made in 40 different workplaces, is about health and safety
   hazards faced by women workers. It ably documents both the jobs traditionally held by women and jobs into which women are beginning to
   move. This film also looks at the ways women are actively and collectively
   fighting to improve working conditions.

Workplace Hustle (USA 1981, Clark Communications. 30 min., colour, 16mm.
   Women's Bureau, Ontario Ministry of Labour [loan], International
   Tel-Film [rental])
   Ed Asner narrates this film about sexual harassment that is largely directed
   towards changing men's behaviour towards women. The film argues that

women want to separate sexuality and work in order to improve both and
that men must support women in this.

Yes I Can (Canada. 30 min., colour, 16mm. Women's Bureau, Ontario
Ministry of Labour)
This film about women in non-traditional jobs such as truck driving, tool
and die making and carpentry, deals not only with the work these women
do, but also with how they feel about their jobs.

Yes We Can! (Québec 1981, VidéoFemmes. 30 min., b/w, ¼ inch videocassette,
Women in Focus)
A translation of the original French tape, Six Femmes A Leur Place,
described in the French-language section of this list.

FRENCH LANGUAGE RESOURCES

Les bucheronnes (Québec 1978, V. Pelletier and J. Bouffard. 28 min., colour,
16 mm. Cinéma Libre)
A film about the daily lives of two women, mother and daughter, who
have been woodcutters all their lives – not for recreation or exercise, but
for a livelihood. They have a lot to say about women's liberation, the
relationships between men and women, and equal pay for work of equal
value.

Ce serait donc mieux (Québec 1975, ONF/NFB. 25 min., b/w, video, ½ inch
betamax. Réseau Vidé-elles des Femmes)
Made by and for secretaries. They talk of the monotony of their jobs and
how what they do undervalues their potential. As one of them says.
"Secretaries: we can think too …"

Les championnes du "cheap labour" c'est nous (Québec 1979. 57 min., colour,
¾ inch video. TVC Bois Francs)
An interview with two garment workers in the Bois Francs region. They
talk about the considerations of their work and the madness of their
employer's obsession with profitability, which determines the nature of
their work.

D'abord ménagères (Québec 1978, Luce Guilbeault. 90 min., colour, 16mm.
Cinéma Libre)
Luce Guilbeault maintains throughout the film that it's not enough for a
woman to work in order to attain real freedom or fulfillment. She does
not undervalue women's work in the home and states clearly that to find
a job similar to housework in no way changes the situation or traditional
role of women. In the final interview, the heart of the film, a woman
affirms that change will be possible when women reorganize themselves
and share in common their individual experiences.

De fil en aiguille (Québec 1976, La Ligue des Femmes du Québec. 45 min. b/w, ½ inch betamax or ¼ inch videocassette. Vidéographe)

Textile workers are the heroines of this video, which uses personal testimonies to illustrate their unbearable working conditions. The video talks about the particular exploitation of home workers, piecework, the need for day care centres both in factories and in schools, the need for equal pay, and for a 30 hour week — issues often discussed but rarely articulated as demands by those workers who are the least protected.

Elles ont relevé le défi (Québec 1977, Claire Couture. 52 min., b/w, ½ inch betamax. Vidéo Femmes and ROCCQ)

A video on the courage of women who have decided to use completely different skills from the ones traditionally designated for women.

L'Etat employeur (Québec 1975, SCRAM. 55 min., ½ inch betamax or ¼ inch videocassette. G.I.V.)

Workers at a hospital in Saguenay-Lac-St. Jean demand decent wages, remember the formation of the Common Front in 1972 and talk of the importance of political struggle in defending the interests of workers.

Les femmes dans la grève de l'amiante (Québec 1975. 22 min., b/w, ½ inch betamax. Vidéographie)

On March 18, 1975, 3,500 miners went on strike at Thetford Mines. This video shows the active solidarity given by miners' wives when they formed a strike support committee independent of the union.

Les femmes et le syndicat (Québec 1981, 16 min., colour, ¼ inch videocassette TVCRA)

As part of a live broadcast on International Women's Day, two women active in the CSN and CEQ talk about the role of women in the unions, the struggles they both have lead, and the rights they have won over the years.

La lutte des femmes, combat de tous les travailleurs (Québec 1979. 35 min., b/w, ½ inch betamax. TVCRA)

A video explains the position of the CSN on the "Equality and Independence" report by the Status of Women Council.

Les métiers non-traditionnel (Québec 1981. 28 min., colour, ½ inch betamax or ¼ inch videocassette. Femmes en Focus)

This video evaluates the non-traditional skills that women are starting to use in their work.

Où est Anne (Québec 1978, CECM. 50 min., b/w, ½ inch betamax. CECM and Vidéo Femmes)

The story of a woman who works outside her home, this video documents the new division of domestic and family tasks when both members of a couple work.

La perle rare (Québec 1980, Diane Poitras. 30 min., b/w, ½ inch betamax or
¼ inch videocassette. G.I.V. and Vidéo Femmes)
The secretary at work plays the same role as she does at home – she is
a stabilizing force. To be a secretary is to define oneself in an indeter-
minate role between object-woman and wife-mother, between decor-
ative and practical functions. A rare pearl (a description often used of
domestic workers) is a subordinate, an adjunct or assistant, the feminine
presence behind all great accomplishments.

Piquez sur la ligne bisée (Québec 1976, France Renaud. 13 min., b/w, ½ inch
betamax G.I.V. and Vidéographe, 16 mm. Les Films du Crépuscule)
A film that counterpoints the rhythm of women workers at their
machines with the soundtrack of a record by Dr. Gendron on "Preparation à l'amour." The clash between these images points out the contradiction between the real conditions of women's work and the traditional stereotypes of femininity.

Point d'ordre (Québec 1978, CV Pop Lévis. 30 min., b/w, ½ inch betamax. CV
Pop Lévis and Vidéo Femmes)
How can we get involved with a union or popular group without jeopard-
izing our marriages? Are militancy and family life incompatible? Does
any decision to get involved politically at the workplace concern the rest
of the family? Do wives feel well informed at the beginning of a union
conflict? Militant couples and couples no longer involved try to answer
all these questions. One of them concludes that "the personal *is* political."

Les poissoneries au nord-est (Canada 1976, Télé Publik de Bathurst, N.B. 28
min., b/w, ½ inch betamax, Réseau Vidé-elle des Femmes)
A video on the working conditions of women at the fish plants of New
Brunswick.

Retour an travail: project d'integration des au travail (Québec 1981, Josée
Belleau, 30 min., colour, ¼ inch videocassette. Vidéo Femmes)
Economic independence is the first step towards autonomy. The P.I.F.
offers services to assist women returning to the labour force and this
video outlines their program.

Rien qu'une secrétaire (Québec 1978, Lynda Roy. 53 min., b/w, ½ inch
betamax, CV Lévis and Vidéo Femmes)
Examines the myths and realities of a secretary's job and the conditions
of this work. It shows the different views of students, guidance counsel-
lors, personal directors, employers and a representatives of the Crossroads Association for Clerical Employees.

Se tailler une place au soleil (Québec 1977, Claire Couture and Rose-Marie
Joncas. 45 min., b/w, ½ inch betamax. ROCCQ and Vidéo Femmes)
Traditionally women stay at home caring for their husband and

children. What happens when they want to leave this role and rejoin the labour force? What are the options open to them for retraining or professional training? Is it easy to find a place in the sun?

Six femmes à leur place (Québec 1981, Louise Giguère and Louise LeMay. 30 min., ½ inch betamax and ¾ inch videocassette. Vidéo Femmes)
The orginal French version of *Yes We Can*. From garbage collector to electrician, where do we situate women in traditionally male jobs? Six women talk about the difficulties they face, the changes they wish for, the fulfilment and affirmation that doing these unusual jobs gives them.

Le syndicalisme au Québec: la condition de la femme au travail (Québec 1975, Francine Rochon and Lise Lebel. 30 min., b/w, ½ inch betamax and ¾ inch videocassette. CEQ)
This video outlines the FTQ's approach to the problems of women workers and their priorities for action. It highlights the Laure Gaudreault Committee of the CEQ and its emphasis on the issue of maternity leave.

Tout ce qui sort de l'ordinaire: j'aime ça la faire (Québec 1979. 45 min., b/w, ½ inch betamax. Réseau Vidé-elle des Femmes)
A video on non-traditional work.

Les voleurs de job (Québec 1980, Tahni Rached. 68 min., 16mm. NFB)
A film that demolishes the myth that immigrants steal jobs from Canadians. The film shows immigrants at work in jobs such as night cleaner, hotel maid, dishwasher and unskilled factory work. They talk of their understanding of Canada's needs for immigrant workers in low-paid, unskilled jobs and of their frustrated quest for freedom and economic opportunity that brought them to Canada.

Vous repasserez (Québec 1973, 30 min., b/w, ½ inch betamax or ¾ inch video. Vidéographie)
Women have children to carry, to feed, to clothe, to care for, to reprimind and to console. They also have other jobs as administrator, counsellor, cook and laundress. But when they demand the right to use one of these skills in a job outside the home, they are inevitably told to "move along."

DISTRIBUTORS

Amelia Productions, c/o Ellen Frank, 1774 Grant Street Apt. 3., Vancouver, B.C.
BBC, Manulife Centre, Suite 510, 55 Bloor Street West, Toronto, Ontario (416)925-3891
Canadian Filmmakers Distribution Centre, 406 Jarvis Street, Toronto, Ontario (416)593-1808

CLC Labour Education and Studies Centre, 2841 Riverside Drive, Ottawa, Ontario (613)731-3052

Cross Cultural Communications Centre (CCCC), 1991 Dufferin Street, Toronto, Ontario (416)653-2223

CUPE, 233 Gilmour Street, Ottawa, Ontario

DEC Films, 427 Bloor Street West, Toronto, Ontario M5S 1X7 (416)964-6560

Idera Films, 2524 Cypress Street, Vancouver, B.C., V6J 3N2 (604)738-8815

International Tele-Film, 47 Densley Avenue, Toronto, Ontario M6M 2P5 (416)241-4483

Labour Advocacy and Research Association, 2520 Triumph Street, Vancouver, B.C.

McIntyre Educational Media Ltd., 30 Kelfield, Rexdale, Ontario (416)245-7800

NFB(National Film Board) has regional distribution centres in most Canadian cities. Contact the one nearest you.

Red River Community College, A/V Department, Notre Dame Avenue, Winnipeg, Manitoba

Sky Works, 566 Palmerston Avenue, Toronto, Ontario M6G 2P7 (416)536-6581

Steelworkers National Office, 55 Eglinton Avenue East, Toronto, Ontario (416)487-1571

Vancouver Status of Women, 400A West 5th Avenue, Vancouver, B.C. V5Y 1J7

Women In Focus, Suite 204, 456 West Broadway, Vancouver, B.C. V5Y 1R3

Women's Bureau, Ontario Ministry of Labour, 400 University Avenue, Toronto, Ontario M7A 1T7 (416)965-9500

Working Women's Centre, 1072A Bloor Street West, Toronto, Ontario (416)532-2824

French Language Distributors

C.E.Q. Centre audio-visual, 2334, chemin Ste Foy, Ste Foy Québec G1V 4ES (418)658-57711 x120

Cinéma Libre, 4872 rue Papineau, Montréal, Québec H2H 1V6 (514)526-0473

C.V-Pop Lévis (Centre vidéo populaire) 17 rue Notre Dame, C.P. 1104, Lévis, Québec G6V 4A3

Femmes en Focus, C.P. 124, Bathurst, New Brunswick, E2A 3Z2 (506)548-3717

G.I.V. (Groupe D'Intervention Vidéo), 3963 St. Denis, Montréal, Québec (514)849-4044

ONF (National Film Board), 550 Sherbrooke Street West, Montréal, Québec (514)333-3333

Réseau Vidé-elle des Femmes R.R. No. 1, Rang 8, St.-Adrian-de-Han Québec

ROCCQ (Regroupment des organismes communautaires de communication du Québec) 835 rue Brown, local 305, Québec, Québec G1 5 4S1 (418)681-0651

TVC des Bois Franc, 37 rue Dubord, Victoriaville, Québec G6P 7Z9 (418)544-6869

TVC R.A. (Région de l'amiante) 22 rue de la Fabrique, Thetford Mines Québec G6G 2N2 (418) 380-8444

Vidéo Femmes, 10 rue McMahon, Québec, Québec G1R 3S1 (418)692 3090

Vidéographie, 4550 Garnier, Montréal, Québec H2J 3S6 (514)521-2116

TRADE UNION RESOURCES ON WOMEN

Linda Briskin

This bibliography was compiled through library research and by soliciting material directly from unions. A letter containing an initial draft of the bibliography was sent to the largest unions in Canada, both Canadian and international, and to those unions with the greatest number of women members. Approximately 50 letters were sent out and I received 25 responses, 24 from Canadian unions or federations. Only one international union – the United Auto Workers – replied.

Although in 1980 only 18.5% of the Canadian membership in international unions were women, this represented 30.8% of all women trade unionists in Canada. Therefore the lack of response from the international unions was disappointing. However, the branch plant nature of the international unions' operation in Canada may mean that they have little material available in their Canadian offices and/or few staff to process requests.

As evidenced in the following pages, extensive material emerged from the Canadian unions and federations. This is a reflection of the growing militancy of women trade unionists and of the increased pressure being put on unions to take up women's issues in a serious way.

When I began this project I was surprised to discover that no union, federation nor even the Women's Bureau of the Canadian Labour Congress was cataloguing and distributing material produced on women's union issues. This is unfortunate, for trade unionists across the country should be sharing policy statements and research. Not only would this save time, effort and money but it would also have important political ramifications. A policy paper or a convention resolution is always the result of a political, organizational and educational process. Both the political lessons and the strategy learned during this process need to be articulated and shared. And, during a battle on the convention floor over a controversial issue, being able to invoke a policy on that issue passed by another major union is a persuasive and effective strategy.

The resource list shows the evolution of concern with women's union issues over the past ten years and it also helps to identify the significant issues in any given time period. For example, many of the recent entries, from a number of unions and from across the country, deal with the impact of microtechnology. This commonality of concern with the new technology suggests both the need for and the possibility of a coordinated strategy across Canada.

The bibliography is not exhaustive, but to my knowledge represents the most comprehensive list available at this time. It is organized alphabetically. Within the listing for each union, the most recent materials are noted first. There is a wide variation in the kinds of materials included: leaflets, government briefs, policy statements from conventions, references from union newspapers and research reports. Each entry contains as much information as possible, but many union publications do not list a specific author or publication date. The end of the list contains a few references to material published by groups of trade unionists not working directly under the auspices of their unions.

I hope this bibliography will facilitate contact between Canadian women trade unionists. I would like to thank all the unions who responded to my request for material and John Ford of the Ontario Ministry of Labour Library for his assistance.

Alberta Union of Provincial Employees (AUPE)
10975-124th Street
Edmonton, Alberta T5M 0J2
1 *Impact*. News magazine of AUPE, occasional coverage of women's issues.

British Columbia Federation of Labour (BCFL)
Women's Rights Committee
3110 Boundary Road
Burnaby, B.C. V5M 4A2
1 "Submission to the Federal Task Force on Microelectronics," July 23, 1982.
2 "Women and Technological Change: A Background Paper," 1981.
3 "Why do Women Join Unions?", nd (leaflet).
4 "Affirmative Action," Policy Paper, 1980.
5 "Equal Pay for Work of Equal Value," Policy Paper, 1980.
6 "Sexual Harassment," Policy Paper, nd.
7 "Sexual Harassment in the Workplace – A Discussion Paper," B.C. Federation Women's Rights Committee and Vancouver Women's Research Centre, nd.
8 "Annual Report of the B.C. Federation of Labour, Committee on Women's Rights," 1971.

9 *Sisterhood.* Publication of Women's Rights Committee (subscription free on request).

British Columbia Government Employees Union (BCGEU)
4911 Canada Way
Burnaby, B.C. V5G 3W3

1 "Women in the BCGEU," Women's Committee, nd (leaflet).
2 *Bargaining for Equality* – A Calendar of Contract Clauses of Interest to Women Workers, 1982.
3 *Toward Equality* – A Calendar of Women in the Labour Movement, 1981.

British Columbia Teachers Federation (BCTF)
2235 Burrard Street
Vancouver, B.C. V6J 3H9

1 *Status of Women Bargaining Issues,* September 1982 (booklet).

Canadian Air Line Employees Association (CALEA)
6520 Viscount Road
Mississauga, Ontario L4V 1H3

1 *Skyways.* Bi-monthly publication of CALEA, occasional coverage of women's issues.

Canadian Labour Congress (CLC)
Women's Bureau
2841 Riverside Drive
Ottawa, Ontario K1V 8X7

1 "Special Issues for Union Women Today," "Running Uphill: The Effects of Economic Crisis on Women Workers," "Our Changing Unions." Documents from CLC Women's Conference, March 1983.
2 "Report of the Committee on Equality of Opportunity and Treatment of Women Workers," Document 9, CLC Convention, May 1982.
3 "Resolutions No. 421-449 Submitted on Equality of Opportunity," Background to Document 9, CLC Convention, May 1982.
4 "Report of the Women's Bureau," contained in the Report of the Executive Council, CLC Convention, May 1982.
5 "Clerical and Office Hazards: An Inventory," *Issues in Health and Safety,* No. 2, nd.
6 *Equal Partners for Change – Women and Unions* (kit) contains "Women and the Canadian Labour Congress," "To Seize the Good: History of Women in Unions," "Here to Stay: Women in the Workforce," "Speak Up: Sexual Harassment on the Job," Bread and Roses," "Reaping the

Benefits," "Fit to Work: Health on the Job," "Using Your Unions," "Dealing with Change: The Challenge of Microelectronics," "Who Will Mind the Children."

7 "We've Had Enough," Brief presented by locked-out employees of the Canadian Imperial Bank of Commerce (East Angus Branch) to the CLC Conference on Equal Opportunity and Treatment of Women, December 1980.

8 "Report of the Committee on Equality of Opportunity and Treatment of Women Workers," Document 16, 13th Constitutional Convention, 1980.

9 "Equal Pay for Work of Equal Value," Policy Paper, CLC Convention, 1980.

10 "Equality of Opportunity and Treatment of Women Workers," Conference Report, January 1978.

11 "Paid Educational Leave," Policy Statement, CLC Constitutional Convention, 1976.

12 "Equality of Opportunity and Treatment of Women Workers," Policy Statement, 11th Constitutional Convention, 1976.

13 "Women Trade Unionists," Conference Resolutions, March 1976.

14 *Canadian Labour.* Monthly publication of CLC (subscription free on request). Regular coverage of women's issues. Special issues on women: Vol. 24 (December 1979), Vol. 21 (September 1976), Vol. 20 (June 1975).

Canadian Union of Postal Workers (CUPW)
280 Metcalfe Street
Ottawa, Ontario K2P 1R7

1 "Address by Jean Claude Parrot to Conference on Work and the Quality of Family Life," Toronto, April 1982.

2 "Parental Rights," *Negotiations*, March 1981.

3 CUPW. National newspaper, occasional coverage of women's issues.

Canadian Union of Public Employees (CUPE)
21 Florence Street
Ottawa, Ontario K2P 0W6

1 *Le harcèlement sexuel — guide syndical pour la prévention et le règlement des problèmes de harcèlement sexuel en milieu de travail,* Comité de condition féminine, conseil du Québec Syndicat canadien de la fonction publique, décembre 1982.

2 "Technological Change and Working Women," CUPE Research Department, February 1981.

3 "Daycare Where People Care," Education Department, nd (bilingual leaflet).

4 "Affirmative Action – Putting a Stop to Sex Discrimination: An Outline for Locals," nd.

5 *Equal Opportunity at Work: A* CUPE Affirmative Action Manual, Education Department, nd.

6 "Are You Being Discriminated Against?", Education Department, nd (bilingual leaflet).

7 "The 'New' Status of Women in CUPE," Education Department, nd.

8 "The Status of Women in CUPE," Special Report, CUPE National Convention, September 1971.

9 *The Facts,* regular newsletter of CUPE.
"Bargaining for Equality: How to Eliminate Discrimination through Negotiation," Vol. 4, No. 5 (May 1982), p. 15.
"Day Care in Crisis," "Sexual Harassment – why it's important to negotiate clauses on this issue," Vol. 4, No. 3 (March 1982), pp. 7, 19.
"Parental Leave – Leave to Love our Children," "Equal Pay – Striking Back in B.C.," Vol. 4, No. 1 (September 1981), pp 12, 20.
"Women – the Growing Problems at Work," Vol. 3, No. 2 (March 1981), p. 9.
"Part Timers – They Deserve Full Time Rights," Vol. 3, No. 1 (November 1980), p. 11.
"Technological Change – Changing Ourselves to Meet the New Technologies," "Parental Leaves of Absence – Quebec Public Employees Win Important Gains," "Cutback Reports – The Federal Cutback Attack on Women," Vol. 2, No. 9 (June-July 1980), pp. 146, 160, 161.
"Volunteers," "Technological Change – The Little Machines that Bring Big Layoffs," Vol. 2, No. 8 (May 1980), pp. 127, 129.
"Sexual Harassment – The Social Disease and How to Fight It," Vol. 2, No. 7 (March 1980), p. 107.
"Technological Change – Machines are Taking our Jobs," "Women Workers – Writing Non-Sexist Contracts," Vol. 2, No. 4 (September 1979), pp. 66, 69.
"New Office Technology," Vol., 2, No. 3 (August 1979), p. 4.
"International Women's Day – Counting Up Victories and Facing Challenges," Vol. 1, No. 9 (February-March 1979), p. 137.
"Pensions and Women, "Vol. 1, No. 4 (June-July 1978), p. 53.

10 *The Public Employee.* Journal/magazine, published five times a year. Brief news items; regular coverage of women's issues.

Centrale de l'enseignement du Québec (CEQ)
2336 rue Chemin Sainte-Foy
Sainte-Foy, Québec G1V 4E5

1 *Le droit au travail social pour toutes les femmes,* 27ième congrès, 1980.

Communication Workers of Canada (cwc)

25 Cecil Street, 2nd Floor
Toronto, Ontario M5T 1N1

1 "Women Workers," "Part Time Workers," "Parental Rights," Policy Statements, cwc Convention, June 1982.

Confédération des syndicats nationaux (csn)

1601 rue Delorimier
Montréal, Québec H2K 4M5

1 *Les femmes à la csn n'ont pas les moyens de reculer,* rapport du Comité de la condition féminine, 51ième Congrès, 1982.

2 "Un vieux problème, la discrimination, un noveau moyen, l'action positive," par la service de la condition féminine, 1982.

3 *On n'a pas les moyens de reculer! Les conséquences de la crise sur la femme,* Dossiers Spéciaux, le Comité de la condition féminine, 1981.

4 *La lutte des femmes, une lutte permanente, une lutte collective,* rapport du Comité de la condition féminine de la csn, 50ième Congrès, mai 1980.

5 *Garderies – pour un réseau universel gratuit,* Dossiers Spéciaux, 1980.

6 *La lutte des femmes pour le droit au travail social,* Deuxième rapport du Comité de la condition féminine, 49e Congrès de la csn, juin 1979.

7 *Les travailleuses et l'accès de la syndicalisation,* Dossiers Spéciaux, le Comité d'action accès à la syndicalisation et normes minimales d'emploi, des Etats généraux II des travailleuses salariées québécoises, 1978.

8 *La lutte des femmes, combat de tous les travailleurs,* rapport du Comité de la condition féminine, 47e Congrès, 1976 (2ième èdition, 1977).

9 *Les Conditions de travail des femmes,* Comité d'action des Etats généraux II des travailleuses salariées québécoises, 1978.

10 "Pour des congés de maternité payés," Le Service d'action politique et la service de la condition féminine, nd.

11 "Le congé de maternité," nd (brochure).

12 "Pour les femmes: égalité dans l'emploi," nd (brochure).

13 "Plateforme des Etats généraux II," nd.

14 "Bulletin du Front Commun sur les droits parentaux," nd.

Fédération des affaires sociales (fas)

1601, rue Delorimier
Montréal, Québec H2K 4M5

1 "Rapport du comité de la condition féminine de la fédération des affaires sociales," Congrès d'orientation, May 1983.

Fédération des travailleurs de Québec (FTG)

Le comité de la condition féminine de la FTG
2100 rue Papineau
Montréal, Québec H2K 4J4

1 "8 mars Journée Internationale des femmes," 1983 (brochure).
2 *Les syndicats et le congé-maternité,* Service d'éducation, 1982.
3 *Comité de la condition féminine – guide pratique,* nd.
4 "La présence des femmes dans les syndicats," 17e Congrès, novembre 1981.
5 "Les femmes à la FTQ: 1 sur 3," Document d'information No. 10, 17e Congrès, novembre 1981.
6 *Congé-Maternité,* 1981.
7 "Déclaration de politique sur la condition féminine," 16e Congrès, novembre 1979.
8 "Une double exploitation, une seule lutte," 1979.
9 "Politique familiale," déclaration de principe de la FTQ, 15e Congrès, décembre 1977.
10 *Travailleuses et syndiquées,* 13ième Congrès, décembre 1973.
11 "Le combat syndical et les femmes," 14ième Congrès, décembre 1975.

Manitoba Federation of Labour

Equal Rights and Opportunities Committee
570 Portage Avenue, Suite 104
Winnipeg, Manitoba R3C 0G4

1 "Women, Work and Unions," Equal Rights and Opportunities Committee, nd (leaflet).

Manitoba Government Employees Association (MGEA)

360 McMillan Avenue
Winnipeg, Manitoba R3L 0N2

1 "Women in the M.G.E.A.," Equal Opportunities Committee, 1981.
2 "Plans for Action," Status of Women Committee, out of print.

National Union of Provincial Government Employees (NUPGE)

204-2841 Riverside Drive
Ottawa, Ontario K1V 2E1

1 "The Report of the Task Force on Micro-electronics and Employment – NUPGE's Response," Research Report No. 12, November 1982.
2 "Sexual Harassment," Policy Statement, nd.
3 "Affirmative Action," Policy Statement, nd.

4 *Microtechnology,* 1982 (booklet).
5 *Bargaining for Equality,* 1982 (booklet).
6 *Sexual Harassment at Work,* nd (booklet).
7 "Stress at Work," Research Report No. 11, March 1980.
8 "The Challenge of New Technology," Research Report No. 10, March 1980.
9 "Affirmative Action," Research Report No. 9, March 1980.
10 "Parental Leave," Collective Agreement Information System, March 1980.
11 "Myths about Sexual Harassment," Research Report No. 8, November 1979.
12 "Sexual Harassment in the Workplace," Research Report No. 7, November 1979.
13 "Women in the Labour Force – The Truth Behind the Myths," Research Report No. 6, June 1979.
14 "Government Cutbacks – Women as Targets," Research Report No. 4, March 1979.

Nova Scotia Federation of Labour
Women's Committee
P.O. Box 3045
Halifax, Nova Scotia B3J 3G6

1 *Women and Work Kits,* sponsored by the Nova Scotia Federation of Labour, Canadian Research Institute for the Advancement of Women, A Woman's Place and Dalhousie University, 1982. Four kits are available: *Women and the Nova Scotia Economy, Equal Pay for Work of Equal Value, Child Care Resources, Women and Unions.* Each kit contains a working paper, a course outline and a series of handouts.

Ontario Federation of Labour (OFL)
Women's Committee
15 Gervais Drive, Suite 202
Don Mills, Ontario M3C 1Y8

1 "Statement on Women and Affirmative Action," Policy Paper, OFL Convention, November 1982.
2 "Our Fair Share: Affirmative Action and Women," Discussion Paper, OFL Conference on Affirmative Action, May 1982.
3 *Parental Rights and Daycare – A Bargaining Guide for Unions,* April 1982.
4 "Daycare Deadline 1990," Brief to government of Ontario OFL *et al.,* 1981.
5 "When We Stand Together, We All Win," nd (leaflet describing activities of the OFL Women's Committee).

6 "Statement on Daycare," 24th Annual Convention of OFL, November 1980.

7 "Sharing the Caring," Discussion Paper, OFL Conference on Daycare, October 1980.

8 "A Woman's Place is in Her Union," Policy Statement 22nd Annual OFL Convention, November 1978.

10 *Women's Rights Bulletin.* Quarterly publication of the OFL Women's Committee (subscription free on request).

11 *Ontario Labour.* Bi-monthly publication of the OFL; regular coverage of women's issues (subscription free on request).

Ontario Public Service Employees Union (OPSEU)

1901 Yonge Street
Toronto, Ontario M4S 2Z5

1 "Proposal for a Policy Resolution on Job Sharing," Provincial Women's Committee, May 1982.

2 "Presentation on the Inclusion of Sexual Harassment within the OPSEU Constitution," Provincial Women's Committee, April 1982.

3 "Women in OPSEU – a statistical analysis of participation in union affairs by women," President's Report, February 1982.

4 "Women and Unions ... Stronger Together," 1982 (leaflet).

5 Bob deMatteo, *The Hazards of* VDTs, Special Operations Department, October 1981.

6 "Presentation on Microelectronic Technology and Jobs," Provincial Equal Opportunities Committee, May 1981.

7 "Maternity Leave/Paternity Leave," prepared by Equal Opportunity Co-ordinator, 1981 (draft).

8 "OPSEU Women's Caucus," 1981 (leaflet).

9 "Submission to General Government Committee Respecting Bill 3 (Equal Value Legislation)," Special Operations Department, January 1980.

10 "Equal Opportunities Evaluation Report," January 1979.

11 "Report to the President of OPSEU on Equal Opportunities," Interim Equal Opportunities Co-ordinator, March 1978.

Ontario Secondary School Teachers Federation (OSSTF)

60 Mobile Drive
Toronto, Ontario M4A 2P3

1 *Women in Education,* Professional Development Committee, OSSTF, 1982 (monograph).

2 "Ratio of Men to Women Applicants to Provincial Standing Committees and Councils," Fact Sheet, Status of Women Committee, 1981-82 and 1982-83.

3 *Negotiating for Equal Working Conditions;* "OSSTF Status of Women
   Committee: One Year Later" (leaflet); "Affirmative Action: Count Me
   In" (leaflet); "Count Me In," Fact Sheet; Status of Women Committee,
   1982.
4 "Participation of Women in OSSTF Offices," Fact Sheet, 1981.
5 *Suggestions for Organizing District Status of Women Committees,* Status of
   Women Committee, 1981.
6 *The Effect of Sexism on the Career Development of Teachers,* Task Force
   on Women, OSSTF, 1975.
7 *Forum.* OSSTF journal, regular coverage of women's issues.

Public Service Alliance of Canada (PSAC)

233 Gilmour Street
Ottawa, Ontario K2P 0P1

1 "Technological Change – Office Automation," Policy Paper, 1982.
2 "Equal Opportunity," 1982 (leaflet).
3 "Equal Opportunity," Policy Paper No. 20, 1979.
4 "Paid Educational Leave," Policy Paper No. 19, 1979.
5 "Equal Pay for Work of Equal Value," Policy Paper No. 15, 1979.
6 "Recommendations of the PSAC Women's Committee on Equal
   Opportunities to the PSAC Board of Directors," 1977.
7 *The Civil Service Review.* Regular publication of PSAC, occasional
   coverage of women's issues.

Saskatchewan Federation of Labour (SFL)

Women's Committee
2709-12th Avenue, Room 103
Regina, Saskatchewan S4T 1J3

1 "Daycare," "Affirmative Action – A Program to Combat
   Discrimination," "Sexual Harassment," Policy Statements, nd.

United Auto Workers (UAW)

205 Placer Court
Willowdale, Ontario M2H 3H9

1 "Paid Educational Leave is an Equal Opportunity Program," 1982
   (leaflet).
2 "A Women's Committee Can Make Your Union Work for You," 1981
   (leaflet).
3 "Policy on the Elimination of Sexual Harassment at the Workplace," UAW
   Administrative Letter, Vol. 33, No. 1 (January 15, 1981).
4 "Submission to the Standing General Government Committee regarding
   Bill 3 (An Act to Amend the Employment Standards Act)," Canadian UAW
   Women's Advisory Council, January 30, 1980.

5 *Solidarity.* National magazine of UAW, Canada. Occasional coverage of women's issues; special issue on women, September 1980.

United Steel Workers of America (USWA)

55 Eglinton Avenue East
Toronto, Ontario M4P 1B5

1 "Women of Steel – Equality in the Economy, on the Job and in the Union," Research Report, March 1983.
2 "Equal Rights for Women," Policy Statement, 1981.
3 *Steel Shots.* Newspaper of Local 1005, Stelco, Hamilton; occasional coverage of women's issues.

TRADE UNION GROUPS

Organized Working Women (OWW)

15 Gervais Drive, Suite 301
Don Mills, Ontario M3C 1X8

1 "Unions and the Fight for Daycare," Background Paper, OWW Conference on Day Care and the Union Movement, March 1980.
2 *Union Woman.* Newspaper. Subscription rates available on request.

Saskatchewan Working Women (SWW)

P.O. Box 7981
Saskatoon, Saskatchewan

1 "Saskatchewan Working Women," nd (leaflet).
2 "Daycare," *Working Woman*, April 1980.
3 "Women at Work," *Working Woman*, April-May 1979.

Equal Pay Information Committee (EPIC)

P.O. Box 4237
Vancouver, B.C.

1 *Of Epic Proportions – Achieving Equal Pay for Work of Equal Value* (kit), contains: "The Position of Women in the Workforce," "The Struggle for Equal Pay," "The Opposition to Equal Pay."

Institut de recherche appliquée sur le travail

3290 rue Lacombe, CP 6128
Montréal, Québec H3C 3J7

1 *Le travail à temps partial, février 1978.*

ADDENDA TO TRADE UNION RESOURCES ON WOMEN
Updated, June 1985
See original listing for union addresses.

Canadian Labour Congress

1. "Women and Affirmative Action," Document 25, 15th Constitutional Convention, 1984.
2. "Unions and Affirmative Action," discussion paper, prepared by Hana Aach, 1984.
3. Leaflet Series (bilingual): "Women and Unions," "Women and Pensions," "Sexual Harassment," "Women and Affirmative Action," "Women and Health and Safety," "Women and Technological Change," "The CLC Women's Bureau."

Canadian Union of Public Employees

1. *Equal Opportunities Kit* contains CUPE *Women: Survival in Crisis*, submitted by the National Executive Committee to 1983 Convention (bilingual booklet), *Equality Resources List* (booklet), "A decade of Breaking Through at the Bargaining Table," "Affirmative Action: Putting a Stop to Sex Discrimination: an outline for Locals," "Are You Being Discriminated Against?" (bilingual leaflet).

2. CUPE: *The Facts,* Special Women's Issue, Vol. 7, No. 3, May / June 1985.

National Union of Provincial Government Employees

1. "Women in NUPGE," NUPGE *Notes,* Vol. 10, #1, Spring 1985, pp. 4-13.

Ontario Federation of Labour

1. *Making Up the Difference, Ontario Women Speak Out,* Brief to the Government of Ontario on the Results of the OFL Campaign on Women and Affirmative Action, April 1984.

2. "Affirmative Action," *Ontario Labour* Fall / Winter 1983, pp. 4-8.

Ontario Public Service Employees Union

1. "Equality Before the Year 2000," A Policy Paper on Women and Affirmative Action, Convention 1984.
2. "Presentation to the OFL Affirmative Action Forum," October 1983.

Public Service Alliance of Canada

1. "Personal / Sexual Harassment Policy," January 1984.
2. "The PSAC Working for Women," 1984 (bilingual leaflet).
3. *Ca m'agace*, Journee internationale de la femme, SEIC / PSAC, 1984.
4. "Affirmative Action in the Public Service – More Talk than Action," a
   report of the Public Service Affirmative Action Strategy, by Bonnie
   Carroll, May 31, 1983.

WOMEN AND UNIONS: A SELECTED
BIBLIOGRAPHY

Lynda Yanz

The focus of this bibliography of books and articles about women and unions is Canadian. It is limited to English materials and thus does not represent the rich experience of women in Quebec.

Women and unions is a difficult topic to define; many sources on women and work touch on the issue of unions and some general labour histories mention women. I have tried to limit this bibliography to resources that focus specifically on some aspect of "women and unions." The bibliography is divided into two sections: contemporary and historical. The historical section also includes reference to a few, particularly important studies of women and unions in the U.S. and England. People doing work in this area will want to look at the more general materials, examine existing archival and union documents (see Linda Briskin's "Trade Union Resources on Women" in this book), and, where possible, supplement what exists with oral history.

CONTEMPORARY

Acheson, Shelly. "Affirmative Action at the C.L.C." in *Our Times*, 3:6 (July / August 1984), p. 10.

Adams, Jane and Julie Griffin. "Bargaining for Equality," in *Union Sisters: Women in the Labour Movement*, eds. L. Briskin and L. Yanz. Toronto: Women's Press, 1983, p. 182-197.

Ainsworth, Jackie, Ann Hutchinson, Susan Margaret, Michele Pujol, Sheila Perret, Mary Jean Rands, Star Rosenthal. "Getting Organized ... in the Feminist Unions," in *Still Ain't Satisfied: Canadian Feminism Today*, eds. M. FitzGerald, C. Guberman and M. Wolfe. Toronto: Women's Press, 1982, p. 132-140.

Attenborough, Susan. "Sexual Harassment: An Issue for Unions," in *Union Sisters: Women in the Labour Movement*, eds. L. Briskin and L. Yanz. Toronto: Women's Press, 1983, p. 136-143.

Baker, Maureen and Mary-Ann Robeson, "Trade Union Reactions to Women Workers and Their Concerns," in *Canadian Journal of Sociology*, 6:1 (Winter 1981), p.19-31.

Bank Book Collective. *An Account to Settle: The Story of the United Bank Workers* (SORWUC). Vancouver: Press Gang, 1979.

Bannon, Sharleen. "Women Unionists Demand Their Share," in *Labour Gazette*, April 1976, p.201-204.

Beattie, Margaret, "A Note on CEQ's Policy on Women," in *Women and Trade Unions*, an issue of *Resources For Feminist Research*, 10:2 (July 1981), p.40-43.

Beattie, Margaret. "Women and Factional Politics in a Teachers' Union," in *Atlantis*, 8:1 (Fall 1982), p.34-43.

Berry, Janet. "Telling the B.C. Tel Sit-in Story," in *Kinesis*, (Vancouver Status of Women), March 1981, p.13.

Briskin, Linda and Lynda Yanz, eds. *Union Sisters: Women in the Labour Movement*. Toronto: Women's Press, 1983.

Briskin, Linda. "Women and Unions in Canada: A Statistical Overview," in *Union Sisters: Women in the Labour Movement*, eds. L. Briskin and L. Yanz. Toronto: Women's Press, 1983, p.28-43.

Briskin, Linda. "Women's Challenge to Organized Labour," in *Union Sisters: Women in the Labour Movement*, eds. L. Briskin and L. Yanz. Toronto: Women' Press, 1983, p.259-271.

Chaison, G.N. and D. Andiappan. "Characteristics of Female Union Officers in Canada," in *Relations Industrielles*, 37:4 (1982), p.765-799.

Colley, Sue. "Free Universal Day Care: The OFL Takes a Stand," in *Union Sisters: Women in the Labour Movement*, eds. L. Briskin and L. Yanz. Toronto: Women's Press, 1983, p.307-321.

Cornish, Mary. "Women in Trade Unions," in *This Magazine*, 9:4 (1975).

Cornish, Mary and Laurell Ritchie. *Getting Organized: A Worker's Guide to Building a Union*. Toronto: Women's Press, 1980.

Cumsille, Alejandra, *et al.* "Triple Oppression: Immigrant Women in the Labour Force," in *Union Sisters: Women in the Labour Movement*, eds. L. Briskin and L. Yanz. Toronto: Women's Press, 1983, p.212-221.

Cuthbertson, Wendy. "Fleck: The Unionization of Women," in *Canadian Women Studies*, 1:2 (Winter 1978-79), p.17-32.

Cuthbertson, Wendy. "Demanding Daycare: Autoworkers Win Historical Agreement on Childcare," in *Our Times*, 3:1 (Feb. 1984), p.12-13.

Darcy, Judy and Catherine Lauzon. "The Right to Strike," in *Union Sisters: Women in the Labour Movement,* eds. L. Briskin and L. Yanz. Toronto: Women's Press, 1983, p. 171-181.

David, Francoise, "Women's Committees: The Quebec Experience," in *Union Sisters: Women in the Labour Movement,* eds, L. Briskin and L. Yanz. Toronto: Women's Press, 1983, p. 285-292.

David, Hélène. "'Action Positive' in Quebec," in *Union Sisters: Women in the Labour Movement,* eds. L. Briskin and L. Yanz. Toronto: Women's Press, 1983, p. 87-102.

Dofny, Jacques. "Sex and Class Struggle," trans. Paul Cappon, in *The Working Sexes: Symposium Papers on the Effects of Sex on Women at Work.* Vancouver: The Institute of Industrial Relations, 1976.

Egan, Carolyn and Lynda Yanz. "Building Links: Labour and the Women's Movement," in *Union Sisters: Women in the Labour Movement,* eds. L. Briskin and L. Yanz. Toronto: Women's Press, 1983, p. 361-375.

Epstein, Rachel. "Domestic Workers: The Experience in British Columbia," in *Union Sisters: Women in the Labour Movement,* eds. L. Briskin and L. Yanz. Toronto: Women's Press, 1983, p. 222-237.

Equal Pay Information Committee (P.O. Box 4237, Vancouver, B.C.). *Of Epic Proportions, Achieving Equal Pay for Work of Equal Value,* 1982.

Field, Debbie, "Coercion or Male Culture: A New Look at Co-worker Harassment," in *Union Sisters: Women in the Labour Movement,* eds. L. Briskin and L. Yanz. Toronto: Women's Press, 1983, p. 144-160.

Field, Debbie. "The Dilemma Facing Women's Committees," in *Union Sisters: Women in the Labour Movement,* eds. L. Briskin and L. Yanz. Toronto: Women's Press, 1983, p. 293-303.

Fisher, Christine. "CLC Ottawa Conference – Women's Battle for Equal Rights," in *Labour Gazette,* May 1978, p. 199-202.

FitzGerald, Maureen. "Whither The Feminist Unions? SORWUC, AUCE, and the CLC," in *Women and Trade Unions,* an issue of *Resources for Feminist Research,* 10:2 (July 1981), p. 19-20.

Gallagher, Deirdre. "The Struggle for Union Recognition: A Feminist Issue," in *Women and Trade Unions,* an issue of *Resources for Feminist Research,* 10:2 (July 1981), p. 14-15.

Gallagher, Deirdre. "Getting Organized ... in the Canadian Labour Congress," in *Still Ain't Satisfied: Canadian Feminism Today,* eds. M. FitzGerald, C. Guberman and M. Wolfe. Toronto: Women's Press, 1982, p. 152-162.

Geoffroy, Renée and Paule Sainte-Marie. *Attitudes of Union Workers to Women in Industry.* Vol. 9 of Studies of the Royal Commission on the Status of Women in Canada, Information Canada, 1971.

Genge, Susan. "Lesbians and Gays in the Union Movement," in *Union Sisters: Women in the Labour Movement,* eds. L. Briskin and L. Yanz. Toronto: Women's Press, 1983, p.161-170.

Gray, Charlotte, "What Will Unions Do for Women in the 1980s?" in *Chatelaine,* May 1981, p.54.

Gray, Stan. "Sharing the Shop Floor," in *Canadian Dimension,* 18:2 (June 1984), p.17-32.

Guberman, Nancy. "Working, Mothering and Militancy: Women in the CNTU," in *Union Sisters: Women in the Labour Movement,* eds. L. Briskin and L. Yanz. Toronto: Women's Press, 1983, p.272-284.

Hartman, Grace. "Women and Unions," in *Women in the Canadian Mosaic,* ed. Gwen Matheson. Toronto: Peter Martin, 1976, p.243-255.

Hastings, J. "Assertiveness Training for Union Women," in *Canadian Women's Studies,* 2:2 (1980), p.76.

Howell, Shelly and Margaret Malone. "Immigrant Women and Work," in *Rikka,* 7:1 (Spring 1980), p.35-41.

Jackson, Nancy. "Trade Unionists and Academics: Strategies for Collaboration," in *Women and Trade Unions,* an issue of *Resources for Feminist Research,* 10:2 (July 1981), p.6-7.

Johnston, Wendy. "Women's Struggle for Non-Traditional Jobs," in *Women and Trade Unions,* an issue of *Resources for Feminist Research,* 10:2 (July 1981), p.16-17.

Kates, Joanne and Jane Springer. "Organizing Freelancers in the Arts," in *Union Sisters: Women in the Labour Movement,* eds. L. Briskin and L. Yanz. Toronto: Women's Press, 1983, p.238-255.

Kinesis, an issue on *Women in the Labour Movement.* (Vancouver Status of Women), February 1984.

Kouri, Denise. "Getting Organized ... in Saskatchewan Working Women," in *Still Ain't Satisfied: Canadian Feminism Today,* eds. M. FitzGerald, C. Guberman and M. Wolfe. Toronto: Women's Press, 1982, p.163-167.

Koziara, K.S. and P.J. Insley. "Organizations of Working Women Can Pave the Way for Unions," in *Monthly Labor Review,* 105:6 (June 1982), p.53-54.

Kuyek, Joan. *The Phone Book: Working at the Bell.* Toronto: Between the Lines, 1979.

Kuyek, Joan, Madeleine Parent, Judy Darcy, Linda Briskin. *Strong Women, Strong Unions: Speeches by Union Women.* Toronto: Participatory Research Group and Canada Employment and Immigration Union, 1985.

Labour Gazette. "Women in Trade Unions," October 1971, 682-685.

Landsberg, Michele. "How Trade Unions Let Women Down," in *Chatelaine,* March 1971, p.40.

Lane, Arja. "Wives Supporting the Strike," in *Union Sisters: Women in the Labour Movement,* eds. L. Briskin and L. Yanz. Toronto: Women's Press, 1983, p.322-332.

Legowski, T. "Dignity in the Workplace: Women and Unionization," in *Northern Woman Journal,* 6:6 (Aug. 1981), p.4, 6, 11.

Larkin, Jackie. "Out of the Ghettos: Affirmative Action and Unions," in *Union Sisters: Women in the Labour Movement,* eds. L. Briskin and L. Yanz. Toronto: Women's Press, 1983, p.67-86.

Lowe, Graham S. "The Canadian Union of Bank Employees: A Case Study," in *Working Papers.* Centre for Industrial Relations, University of Toronto, 1979.

Luxton, Meg. "From Ladies' Auxiliaries to Wives' Committees," in *Union Sisters: Women in the Labour Movement,* eds. L. Briskin and L. Yanz. Toronto: Women's Press, 1983, p.333-347.

Marchak, Patricia. "Women, Work and Unions in Canada," in *International Journal of Sociology,* 5:4 (Winter 1975/76), p.39-61.

Marchak, Patricia. "Women Workers and White Collar Unions," in *Canadian Review of Sociology and Anthropology,* 10:2 (May 1973), p.134-147.

Marie, Gillian. "Civic Workers Strike in Lower Mainland: Demand Equal Pay for Work of Equal Value," in *Kinesis,* (Vancouver Status of Women), March 1981, p.12-13.

McCune, Micki. "Fighting For Our Rights: The 1980 CLC Women's Conference," in *Women and Trade Unions,* an issue of *Resources for Feminist Research,* 10:2 (July 1981), p.11-12.

McFarland, Joan. "Women and Unions: Help or Hindrance," in *Atlantis,* 4:2 (Spring 1979), p.48-70.

McShane, S.L. "Women in Unions: Their Numbers Are Growing," in *Worklife,* 2:2 (1981), p.10-11.

Ng, Winnie. "Organizing Workers in the Garment Industry," in *Rikka,* 7:1 (Spring 1980), p.30.

Pappert, Anne. "The Unions Make Us Strong," in *Quest*, Oct. 1982, p.84-90.

Pollock, Marion. "The CLC 1980 Convention Appraised: Sexism was Everywhere but Feminist Presence Growing," in *Kinesis*, (Vancouver Status of Women), June 1980, p.16.

Pollock, Marion. "Under Attack: Women, Unions and Microtechnology,"in *Union Sisters: Women in the Labour Movement*, eds. L. Briskin and L. Yanz. Toronto: Women's Press, 1983, p.103-118.

Posner, Judith. "YUSA Strike Report, Ladies Last – the 6% Solution," in *Canadian Women's Studies*, 1:2 (Winter 1978-79), p.64-65.

Rands, Jean. "Toward An Organization of Working Women," in *Women Unite: An Anthology of the Canadian Women's Movement*. Toronto: Women's Press, 1972, p.141-148.

Rankin T. "Can the Union Make Us Strong?" in *Quest*, 5:4, (1982), p.13-24.

Renholm, Marie. "How They Won at Kenworth, CAIMAW Activist Describes Equal Pay for Work of Equal Value," in *Kinesis*, (Vancouver Status of Women) May 1981, p.6.

Resources For Feminist Research, an issue on *Women and Trade Unions*, 10:2 (July 1981).

Richmond, Penny. "Affiliates Affirm Action," in *Our Times*, 3:8 (Oct. 1984), p.34-37.

Ritchie, Laurell, "Why Are So Many Women Unorganized?" in *Union Sisters: Women in the Labour Movement*, eds. L. Briskin and L. Yanz. Toronto: Women's Press, 1983, p.200-211.

Routledge, Janet. "Women and Social Unionism," in *Women and Trade Unions*, an issue of *Resources for Feminist Research*, 10:2 (July 1981), p.17-18.

Sarra, Janis. "Trade Union Women and the NDP," in *Union Sisters: Women in the Labour Movement*, eds. L. Briskin and L. Yanz. Toronto: Women's Press, 1983, p.348-360.

Sceviour, Carrol Anne. "Power Plays: Sexual Harassment in the Workplace," in *Our Times*, 2:4 (Nov. / Dec. 1983), p.8-10.

Spinks, Sara. "Women on Strike: Dare and Wardair," in *This Magazine*, 7:1 (May / June 1973), p.23-27.

Sufrin, Eileen Tallman. *The Eaton Drive: The Campaign to Organize Canada's Largest Department Store*. Toronto: Fitzhenry and Whiteside, 1983.

Thompson, Joey, "Nannies Aren't Going to Take it Any Longer: They're Organizing" in *Kinesis*, (Vancouver Status of Women), July 1980, p.3.

Tolmie, Ellen, "Fleck – Profile of a Strike," in *This Magazine*, 12:4 (Oct. 1978), p.22-29.

Townson, Monica. "Organizing Women Workers," in *Labour Gazette*, 75:6 (June 1975), p.349-353.

Valverde, Mariana. "Union Maid, Union Made," in *Broadside*, 2:10 (Aug. 1981), p.8.

Vickers, Jill and Patricia Finn. " 'And the Winner is ... for Norma Rae' – Is Unionism Effective in the Fight for Women's Economic Equality?" in *Perception*, 3:6 (July / August 1980), p.17-22.

Vohanka, Sue. "Getting Organized ... in the Confederation of Canadian Unions," in *Still Ain't Satisfied: Canadian Feminism Today*, eds. M. FitzGerald, C. Guberman and M. Wolfe. Toronto: Women's Press, 1982, p.141-151.

Vukman-Tenebaum, Marijana. "Organizing Domestics in Ontario," in *Women and Trade Unions*, an issue of *Resources for Feminist Research*, 10:2 (July 1981), p.32-33.

White, Julie. "Part-time Work, Women and Unions," in *Union Sisters: Women in the Labour Movement*, eds. L. Briskin and L. Yanz. Toronto: Women's Press, 1983, p.119-135.

White, Julie. *Part-Time Work: Women, Unions and Legislation*. Ottawa: Advisory Council on the Status of Women, 1983.

White, Julie. *Women and Unions*. Ottawa: Advisory Council on the Status of Women, 1980.

Women's Committee, United Farmworkers and Allied Workers Union. "Sex Discrimination is Being Fought Through the Union," in *Kinesis*, (Vancouver Status of Women), Feb. 1980..

HISTORICAL

Canada

Bacchi, Carol. "Divided Allegiances: The Response of Farm and Labour Women to Suffrage," in *A Not Unreasonable Claim: Women and Reform in Canada 1880s-1920s*, ed. L. Kealey. Toronto: Women's Press, 1979.

Campbell, Marie. "Sexism in British Columbia Trade Unions 1900-1920," in *In Her Own Right: Selected Essays on Women's History in* B.C., eds. B. Latham and C. Kess. Victoria: Camosun College, 1980.

Cook, Ramsay and Wendy Mitchinson, eds. *The Proper Sphere: Women's Place in Canadian Society.* Toronto: Oxford University Press, 1976.

Diamond, Sara. "You Can't Scare Me I'm Sticking to the Union: Union Women in British Columbia during the Great Depression," in *Kinesis,* (Vancouver Status of Women), June 1979, p.13-17.

Diamond, Sara. *Women's Labour History in British Columbia: A Bibliography, 1930-48.* Vancouver: Press Gang, 1982.

Frager, Ruth. "No Proper Deal: Women Workers and the Canadian Labour Movement, 1870-1940," in *Union Sisters: Women in the Labour Movement,* eds. L. Briskin and L. Yanz. Toronto: Women's Press, 1983, p.44-64.

French, Doris. *High Button Bootstraps: Federation of Women Teachers' Associations of Ontario, 1918-1969.* Toronto: Ryerson, 1968..

Kidd, Dorothy. "Women's Organization: Learning from Yesterday," in *Women at Work in Ontario, 1850-1930,* eds. J. Acton *et al.* Toronto: Women's Press, 1974, p.331-361.

Klein, Alice and Wayne Roberts. "Besieged Innocence: The 'Problem and Problems of Working Women – Toronto 1896-1914," in *Women at Work in Ontario, 1850-1930,* eds. J. Acton *et al.* Toronto: Women's Press, 1974, p.211-253.

Kojder, Apolonja. "The Saskatoon Teachers Association: A Demand for Recognition," in *Saskatchewan History,* 30:2 (Spring 1977).

Kouri, Denise and Don Kossick. "A History of Courage: Women in Saskatchewan Have A Long History of Organizing for Their Rights," in *Briarpatch,* 9:8 (Nov. 1980), p.20-21.

LaVigna, C. *Women in the Canadian and Italian Trade Union Movements at the Turn of the Century: A Comparison.* The Italian Immigrant Woman in North America: Proc. 10th Annual Conference of the American Italian Historical Association. Toronto: Oct. 1977, p.28-29, eds. B.B. Caroli, R.F. Harney, and L.F. Tomasei. Toronto: Multicultural History Society of Toronto, 1978, p.32-42.

Macleod, Catherine. "Women in Production: The Toronto Dressmakers' Strike of 1931," in *Women at Work in Ontario, 1850-1930,* eds. J. Acton *et al.* Toronto: Women' Press, 1974, p.309-329.

Montero, Gloria. *We Stood Together, First-Hand Accounts of Dramatic Events in Canada's Labour Past.* Toronto: James Lorimer, 1979.

Roberts, Wayne. *Honest Womanhood: Feminism, Femininity and Class Consciousness Among Toronto Working Women, 1893 to 1914.* Toronto: New Hogtown Press, 1976.

Roberts, Wayne ed. *Where Angels Fear to Tread: Eileen Tallman and the Labour Movement.* Publication of the Labour Studies Program, McMaster University, Hamilton, nd.

Rosenthal, S. " 'Union Maids': Organized Women Workers in Vancouver 1900-1915," in B.C. *Studies,* Issue 41 (Spring 1979).

Sangster, Joan. "The 1907 Bell Telephone Strike: Organizing Women Workers," in *Labour / Le Travailleur, Journal of Canadian Labour Studies,* Vol. 3 (1978), p. 109-130.

Sangster, Joan. "Women and Unions in Canada: A Review of Historical Research," in *Women and Trade Unions,* an issue of *Resources for Feminist Research,* 10:2 (July 1981). p. 2-6.

Smith, Dorothy E. "Women and Trade Unions: The U.S. and British Experience (Review Essay)," in *Women and Trade Unions,* an issue of *Resources for Feminist Research,* 10:2 (July 1981). 53-60.

Strong-Boag, Veronica. "The Girl of the New Day: Canadian Working Women in the 1920s," in *Labour / Le Travailleur, Journal of Canadian Labour Studies,* Vol. 4 (1979), p. 131-164.

Wade, Susan. "Helena Gutteridge: Votes for Women and Trade Unions," in *In Her Own Right: Selected Essays on Women's History in* B.C., eds. B. Latham and C. Kess. Victoria: Camosun College, 1980.

Woywitka, Anne B. "A Pioneer Woman in the Labour Movement," in *Alberta History,* 26:1 (Winter 1978).

England

Boston, Sara. *Women Workers and the Trade Unions.* London: Davis-Poynter, 1980.

Lewenhak, Sheila. *Women and Trade Unions: An Outline History of Women in the British Trade Union Movement.* London: Ernest Benn, 1977.

Middleton, Lucy. *Women in the Labour Movement: The British Experience.* London: Croom Helm, 1977.

United States

Dye, Nancy Schrom. *As Equals and As Sisters: Feminism, the Labor Movement and the Women's Trade Union League of New York.* Columbia: University of Missouri Press, 1980.

Foner, Philip S. *Women and the American Labour Movement From Colonial Times to the Eve of World War I.,* Vol. I. New York: The Free Press, 1979.

Foner, Philip S. *Women and the American Labour Movement From World War I to the Present*, Vol. II. New York: The Free Press, 1980.

Kenneally, James J. *Women and the American Trade Unions*. Montreal: Eden Press, 1978..

Tax, Meredith. *The Rising of the Women: Feminist Solidarity and Class, 1880-1917*. New York: Monthly Review, 1980.

CONTRIBUTORS

JANE ADAMS is a Toronto union educator with a background as an organizer and a negotiator with CUPE and FOCAS (a social service workers' union). She also designs and leads educational workshops for unions and other public interest groups.

SUSAN ATTENBOROUGH is on staff at NUPGE, where she has authored several booklets on women's issues, including "Sexual Harassment at Work." She is also a member of the Equality of Opportunity and Treatment of Women Workers Committee of the Canadian Labour Congress.

LINDA BRISKIN is an activist in OPSEU and a community college teacher in Toronto. She co-authored *The Day the Fairies Went on Strike,* a non-sexist fairy tale for children, and co-produced *Rising Up Strong: Women in the* 80's, an hour-long video documentary on the women's movement in Ontario.

SUSAN COLLEY is a day care parent and a member of Action Day Care in Toronto. She has been active in the women's movement and the day care movement in Canada for many years.

ALEJANDRA CUMSILLE works with the Working Women Community Centre and is a member of the labour committee of Women Working With Immigrant Women. She is from Chile and lives in Toronto.

JUDY DARCY is a Toronto library clerical worker, union activist, socialist and feminist. She was first involved in the Toronto Women's Liberation Movement in 1969, and has been active in CUPE and the labour movement since 1972. She is an executive member of her local union and the CUPE Metro Toronto District Council.

FRANCOISE DAVID has worked with various citizen's groups in Montreal, including child care centres, food co-ops and social assistance programs. She has been active in the trade union movement for the last four years and in the Social Affairs Federation's (FAS) women's committee since it began in 1980. She is a sole-support mother of a two-year-old child.

HELENE DAVID does research for the labour movement in Quebec at the Institut de recherche appliquée sur le travail (IRAT). She was president of the CNTU's national women's committee in 1976 when the committee submitted its first report, *Women's Struggle, the Fight of all*

Workers, which has since become the basis for the CNTU's involvement in the struggle against women's oppression.

CAROLYN EGAN has been an activist in the women's liberation movement for the past thirteen years. She works at the Birth Control and Venereal Disease Clinic in Toronto, is involved in the International Women's Day Committee, and is a member of the Labour Committee of Women Working With Immigrant Women.

RACHEL EPSTEIN was a founding member of the Labour Advocacy and Research Association (LARA) in 1975, worked with the British Columbia Domestic's Association (BCDA) and was on the coordinating committee of the Committee for the Advancement of the Rights of Domestic Workers (CARDWO). She currently works for Press Gang Printers and Publishers in Vancouver and is part of the Acting Up theatre group.

DEBBIE FIELD works at the Development Education Centre in Toronto and is active in Canadian Action for Nicaragua. She helped build OPSEU's first women's caucus and was their first Equal Opportunity Coordinator. After the Women Back Into Stelco Campaign, she worked in the coke ovens at Stelco for a year and was the chairperson of the USWA Local 1005 women's committee.

DINAH FORBES tries to be a socialist, feminist, part-time mother of two boys and a full-time worker at the Development Education Centre in Toronto. She has worked in book publishing and distribution for the past ten years and was co-producer of the slide show *On the Bias.*

RUTH FRAGER is an active member of the Canadian Union of Educational Workers and is writing a thesis on the history of Toronto's garment workers.

SUSAN GENGE is a library worker and union activist in Toronto. She is a member of the women's committee of the Ontario division of CUPE and president of her local union. She is a member of the International Women's Day Committee and co-mother of a daughter.

DAINA GREEN works as an educational researcher, freelances as an interpreter and translator for Spanish and French and teaches English as a second language. She is active in OPSEU and has worked on issues important to women as well as in solidarity with Latin American struggles.

JULIE GRIFFIN is chief negotiator of CUPE's 18,000 hospital workers in Ontario. She is staff advisor to CUPE's Ontario division's women's committee and its national Task Force on Women and a member of the OFL women's committee. A long-time union activist, Julie has been a member of the USWA, the UAW and the Canadian Textile and Chemical Workers Union.

NANCY GUBERMAN teaches women's studies and community organizing in the social work department at the Université de Québec à Montréal, and is active with the CNTU women's committee and a local women's community group. She is also a full-time activist in various social and political movements, and now has a third job — as a mother of an eight-month-old girl.

JOANNE KATES is a freelance journalist, author and radio commentator. She is the restaurant critic for *The Globe and Mail,* author of *Exploring Algonquin Park* and was founding president of the Periodical Writers' Association of Canada.

GLADYS KLESTORNY works for the Centre for Spanish Speaking People, is a member of OPSEU and of the labour committee of Women Working With Immigrant Women. She is from Uruguay and lives in Toronto.

ARJA LANE was a founding member of Women Supporting the Strike in Sudbury. She was also a member of Women Helping Women and coordinator of fundraising and publicity for the Sudbury Women's Centre. She has worked as a secretary, an administrative assistant and a seasonal farm labourer. Presently she is living in Thunder Bay with her daughter and writing for the *Northern Woman Journal.*

JACKIE LARKIN is a Vancouver feminist and socialist of revolutionary persuasion. She would still be working in a wood panelling mill in B.C. if she had not been laid off. She foresees continued forced unemployment after completing training as an electronics technician.

MARIA TERESE LARRAIN is coordinator of Women Working With Immigrant Women. She is from Chile and is active in the solidarity community in Toronto.

CATHERINE LAUZON is a former hospital worker and clerical worker who now works as a typesetter. She lives in Hamilton, Ontario and is a journalist for the *Forge* newspaper.

MEG LUXTON is a sociology professor at McMaster University in Hamilton, Ontario. Author of *More Than a Labour of Love: Three Generations of Women's Work in the Home,* she is currently studying working-class families in Hamilton.

FRANCOISE PELLETIER is a sole-support mother and researcher in applied linguistics. She has worked as a teacher of English as a second language and as a freelance translator. She is exploring the area of children's rights and education and maintains an interest in the struggle for women's rights around the world.

MARION POLLOCK is a mail sorter and an executive member of the Vancouver local of the Canadian Union of Postal Workers. She is also a member of the Equal Pay Information Committee (EPIC).

LAURELL RITCHIE is an organizer with the Canadian Textile and Chemical Union (Confederation of Canadian Unions) and a member of the Equal Pay Coalition. She co-authored an organizing manual with lawyer Mary Cornish, entitled *Getting Organized: Building a Union.*

JANIS SARRA does research and advocacy in occupational health and safety and women's issues. Based in Toronto, she is a member of the OFL women's committee, an active trade unionist and feminist. Best of all, she is mom to daughter Sam.

DAVID SMITH is a Marxist economist whose work focuses on trends in women's labour force participation. He is active in an anti-sexist men's group in Toronto and is a member of a working group on micro-technology and women.

JANE SPRINGER is a Toronto freelance editor and founder of the Freelance Editors' Association of Canada. She is a member of the Marxist Institute collective and has been working with the Women's Press for eight years.

JULIE WHITE came to Canada from England in 1975 with a background in sociology and social work. Since 1977 she has worked as a freelance researcher in Ottawa, focusing on aspects of women's participation in the labour force. She is author of *Women and Unions* and *Part-Time Work: Women, Unions and Legislation.*

LYNDA YANZ has been involved in the women's movement for the past thirteen years. She works with the Participatory Research Group and International Council for Adult Education in Toronto, and is active in the International Women's Day Committee.

PHOTO CREDITS